Children's Humour

Children's Humour

Edited by
Paul E. McGhee
Department of Home and Family Life
Texas Tech University

and

Antony J. Chapman
Department of Applied Psychology
University of Wales Institute of Science and Technology

Illustrations by Patty Inkley

JOHN WILEY AND SONS
Chichester · New York · Brisbane · Toronto

Copyright © 1980 by John Wiley & Sons Ltd.

British Library Cataloguing in Publication Data:
Children's humour.
  1. Wit and humor—Psychology
  2. Wit and humor, Juvenile
I. McGhee, Paul Edward
II. Chapman, Anthony J
155.4'18   BF723.W   79–40648

ISBN 0 471 27638 3

Photosetting by Thomson Press (India) Ltd., New Delhi and printed at The Pitman Press, Bath, Avon.

List of Contributors

MICHAEL J. APTER — *Department of Psychology, University College, Cardiff, U.K.*

DAVID M. BRODZINSKY — *Douglass College, Rutgers, The State University of New Jersey, New Brunswick, New Jersey 08903, U.S.A.*

ANTONY J. CHAPMAN — *Department of Applied Psychology, University of Wales Institute of Science and Technology, Llwyn-y-Grant Road, Cardiff CF3 7UX, U.K.*

ANN P. DAVIES — *Department of Psychology, University College, Cardiff, U.K.*

HUGH C. FOOT — *Department of Applied Psychology, University of Wales Institute of Science and Technology, Cardiff, U.K.*

HOWARD E. GARDNER — *Project Zero, Harvard University, Cambridge, Massachusetts 02138, U.S.A. (and Veterans Administration Hospital, Boston, Massachusetts 02130, U.S.A.)*

JACOB LEVINE — *Departments of Psychiatry and Psychology, Yale University, New Haven, Connecticut 06520, U.S.A. (and Veterans Administration Hospital, West Haven, Connecticut 06516, U.S.A.)*

PAUL E. MCGHEE — *Department of Home and Family Life, Texas Tech University, Lubbock, Texas 79409, U.S.A.*

DIANA PIEN — *Department of Psychology, University of Oregon, Eugene, Oregon 97403, U.S.A.*

JONATHAN RIGHTMYER — *Department of Psychology, University of Pittsburgh, Pittsburgh, Pennsylvania, U.S.A.*

JUDITH ROBILLARD — *Department of Human Communication Disorders, McGill University, Montreal, PQ, Canada.*

MARY K. ROTHBART — *Department of Psychology, University of Oregon, Eugene, Oregon 97403, U.S.A.*

THOMAS R. SHULTZ — *Department of Psychology, McGill University, Montreal, PQ, Canada H3A 1B1.*

JEROME L. SINGER — *Department of Psychology, Yale University, New Haven, Connecticut 06520, U.S.A.*

JEAN R. SMITH — *Department of Applied Psychology, University of Wales Institute of Science and Technology, Cardiff, U.K.*

RONI BETH TOWER — *Department of Psychology, Yale University, New Haven, Connecticut 06520, U.S.A.*

Contents

Preface   xi

Chapter 1   Incongruity Humour, Play, and Self-Regulation of
Arousal in Young Children   1
Diana Pien and Mary K. Rothbart
    A Theoretical Model for the Origins of Incongruity
      Humour.   1
    Affective and Locomotor Responses to In-
      congruity   9
    Summary and Conclusions.   21

Chapter 2   Imagination, Interest, and Joy in Early Childhood:
Some Theoretical Considerations and Empirical
Findings   27
Roni Beth Tower and Jerome L. Singer
    The Imaginative Dimension in Cognitive, Social,
      and Emotional Growth.   29
    A Cognitive-Affective Approach to Imaginative
      Play   40
    Some Empirical Findings   45
    Implications of Joy in Play   47

Chapter 3   The Development of Linguistic Humour in Children:
Incongruity through Rule Violation   59
Thomas R. Shultz and Judith Robillard
    Phonology   61
    Morphology   73
    Semantics   76
    Syntax   81
    Pragmatics   83
    Summary   86

Chapter 4   Children's Literary Development: The Realms of Meta-
phors and Stories.   91
*Howard E. Gardner with the collaboration of Robin
Bechhofer, Jane Hanenberg, S. William Ives, Laurence
Meringoff, Shelley Rubin, Jen Silverman, Ellen Winner,
and Dennie Wolf*

vii

Introduction: The Links Between Jokes and
Literary Art.. 91
The Development of Metaphoric Competence .. 94
The Development of Competence with Stories .. 102
Closing Thoughts: Exploring the Relation Bet-
ween the Realms of Humour and Literary
Accomplishment 112

Chapter 5 Development of the Creative Aspects of Humour .. 119
Paul E. McGhee
Creativity and Humour Development 120
Age-related Changes in Created Humour .. 130
Development of the Humorist 135
Concluding Remarks 135

Chapter 6 Humour, Laughter, and Social Interaction 141
Antony J. Chapman, Jean R. Smith, and Hugh C. Foot
Adult Analyses: Processes and Functions .. 142
Social Aspects of Children's Humour 149
Children's Responsiveness in Humour Situations 153
Summary and Conclusions 170

Chapter 7 Individual Differences in Children's Humour Develop-
ment 181
David M. Brodzinsky and Jonathan Rightmyer
A Rationale for Studying Individual Differences in
Children's Humour.. 182
Research Strategies and the Question of Individual
Differences 183
Empirical Studies 185
Conclusions and Implications 204

Chapter 8 Development of the Sense of Humour in Childhood: A
Longitudinal Study 213
Paul E. McGhee
Experimental Procedures 214
Results and Discussion of Findings 216
Summary and Developmental Profile 231

Chapter 9 Humour and its Effect on Learning in Children .. 237
Ann P. Davies and Michael J. Apter
Previous Research on Humour and Learning .. 240
The Cardiff Study. 243

Recommendations for Future Research .   . .   248
Concluding Remarks   251

Chapter 10   The Clinical Use of Humour in Work with Children .   255
               Jacob Levine
               Developmental Assessment   256
               Psychotherapy   263
               The Child's Use of Humour in Therapy .   . .   267
               The Therapist's Use of Humour in Therapy   . .   274
               Other Clinical Uses of Humour   277

Chapter 11   Children's Humour: Overview and Conclusions   . .   281
               Paul E. McGhee and Antony J. Chapman

Bibliography of Studies on Children's Humour, Laughter, and Smiling   307
               Paul E. McGhee and Antony J. Chapman
               Children's Humour   307
               Smiling and Laughter in Infancy   314

Subject Index   319

Preface

This volume represents a further milestone in the resurgence of interest in humour and in humour-related behaviours which has characterized the decade of the seventies. The rate of publications pertaining to such topics as humour, play, make-believe or fantasy, metaphorical thinking, laughter, and smiling continues to spiral upwards. The recent international conferences on humour and laughter held in Cardiff in 1976 and Los Angeles in 1979 support the view that interest in humour research is taking the lead in setting this general research pattern. Part of the revival of interest in studies of humour appears to be due to an increasing awareness that humour touches our lives in many ways. The average person is aware intuitively that the possession of a sense of humour is important and is not likely to appreciate someone's suggestion that he or she lacks a sense of humour or has a poor one. At the national level, we hold a special place in our minds and hearts for those who make us laugh.

Evidence for the position that the study of children's humour and its development has come into its own in the seventies can be garnered from the bibliography presented at the end of this book. A count of the number of publications focusing in some way on children's humour (excluding studies of infant smiling or laughter) indicates a total of only sixty publications in the seven decades of this century prior to 1970. This total results from the following number of publications for each decade: 1900–1909, two; 1910–1919, two; 1920–1929, nine; 1930–1939, twelve; 1940–1949, thirteen; 1950–1959, eight; and 1960–1969, fourteen. Even in the peak years of interest in humour development in the 1930s and 1940s, there was an average of only one publication per year dealing with the topic. In sharp contrast to these figures, there have been one hundred and six publications thus far in the 1970s focusing on various aspects of humour development.

To some extent, the renewed attention to humour development may be attributed to the fact that developmental changes in humour and laughter reflect underlying basic developmental trends in cognitive, social and emotional development. Indeed studies of the cognitive and social aspects of humour development have led the way in increasing our knowledge in this area. These studies, in combination with studies of personality and other individual difference factors, have made us increasingly aware of the complexity of the humour experience in children (and adults); also, they have made us appreciate the significance of this often overlooked aspect of human development for our general adaptation to the physical and social world. Because of the extension of humour to so many aspects of the child's life and development, progress toward a

xi

fuller understanding of humour development is tantamount to the achievement of a fuller understanding of children and their development generally.

Our primary aim in planning this book was to summarize existing research and theory on children's humour. In the process both the contributors and the editors have attempted to draw attention to key issues and provide an impetus for further research. In support of the latter goal, we have included chapters by investigators studying children's make-believe and metaphor development, since we believe the research findings in these areas (obtained outside the context of humour research) have important implications for understanding humour development.

It is appropriate that the first chapter of a book on children's humour deals with the basic issue of the point in development at which the capacity for humour first appears. Pien and Rothbart discuss the meaning of smiling and laughter in infancy, along with the role of such factors as playfulness, arousal, incongruity, and cognitive processes in the earliest occurrences of humour. They also present findings of a study of two-year-olds' smiling, laughter, and other reactions to incongruous and arousing events. Chapter 2, by Tower and Singer, marks an attempt to draw attention to the importance of imaginative play and positive emotionality in children for humour development. Singer's extensive prior work in this area has not been directed toward understanding humour, but it is our belief that a full understanding of children's humour and its development requires an advancement of knowledge in these areas.

Chapters 3 and 4 focus on the role played by language in children's humour. Shultz and Robillard have systematically analysed the implications of phonological, morphological, semantic, syntactic, and pragmatic aspects of language development for humour development, focusing on the relationship between humour and rule use and rule awareness in each case. Chapter 4, by Gardner and his associates at Harvard's Project Zero, focuses on recent studies of different aspects of literary development, including story-telling and the comprehension and production of similes and metaphors. It is important for investigators studying humour development to be aware of this rich and growing body of literature, since the cognitive prerequisites for comprehension and appreciation of metaphors and other literary devices are identical to those required for comprehension and appreciation of many forms of humour.

Chapter 5 by McGhee examines the general relationship between creativity and humour development, focusing on the cognitive processes involved in humorous and non-humorous forms of creativity, age-related changes in the ability to create humour (along with the role of cognitive development in producing those changes) and the importance of fantasy play and a general 'style' of playfulness. The issue of the origins of humour, raised in Chapter 1 by Pien and Rothbart, is discussed again here in connection with whether the earliest form of humour experienced by children is of a self-constructed or reactive nature.

Chapman, Smith, and Foot draw attention in Chapter 6 to the fact that humour is most likely to occur in a social context. Their research has provided important first steps toward filling the void of social psychological research on children's humour and its development. They draw from social facilitation and social intimacy theory in interpreting findings related to such factors as number of companions present, sex and degree of friendship among those present, physical distance between those present, amount of laughter exhibited by companions, and the effect of presence or absence of an experimenter. The influence of social factors on children's humour might be conceptualized as a source of individual differences in children's humour. Brodzinsky and Rightmyer summarize in Chapter 7 the available research findings related to other important sources of individual differences, such as cognitive style and other personality dimensions, IQ and other measures of cognitive status, and sex of subject. Relative to research on the cognitive and social aspects of humour development, studies of individual differences in children's humour have been neglected. Chapter 8 presents the findings of a long-term longitudinal study of the antecedents (in prior maternal and child behaviour) of humour appreciation and initiation. These data, obtained by McGhee, mark the first attempt to relate actual observations of early parent and child behaviour to the subsequent development of individual differences in children's sense of humour.

Chapters 9 and 10 deal with two important practical applications of humour with children. In Chapter 9, Davies and Apter discuss issues and research findings related to the effects of humour upon learning and retention in children. In spite of the fact that humour is an important element in such programmes as *Sesame Street* and *The Electric Company* (which are aimed at promoting learning), it is not at all clear that humour helps rather than interferes with the learning-retention process. The success and failure patterns of recent television commercials in the United States using humour suggest that this relationship will not prove to be a simple one. Davies and Apter present findings from an extensive study relating to these issues, and discuss related theoretical views pertinent to existing data.

In Chapter 10 Levine discusses the clinical uses of humour with children. In addition to noting psychoanalytic interpretations of joking and other forms of humour initiated by children, he discusses the potential hazards and usefulness of humour when used by therapists during therapy sessions, the significance of humour initiated by children during therapy, and the use of humour 'tests' both as a diagnostic tool and a means of assessing cognitive level or intelligence. This chapter helps clarify many of the issues related to the old question of whether the possession of a good sense of humour (there is no common agreement on the meaning of this term) can be used as an index of good mental health.

Finally, Chapter 11 is used as an opportunity for the editors to assess the contributions made by the individual chapters of this volume. An attempt is made to underscore both the strengths and limitations of the views and data presented. This final chapter is not intended to summarize the contents of each chapter, but rather to draw attention to especially important contributions, point out areas of continued or new controversy, and help give direction to new research and theoretical developments in a now rapidly expanding field.

PAUL E. MCGHEE

ANTONY J. CHAPMAN

CHAPTER 1

Incongruity Humour, Play, and Self-Regulation of Arousal in Young Children

DIANA PIEN
and
MARY K. ROTHBART

In this chapter, we discuss two separate but related issues in the study of humour and affect in young children. First we present a theoretical model of the origins of incongruity-based humour and the relationship between incongruity-based humour and the development of play abilities. We propose that by about the age of four or five months infants are capable of evaluating incongruous stimuli as humorous. In the second part of the chapter, we discuss humour appreciation as one aspect of positive affect and we examine the relationship between affect and approach-avoidance behaviours. In connection with this second issue, we present an experimental study of children's humour, affect, and approach-avoidance behaviours as they occur in a naturalistic play situation. These three types of responses are discussed in terms of subjects' level of arousal and their self-regulation of arousal.

A THEORETICAL MODEL FOR THE ORIGINS OF INCONGRUITY HUMOUR

It has been frequently proposed that the perception of incongruity (i.e. of an event that violates an individual's expectation) is a necessary condition for the experience of humour (Berlyne, 1960, 1972; Fry, 1963; Koestler, 1967; McGhee, 1971; Shultz, 1972, 1976). Incongruity represents one of the 'collative' variables Berlyne (1960) has identified as involving a person's comparison or collation of information from two or more sources (e.g. a person's reactions to sudden-ness, novelty, complexity, and incongruity of stimuli). Berlyne argued that both collative variables and stimulus intensity tend to raise an individual's level of arousal.

Berlyne (1969, 1972) proposed that both arousal boosts (i.e. moderate increases in arousal level) and arousal jags (i.e. sharp decreases in arousal from previously high levels of arousal) are rewarding. Berlyne (1972) also proposed that smiling occurs with moderate increases in arousal but that only arousal jags lead to laughter and the experience of humour. For humorous stimuli, an arousal jag is produced by increases in arousal level due to incongruity and/or to drive conditions such as anger and sexual urges, while subsequent decreases in arousal level are produced by resolution of the incongruity or a playful, non-serious interpretation of the incongruity. Other theorists (e.g. Flugel, 1954; Fry, 1963; McGhee, 1972) have also stressed the importance of a playful attitude in humour appreciation.

Rothbart's arousal-safety theory (1973, 1976, 1977) modified Berlyne's arousal jag concept to predict that smiling and laughter will occur in situations where there is high arousal and subjects judge the situation as safe or non-threatening. She predicted positive affect in such 'safe' situations even without a reduction in arousal level.

Theorists generally agree with the definition of humour as a response to the perception of incongruity in a playful context that may or may not be accompanied by smiling and laughter. They differ, however, in the cognitive processing they consider necessary for a humour experience to occur, and in their interpretation of when in the developmental sequence children will first be able to experience humour.

McGhee (1971, 1977) and Shultz (1976) both propose that incongruity-based humour is one of the earliest forms of humour in young children, and that appreciation of incongruity humour depends on the development of infants' symbolic play capacities. They predict that when infants become capable of symbolic play at about eighteen months of age (Piaget, 1962), they also become capable of experiencing incongruity humour. Shultz and McGhee, however, differ in their interpretations of the function of symbolic play skills in incongruity humour.

McGhee (1971, 1977) proposes that an incongruous stimulus will be evaluated as humorous only when the stimulus is recognized as inconsistent with one's past experience, and when no attempt is made to alter one's existing cognitive structures to fit the discrepant event (i.e. the condition of fantasy assimilation). Smiling and laughter may result from successful attempts to alter existing structures to fit the novel or discrepant event (i.e. reality assimilation), but such reactions reflect only pleasure in mastery, not humour. McGhee proposes that the ability to fantasy-assimilate incongruous events does not develop until the child is capable of symbolic play as defined and described by Piaget (1962).

According to Piaget, symbolic play involves the child's awareness of make-believe and pretence. Piaget argues that symbolic play develops early in the second year of life, and involves children's production of pretend or make-believe events when they symbolically apply familiar schemas to new unrelated objects, thereby producing incongruity. Piaget (1962) described the first example of his daughter's symbolic play as she pretended that a cloth is a pillow:

> . . . she saw a cloth whose fringed edges vaguely recalled those of her pillow; she seized it, held a fold of it in her right hand, sucked the thumb of the same hand and lay down on her side, laughing hard. She kept her eyes open, but blinked from time to time as if she were alluding to closed eyes. Finally, laughing more and more, she cried 'Néné' (Nono). The same cloth started the same game on the following days. At 1; 3(13) she treated the collar of her mother's coat in the same way. At 1; 3(30) it was the tail of her rubber donkey which represented the pillow.' . . . (Piaget, 1962, Observation 64(a), p. 96)

Shultz (1976), like McGhee, proposes that incongruity humour depends on the development of symbolic play capacities and begins at about eighteen months. In contrast to McGhee, however, Shultz suggests that until infants develop symbolic play, they are only capable of perceiving novelty, and are unable to perceive incongruity, presumably because they cannot yet form specific expectations about future events. The reaction to an incongruous stimulus is cognitively more complex than the reaction to novelty, because an incongruous stimulus is *mis*expected, (i.e. specific expectations are formed and then violated), while a novel stimulus is *un*expected (i.e. no specific expectations about the stimulus are formed; see Charlesworth, 1969).

Shultz (1976) also differs from McGhee in proposing that primitive forms of humour may involve any activity producing a biphasic sequence of arousal increases and decreases (i.e. arousal jags) that are similar to arousal jags produced by identifying and resolving incongruity. Shultz proposes that since pleasure in mastery produces arousal jags, it is therefore a primitive form of humour. He states that pleasure in mastery 'represents a primitive stage of humour which is qualitatively distinct from the earlier stages of incongruity and resolvable incongruity' (1976, p. 30). Infant games producing arousal increases and decreases (e.g. peek-a-boo and chasing) are also considered by Shultz to be early forms of humour if they elicit smiling and laughter.

Our position regarding the origins of incongruity humour differs from both Shultz's and McGhee's. We argue that the development of symbolic play capacities and fantasy assimilation are *not* necessary for the appreciation of incongruity humour. Instead we propose that incongruity humour involves only the recognition of incongruity and a playful interpretation of incongruity, and we argue that both these abilities are present by the fourth month of life.

Our position that infants recognize incongruities and violations of expectancies during the first year of life prior to the development of symbolic play capacities is supported by recent work concerning the object concept. Bower has extensively used surprise as a means of studying infants' conceptions of objects. To determine what properties two-to-five-month-old infants use to define objects, Bower, Broughton, and Moore (1971) used objects moving behind a screen and changed either the perceptual features of the objects or the speed of objects when they re-emerged from behind the screen. If infants had specific expectations about the properties of objects and these expectations were violated, it was expected that they would view the re-emerging object as a new object and show surprise by looking back for the original object. Four-and-five-month-old infants in fact showed surprise and disruption of their tracking when either the perceptual features or the speed of the object were altered; infants less than four-months-old also showed surprise, but only when the speed of the object was altered. Similar paradigms have been used by Bower (1971, 1974) to examine other aspects of infants' object and perceptual development. His results indicate that infants as young as four months of age can form specific expectations and recognize violations of their expectations. Certainly there are developmental changes concerning the content of expectations but, contrary to Shultz (1976), the recognition of incongruity *per se* appears (a) to be present early in the first year of life, and (b) to be independent of the emergence of symbolic representation and symbolic play.

Next we argue that the perception of incongruous events as humorous requires only a safe, playful context for such events and does *not* require symbolic play capacities. Our position is in direct opposition to McGhee's theory (1971, 1974, 1977). He proposes that the perception of humour depends on symbolic play capacities and the processes of assimilation and accommodation. The terms assimilation and accommodation come from Piaget's model of cognitive development (1963). Assimilation refers to the incorporation of a new event into a pre-existing schema without altering that schema. For example, an infant when presented with a novel object like aluminium foil might suck the foil and thereby assimilate the foil into a pre-existing schema of suckable objects. Accommodation refers to the modification of an existing schema to fit the properties of the new event. In the case of the foil, an older infant might cease to suck the foil on future trials and thereby accommodate the schema of suckable objects to exclude aluminium foil.

According to McGhee, realization that an incongruity is incompatible with reality and is only 'make-believe' results in fantasy assimilation and no accommodation of existing schemas. In contrast, successful attempts to resolve a non-make-believe discrepancy lead to changes in existing schemas to accommodate the discrepancy. This process is called 'reality assimilation' by McGhee, but the term 'reality accommodation' would be more appropriate, since accommodation of schemas occurs in reality assimilation but not in fantasy assimilation. In fantasy assimilation the person considers the possibility of an incongruous event actually occurring to be zero; the event can only occur as a fantasy or make-believe event. For example, before knowledge of the actual existence of a lungfish, an air-breathing fish may be considered to be a fantasy creature. If the lungfish is thought to be make-believe, there will be no conflict between knowledge of the lungfish and one's conception of real fish as only having gills and existing in water. Knowledge of real lungfish produces reality assimilation in which acceptance of the incongruous stimulus as a real object conflicts with one's conception of fish. Resolution of the conflict requires accommodation of one's schema of fish to allow for fish that have lungs and can breathe air.

According to McGhee, children in Piaget's concrete operational stage (i.e. around the age of seven or eight) and adults evaluate both fantasy and real life incongruous events as humorous. Incongruity, however, is evaluated as humorous by children under seven or eight only when it is seen as make-believe and the child fantasy assimilates the event. Thus in McGhee's theory the distinction between real versus make-believe or pretend situations is necessary before an incongruous event is evaluated as humorous by young children. The reality–make-believe distinction depends on the development of symbolic play (Piaget, 1962).

Unlike McGhee we consider the reality–make-believe distinction to be a non-essential component of humour for young children as well as adults. Real-life incongruities may be humorous if they occur in a safe and playful context. For example, a person really slipping on a banana peel may be funny if the person is not hurt. Children often laugh at people wearing large hats or wearing unusual clothes. Berlyne (1972) and Rothbart (1976) proposed that humour involves the perception of incongruity in a non-serious, non-threatening situation where there is no danger, as in the hat and banana peel cases, and where there is no serious, difficult problem-solving. Thus we propose that only a playful interpretation is necessary for a humorous response to occur independent of a make-believe interpretation.

A playful interpretation of incongruous events depends on the development of an infant's play capacity. Piaget (1962) defined play as the assimilation of a stimulus that involves little or no serious attempt to accommodate existing structures to fit the stimulus. Play activities are initiated 'for fun', 'for the pleasure of the activity and without any effort at adaptation to achieve a definite end' (Piaget, 1962, p. 92). Early forms of play appear about the fourth month and consist primarily of repetition and ritualization of schemas for the pleasure of the activity. The early forms of play do not necessarily involve incongruous events; practice play may involve repetition of familiar schemas. Symbolic play, as we have mentioned, develops during the second year of life, and is seen when the child produces 'pretend' events by applying well-practised schemas to new and unrelated objects, creating symbolic incongruities.

While we agree with Piaget and McGhee that the distinction between reality and make-believe occurs with the development of symbolic play capacities, we consider incongruity humour to require only a playful attitude as shown by an absence of serious accommodation of existing schemas to fit the incongruous event (Rothbart, 1976). In our view, only cognitive capacities associated with early forms of play are necessary for incongruity humour appreciation.

Our position is supported by Sroufe's work with infants (Sroufe, Waters, and Matas, 1974; Sroufe and Wunsch, 1972). Sroufe and his associates found smiling and laughter in a small sample of seven-, ten-, and twelve-month-old infants to incongruous events presented in safe situations (i.e. by the infant's mother in the home). While they do not identify the displays of positive affect as indicators of humour appreciation, their stimuli fit current definitions of incongruity humour (i.e. events involving violation of expectancies and discrepancies). Sroufe and Wunsch (1972) report, for example, that twelve-month-old infants smile most at visual and social events that involve discrepancy from a familiar schema; *viz* the mother walking like a penguin, the mother wearing a human-like mask, the mother sucking on a baby's bottle, or presentation of a cloth dangling from the mother's mouth. With all of these stimuli, infants expect to see the familiar face and action schemas of Mother, and the stimuli presented violate these specific expectations. The necessity of a safe, non-threatening situation for incongruity humour is suggested by pilot data reported by Sroufe and his associates, where ten-month-old infants smiled and laughed more at their mother's wearing a mask than at a stranger's wearing the same mask (reported in Sroufe *et al.*, 1974). The presence of a stranger may create a threatening situation for infants.

If Sroufe's data may be interpreted as examples of incongruity humour as we have argued, then incongruity humour certainly appears before the existence of symbolic play capacities, which do not develop until early in the second year of life. We have argued that all the components for incongruity humour are present by at least the first four months of life, and we therefore propose that young infants are capable of appreciating incongruity-based humour. Four- and five-month-old infants have developed early forms of play in which they initiate activities for the pleasure of the activity without any attempts at serious accommodation. In our theory, smiling and laughter at incongruous events by four-month and older infants indicate humour appreciation in those infants.

We might expect, however, that the first expressions of incongruity humour would involve smiling and laughter at incongruity produced by another person. Wolfenstein (1953, 1954), for example, observed that in school-age children appreciation of humour generally precedes production of humour. Sroufe and Waters (1976) anecdotally reported that younger infants smiled and laughed at incongruous events, while older infants smiled and laughed during their own production of discrepant events. When mothers removed cloths dangling from their mouths, twelve-month-old infants would reproduce the incongruity by stuffing the cloth back in their mothers' mouths. Sroufe and Waters reported that older children smiled and laughed more when they performed this action than when their mothers performed the same action.

Pleasure in mastery

The relationship between pleasure in mastery and humour appreciation has not been completely specified. Pleasure in mastery certainly contributes to humour appreciation in the resolution of incongruity (McGhee, 1972; Rothbart and Pien, 1977; Shultz, 1972; Zigler, Levine, and Gould, 1966). In addition, if mastery includes stimulus recognition, then identification of incongruity in the humour situation itself constitutes mastery, e.g. noting that a man is wearing an especially tiny hat (see Rothbart, 1977). The distinction between pleasure in mastery and humour appreciation is even more unclear concerning infants. As stated earlier, McGhee (1974, 1977) argues that pleasure in mastery is not a form of humour; pleasure in mastery and humour appreciation involve different processes. In contrast, Kagan (1971) does not acknowledge incongruity humour as a process separate from pleasure in mastery. He interprets all smiles following presentation of a novel or discrepant stimulus as resulting from successful assimilation and accommodation of existing schemas to the novel or in-congruous stimulus. Shultz (1976) also fails to differentiate between the two processes in infants under a year old. He equates mastery with practice play as defined by Piaget (1962) and considers pleasure in mastery to be a primitive, early form of humour.

While both Kagan and Shultz use Piaget's theory to support their theories of pleasure in mastery, Piaget (1963) in *The Origins of Intelligence* discusses pleasure in mastery as initially resulting from recognitory assimilation (i.e. the successful identification of a stimulus). He observed smiles as reactions to familiar images in his own children as early as the second month of life (cf. Observations 37–39). In later stages of cognitive development, smiles appear as the result of successful assimilation and accommodation of schemas as when children learn to co-ordinate shaking and looking schemas to shake and observe a mobile suspended above the crib (e.g. Observations 94–104). Piaget differentiates these mastery smiles from smiles during play. As previously mentioned, play involves assimilation with no serious accommodation. Piaget (1962) labels this playful type of assimilation as ludic (i.e. 'playful') and non-adaptive to differentiate it from adaptive, recognitory assimilation. Recognitory assimilation is adaptive since the schemas are applied for a specific purpose (e.g. recognition of the object) and the schemas are adapted to an external reality. In play, assimilation is non-adaptive, since 'this activity is no longer an effort to learn, it is only a happy display of known actions' (p. 93). In play there is no effort at comprehension or mastery of events or actions.

In extending Piaget's theory to humour, we propose that incongruity humour involves only ludic assimilation, while mastery smiles involve adaptive assimilation and sometimes accommodation as well. One difficulty with this distinction is in determining when a stimulus involves ludic versus adaptive assimilation. The context may determine the type of assimilation. In a playful situation an incongruous stimulus may involve ludic assimilation; in a non-playful situation an incongruous stimulus may involve adaptive assimilation. Cues children might use for identifying a playful situation include laughter and smiling by others, brief presentations of incongruity, and the infant's control over the incongruity if incongruity is produced by others, and ritualized stereotyped presentation of incongruity. Naturalistic studies of childminders playing with infants may allow us to clarify the types of contextual cues signifying a 'playful' situation.

Piaget's distinction between mastery smiles and smiles in play is not only useful in separating mastery from incongruity humour, but may also be useful in partially accounting for smiles occurring in social games such as tickling or chasing where no mastery is involved. Kagan's mastery theory does not apply to such games, since there is no successful adaptive assimilation other than recognition that the activity is a game. These games all involve large increases in arousal level and either subsequent arousal reduction and/or evaluation of the situation as safe and playful. Rothbart's (1973) and Berlyne's (1960) arousal theories both predict laughter and smiling in these situations because of arousal boosts or arousal jags, although Rothbart's theory is more compatible with Piaget's play theory, since it allows for smiles with very high levels of arousal in a playful situation.

Thus we propose that smiling and laughter may result from increases in arousal level in playful incongruous situations (incongruity humour) and playful familiar situations (e.g. social games), and from increases and decreases in arousal level in mastery situations.

Implications for future humour studies

We have presented a model of children's humour based on an integration of arousal theories with Piaget's theory of play. We propose that incongruity-based humour develops early in infancy and depends on the perception of incongruity in a playful context. We predict that four-month-old infants may appreciate incongruity-based humour, since they are capable of detecting incongruity and are also capable of ludic assimilation. Sroufe and his associates' informal observations of laughter and smiling in the first year of life provide some evidence for incongruity humour in infants (Sroufe and Waters, 1976; Sroufe et al., 1974; Sroufe and Wunsch, 1972). Their work, however, needs to be replicated with larger samples and more careful observations, for many of their conclusions are anecdotal and are not documented in their original presentation of results.

In addition, future research concerning the types of contextual cues leading to ludic versus adaptive assimilation of incongruity is crucial. Piaget (1962) reported his child playing at three months, and Rothbart (1973) observed that the same stimulus could elicit either laughter or distress reactions depending on the context. At present there is little research concerning when and how infants recognize contexts as safe and playful, and when and how infants recognize play by others. The recognition of play in others may appear after the infant's own production of play. We propose that the following factors may be important in the infant's evaluation of an incongruous stimulus as playful when another person produces the incongruity: ritualized or predictable stimulus presentation by a familiar person; the infant's control over stimulus presentation; brief presentation(s) of the incongruous stimuli; no other needs predominating (e.g. hunger); and evidence of laughter and smiles by other persons present. Detailed observations of very young infants in play situations are necessary for us to understand the origins of humour and also the nature of social interaction and emotional development.

AFFECTIVE AND LOCOMOTOR RESPONSES TO INCONGRUITY

In the section above, we described incongruity as an important stimulus variable producing positive affect in young children. The perception of incongruity may lead to ludic assimilation and humour appreciation or to reality assimilation and pleasure in mastery. However, the perception of incongruity may also lead to negative affective responses (cf. Hebb, 1946; Schaffer, 1966) and exploratory or avoidance responses (cf. Berlyne, 1960). In the second part of this chapter we examine both positive and negative affect resulting from the perception of incongruity, and relate children's approach and avoidance of incongruous stimuli to their positive and negative affective responses to the stimuli. We briefly review the literature in this area, and then present detailed naturalistic observations of two-year-old children's affective and exploratory reactions to an incongruous toy.

Hebb (1946) and Schaffer (1966) explained fear reactions as an organism's reactions to extremely incongruous stimuli. Such stimuli are very discrepant from an organism's existing schemas and lead to fear responses (e.g. when a child sees a strange adult or when a model of a chimpanzee's head is presented to other chimpanzees). Berlyne (1960) suggested that extreme incongruity and novelty may activate two competing systems, exploration and fear, resulting in vacillation between approach and avoidance of the stimuli. A graphic example of a raven's conflict and vacillation described by Lorenz is cited by Berlyne:

> A young raven, confronted with a new object, which may be a camera, an old bottle, a stuffed polecat, or anything else, first reacts with escape responses. He will fly up to an elevated perch and, from this point of vantage, stare at the object literally for hours. After this, he will begin to approach the object very gradually, maintaining all the while a maximum of caution and the expressive attitude of intense fear. He will cover the last

distance from the object hopping sideways with half-raised wings, in the utmost readiness to flee. At last, he will deliver a single fearful blow with his powerful beak at the object and forthwith fly back to his safe perch. If nothing happens he will repeat the same procedure in much quicker sequence and with more confidence . . . .(Berlyne, 1960, p. 123).

While Berlyne (1960) states that conflict between approach and avoidance responses to novelty is common, there has been virtually no detailed observation of such conflicts in humans. Berlyne's predictions that both affective responses and approach-avoidance are influenced by increases in arousal suggest that both approach-avoidance behaviour and fluctuations in affect should be present in young children when an incongruous stimulus is presented. Berlyne and other theorists, however, have not specified to what degree approach-avoidance and affective responses might be expected to be temporally related to each other.

Most research to date on children's approach-avoidance and affective responses to incongruous stimuli has focused on children's affective and exploratory responses to strange adults or to novel toys in an experimental setting (e.g. Ainsworth and Bell, 1970; Bronson, 1972; Rheingold and Eckerman, 1973). Unfortunately these studies have frequently failed to differentiate clearly children's affective responses from their exploratory reactions in their response measures of children's reactions to incongruity and novelty. In studies of children's reactions to strangers, experimenters have often assumed that approach behaviours co-occur with smiling and laughter, or assumed that investigatory and approach behaviours are indicators of positive affect (e.g. Bretherton and Ainsworth, 1974; Lewis and Brooks, 1974). Similarly, visual and behavioural avoidance have often been used as measures of negative affect (Bronson, 1972; Scarr and Salapatek, 1970; Waters, Matas, and Sroufe, 1975). For example, Bronson (1972) and Waters *et al.* (1975) use visual avoidance as a measure of wariness of strangers even in the absence of negative facial expressions, behavioural avoidance, or crying. The assumption that greater looking time indicates preference, and that exploratory behaviour indicates positive affect is questionable at best. Berlyne and Lawrence (1964) have reported that college students look longer at more complex stimuli than simpler stimuli, while rating the more complex stimuli as *less* pleasant than the simpler stimuli. In addition, children and adults look longer at stimuli they have rated as unpleasant than at stimuli they rated as pleasant or neutral (Faw and Nunnally, 1967, 1968). Even monkeys repeatedly perform instrumental responses in order to view a frightening stimulus, for example, an anaesthetized monkey (Butler, 1964).

In the present study, we wished to study the relation of approach and avoidance to smiling, laughter, and negative affect associated with an incongruous toy, and to study the temporal relation between positive and negative affect and approach and avoidance responses. We also wished to test predictions about the occurrence of positive and negative affect from arousal-safety theory.

In the next sections we present our observational study, and then relate our findings to an arousal-safety theory and to theories of avoidance and self-regulation of arousal levels.

Procedure

Subjects were four boys and four girls from white middle-class families. Their ages ranged from twenty-four months to twenty-eight months, with a mean age of twenty-six months. Mothers brought their children to a laboratory observation room, where each child was seen individually. The 2.8×4.2 metre observation room was comfortably furnished and carpeted. The floor of the room was marked into 0.9 metre squares with masking tape. The experimenter sat in the far-right corner of the room, with the mother in the far-left corner, 0.30 metres to the left of the child. A one-way mirror, video-camera and camera operator were located at the opposite end of the room facing the child, mother, and experimenter. The complete session consisted of the child's initial familiarization with the room and subsequent play with three toys: a Jack-in-the-box, a toy vacuum cleaner, and a remote-controlled barking and walking toy dog. Since only children's reactions to the Jack-in-the-box have been coded and are reported in this chapter, only the procedures during familiarization and presentation of the first toy are described here.

At the beginning of the session, a yellow toy school-bus and a squeaking penguin toy were placed on the floor near the mother's chair. During the familiarization episode, the experimenter showed the two toys to the child, and the mother was instructed to interact with the child in her normal fashion. The child was allowed to play with these toys for four to six minutes; then the experimenter told the child she would now show a different toy. The bus and penguin were removed from the room, and a Jack-in-the-box operated by a push button was brought into the room and placed on 61×61 centimetre table in front and to the right of the mother. Six of the children had never seen or played with any type of Jack-in-the-box; one had operated a crank but never a push-button Jack-in-the-box. The Jack-in-the-box was initially presented to the child by the experimenter with the lid open and the clown upright. The experimenter introduced the toy by saying, 'Let me show you this funny man. He makes a funny noise. See (squeaks the toy)?'. Unless the child started to push the clown back into the box, the experimenter pushed the clown several times, whereupon the child was asked if s/he would like to push the clown and make him talk. Then the experimenter sat down in her chair 1.6 metres away from the toy. Children were allowed to interact freely with the toy until they lost interest in it and either said they wanted a new toy when asked by the experimenter or spontaneously stated they wanted another toy. The length of the Jack-in-the-box session varied from five to twenty-one minutes.

Coding

Each child's entire session was video-taped, and time in tenths of seconds was superimposed on the lower left-hand corner of the videotapes. Three trained coders then coded the video-tapes using the categories described below. Onset, duration, and offset of events in each category were coded sequentially on sheets divided into one-second intervals. The video-tape record was supplemented by the coding of the child's looking responses by an observer during the observation session. The following coded information was recorded on separate lines: locomotor responses, looking responses, facial expressions, and vocalizations. The child's actions involving the toy were also recorded. Behavioural items coded within each of these broad categories are listed in Appendix A.

Reliability among the three coders was at least 0.90 for all categories in randomly selected three-minute periods for each child. In addition, each segment of the tape was coded by at least two coders and disagreements resolved between them. This coding was extremely time-consuming, and limited the number of subjects that could be studied in this project.

Smiling, laughter, and locomotor responses

We first discuss the co-occurrence of arousal-increasing events with smiling and laughter, and then discuss the relationship between children's affective responses and approach-avoidance behaviours. The results are mainly descriptive due to the small number of subjects in the study.

Arousal-increasing events. Arousal theories predict that smiling is more likely after arousal-increasing events than after low-arousal events (e.g. Berlyne, 1960, 1972; Rothbart, 1973, 1976). We identified toy-related events as arousal-increasing based on two factors: (a) the collative properties of events and (b) the difficulty and amount of effort involved in producing the events. We expected that effort and task difficulty might increase arousal level independent of collative properties. In our view, however, only high-arousal events involving incongruity would be potential humorous events; high-arousal events involving only serious problem-solving and effort would not be humorous (Berlyne, 1972; Rothbart, 1977). In the following analyses we are concerned only with the highest arousal incongruous event (i.e. the pop-up); the highest arousal mastery event (i.e. the successful lid close); and the two lowest arousal events (i.e. the child touching the box and approaching the toy).

All types of pop-ups were judged to be the most arousal-increasing incongruous events based on their collative properties and intensity. The noise and sight of the clown associated with the pop-up was loud, sudden, and incongruous. Since the incongruities were produced in a playful situation, pop-ups were judged to be humour stimuli. Successful lid closes were judged to be the highest arousal mastery events. Closing the lid required considerable expenditure of strength for a two-year-old along with co-ordination of two hands. Since closing the lid did not produce incongruity, it was judged not to involve humour. The two lowest arousal-producing events, touching the box and approaching the toy, involved proximity or contact with the toy but little effort was involved for the child and these events did not produce sudden or incongruous stimulation. (For detailed definitions of the behaviour categories coded, see Appendix.) Children in the present experiment were in contact with the Jack-in-the-box for an average of seventy-five per cent of the toy episode.

Smiles. All but one of the children smiled during the Jack-in-the-box episode. All of the following analyses concern only the seven children who smiled. The percentage of time children smiled ranged from eight per cent to thirty-six per cent of the session. The mean per cent of time smiling for all seven children in the first third of the session was eighteen per cent, increasing to twenty-eight per cent in the middle third of the session, and then decreasing to fifteen per cent in the last third of the session.

Incongruous events associated with onset of smiling. In the present experiment, we predicted that smiles would occur more often after high arousal incongruous events (i.e. pop-ups) than after low arousal non-incongruous events (i.e. approach or touch box). To test this prediction, we defined the association of an event and a smile as the initiation of a smile during or within two seconds following the event. For all seven children who smiled, each child's probability of

Table 1.1 Overall conditional probabilities for children's reactions

1A	Event			
	Pop up	Touch or approach toy	Successful lid close	Unsuccessful lid close
p (event/smile onset)[a]	0.28(63/224)[b]	0.08(19/224)		
p (smile onset/event)	0.94(63/67)	0.23(19/82)	0.54(43/79)	0.21(6/29)
p (event/laugh)	0.31(17/54)	0.09(5/54)		

1B	Event	
	Pop up or lid close	Touch or approach toy
p (event/avoidance)	0.34(40/119)	0.03(3/119)
p (event/smile-avoidance pair)	0.49(33/68)	0.04(3/68)

[a] The conditional probability $p(x/y)$ refers to the probability of x occurring during y, or two seconds before y.
[b] Numbers in parentheses refer to the proportion of x events to y events.

a pop-up being associated with a smile was larger than the child's probability of touching or approaching the toy being associated with a smile ($7/7$, $p < 0.02$, sign test). Table 1.1 presents the overall probabilities across all subjects for this and all subsequent analyses. In addition, for pop-ups not already preceded by smiles, each subject's probability of a smile's being initiated during or within two seconds after a pop-up was larger than the probability of a smile's being terminated ($7/7$, $p < 0.02$, sign test). The probability over all children of a smile terminating during a pop-up was 0.19, while the probability of a smile onset was 0.94. The results clearly indicated that smiles were more likely to be initiated during or following high-arousal incongruous events than during or following low-arousal events.

Mastery events associated with smiles. Smiles frequently occur in non-humorous situations involving mastery or successful completion of tasks requiring effort (e.g. Harter, 1974; Kagan, 1971). To determine whether mastery smiles occurred in the present study, we compared the probability of smiles being associated with (i.e. initiated during or within two seconds after) successful lid closes not already preceded by smiles with the probability of a smile onset during or after non-mastery events. For six children, each child's probability of a smile's being associated with a successful lid close was larger than the probability of a smile's onset associated with an unsuccessful lid close or a lid close by the mother or experimenter (one child had none of the latter events and was not considered in this analysis), $6/6$, $p < 0.04$, sign test. In addition, the Mann–Whitney U-test indicated that the overall probability of a smile onset tended to be greater after a successful lid close than after non-mastery low arousal (i.e. approach or touch box) events (U (7, 7) $= 9.5$, two-tailed $p < 0.06$). The Mann–Whitney U-test assumes independent samples, and is conservative when there is a positive correlation between scores, which was true in the present study.

Our interpretation of smiles initiated after successful lid closes as mastery smiles was further supported by two children's hand movements, which occurred only after these events. One subject said, 'I did that', clapped her hands, and smiled after four successful lid closes. Another subject smiled and clasped her hands after five successful lid closes.

Laughter. Since only five of the eight children laughed, there were not enough data for a meaningful analysis of the relation between arousal and laughter.

Avoidance events. We defined avoidance as events which terminated the child's visual or physical contact with the toy or events which increased the distance between the child and toy. Based on current fear of strangers research (see Bretherton and Ainsworth, 1974; Bronson, 1972; Morgan and Ricciuti, 1969; Waters *et al.*, 1975), we designated the following behaviours as visual avoidances: gaze aversion (looking away from the toy but not looking at the mother or any person in the room); closing the eyes; and head turned away from the toy but not looking at the mother or another person (see Appendix, part IV). We defined locomotor avoidance as any motor movements away from the toy but not toward the mother. The preceding definitions excluded events which terminated the child's contact with the toy by initiating contact with mother (i.e. approaching the mother and moving away from the toy, turning away from the toy and looking at the mother, hiding the face in the mother's lap or behind the mother). It should be noted that these proximity-to-mother behaviours have almost always been considered avoidance behaviours in the fear of strangers literature (e.g. Bretherton and Ainsworth, 1974; Bronson, 1972; Lewis and Brooks, 1974; Scarr and Salapatek, 1970), even though these responses may primarily be initiated for social interaction rather than for avoidance of the toy. Because of the ambiguous nature of such responses, we did not code them as avoidance responses.

Arousal events associated with avoidance behaviours. According to Berlyne's arousal theory (1960, 1972) and Rothbart's arousal-safety theory (1973), avoidance events should be associated with high-arousal-producing events more frequently than with low-arousal-producing events. This prediction was confirmed in our observations. All eight children initiated avoidance behaviours. For all eight children, each child's probability of a pop-up or close of the lid's being associated with an avoidance event was larger than the probability for an associated low-arousal event ($8/8$, $p < 0.01$, sign test). As was the case for smiles, avoidance events were more likely to occur during or after very high-arousal events than during or after low-arousal events.

Relationship between smiles and avoidance behaviours. Examination of the facial expressions associated with avoidance behaviours revealed an unexpected relationship between avoidance events and smiles. Avoidance has commonly been assumed to indicate distress and negative affect (e.g. Bronson, 1972; Waters *et al.*, 1975); however, in the present experiment thirty per cent of all smiles occurred either during or within two seconds of at least one avoidance event. Of all avoidance events where children's facial expressions were visible, over sixty per cent occurred either during a smile or within two seconds of a smile.

High-arousal-increasing events may have led to this pairing of smiles and avoidance events, since both types of responses were more likely to occur after high-arousal events than after low-arousal events. We calculated the probability of a high-arousal event occurring during or within two seconds prior to a smile-avoidance pair of events. To determine whether the pairing between smiles and avoidance behaviours was related to arousal-increasing events, we compared the above probability with the probability of a low-arousal event given a smile-avoidance pair. For all seven subjects who smiled, each child's probability of a high-arousal event's being associated with a smile-avoidance pair of events was larger than the probability of a low-arousal event given the pair, 7/7, $p < 0.02$, sign test.

The results indicated that avoidance events are not incompatible with smiles and frequently occur in close temporal succession after high-arousal events.

Negative facial and vocal reactions. In the present study, we coded only distress faces (i.e. frowning and/or lower lip protrusion) as negative facial expressions. Crying was used as our measure of negative vocalization.

No crying occurred during any of the Jack-in-the-box episodes and only four children showed distress faces. The number of distress faces was minimal. Across all children there were twenty distress faces compared to two hundred and thirty-five smiles. The onsets of distress faces were not related to either high-arousal-increasing or to avoidance events.

Theoretical perspectives

Positive affective reactions. Our results in general support arousal theories of humour and smiling. We found evidence for incongruity humour in two-year-old children, for these children smiled and laughed at the incongruous sight and sounds of the clown, especially the clown's popping up. One child spontaneously stated that such events were funny, saying 'It's funny' or 'He is so funny' four times during the session.

Our observations also indicate that pleasure in mastery can lead to smiling in children. We found the children were more likely to smile after successfully closing the lid of the Jack-in-the-box in comparison to their unsuccessful attempts. Children were also more likely to smile when they successfully closed the lid than when the mother or experimenter closed the lid. These results are consistent with research and theories concerning pleasure in mastery (e.g. Harter, 1974; Harter, Shultz, and Blum, 1971; Kagan, 1971).

Our observations fail to support Sroufe and his associates' proposal that smiles represent the end point of a positive evaluation process (Sroufe *et al.*, 1974). They report that in their study of infant smiling to masks, smiling 'preceded or was concurrent to the reach toward the mask, never subsequent to it' (Sroufe *et al.*, 1974, pp. 63–64). Sroufe *et al.* propose that smiling allows previously inhibited release of overt behaviour toward incongruous stimuli. The evaluation process Sroufe and his associates describe involves initial inhibition of approach to the stimulus, followed by either a negative or positive appraisal of it:

> When the infant is confronted with a novel, incongruous situation, appropriate to its cognitive-developmental level, behavioral fixation occurs and 'tension' develops. Within a positive context—for example, in the home with mother as stimulus agent—the infant will smile or laugh, perhaps reach, and seek to reproduce the situation. Within a negative context the same 'stimulus' will produce crying or

behavioral avoidance. That is, infants have *both* a strong disposition to approach *and* to avoid novel stimulation, but neither crying nor laughter is an expression of ambivalence. Rather both crying and laughter occur following the resolution of indeterminacy, with laughter occurring when there is a positive 'evaluation' as well as considerable 'tension' due to discrepancy (Sroufe *et al.*, 1974, pp. 50–51).

We did not find that smiling appeared to represent an 'end point' of evaluation; rather, if evaluation were involved in smiling, it appeared to represent continuing *re*-evaluation of the situation by the child. Contrary to Sroufe's statements and our own initial expectations, smiles were in fact very frequently associated with avoidance events: over sixty per cent of all avoidance events were associated with smiles, while thirty per cent of all smiles were associated with avoidance behaviours. Further analysis indicated that high-arousal-increasing events tended to be associated with both smiles and avoidance behaviours. These results suggest that avoidance behaviours and smiling are not necessarily two incompatible results of an evaluation process, and that neither avoidance nor smiling reliably indicates the termination of the stimulus evaluation process.

Negative affective reactions. The amount of negative affective reactions shown by the children in playing with the Jack-in-the-box depends on the response measure used. Scarr and Salapatek (1970) infer fear from fleeing to mother, crying, and sobering; they do not define sobering, but other experimenters define sober as a neutral face (e.g. Morgan and Ricciuti, 1969; Waters *et al.*, 1975). If their measures of fear excluding sobering (proximity to mother, avoidance, pouting, crying, frowning) are applied to our data, then our children show frequent negative reactions to the Jack-in-the-box. If, however, only frowning, pouting, and crying are used as measures of negative affect, then our subjects rarely show negative reactions. Thus conclusions from this experiment vary greatly depending on the definition of negative affect employed.

While most experimenters do not regard sobering as an index of negative affect (e.g. Lewis and Brooks, 1974; Morgan and Riciutti, 1969), many experimenters regard any type of visual and behavioural avoidance of the stimulus as an indication of wariness or distress (Bretherton and Ainsworth, 1974; Bronson, 1972; Sroufe *et al.*, 1974). Bronson (1972) proposes that visual avoidance of strangers is a valid indicator of wariness, since visual avoidance rarely occurs in episodes in which infants frequently smile at a stranger. Sroufe and his associates (Sroufe *et al.*, 1974; Waters *et al.*, 1975) also propose that visual avoidance of a stimulus indicates wariness and a negative evaluation of the stimulus. We failed to replicate these observations in our present study.

The frequent co-occurrence of avoidances with smiles in this study suggests that avoidance events were not definitive expressions of lack of preference and/or negative affect. Children in a naturalistic setting often show avoidance *and* smiling in reaction to high-arousal events, and may be modulating their own arousal levels through the avoidance behaviours. In doing so, they may be either creating an arousal jag or establishing safety in the situation. Further, evaluation seems *not* to be an all-or-nothing affair; the child seems to continue to re-evaluate the situation throughout the session of interaction with the toy. In a relatively non-threatening situation such as the present experiment, avoidance events may function to control high levels of arousal by either reducing arousal to a pleasurable level (see Berlyne, 1960; Stern, 1974a, 1974b) or to define high levels of arousal as non-threatening and pleasurable (cf. Rothbart, 1973). In either case positive affect is associated with avoidance events. In contrast, in situations which are threatening or potentially threatening (e.g. fear of stranger experiments), avoidance events may control very high levels of arousal only enough to reduce the magnitude of the distress reaction or to produce a neutral reaction. On the basis of our data, we wish to extend Bronson's (1972) conclusion that visual avoidance aids infants in maintaining composure in the presence of a disturbing stranger. We propose that avoidance may primarily function to control high levels of arousal which can lead to either positive or negative affect, depending on the context and level of arousal.

Given our admittedly *post hoc* interpretation of avoidance behaviours, we have concluded that only frowning, pouting, and crying are valid indicators of negative affect in the present experiment. Our results indicate little negative affective reaction to the Jack-in-the-box, with all children except one displaying positive affect to the toy.

Self-regulation of arousal levels. Our results concerning the co-occurrence of smiling and avoidance responses are strikingly similar to Stern's (1974a, 1974b) detailed and extensive observations of three-to-four-month-old infants engaged in playful interactons with their mothers. Stern notes that gaze aversions are frequent on the part of infants while mothers tend to gaze at their infants for longer periods. Infants alternate between gazing-at mother and gazing-away from mother when they seek contact with mother as well as when they avoid contact. He interprets the infant's visual avoidances as a means of controlling perceptual input, thereby keeping the infant at an 'optimal' state of arousal. Stern hypothesizes that visual avoidance is engaged in when the child's arousal level becomes too high and affect becomes negative rather than positive.

Stern also has observed both rapid alternations of positive and negative affect in connection with gaze aversions and simultaneous gaze aversion and smiling in three- to four-month-old infants. He describes a frequently occurring 'pre-peek-a-boo' game between infants and their mothers which he characterizes as follows:

> It consists of the infant looking at the mother, smiling, vocalizing, and showing other signs of mounting arousal and positive affect, including increasing motor activity. As

the intensity of his state increases, he begins to show signs of displeasure, momentary sobering, and a fleeting grimace, interspersed with the smiling. The intensity of arousal continues to build until he suddenly averts gaze sharply with a quick but not extensive head turn which keeps the mother's face in good peripheral view, while his level of 'excitement' clearly declines. He then returns gaze, bursting into a smile, and the level of arousal and affect build again. He again averts gaze, and so on. The infant gives the clear impression of modulating his states of arousal and affect within certain limits by regulating the amount of perceptual input. (Stern, 1974b, pp. 208–209)

While the above example illustrates alternation between gaze aversion and smiling, Stern (1974a) also observed simultaneous gaze aversion and smiling, reporting that he often cannot predict whether gaze aversions will be accompanied by sobering or smiling. We observed a similar pairing of avoidance and smiling in our two-year-olds' reactions to the Jack-in-the-box, as illustrated in the following sequence of one child's behaviours after the first fast pop-up: simultaneous startle and neutral face with the child hitting the clown as it pops up, followed by smile and simultaneous gaze aversion (i.e. child does not look at the toy or the mother), followed in turn by approach, big smile, and retreat. All of these behaviours occurred within three seconds of the pop-up.

Tennes, Emde, Kisley, and Metcalf (1972) have also investigated the development of the infants' capacity to regulate their level of arousal. Based on Benjamin's theory (1965), they suggest a neurological basis for the infant's capacity to modulate arousal, with the capacity of inhibiting or controlling responses developing during the third or fourth month and rapidly maturing thereafter. In Tennes et al.'s view, these regulatory mechanisms allow the infant to shut out stimuli; before three or four months, infants cannot actively avoid stimulation. In their research, Tennes et al. (1972) found that obligatory looking at a bull's eye or striped target initially develops at around four weeks in the majority of their longitudinal sample of twelve infants. At first, obligatory looking usually leads to distress, but by about the fourth month, infants are able to look at a stimulus, turn away, and then return to the stimulus. Tennes et al. found similar developmental changes in infants' responses to the ringing of a bell and blasts on a toy horn. After fourteen weeks, infants would startle to the sound of the horn, and then avert their heads and become visually attentive to other objects in the room, maintaining their attention without further response to the sounds of the horn. Their observations are similar to Stern's in finding modulation of arousal levels in three- to four-month-old infants; however, Tennes et al. do not ascribe negative affect to the infants' visual avoidances.

The development of regulatory mechanisms to control stimulation and thereby control arousal level may be related both to neurological maturation of inhibitory processes and also to changes in the child's level of cognitive development as described by Piaget (1963). Piaget proposed that during Stage III of sensorimotor development, beginning at about three or four months of age, infants learn to control external stimulation. For example, Piaget observed that his own children at about three or four months learned to move objects suspended above their cribs by striking the objects with their hands. This behaviour was learned only after the child accidentally moved the objects. According to Piaget, this activity is an early form of goal-directed behaviour. Infants during Stage III learn to separate the goal of their behaviour (e.g. looking at moving objects) from the means for achieving that goal (e.g. striking the objects). While Piaget primarily focused on goal-directed activities which produced external stimulation, such activities may also include behaviours which serve to terminate external stimulation. If so, the development of regulatory mechanisms may depend on neurological changes and also on changes in infants' cognitive structures.

Methodological implications. Our results concerning the relationship between affect and approach-avoidance strongly challenge the common assumption that visual and/or behavioural avoidance indicates negative affect. Avoidance may sometimes indicate negative affect, but it may also function to control subjects' arousal levels independently of their affective states. Our data indicate that avoidance responses alone are ambiguous and can only be interpreted in association with a person's facial expression and subsequent approach-avoidance and facial responses. The data provide strong evidence supporting Lewis and Rosenblum's (1974) and Rheingold and Eckerman's (1973) warnings about the danger of inferring fear, wariness, or anxiety too freely from subtle or ambiguous responses. The majority of studies of infants' reactions to novel persons assume that infants' looks to their mothers and/or visual avoidances of a stranger indicate fear or wariness of the stranger. Recent studies of fear of strangers which separate visual avoidance and looking at mother from overt facial or vocal distress (i.e. frowning, crying), however, have found that the latter types of distress are rare (Bretherton and Ainsworth, 1974; Bronson, 1972; Rheingold and Eckerman, 1973; Sroufe *et al.*, 1974). For example, Bronson (1972) observed only ten instances of crying in sixty-three stranger episodes with nine-month-old infants. The conclusion that nine- to twenty-four-month-old infants generally show fear of strangers is based primarily on infants' visual and/or behavioural avoidance of strangers. Furthermore, even these behaviours are usually not distinguished from proximity-to-mother behaviours; contact with mother is assumed to serve an avoidance function. Given our data and those of Stern (1974a) that three- and four-month-old infants show gaze aversion interspersed with smiles and laughter in play sessions with their own mothers, we strongly question the conclusion that a majority of infants show fear of strangers. Such conclusions can only be made given detailed observations of both affective and approach-avoidance responses and the pattern and sequence of these responses (see also Lewis and Rosenblum, 1974).

Our data also question Bronson's (1972) and Bretherton and Ainsworth's (1974) proposals that strangers activate two separate systems, an affiliative system, which they define as friendliness to a person other than an attachment figure, and a wariness system. If smiling indicates positive affect and avoidance negative affect, then two independent systems (e.g. affiliation and wariness) are necessary to account for instances in which infants simultaneously smile and avoid strangers. If, however, avoidance does not indicate negative affect, then there is no need to postulate two systems to account for instances in which infants smile and simultaneously avoid strangers. Even given the assumption that independent affiliative and wariness systems exist, these two systems cannot account for our data indicating smiling and avoidance with an inanimate object, since as Bretherton and Ainsworth (1974) define it, an affiliative system should only be activated with animate objects. To explain our data using the assumption that avoidance indicates negative affect, still another system must be proposed. We will leave proponents of the avoidance-negative affect assumption to specify this other system. Instead, we have proposed that avoidance alone does *not* indicate negative affect, and therefore smiles and avoidance are compatible with a single affective system. Based on our own research and research by Tennes *et al.* (1972) and Stern (1974a, 1974b), we would instead argue that both smiles and avoidance may be elicited by high levels of arousal, and avoidance responses may be used to prevent arousal from reaching high aversive levels or to prevent the situation from becoming threatening.

SUMMARY AND CONCLUSIONS

In this chapter we have discussed young children's affective responses to incongruity. In our observational study of two-year-old children's reactions to an incongruous toy, children showed both humour responses and pleasure in mastery to the toy. We differentiated incongruity humour from pleasure in mastery based on Piaget's distinction between ludic and reality assimilation of incongruous events. In our model of the origins of incongruity humour, we argued that the capacity for symbolic play as defined by Piaget is not necessary for the appreciation of incongruity humour. Pre-symbolic infants should appreciate incongruity humour when they are capable of ludic assimilation of incongruous events (i.e. by about four months of age).

In our observational study we unexpectedly found that avoidance responses were associated with high-arousal events and with smiles to high-arousal events. The co-occurrence of smiles and avoidance behaviours suggested that avoidance may serve to modulate high levels of arousal. Avoidance responses by themselves may not necessarily indicate negative affect; in relatively safe, non-threatening situations such as the present toy setting, avoidance may prevent high levels of arousal that are pleasurable from reaching very high, aversive levels. In potentially threatening situations such as a fear-of-stranger experiment, avoidance may prevent high, potentially aversive arousal levels from becoming higher and aversive. Control of arousal levels is possible not only through children's avoidance of the arousal-increasing stimulus, since contextual cues may also serve to define a situation as safe and non-threatening. Further research is necessary with children to determine the cues that children use to define a situation as safe. Such research will be beneficial not only in increasing our understanding of origins of humour appreciation, but also in understanding further the relationship between cognitive and emotional development.

APPENDIX A

Behavioural categories

   I. Actions involving toy
1. Close lid. Child snaps lid closed on toy.
2. Hold lid. Child depresses lid somewhat but does not close it.
3. Touch lid.
4. Touch or push button.
5. Touch or push lever.
6. Touch or push clown resulting in noise.
7. Touch or push clown with no noise.
8. Touch or hold box.

   II. Major facial expressions
1. Smile. Corners of mouth upturned; teeth may or may not be showing.
2. Big smile. Corners of mouth drawn as far upwards as possible; usually with open mouth.
3. Distress face. Corners of mouth turned down as in a frown or lower lip protruded as in pout.

(The following facial expressions were scored but are not distinguished from each other in this chapter):
4. Open mouth. Jaw dropped more than in relaxed open mouth position.
5. Extended mouth. Mouth tautly pulled back so lips are level.
6. Neutral. Face relaxed.
7. Grimace. Furrowed brow accompanied by extended mouth or smile (if smile alone does not precede or follow furrowed brow).
8. Wry face. One corner of mouth up, other corner level or turned down.
9. Self-stimulation. Manipulation of lips or jaw, e.g. lip biting, tongue between lips.
10. Manual self-stimulation. Any hand to mouth behaviour such as thumb sucking, finger in mouth.

   III. Minor facial expressions
These behaviours could occur simultaneously with major facial expressions. (These expressions were scored but are not reported in the present chapter.)

1. Surprise. Reaction to pop up; eyes widening or eye blink alone.
2. Startle. Reaction to pop up; sudden jerk of head. shoulders, hands. May include blink or eyes widening.
3. Furrowed brow. Eyebrows drawn together or knitted.
4. Brow raise. Eyebrows lifted and horizontal wrinkling of forehead.
5. Nose wrinkle. Nostrils drawn up resulting in horizontal wrinkling of bridge of the nose.
6. Body self-stimulation. Repetitive body movements such as leg swinging, rubbing body against chair.

IV. Looking responses
1. Look at clown, button, lid, toy in general.
2. Look at experimenter or camera operator.
3. Look at mother.
4. Gaze aversion. Looks downward and away from toy but not at anyone.
5. Eyes closed. Eyes must be closed for half-second or more.
6. Look around. Looks aways from toy; gaze is level or upward.
7. Hide eyes. One or both eyes are covered by arm or hands.
8. Head turn. Child turns head away from toy, but does not look at anyone.
9. Head turn toward mother. Child turns head away from toy and looks at mother.
10. Hide face. Face hidden behind mother or in mother's lap.

V. Locomotor behaviour, claps, and handclasps
1. Approach. Child leans or moves toward toy in a direct line. (Number of lines crossed was noted.)
2. Retreat. Child leans or moves away from toy in direct line. (Number of lines crossed was noted.)
3. Side. Child moves but no direct movement toward or away from toy.
4. Touch mother.
5. Move with toy.
6. Clap hands.
7. Clasp hands.

VI. Vocalizations
1. Laughter ranging from giggles to guffaws by mother or child.
2. All utterances transcribed.

VII. State of toy
1. Noise. Noise produced by depressing clown.
2. Fast pop up. Clown pops up after button is pushed.

3. Slow pop up. Clown pops up after button is pushed, but child has hand on lid so pop up is slower than fast pop up.
4. Horizontal pop up. Box turned on side so clown pops out horizontally.

NOTE

This research was sponsored in part by BSRG Grant RB 07080 awarded by the Biomedical Research Support Grant Program, Division of Research Resources, National Institute of Health. We wish to thank Myron Rothbart for his helpful comments and criticisms on earlier versions of this paper.

REFERENCES

Ainsworth, M. D. S., and Bell, S. (1970). Attachment, exploration and separation: illustrated by the behavior of one-year-olds in a strange situation. *Child Development*, **41**, 49–67.

Benjamin, J. (1965). Developmental biology and psychoanalysis. In N. Greenfield and W. Lewis (Eds.), *Psychoanalysis and Current Biological Thought*. Madison: University of Wisconsin Press.

Berlyne, D. E. (1960). *Conflict, Arousal and Curiosity*. New York: McGraw-Hill.

Berlyne, D. E. (1969). Laughter, humor and play. In G. Lindzey and E. Aronson (Eds.), *Handbook of Social Psychology*. Vol. 3 Reading, Massachusetts: Addison-Wesley.

Berlyne, D. E. (1972). Humor and its kin. In J. H. Goldstein and P. E. McGhee (Eds.), *The Psychology of Humor*. New York: Academic Press.

Berlyne, D. E., and Lawrence, F. H. (1964). Effects of complexity and incongruity variables on G. S. R., investigatory behavior, and verbally expressed preference. *Journal of General Psychology*, **71**, 21–45.

Bower, T. G. R. (1971). The object in the world of the infant. *Scientific American*, **225**, 30–38.

Bower, T. G. R. (1974). *Development in Infancy*. San Francisco: Freeman.

Bower, T. G. R., Broughton, J. M., and Moore, M. K. (1971). The development of the object concept as manifested by changes in the tracking behavior of infants' behavior between 7 and 20 weeks of age. *Journal of Experimental Child Psychology*, **11**, 182–193.

Bretherton, I., and Ainsworth, M. D. S. (1974). Responses of one-year-olds to a stranger in a strange situation. In M. Lewis and L. Rosenblum (Eds.), *The Origins of Fear*. New York: Wiley.

Bronson, G. W. (1972). Infants' reactions to unfamiliar persons and novel objects. *Monographs of the Society for Research in Child Development*, **32** (3, Serial No. 148).

Butler, R. A. (1964). The reactions of rhesus monkeys to fear-provoking stimuli. *Journal of Genetic Psychology*, **104**, 321–330.

Charlesworth, W. R. (1969). The role of surprise in cognitive development. In D. Elkind and J. H. Flavell (Eds.), *Studies in Cognitive Development*. New York: Oxford.

Faw, T. T., and Nunnally, J. C. (1967). The effects on eye movements of complexity, novelty and affective tone. *Perception and Psychophysics*, **2**, 263–267.

Faw, T. T., and Nunnally, J. C. (1968). The influence of stimulus complexity, novelty and affective value on children's visual fixations. *Journal of Experimental Child Psychology*, **6**, 141–153.

Flugel, J. C. (1954). Humor and laughter. In G. Lindzey (Ed.), *Handbook of Social*

Psychology. Cambridge, Massachusetts: Addison-Wesley.

Fry, W. F. (1963). *Sweet Madness: A Study of Humor.* Palo Alto: Pacific Books.

Harter, S. (1974). Pleasure derived by children from cognitive challenge and mastery. *Child Development,* **45,** 661–669.

Harter, S., Shultz, T., and Blum, B. (1971). Smiling in children as a function of their sense of mastery. *Journal of Experimental Child Psychology,* **12,** 396–404.

Hebb, D. O. (1946). On the nature of fear. *Psychological Review,* **53,** 259–276.

Hunt, J. McV. (1961). *Intelligence and Experience.* New York: Ronald.

Kagan, J. (1971). *Change and Continuity in Infancy.* New York: Wiley.

Koestler, A. (1967). *The Act of Creation.* New York: Macmillan.

Lewis, M., and Brooks, J. (1974). Self, other and fear: infants' reactions to people. In M. Lewis and L. Rosenblum (Eds.), *The Origins of Fear.* New York: Wiley.

Lewis, M., and Rosenblum, L. A. (1974). Introduction. In. M. Lewis and L. A. Rosenblum (Eds.), *The Origins of Fear.* New York: Wiley.

McGhee, P. E. (1971). The development of the humor response: a review of the literature. *Psychological Bulletin,* **71,** 328–348.

McGhee, P. E. (1972). On the cognitive origins of incongruity humor: fantasy assimilation versus reality assimilation. In J. H. Goldstein and P. E. McGhee (Eds.), *The Psychology of Humor.* New York: Academic Press.

McGhee, P. E. (1974). Cognitive mastery and children's humor. *Psychological Bulletin,* **81,** 721–730.

McGhee, P. E. (1977). A model of the origins and early development of incongruity-based humour. In A. J. Chapman and H. C. Foot (Eds.), *It's a Funny Thing, Humour.* Oxford: Pergamon Press.

Morgan G., and Ricciuti, H. N. (1969). Infants' responses to strangers during the first year. In B. M. Foss (Ed.), *Determinants of Infant Behaviour.* Vol. 4. London: Methuen.

Piaget, J. (1962). *Play, Dreams and Imitation in Childhood.* New York: Norton. (Original French edition, 1945).

Piaget, J. (1963). *The Origins of Intelligence in Children.* New York: Norton. (Original French edition, 1936).

Rheingold, H., and Eckerman, C. O. (1973). Fear of the stranger: a critical examination. In H. W. Reese (Ed.), *Advances in Child Development and Behavior.* New York: Academic Press.

Rothbart, M. K. (1973). Laughter in young children. *Psychological Bulletin,* **80,** 247–256.

Rothbart, M. K. (1976). Incongruity, problem-solving and laughter. In A. J. Chapman and H. C. Foot (Eds.), *Humour and Laughter: Theory, Research and Applications.* Chichester: Wiley.

Rothbart, M. K. (1977). Psychological approaches to the study of humour. In A. J. Chapman and H. C. Foot (Eds.), *It's a Funny Thing, Humour.* Oxford: Pergamon Press.

Rothbart, M. K., and Pien, D. (1977). Elephants and marshmallows: a theoretical synthesis of incongruity-resolution and arousal theories. In A. J. Chapman and H. C. Foot (Eds.), *It's a Funny Thing, Humour,* Oxford: Pergamon Press.

Scarr, S., and Salapatek, P. (1970). Patterns of fear development during infancy. *Merrill-Palmer Quarterly,* **16,** 53–90.

Schaffer, H. R. (1966). The onset of fear of strangers and the incongruity hypothesis. *Journal of Child Psychology and Psychiatry,* **7,** 95–106.

Shultz, T. R. (1972). The role of incongruity and resolution in children's appreciation of cartoon humor. *Journal of Experimental Child Psychology,* **13,** 456–477.

Shultz, T. R. (1976). A cognitive-developmental analysis of humour. In A. J. Chapman and H. C. Foot (Eds.), *Humour and Laughter: Theory, Research and Applications.* Chichester: Wiley.

Sroufe, L. A., and Waters, E. (1976). The ontogenesis of smiling and laughter: a perspective on the organization of development in infancy. *Psychological Review*, **83**, 173–189.

Sroufe, L. A., Waters, E., and Mates, L. (1974). Contextual determinants of infant affective response. In M. Lewis and L. Rosenblum (Eds.), *The Origins of Fear*. New York: Wiley.

Sroufe, L. A., and Wunsch, J. P. (1972). The development of laughter in the first year of life. *Child Development*, **43**, 1326–1344.

Stern, D. N. (1974a). The goal and structure of mother-infant play. *Journal of the American Academy of Child Psychiatry*, **13**, 402–421.

Stern, D. N. (1974b). Mother and infant at play: the dyadic interaction involving facial, vocal and gaze behaviors. In M. Lewis and L. Rosenblum (Eds.), *The Effect of the Infant on Its Caregiver*. New York: Wiley.

Tennes, K., Emde, R., Kisley, A., and Metcalf, D. (1972). The stimulus barrier in early infancy: an exploration of some formulations of John Benjamin. In R. R. Holt and E. Peterfreund (Eds.), *Psychoanalysis and Contemporary Science*. Vol. I. New York: Macmillan.

Waters, E., Matas, L., and Sroufe, L. A. (1975). Infants' reactions to an approaching stranger: description, validation and functional significance of wariness. *Child Development*, **46**, 348–356.

Wolfenstein, M. (1953). Children's understanding of jokes. In *The Psychoanalytic Study of the Child*, **9**, 162–173. New York: International Universities Press.

Wolfenstein, M. (1954). *Children's Humour*. Glencoe, Illinois: Free Press.

Zigler, E., Levine, J., and Gould, L. (1966). Cognitive processes in the development of children's appreciation of humor. *Child Development*, **37**, 507–518.

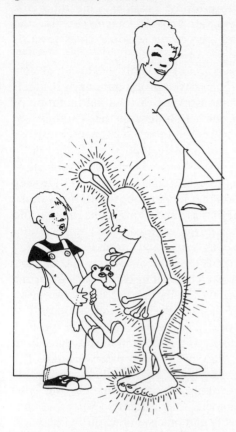

CHAPTER 2

Imagination, Interest, and Joy in Early Childhood: Some Theoretical Considerations and Empirical Findings

RONI BETH TOWER

and

JEROME L. SINGER

What is it about children that makes them so 'cute' and lovable—at least at those moments when we adults are not so hard-pressed by chores and worries and can take the trouble of observing them? Of course they are small and powerless and even the most inept adult can often take some satisfaction from the contrast in size and strength. Children are gullible, too, because they lack experience. The small-minded among us can tease children, repeatedly pretending to pull off their noses (displaying the removed organ to them by inserting our thumb through our other fingers) or can threaten to flush them down the toilet, laughing uproariously as older cousins used to when the smallest was trundled shrieking with terror towards the bathroom.

Probably, however, it is not the child's vulnerability or potential victimization that accounts for its appeal to reasonably mature adults. It is much more likely to be the playfulness, the miniaturization of complex adult affairs into make-believe games and the quaintness of phraseology. Most of all, perhaps, there are the ready smiles and laughs, those predictable and universal symbols of joy which rarely fail to melt our toughened veneers. Since humour (at least beyond the 'horseplay' stage) involves some attitude towards the 'possible', a metaphor or a 'what if?', we are proposing that the interaction between imaginative play and positive emotionality in early childhood may provide some clues towards ultimate humour development.

We know now that the smiling response is almost certainly innate—or at least well prepared for by the child's neuromuscular development quite early in life. If Meltzoff and Moore's (1977) research demonstrating early infant imitation of adult facial expressions is supported by further studies, the baby's ability to translate a perceived physiognomic response into its own neuromuscular expression emphasizes even more than had been realized the adult's role in generating particular affects such as the smile. Michael Lewis' (1977) studies of infant–mother interactions also point up the significance for the child's growing sense of self through its seeming recognition that it can evoke the mother's smile.

In this chapter we seek to examine some of the foundations in imagination and joyful play for the later development of humorous expression and appreciation. We emphasize situations of spontaneous play—the normally occurring activities in a society like ours which demands little else of children—a contrast, of course, with other cultures which involve children in chores as part of the work-force at quite early ages (Feitelson, 1977). By positive affects we mean primarily interest or curiosity and joy, following the theoretical proposals of Tomkins (1962, 1963) as recently elaborated by Izard (1977). The positive implications for self-development of curiosity and interest in novelty have been suggested by the findings of Maw and Maw (1970) with older children. The position we present implies that imaginative play in early childhood represents an especially significant vehicle for evoking not only interest but also considerable joy and smiling in pre-schoolers. One cannot as yet prove that children who show absorption and curiosity and much smiling during play will grow up to be happy adults. We can, however, take comfort in the openness of affective expression in childhood and propose that those children who show a stronger predisposition to engage in imaginative play—in pretending and make-believe games—may at least be enjoying their childhood more than children who show very little make-believe in their play repertory.

Scientific interest in the spontaneous play of the pre-school child is a relatively recent phenomenon. The few early theories attributed play to an excess of energy, to a vague 'instinct', to a need for each species to recapitulate its evolutionary history, or to some hypothesized inherent tendency of organisms to practise behaviours which would be useful in later life. Several extensive reviews of theories and research on play have recently been published (see Ellis, 1973; Millar, 1968; Singer, 1973) along with two outstanding collections of articles (Bruner, Jolly, and Sylva, 1976; Heron and Sutton-Smith, 1971). The increased interest in play reflects the growing understanding of its role in a child's cognitive, social, and emotional development. There is also increasing awareness that the natural development of play behaviours outlined by Piaget (1962) as part of cognitive expansion may not occur for many children without some adult support or systematic parental input (Smilansky, 1968).

One can distinguish perhaps four types of early childhood play, each associated somewhat differently with positive affects of interest and joy. Pure sensory play (the pleasure of stroking soft wool, or reaching for sunbeams, or kissing and cuddling) involves some exploration and much smiling. Mastery play (the emerging competencies of walking, talking, manipulating) is linked closely with strong interest-affect and curiosity, with joy emerging when a goal is accomplished. Symbolic play (imagining and pretending) seems closely tied both to interest and curiosity as well as to joy. Games with rules ('Red Light' or 'Giant Steps'), the fourth type of play, may involve some exploration but predominantly the joy of success. Clearly joy, the major positive affect linked in information-processing terms to the reduction of incongruities and to making the novel familiar (Izard, 1977; Tomkins, 1962, 1963), is central to most play with moderate amounts of the positive affects of interest and surprise involved to varying degrees as well.

Our emphasis in this chapter is upon the origins and significance of play which is imaginative or symbolic, particularly as it relates to the affective experience of the pre-school child. While some prototypes of humour may reflect elements from mastery or rules games (as in tongue-twisters, puns, pratfalls, or sudden breaks in formalities), we believe that the most extensive and complex forms of humour development and humour appreciation may be related to the 'as if' and imagery characteristics of symbolic play.

THE IMAGINATIVE DIMENSION IN COGNITIVE, SOCIAL AND EMOTIONAL GROWTH

Origins of imaginative play

A curious shift in the play of the small child emerges when, at around eighteen months of age (Fein, 1975), the toddler lifts an empty seashell to the mouth of her teddy-bear as if to serve him tea. The child has learned to have one object symbolize another. This representation reflects an ability to schematize information in a qualitatively new way—that is, by imagery, memory of that which is known from previous sensorimotor experience. As Piaget has so clearly described (Piaget, 1962; Pulaski, 1971), the pre-school child uses the accommodation-assimilation process to develop and refine its inborn capacities to form visual, tactile, and auditory images of events.

These representational abilities, although closely paralleling the development of linguistic skills in most children, serve quite different functions than the abstraction language permits and may even take place in a separate hemisphere of the brain (Rose, 1975; Singer, 1974; Witelson, 1975). They may facilitate the development of a host of cognitive, affective, and social skills.

Through the practice of imagery skills in play, the pre-school child may be developing its abilities to maintain attention, distinguish between internally- and externally-generated information, organize the information, rehearse and retain it, reflect on it, correct faulty perceptions and cognitions, elaborate on them, make plans, and integrate the entire experience. In addition, there is reason to believe that these benefits are magnified through the effects which imagery has on language development.

Cognitive benefits of imagery

Attention span. Ample evidence suggests that children maintain imaginative play for longer periods of time than they do predominantly mastery play (Marshall and Hahn, 1967; Singer and Singer, 1976a; Smilansky, 1968). While the source of such attention is probably the positive affective feedback, to be discussed shortly, its effect is to permit sustained concentration to develop. Correlations between imaginativeness of play and concentration during play have been consistently high (Singer and Singer, 1976a, 1976b, 1977; Tower, Singer, Singer, and Biggs, 1978).

Indeed, if one accepts Klinger's evidence and arguments that imaginative play is later internalized as daydreaming (Klinger, 1971; Singer, 1973, 1975), an intriguing relationship between imagery and attention becomes clear: it is just those people who report the least imagery and fantasy who are the most distractible (Singer, 1974, 1975; Singer and Brown, 1977). In studies of pre-school children, Gould has reported that the child who cannot pretend may be aggressive, disruptive, and generally unable to sustain attention (Gould, 1972). These data fit well with the recognized deficit in fantasy skills and attention span in schizophrenics (Blatt and Wild, 1976; Buss and Buss, 1973; Singer, 1975). Starker (1977) found that young adults who reported problems of distractibility and mindwandering in daytime thought experienced more distress and negative affect in night dreams in contrast to those whose daytime fantasies were positive and vivid.

Distinguishing internally-generated from externally-generated information. The child who is skilled in symbolic play develops an ease in differentiating between that which is provided for it by the environment and that which he or she creates in his or her own head. The child who pins a dish towel around its shoulders and announces 'I'm Batman!' may be developing a greater sense of reality than the child who cannot risk its sense of self in role-playing for fear that proclaiming a separate identity will make it materialize permanently. Interestingly, Levin and Wardwell (1962) found imaginative children better able to make *perceptual* distinctions between internal and external information; they performed more accurately in Witkin's classic rod-and-frame and tilted-room tests of field dependence-independence. Tucker (1975) found imaginative children less likely to distort the events of stories in recalling them. The children who showed more imaginativeness of play revealed less tendency to fuse internally-generated and externally-presented information than their less imaginative peers.

Organization of information. Piaget has been a significant force in stressing the organizational functions of imagery (Piaget, 1962; Piaget and Inhelder, 1971) along with Klinger (1971) and Singer (1966, 1973, 1975). In their views, imagery permits the *assimilation* of information, a requisite role in the creation and refinement of schemata. To these researchers, a primary function of symbolic play lies in this integration of the child's internalized experiences with the constraints of reality. Clearly, the more facile a child is in such assimilation or play, the more ease he or she will have in progressing to higher levels of organization. As Harlow (1949) suggested, in his early experiments on 'learning sets' in monkeys, *strategies* for processing information are developed, making integration of new information far easier. In the child, the act of approaching information with a 'set' towards using it in a sociodramatic game may evoke principles of organization that can aid in effective coding and later retrieval (Singer, 1973).

Rehearsal and retention of information. Pretend play requires that a child rehearse the information which s/he has stored. Tooting a cardboard tube as if it were a trumpet assumes that the child has some notion of 'trumpet'. In addition, each rehearsal of a stored image by bringing it into ongoing play adds new associations to it and increases its likelihood of being remembered subsequently. The child who integrates a pretend trip to the zoo into an ongoing sequence of 'house' is using stored experiences in a new context. The child who has the role of 'Mommy' may suggest feeding bananas to the elephant—an image from her experiences—which permits the new association of bananas-as-elephant-food to be made by another child playing 'Daddy' or 'baby'.

Reflectivity. An emerging literature on reflectivity-impulsivity as a cognitive tempo or cognitive style has been reviewed recently elsewhere (Messer, 1976; Kogan, 1976). While reflectivity applies to a variety of problem-solving situations, we will limit our discussion here to the role of *imagery* in the development of cognitive reflection. As Nahme-Huang, Singer, Singer, and Wheaton (1977) and Franklin (1975) have found, imaginative pre-school children show a greater tendency to inhibit response while considering alternatives as measured by the pre-school version of Kagan's Matching Familiar Figures Test. Two explanations suggest themselves: that the imaginative child simply has had more practice in matching images and therefore does it more comfortably, or that the imaginative child knows the positive affect which results from the reduction in novelty produced by matching to stimuli. The latter theory is discussed in more detail shortly.

Transformation of information. Symbolic play is by definition the transformation of reality—it is using one stimulus or situation 'as if' it were another; it is transcending the constraints of present time and space. As a cognitive skill, such transformation permits the creative uses of materials and ideas. Marshall and Hahn (1967), and Franklin (1975) as well as Feitelson (1972), found imaginative children or children who had been trained in imaginative skills to be more able to transform play materials into a variety of objects and uses. Lieberman (1965, 1977) found playful children more able to transform ideas, as they generated more abundant and original ones in response to divergent-production tasks. Dansky (1976) also reported more evidence of creative behaviour in imaginative children.

Correction of faulty perceptions and cognitions. Imagery is the source of a child's ability to match prior experience with present reality. The child who has known rides over a small bridge as 'bridge' and then travels over the Golden Gate to San Francisco could perceive that bridge as something totally new and unrelated to anything from past experience or match the experience and expand his understanding and image of 'bridge' to include the larger. Only if the child has already stored an image of 'bridge' is the second alternative possible. Indeed, the behaviour modification work of Homme, C'de Baca, Cottingham, and Homme (1968) relies heavily on just this process: new imagery is used as corrective of distorted images which cause the child to have difficulties.

Elaboration of perceptions and cognitions. Pretend play requires the elaboration of internally-generated content or it disintegrates. The child who has built an elaborate parking lot with toy cars, trucks, people, and buildings can suddenly become stuck in its play, as if to say 'what do I do now?'. In order to keep going the pleasant environment s/he has created, the child must either elaborate upon it or shift to a new direction. Because of the positive affect engendered by the play, the child has a vested interest in learning to embellish its ideas. As a cognitive skill, this elaboration can be seen in the imaginative child's ability to recall stories in greater detail (Tucker, 1975) and to show more flexibility in its own story-telling (Pulaski, 1973). The transfer of these skills can, again, also be seen in Lieberman's (1965, 1977) studies of divergent thinking processes.

Making plans. The abilities of the child to play imaginatively ultimately result in an ability to generate alternatives, consider their consequences, select a plan and organize implementation of it. While the decision of a pre-school child to set up toy soldiers and enact a battle more reminiscent of a poorly understood television documentary than an actual war seems far removed from the young adult's selection of a career, the former is in some respects a preparation for the latter. First the child must consider options—what possibilities for play actually exist at that time? What themes can be called to mind? Next, resources must be collected, evaluated, and distributed. If the child has been in a room void of soldiers but filled with cars, its play might be different. Gump and Sutton-Smith (1971) have shown the enormous effect of environmental conditions on the play that actually takes place. Potential benefits must be considered: the child who anticipates loss of self-esteem or control in its play is unlikely to engage in it. Finally the child must gain experience in translating its ideas into actions.

Integration of experiences. Finally, imagery skills help a child integrate its experiences, arriving at new schemata. The constant matching and rematching of experience and stored imagery permits not only the exercise—and hence likelihood of later recall—of the latter, but the enhancement of the former, as experience is enriched by one's associations.

Imagery and language. There is evidence that the pre-school children do not simultaneously encode information both verbally and visually (Forisha, 1975; Mowbray and Luria, 1973; Reese, 1975; Tversky, 1973). Whereas verbal encoding is used more as children age (Kendler, 1963) and the systems appear to be integrated and mutually supportive by a mental age of nine years (Forisha, 1975), the small child is at least as likely to use visual encoding as verbal (Tversky, 1973) if not actually more likely (Perlmutter and Myers 1975; Reese, 1975; Wilgosh, 1975).

The importance of imagery in early childhood as a means of actually obtaining information which can be later labelled by the child is clear. The child to whom 'dog' means 'my collie' can match that image against future information of similar labels and thus learn both generalization (for example, to 'furry animals that bark') and discrimination ('but not if they have no legs and swim in water'). A rich fund of imagery and practice in matching new information to stored images accelerates language and concept development.

Second, imaginative play facilitates the development of verbal skills by providing opportunities to try out novel combinations in a non-evaluative context. Children can often be overheard singing to their dolls and teddy-bears before they are willing to sing with the family. Similarly, they gain mastery over novel sounds and rhythms, an essential dimension of communicative speech, through duplicating those in their personal environments as they play. The 'vroom, vroom' accompanying a Tonka truck or 'eeeee' of a fantasized fire engine reflect the child's accurate perception that sounds can have meanings.

Finally, language is above all a means of communication. And it is in social play that the relationships between imaginative play and linguistic development can be most clearly seen. Children who are skilled at sociodramatic play, whether by predisposition (Singer, Caldeira, and Singer, 1977) or training (Lewis, 1973; Lovinger, 1974; Marshall and Hahn, 1967; Smilansky 1968) have larger vocabularies, use longer sentences, and create more complex sentences. As these researchers have pointed out, the assumption of a role in a pretend game with other children requires one to express the dimensions s/he assigns to that role. In the interest of maintaining the play, speech becomes more effective. And in the increased mastery of pronounciation, parts of speech and syntax linked to games of pretend and a general playfulness (Lieberman, 1977) may lie the beginnings of the verbal twists and metaphoric thrusts that become jokes and humorous phraseology.

Perhaps the child who enjoys imaginative play also becomes eager for more potential input—and thus more alert to stories, films, aesthetic experiences. From the richness of these sources, the child can learn new words to label experiences, new nuances of inflection to use in character portrayal, and, quite often, new phrases to be applied both appropriately and inappropriately to novel situations. A four-year-old, assuming the role of a quite adult expert, announced to her father, 'You know, you shouldn't smoke'. When asked 'Why not?' she paused, thoughtfully, and then authoritatively announced, 'Because you could burn up'. The style and message of the anti-smoking commercial had been clearly communicated but its rationale was beyond her.

Social benefits of imagery

As children progress in their pre-school development, changes in the content, context, and elaboration of pretending are striking. The two-year-old who fleetingly offered her teddy-bear a stone as a cupcake becomes the three-year-old who can play a game of 'house' and assume the role of mother or sister or baby herself and, later, who can create characterisitcs of the role-players and story-lines to act out.

Such sociodramatic play improves a child's sensitivity to other children, empathy for them, poise in front of them, and it increases ways of interacting with them. It is equally helpful in relationships with adults, providing a common arena for interactions with parents, yielding sophisticated combinations of behaviour useful in eliciting adult approval, facilitating self-entertainment when adults are preoccupied with other matters, and, as Stone (1971) has suggested, providing acculturation into the myths and traditions of their culture. Finally, imaginative play can serve as a communication system through which an adult can reach an otherwise unreachable child.

Sensitivity to others. As Marshall and Hahn (1967), and Smilansky (1968) found, sociodramatic play increases a child's sensitivity to the behaviour of other children—both verbal and non-verbal. Interpretation of the usually non-verbal message 'this is play' (Bateson, 1955) is necessary if children are to be able to create and develop 'scripts'. Here we may also see some origins of the signal 'this is a joke'.

Increased empathy. When the small child imagines itself to be a salesperson or customer, a parent or sibling, the child can try out a segment of life from another's point of view. By experiencing a situation the way the child imagines a person in the designated role would experience it, the child gains empathy for feelings of another in that role. Thus, s/he might learn that even though a fireman with a cut knee does not cry, the fireman still feels pain, or that having a whining baby in the room can become very annoying and make a parent feel angry and frustrated. Gould (1972) has elaborated on such situations. Saltz's (1976) fine studies of training urban ghetto children in thematic fantasy play also demonstrate that such children increase in the ability to identify others' emotions relative to a control group. Empathy expands the role-taking capacity. Indeed the humorist's skill often lies in playing the part of the underdog or the bedevilled, for example Woody Allen's representing a hopeful spermatozoa in his 'sex' movie.

Poise. The possibility that play facilitates poise has been suggested by Sutton-Smith (1971). And, indeed, when one watches the tenacity with which a child recreates a baffling or embarrassing experience in play, this benefit is clear. By living a first vacation or visit to the hospital through in pretend play, the child may learn what is expected of him or her in the new situation and may practise rising to those expectations. Similarly, alternative responses to a situation where the child felt incompetent can be tried out through play. The small child's delight in slapstick humour reflects an appreciation of a loss of poise—especially when it's all in fun.

Avenues for interaction. One of the most delightful applications of imaginative play is in providing a child with a variety of ways to interact with others. As Parten found as early as 1933 (Parten, 1971) and as Rubin, Maioni, and Hornung (1976) recently replicated, imaginative play surpasses motor or manipulative play in popularity as pre-school children grow. Part of the reason for this is surely that role-play provides easy access to others. By announcing, 'I'll be the newspaperman' or 'I'm the painter come to paint your house', the small child has an efficient means of joining the ongoing play of others. In addition, his or her own ideas become valuable to the other children and co-operation flourishes. One wonders how many comedians got their early identification by volunteering for clownish or oafish roles eschewed by other children.

Play with parents. When a child engages in imaginative play with a parent, a very special phenomenon is taking place: the child is generating and executing ideas based on its own experience in a context of mutual respect, interest, and absence of criticism. Parent and child are free to experience each other in terms of possibilities. Constraints inherent in the usual roles they play in relation to each other may be temporarily put aside. The give and take of laughter and of shared 'dangers' or 'rescues' may enhance a positive sense of communion. Parents often have lost touch with their own childhood joys in fantasy play and can regain some of that excitement through play (Singer and Singer, 1977).

Sophisticated combinations of behaviour. Quite commonly children transfer skills developed in make-believe play to real-life situations, much to a parent's delight. Routines created, elaborated, and polished in pretend play may easily be brought into a child's behaviour in a restaurant, while shopping, or during a visit to grandparents. The little scenes from play (often those initially based on childhood misunderstandings) which evoked good-humoured laughter may also form the basis for repetition in the interest of 'getting a laugh'.

Self-entertainment. A common source of friction between parents and children occurs when children are called upon to withstand boring or redundant situations. Waiting for a turn in the barber's chair or for Mother to get off the telephone can easily lead to frustration and attention-getting activity in the small child. Frequently, parents then respond with anger and the child, feeling increasingly powerless, escalates the annoying behaviour. Being skilled at pretending can enable a child to create an alternative setting to the actual one and to amuse himself or herself with it. In an experiment in waiting behaviour, Singer (1961) found that children who pretended to be spacemen when seated in a 'space capsule' endured the wait with far less difficulty than those who remained attuned to the external situation. The child who can begin a game of store or train while Mother is on the phone is going to get along better with Mother than the one who spends the time tugging at her or emptying the bureau drawers.

Acculturation. Stone has suggested that imaginative play serves to 'maintain and keep viable the past of the society—its myths, legends, villains, and heroes' (Stone, 1971, p. 10). Thus, pre-school children recreate the American Revolutionary War with toy soldiers and act out the tales of 'Cinderella' and 'Snow White'.

Not only does play serve acculturation by transmitting the myths of a society, but, as Sutton-Smith has stressed (1971), a critical skill for effective functioning in society is that of effective 'boundary behaviour'—being able to play and not play, and to distinguish between contexts appropriate to both. In this social application of the cognitive real/not-real discrimination discussed earlier, the child learns to regulate its own movement in and out of play in accordance with the activities and setting around it. This discrimination may be crucial later in being able to signal to others that a behaviour or verbal sequence is humorously intended and also in detecting humorous behaviour in others.

A bridge in communication. Finally, in the disturbed child, imaginative play may be the most effective bridge between the child and a therapeutic adult. Thus Singer (1973, 1974) discusses the extensive therapeutic uses of imagery and Gardner (1971) and Kritzberg (1975) have developed 'mutual storytelling' techniques as a means for adult and child to create experiences which can then be used therapeutically. The use of a 'clown' identity has been shown to be an extremely promising approach with very disturbed, hospitalized children (Nahme-Huang *et al.*, 1977).

Affect and imaginative play

The relationship between imaginative play and the emotional life of the child is especially intriguing. Three different themes can be discerned: emotions as the motivating source of play; improved emotional well-being as a result of imaginative play; and the facilitation of behavioural change through exploitation of the cognitive-affective implications of imaginative play. Since the role of affect in stimulating and maintaining play is discussed thoroughly in the next section, only the latter themes will be considered here.

Improved emotional well-being. The emotional benefits of imaginative play to the child are well known. Pretending can lead to an increased repertoire for expressing feelings, more spontaneity in their expression, reduced fear and anxiety, an increased sense of mastery, and a range of benefits that are associated with the increased positive affect yielded by imaginative play—more ease in delaying gratification, greater self-reward, more generosity, more self-control, and healthy self-interest (Singer and Singer, 1976a).

Increased avenues of expression. The imaginative child spends much time interpreting situations with their accompanying thoughts and feelings, fear, anger, sadness, or digust. Because 'pretending' is often more acceptable to parents than direct expression of these negative affects, the child who can assimilate its unpleasant experiences by translating them into play is more likely (a) to feel free to experience the feelings and (b) to develop a variety of methods of expression. For example, anger could appear in make-believe as a 'Mommy' tirading, a 'baby' throwing a tantrum, a 'monster' stomping, or an 'army guy' barking orders. We do not wish here to endorse the catharsis hypothesis of fantasy (i.e. that associative thought arises out of an intense drive state and serves to release the pent-up emotions of that state). Rather, we are suggesting that fantasy provides a fund of alternatives for expressing emotions as they occur in daily living. Surely the full expression of one's affect, as Tomkins has claimed (1962), is a potential wired into the human being. Tomkins has proposed that we are basically motivated to maximize positive affects, minimize negative affects, express affects as fully as possible, and yet also control them. *Play provides*

the child with a miniature theatre for expressing yet controlling affect.
It might follow from this approach that humour, at least in its somewhat subtler forms, is a special case of imaginative play. It provides a miniaturized, clearly delineated theatre for expressing a range of possibilities that, presented directly, might lead to conflicts and resentments. The medieval and renaissance buffoon or jester, adorned in cap and bells, could speak the unspeakable because his costume and role suggested 'make-believe'. The Fool in *King Lear* says the simple truth in playful terms and in this miniaturized form that truth can be tolerated. Humour may indeed maximize positive affect, minimize negative, yet give the appearance of controlled expression much as does the child's playing of battles or combats with monsters.

Increased spontaneity. Having an increased repertoire to draw from in responding to situations, the imaginative child is likely to feel more comfortable in expressing itself. In addition, the likelihood that the child has incurred fewer negative reactions from the adults in its life for such expressions, as previously discussed, increases the likelihood that it will, finding its behaviour inherently rewarding, engage in it more freely. By feeling good about his or her own ability to deal with experience—a direct result of facility with assimilation—the child is free to respond to new experiences with a minimum of inappropriate internal constraints. Play, since it allows a variety of possibilities, increases the range of the child's potential reactions. Thus the child experienced in imaginative play may be less likely to express cliché or repetitive responses.

Reduced fear and anxiety. According to Tomkins' theory of affects (1962, 1963), fear is triggered by the too sudden introduction of novel information. Thus an unfamiliar adult may make a distorted face at a baby and watch the infant shrink back in fear, while the same face leads to interest and then laughter in older children who have some preparation for the contextual situation. Similarly, the child's first experience with nursery school is likely to evoke fear to the extent that the child is unfamiliar with the qualities of the setting—the place, the objects in the room, the other children, the activities, the teachers, and the expectations the teachers hold for it. The child who is skilled at pretending can replay the novel experiences and, in so doing, reduce their novelty. This familiarization serves, as Erikson (1940) suggested, to restore a sense of mastery to the child. And, indeed, imaginative children have been shown to be less fearful than their more stimulus-bound peers (Halverson and Waldrop 1974; Singer and Singer, 1977). Studies by Gould (1972) and observations by Singer (1973) suggest that the fearful child is likely to be inhibited in ability to express itself through fantasy play. Perhaps Axline's (1965) belief that the power of play therapy lies not in interpretations, but in the act itself, reflects the enormous self-regulative power of play.

Not only can pretending reduce fear of the novel through making it familiar, as

Peller has suggested (1971), but it can serve to transform the traumatic, to rework the experience that is indeed unassimilable in its initial form. The child who has had his or her tonsils removed frequently plays hospital; the child who experiences the death of a relative may repeat the theme in play. A five-year-old overheard his mother telling his father over the telephone of John F. Kennedy's assassination. He ran to the record player and put on a recording of a comedian's mimicry of the Kennedy family and played it over and over again on that bleak November afternoon.

Increased sense of mastery. The child's ability to pretend leads to increased feelings of mastery and increased control. This most important benefit results from (a) an ability to transcend the constraints of reality through play; (b) an increased repertoire for dealing with novel situations; (c) greater impulse control; (d) techniques readily available for dealing with boredom and redundancy in the environment.

Increased positive affect. There is an increasing body of evidence that imaginative children are happier in their play, showing more smiling and laughing and sustained interest, than less imaginative children (Marshall and Hahn, 1967; Singer, 1973; Singer and Singer, 1977; Tower, Singer, Singer, and Biggs, 1978). Research on the implications of such happiness are only now beginning. But in an intriguing series of studies, investigators have been sorting out the benefits of positive affect itself from a more broad series of studies on the benefits of feelings of success. By having children 'think happy' or 'think sad' and giving control groups neutral tasks such as counting exercises, they have found that *thinking happy thoughts in itself* leads to increased sharing and thoughtfulness of others (Moore, Underwood, and Rosenhan, 1973), greater delay of gratification (Moore, Clyburn, and Underwood, 1976), a tendency to reward onself more generously (Underwood, Moore, and Rosenhan, 1973; Vanty and Vaillant, 1975), and a willingness to think ahead in order to maximize one's benefits (Moore, Clyburn, and Underwood, 1976). Clearly a child's mood can influence its behaviours and, through repetition, most likely its set towards itself—its self-esteem. It would be intriguing to study if the ease of generating positive affect through play yields children with more positive self-concepts later in life.

Is it possible that the practice in sustained interest, laughing, and smiling which children obtain through imaginative play prepares them better to be 'receivers' of humorous messages? While laughter is inborn, there are wide individual differences in how easily people smile or guffaw, how open they are to seeing possibilities for absurdity, for noticing novel twists in language or gesture and feeling able to acknowledge these perceptions by overt affective responses. We might again speculate that children who play at make-believe can later enjoy humour and express their joy.

Self-control. An emerging body of work attests to the role of imagery in the young child's development of self-control. Donald Meichenbaum and his associates have amply demonstrated the uses of imagery in helping impulsive children slow down (Meichenbaum, 1971, 1976, 1977). By having them conjure up mental pictures of 'a slow turtle', and accompany the imagery with self-instructions concerning sequences of action, the researchers have been able to help the children develop self-control. Interestingly, Meichenbaum reports that his techniques are most effective with young children when they are worked into the ongoing play of the child.

In a different type of experiment, Lazarus and Abramovitz (1962) and Lazarus, Davison, and Polefka (1965) have used imagery as a means of helping young children to cope with intense fears. By placing the terrifying event in a familiar—and therefore usually incongruous—context, they managed to help children eliminate phobias. A rendezvous with Superman in the dark or an appointment to accompany Batman to the dentist did wonders for formerly terror-stricken children.

Finally, a series of experiments with delinquent adolescents has shown not only that the youths are deficient in imaginative skills, but that training such skills increases their understanding of and respect for the feelings and actions of others (Chandler, 1973). Chandler had the youths make up stories about people their age and then act them out in movies, alternating roles.

In summary, the power of imaginative play is great indeed. It yields cognitive, social and affective benefits to the child skilled in its use, enabling it to deal with its world as a coping, competent, responsive being.

A COGNITIVE-AFFECTIVE APPROACH TO IMAGINATIVE PLAY

Tomkins' theory of affect

For much of this century psychology has focused attention on negative affective experiences as motivational variables: for example, upon efforts to reduce anxiety or guilt or simply to satisfy presumed biological need states such as hunger, thirst, sex, or, for some, aggression. Indeed, Freud, whose very name in German suggests the emotion of joy, rarely examines the importance of positive affects.

A major systematic change in thinking about emotions as motivators of behaviour was initiated by Tomkins (1962, 1963), who emphasizes the role of positive affects of interest-excitement and joy-smiling. Tomkins' theory, influenced by Darwin's early insights on the evolution of emotion, stresses the principle that humans have developed a limited but differentiated series of affects which are experienced differently and expressed primarily through clearly delineated facial musculature. Indeed, the facial expression with its selective muscular feedback *is* the emotion which serves to amplify cognitive or drive system messages as well as to communicate to others motivational information. Support for this theory, and further elaboration of its implications, has emerged in an increasing body of research by Izard (1971, 1972, 1977), by Ekman and various collaborators (Ekman and Friesen, 1975; Ekman, Friesman, and Ellsworth, 1971), and by Schwartz and his associates (Schewartz, Fair, Greenberg, Freedman, and Klerman, 1974; Schwartz, Fair, Salt, Mandel, and Klerman, 1976).

Of special relevance to the issue of play is Tomkins' linkage of affects to the very nature of the information-processing tasks we continuously confront. He proposes that the innate activators of emotions can be expressed in terms of gradients of evoked or reduced density of neural firing over time. Thus, a sudden unexpected loud noise may evoke *startle* or extreme *fear*. If the noise persists and the recruitment of neural firing continues over time at a very high level, one would experience *anger*. At a somewhat lower level of density over time one might rather feel *sadness* or *distress*. A *moderate* rise in density of neural firing should evoke the positive affects of *interest* and *excitement* while a sharp decrease in density of neural firing would evoke *joy*, *laughter*, or the *smiling response*.

Because of the difficulty of operationalizing *density of neural firing*, it might seem more useful initially to translate this notion into a form such as assimilation of novel information (Singer, 1973, 1974). Let us assume that we differ in the number, differentiation, and integration of cognitive schemata which we bring to each new situation. We may also be viewed as bringing to bear on each new setting a number of anticipatory plans (which allow a series of motor subroutines to be run off relatively smoothly) or more complex anticipations (often in the form of images) and, indeed, even relatively long-term 'scripts' (Schank and Abelson, 1977). We are continuously matching each new set of information we confront with such plans or anticipations and then assimilating new data into our established images or schemata.

From this vantage point, a sudden, unexpected noise (an explosion or pistol shot) or even a grossly unexpected visual stimulus such as the appearance at the door of a deformed midget when we had been expecting from a prior telephone conversation a person of average size and carriage, can evoke startle or fear-terror. The persistence over time of a high degree of information in a situation which was not anticipated and cannot easily be assimilated to established schemata should evoke anger or deep sadness. The teacher who returns to a classroom to find a favourite, trusted pupil cheating in an examination may be angered as the evidence piles up that previous evidences of the child's trustworthiness, from which the teacher had built a kind of script, are now possibly all inaccurate. Later, even after expressing wrath or punishing the child, the teacher may still be unable to assimilate this new information into well-established schemata. Having believed for years that children were basically 'good' and incapable of deception without an adult's encouragement, the teacher must now fit these new facts into his system and he experiences sadness. Recall

Freud's depression when he came upon indications that his theory of early childhood sexual seductions as a major aetiological factor in neurosis was based on grossly inaccurate statements of several patients. Freud was able to break out of the depression and experience the joy of continued investigation only when he recognized that the early childhood *fantasy* of parental seduction could explain his findings, thus saving the broader theory and reducing the incongruity of his new information.

However, moderate degrees of novelty in a situation are interesting and pleasing. They evoke excitement and exploratory behaviours as the child seeks to assimilate the novel material. One thinks here of Weisler and McCall's (1976) and Hutt's (1970, 1977) emphasis on moderate arousal to explain curiosity. What makes for moderate assimilability is the fact that some schemata or anticipatory plans are already available in a given situation. If the doorbell rings and one opens it to find a Dracula-like creature outside, one might be startled or frightened. If, however, one already knew it was Halloween, the reaction might be more one of curiosity and interest—who could have got together such a realistic costume?

Exploration then involves gradual assimilation of novelty into some organized relation to established schemata. A sharp drop from a high level of novel information may evoke the experience of joy or the response of smiling and laughing. A husband returns home late at night. When he pulls away the bed covers from her face he sees, instead of his wife's features, those of a wrinkled, ugly crone. He leaps back in fright but at the sound of her familiar voice saying 'trick or treat, darling', he experiences joy and pulls off her mask to kiss her as they both laugh.

While Tomkins has not elaborated a specific theory of humour, we can extrapolate from his general scheme a possible relationship between humour and imaginative play. The make-believe games of children are generally linked to specific verbal and postural signals: 'Let's play "school"! You be the "kid", I'll be the "teacher"!'. This signal establishes a cognitive structure in which whatever novelty occurs does so within a delimited, well-understood context. Thus the novelty is moderate and evokes the affect of interest which, when material is soon assimilated, leads to joy or the smiling response.

Humour is often clearly delineated by some prior signal which alerts one to the fact that whatever novelty may occur will come within the framework of a 'plan' we have, namely to expect some novelty. The 'stand-up' comedian by definition prepares us to anticipate novelty and so we are not likely to experience startle but rather surprise-interest when he puts forward an outlandish proposition such as the 'fact' that Adolf Hitler is alive and well and living in Israel under an Argentinian pseudonym. Just as the child signals by saying 'Let's make-believe' and reduces all subsequent 'dangers' to a miniaturized, assimilable form, so too do we prepare even the prudish for the salacious by asking if they have heard the latest joke. A considerable amount of humour may indeed occur under circumstances in which, having accepted the premise of a 'just suppose', new information or decontextualized novelty that might otherwise shock or frighten now arouses lively interest and then, as it is assimilated, evokes the smiling or laughing response.

In general, the cognitive-affective differential emotion theory stresses the close tie between information-processing and motivating emotional experiences. Tomkins suggests that we seek to repeat positive affective experiences (interest and joy), to minimize the occurrence of negative affects (such as anger, fear, sadness, shame, or humiliation), to express our affects and yet also to control them. As we have already suggested, the symbolic play of the pre-schooler provides the child with a major vehicle for experiencing and expressing positive emotions and also for minimizing or controlling negative experiences. Let us take a closer look at play from this vantage point.

Interest and joy in imaginative play

It might be argued that most of the moments of true happiness in human experience depend upon optimal evocations of interest and joy. In his studies of 'flow', those treasured moments when we engage in action or thought so naturally wedded to challenge and capacity that self-consciousness is abolished, Csikszentmihalyi (1976) has obtained extensive reports from groups as diverse as rock climbers, surgeons, and artists. The flow experience comes when a situation of difficulty exists, yet one which is clearly not beyond one's powers, and when it is met by a full use of one's learned or inborn skills. Children of course show such experiences in the course of mastery play—the thrill of managing a tricycle—the cry of 'Look, Mom! No hands!'.

Make-believe play also affords many such opportunities for the child. For example, a boy has been told by parents or older children about recent space explorations. Perhaps, too, he has visited a local museum and seen full-scale reproductions of prehistoric dinosaurs. With his limited range of cognitive schema, he cannot grasp all the details or implications of these events, yet their novelty arouses interest. In the block corner at nursery school he finds two plastic dinosaurs. He recognizes them as miniatures of what he had seen in the museum and is intrigued at the chance to look at them close up. He remembers too what he has just heard about space travel and so he attempts to relate these novel experiences by devising an adventure—an astronaut lands on the moon and finds dinosaurs there, etc. The child uses the playschool blocks whose geometric features lend themselves to a variety of constructs and, choosing a cylindrical block as a rocket, builds a rudimentary space station, a moon surface of 'rocks' in which the dinosaurs are hidden and a few small plastic 'soldiers' or 'cowboys' act as astronauts. Little of what the child has constructed looks much like a rocket gantry or the lunar terrain but at least, when supplemented by his imagery, it is moderately recognizable as such to him.

The child begins his adventure—a countdown and take-off—without quite knowing what comes next. Yet since the game is his and under his control, its incongruity is not excessive. Thus he remains interested, curious about what can or will happen to his astronauts, getting excited as he brings them close to danger and laughing when they finally 'zap' one of the dinosaurs or when he manages to bring them back safely. In miniaturized form the child has reduced the much more complex, potential fright of space travel to a moderate level of interest and has also, by the working out the plot, incorporated a new set of organized experiences into his own cognitive schema. He may want to replay this game a number of times before its novelty will fade.

Inherent in the play situation is a prescribed sequence or plot, often rather scattered and fragmented to an adult but still obedient to an internal logic, as Sutton-Smith's studies of children's story-telling suggest (Abrams and Sutton-Smith, 1977; Sutton-Smith, Abrams, Botvin, Caring, Gildesgame, and Stevens, 1975). The inherent plot is present yet ambiguous and draws the child ahead. Thus make-believe play should lead to longer play sequences, more concentration, more evidence of affects of interest and joy as the child moves through the plot and finally provides it with an outcome s/he can comprehend. Even sudden opposite behaviours, the reversal of roles, the emergence of the 'trickster', the simulation amid great joy of menacing growls of the dinosaur or of the canny laughter of a villainous moon man reflect *controlled* novelty and, by the very use of *opposites*, expansion of the child's awareness of *possibility* (Abrams and Sutton-Smith, 1977).

While three- or four-year-olds can rarely sustain a make-believe game for very long, especially when playing together, five- and six-year-olds move into far more extended and complex plots with multiple role assignments. Here, too, one child may lead and assign parts or roles and provide a sketchy plot but soon spontaneous invention is rampant and so, again, moderate novelty and curiosity are shared until a final resolution leaves the children with a sense of happiness. Tensions do arise in group games when a child unfamiliar with the general run of plots or with his or her own role introduces behaviour of extreme novelty that cannot be incorporated into the plot. Here one soon sees anger and distress and occasionally a sad withdrawal from the game by its initiator who may feel that it is safer to play the whole game out by oneself rather than rely on 'those dummies'. Such frame-breaking can also be seen in humour when a comedian 'goes too far'; an irreverent reference to religion or the sex life of the President or the Queen can evoke startle and anger rather than laughter.

In effect, then, fantasy play provides a situation of moderate novelty, a chance to create new controlled novelty, and also ample opportunity to incorporate this new material into established schemata or to form new schemata under controlled conditions. Since there is so much that is new and strange for the pre-schooler, make-believe play affords an opportunity for reducing much novelty to manageable proportions and opens the way for rapid cognitive differentiation and integration. The child who has the privacy as well as the parental acceptance and occasionally active encouragement for more imaginative play is therefore more likely to be continuously interested, exploring in a controlled way, and generally learning more as well as just plain happy.

SOME EMPIRICAL FINDINGS

Until the nineteen-seventies there was almost no systematic research examining affective patterns during spontaneous play. Recently a series of investigations has begun to record ongoing play and to score protocols according to pre-defined variables such as imaginativeness of play, positive affect (interest and joy), concentration (persistence at a specific activity), overt aggression, specific affects such as anger, sadness, elation, fear, and interaction behaviours such as co-operation with peers and with adults (Singer, 1973; Singer and Singer, 1977). Direct inquiries of children and parents about play patterns, imaginary companions, and related behaviours are thus being supplemented by observations of naturally occurring play.

Studies of imaginary playmates based on parental observations and children's self-reports have indicated that pre-schoolers who have make-believe friends are also likely to show 'high spirits' or happiness and smiling during spontaneous play (Caldeira, Singer, and Singer, 1978; Manosevitz, Prentice, and Wilson, 1973). Pulaski (1973), Freyberg (1973), and Franklin (1975) in observations of free play either with unstructured playthings or after special training to enhance imaginativeness found an association between pretend play and signs of joy and smiling in early school-age children. Biblow (1973), studying the response of nine-year-olds to aggressive or benign television programmes following induced frustration, found that more imaginative children showed less anger and more elation after seeing the non-aggressive film. The less imaginative children showed persisting high levels of anger when exposed to the benign or aggressive film. Persistent linkages between joy, imagination, and playfulness are also reported by Lieberman (1977).

A series of studies has examined whether children will increase imaginativeness after exposure to adult models or to television programmes designed to foster imagination. Generally, live adult models have yielded the best results, with clear evidence that normal pre-schoolers or older, severely emotionally-disturbed children can increase make-believe play with such stimulation and also regularly show more positive affects, for example smiling and laughing or sustained interest (Nahme-Haung et al., 1977; Singer and Singer, 1976b).

A further study of the relationships of television-viewing to imaginative play and affect was carried out by Tower et al. (1978). Three groups of pre-schoolers watched films or television for half an hour on each of ten consecutive nursery school days. One group watched *Misterogers' Neighborhood*, another saw *Sesame Street*, and a third viewed non-imaginative animal and nature films. The children clearly showed a greater amount of smiling and laughter while watching *Sesame Street*. Those who watched *Misterogers* became more imaginative in their play subsequently, however, while the children who watched *Sesame Street* and the control films did not improve either in imaginativeness or in laughing and smiling. This finding reinforces our view of the role of the interaction of interest and joy in the development of imaginativeness of play: the *Misterogers* children showed a more fluid alternation between the two emotions, with the stress on the more serious affect of interest during most of their viewing time. We are suggesting that the interest aroused in *Misterogers* created a more active viewing behaviour in the child; one which, by practising it during television, the child could then carry back and use in play. The *Sesame Street* viewers, while very amused, appear to have been processing the input more passively. The rapid shifts of sequence that characterize *Sesame Street* may have held their attention but failed to lead to long-term storage of play ideas or attitudes.

In similar studies of the effects of *Misterogers' Neighborhood* on the ongoing play of pre-school children, Friedrich and Stein (1975), Stein and Friedrich (1975) and Stein, Friedrich, and Vondracek (1972) have also found the programme capable of improving imaginativeness and co-operation, nurturance, verbalization of feelings, persistence, and tolerance of delays, among other virtues. The ability to generate and control positive emotions and through them the novelty level of information, apparently affords wide benefits to small children.

In practically every home in the United States television is now a major form of the informational environment for a pre-school child. This ubiquitous 'member of the family' provides an incredible variety of content and form which can be extremely difficult to understand (J. Singer, 1978; Tower, *et al.*, 1978). According to our theory, we might predict that (a) children who show a high level of imaginativeness will show greater positive emotionality in their play regardless of the amount of television they watch, but (b) those who watch a lot of television will show lower levels of positive affect than those who watch little.

One hundred and forty-one children were studied. Regular observations two days apart by independent, hypothesis-blind observers were carried out at two probe periods several months apart. During a two-week span in each probe period parents recorded the children's daily TV-viewing times and programme content. Since this was an opportunity to sample children's affects and tendency towards imaginative play on a number of occasions it is worth noting that ratings of children for *positive affect* correlated $+0.38$ ($p < 0.001$) two days apart and $+0.33$ ($p < 0.01$) more than two months apart. Considering all the possible factors which could influence a child's mood on a given day, such consistency is impressive. *Imaginativeness* of play correlated $+0.33$ ($p < 0.01$) two days apart and $+0.50$ ($p < .0001$) more than two months apart. Other specific affects showed similar patterns: for example *sadness* correlated $+0.25$ ($p < 0.01$) two days and two months apart. Observed *imaginativeness* of play shows consistently significant positive correlations during both February and April probes with *positive affect, concentration, co-operation with peers, liveliness,* and *elation,* and significant negative correlations with *sadness* and *anger.* In general, the data suggest a stability of emotional style and a kind of 'happy child' cluster of imaginativeness, positive affects, persistence, and co-operation with other children. More extensive language usage is also linked to this cluster.

The results for television viewing do not clearly support the second hypothesis. It is true that a high frequency of TV-viewing is significantly associated with *overt aggression* and with *anger* during play periods but the presumed negative link to imagination does not appear at this age level. However, high-frequency TV-viewers are significantly less likely to have imaginary playmates (Caldeira *et al.*, 1978).

In general, the data emerging from a series of studies suggest a continued link between imaginative play and positive emotionality. It should be kept in mind that there is nothing in the definitions of imaginative play or positive affect as rated that should lead to an artifactual association. A child playing at a mastery game such as a form-board or simply piling blocks or riding a tricycle without any indications of a plot or story-line (as manifested by use of onomatopoeic sounds or other verbalizations) might be laughing and smiling. What we actually observe is that children who have not entered into make-believe games are often disruptive of others' play, nagging at the teacher or whining. The imaginative game, by the very logic of its subplot can often hold a pre-schooler's attention better than a mastery game since the latter often quickly ends in failures for three- and four-year-olds. Results of a factor analysis clearly indicate a separate factor linking positive affect, imaginative play, persistence, co-operation with peers, liveliness, and elation. An almost identical result using factor analysis for observations of the play of white South African pre-schoolers has been reported by Shmukler (1978).

IMPLICATIONS OF JOY IN PLAY

A brief summary of the broader implications of our theory is in order. Below we consider some relationships between imaginative play and the activity level of the child, some inferences about how a child learns such play, a consideration of the major environmental variables of socioeconomic class and television, and the ultimate importance of imagination in creativity and a sense of humour.

The activity level of the child

Research suggests an interesting relationship between imagination and behaviour: whereas imagination in school-age children results in a lower level of motoric activity and more planful movements (Singer, 1961; see also Singer, 1973, and Singer and Singer, 1976a), there is a growing body of evidence that imaginative play in the pre-schooler results in more active and lively behaviour (Singer and Singer, 1976b; Tower *et al.*, 1978). Apparently the actual development of imaginative skills which takes place during the pre-school years requires more literally active participation on the part of the child. Still steeped in the associative and perceptual requirements of pre-operational intelligence (Piaget, 1960) and not far removed from a sensorimotor base for understanding, the child appears to need to sound aloud the whinnies and hoofbeats of a horse while he imagines himself one, or to assume the voice and postures of a teacher or librarian. The activity level of the child often seems also linked to humorous pratfalls and posturing—an early form of horseplay joking (McGhee, 1971).

The difficulty arises when a caring adult is unable to accept the liveliness and exuberance of the child's play. Recently Tomkins discussed an elaboration on his theory of emotions (personal communication, 1977). He suggested that 'blocked' affects—emotional reactions that are denied their expression through facial, vocal, and postural demonstrations—require a blockage of breathing to stop the natural expression. When this style of responding becomes common, it creates an elevated level of aversive stimulation, internally generated. Just as prolonged over-optimal external stimulation produces the emotion of distress, so this internally produced emotion is one of distress. Tomkins notes, however, that it is a more diffuse sadness, likely to be expressed inappropriately with excessive crying whenever an opportunity for the realistic expression of distress arises. Thus the child whose parents seek to inhibit its liveliness, laughter, yelling, and general exuberance (all natural to imaginative play) is likely to become saddened over time and to over-react to any incident which might legitimately lead to tears.

It is important to note that the liveliness found in the small child's play is not the same as impulsivity. Rather, as previously discussed, the imaginative child is more likely to develop a reflective cognitive style, simply because it will abet him in the development of his play. Lieberman (1977) notes that playful and imaginative adolescents show more 'prosocial' humour and more witty orientations, while less playful adolescents are more given to teasing and aggressive horseplay.

There is additional evidence that playful, active, lively children are less aggressive than their less imaginative peers, particularly as they reach school age (Biblow, 1973; Singer, 1973; Singer and Singer, 1976b). By being able to respond with appropriate emotions to shifts in the incoming stimulation, they are more able to find alternate means of expressing their anger and frustration than through outright violence. Very recent research even suggests that they may have somewhat of an 'immunity' to the well-known noxious influences of televised violence (Biblow, 1973; Singer and Singer, 1977). The contagious effect of the laughter of the child engaged in active make-believe cannot be minimized. Popularity through evoking laughter can be reinforcing and can begin to establish a pattern of playful engagement that can become a humorous style of social interaction later on.

Learning to play imaginatively

One condition necessary to play's development has just been suggested: the child's natural responses of interest, curiosity, and joy must be respected. In addition, freedom to carry on these activities with some privacy (Feitelson, 1978) and protection from the interference of siblings, particularly when play is in the formative stages, seems necessary (Freyberg, 1973). A 'playful' relationship with a parent seems to be the best help in the development of play (Bishop and Chace, 1971; Shmukler, 1978; Singer and Singer, 1976). Indeed, a major study of children who do and do not have imaginary playmates stressed that children *with* imaginary playmates more often engaged in self-initiated play, that the play was *not* described as 'quiet', and that, while the children with and without playmates spent the same amount of time with their parents, the children with the playmates spent more playful times with their parents. Clearly, a parental attitude of acceptance and respect appears to facilitate the development of imaginative play (Manosevitz *et al.*, 1973; Shmukler, 1978).

In addition, the huge literature on modelling effects in early childhood (see Bandura, 1971) has demonstrated that children tend to imitate adults. Studies such as those by Sroufe and Waters (1976) on the development of smiling and laughing and that of Walters, Leat, and Mezei (1963) in which children would imitate noxious behaviours if they had been modelled with high positive affect reinforce the notion that children are more likely to copy behaviours which are associated with strong expressions of joy in the person being watched. Therefore, the person who shows delight in imaginative activities is likely to be copied by the child. Again, we can speculate that parents or older siblings who model playfulness, humour, or pretending can become the stimulators of fantasy and humorous games and attitudes in the younger children.

Izard (1977) suggests that joy cannot be learned. However, the recent studies of Meltzoff and Moore (1977) suggest that parental smiling may well be imitated early by children. It may be that the opportunities for evoking the affect of joy or the smile can be substantially increased through parental intervention. Our own experiments in training children in imaginative play (Nahme-Huang, *et al.*, 1977; Singer and Singer, 1976; Singer and Singer, 1976b, 1977) and those of others (Friedrich and Stein, 1975; Freyberg, 1973; Lovinger, 1974; Marshall and Hahn, 1967; Stein *et al.*, 1972) have shown that stimulating greater imagination and co-operation behaviour may also yield more positive affect. And with the imagery skills developed in such play, the child gains increased facility in creating internal environments which arouse the emotions of interest and joy. Although some innate parameters of arousability may not be modifiable, a facility within a range of potential responsivity certainly is. The recent follow-up of the children from Thomas, Chess, and Birch's (1968) New York University Longitudinal Study (Cameron, 1977) showed that even the remarkably stable innate temperamental characteristics of the children could be modified by parents' disciplinary and interaction styles. We know too little of how joking and humorous patterns of parent–child interaction are transmitted as yet, but one can surmise that moderate amounts of joke-telling and playful humour can be formative while heavy-handed teasing may create distress or terror.

Environmental variables

Social class. These implications are particularly important for children in lower socioeconomic classes. Since Sara Smilansky published her reports on poor Israeli children in 1968 there has been growing attention to the difficulty which some economically disadvantaged children seem to have in transcending the constraints of reality in play. They simply cannot pick up a stick and pretend that it is a flag. Pavenstadt (1967) has documented some dramatic instances of an absence of imaginative play in severely disadvantaged children. The source of this difficulty may lie in some of the environmental features of the home just discussed—but the implications of modelling's effectiveness are vast. Not only may play-training sessions prove efficacious for poor children in developing some cognitive skills and school readiness (Golumb and Corelius, 1977; Saltz, 1976) but happier, more imaginative children may also develop more methods of interacting with one another and of dealing with their environment. In moderation, it is possible that television *for these children* might possibly provide some of the input that is lacking. Research on *Sesame Street* and *Misterogers' Neighborhood* (for example, see Coates, Pusser, and Goodman, 1976; Singer and Singer, 1976b, 1977; Stein and Friedrich 1975, 1977) suggests that benefits can accrue from spending time with the enigmatic box, *especially if some parental mediation is involved.*

Television. Television is, however, a mixed blessing. As Singer (1977) has reported, it most probably has negative effects on the attention span, differential development of visual and auditory skills and possibly even brain hemispheres, and integration capacities of the child. The young child cannot cope with the complexity of most programmes, their simultaneous verbal and visual messages, and their rapid sequencing. Indeed, a study by Noble (1970) found that *school-aged* children would prefer to slow down programming and give up novelty for familiarity. These findings are similar to those of Friedlander, Wetstone, and Scott (1974) and Wetstone and Friedlander (1974), who learned that children preferred a comprehensible, affectively honest programme to a slick, glossy presentation with little emotional import.

A related issue is that of what children are not doing when they are watching television. There are strong indications that what suffers is play (Lyle and Hoffman, 1972a, 1972b). The passivity permitted may leave a whole generation of children dependent on external stimulation for the modulation of emotion: they may never develop their own skills to respond to and then process information adaptively. Instead of being able to generate joy from within, by responding with interest and then reducing it, television-addicted children may later become addicted to other external agents for 'kicks'. Indeed, a large study of drug abusers has shown that (a) they are dependent on the environment for excitement and pleasure and (b) they have very poor imaginative skills (Huba, Segal, and Singer, 1977). Presumably, had they developed the latter, they would have been able to avoid the former. In our desire to raise healthy, happy, independent children, we must recognize their need to develop and practise play skills.

Creativity and humour

Finally, there is evidence that imaginative play skills in the pre-school years lead to flexibility, adaptability, creativity, and a sense of humour in later years (Dansky and Silverman, 1973, 1975; Getzels and Jackson, 1970; Lieberman, 1965, 1977; Wallach and Kogan, 1965). Since these skills can be considered a major source of success (MacKinnon, 1967, 1970; Taylor and Ellison 1964) in adulthood and similar to the differentiation and integration skills Wexler labels 'self-actualization' (1974), they are useful indeed. The make-believe play of the child who makes a plastic horse suddenly fly (Pulaski, 1973), who has a pretend dragon do a pratfall or burst into tears becomes one prototype for the inventive incongruity of the professional humorist like Woody Allen. But more than just the measurable criteria of 'success' in later life deserve attention. Surely we cannot completely avoid the value of 'happiness' during childhood just because we cannot operationalize it. Would it not be a reasonable goal to raise children who can meet their worlds with curiosity, a free-ranging imagination and a capacity for joy?

We have focused most of our attention on imaginative play. Direct links to the development of humour have not yet been formed. We are proposing, however, that humour, at least in its verbal or subtler non-verbal forms (as against sadistic teasing or beating) is itself an evolution from or a subcategory of the make-believe attitude. Just as children learn by the age of three to signal the onset of pretend sequences, so do they later learn to signal or to interpret signals that an 'as if' humorous story, gesture or behaviour sequence is to follow. The signal is relatively critical, for it avoids the over-stimulation and arousal of negative affect that comes when the humorous stimulus (usually something quite novel or outlandish) is presented. The miracle of early childhood make-believe lies in the fact that the small child learns it can take powerful people, frightening monsters, all kinds of novelty and manipulate them in miniature form once a make-believe stance is assumed. Humour, too, becomes a part of our capacity to adopt an as-if stance. By signalling the humorous sequence we can reduce potentially overwhelming novelty to modest size and respond with the positive emotions of interest and surprise and then, as we match the strange eventuality to earlier schemata or form new schemata and thus reduce the novelty, we respond with the most welcome of human reactions, the smile of joy.

REFERENCES

Abrams, D. M., and Sutton-Smith, B. (1977). The development of the trickster in children's narrative. *Journal of American Folklore*, **90**, 29–47.

Axline, V. (1965). *Dibs: In Search of Self.* Boston: Houghton-Mifflin.

Bandura, A. (1971). *Psychological Modeling.* New York: Aldine-Atherton.

Bateson, G. (1955). A theory of play and fantasy. *Psychiatric Research Reports*, No. **2**, 39–51.

Biblow, E. (1973). Imaginative play and the control of aggression. In J. L. Singer (Ed.), *Child's World of Make-Believe.* New York: Academic Press.

Bishop, D. W., and Chace, C. A. (1971). Parental conceptual systems, home play environment, and potential creativity in children. *Journal of Experimental Child Psychology*, **12**, 318–338.

Blatt, S. J., and Wild, C. (1976). *Schizophrenia: A Developmental Analysis.* New York: Academic Press.

Bruner, J., Jolly, A., and Sylva, K. (Eds.) (1976). *Play: Its Role in Development and Evolution.* New York: Basic Books.

Buss, A., and Buss, E., (Eds.) (1973). *Theories of Schizophrenia.* New York: Lieber-Atherton.

Caldeira, J., Singer, J. L., and Singer, D. G. (1978). *Imaginary playmates: some relationships to preschoolers television-viewing, language and play.* Paper submitted to Eastern Psychological Association.

Cameron, J. (1977). Parental treatment, children's temperament, and the risk of childhood behavioral problems. *American Journal of Orthopsychiatry*, **47**, 568–576.

Chandler, M. (1973). Egocentrism and antisocial behavior: the assessment and training of social perspective-taking skills. *Developmental Psychology*, **9**, 326–332.

Coates, B., Pusser, H., and Goodman, I. (1976). The influence of *Sesame Street* and *Mister Rogers' Neighborhood* on children's social behavior in the preschool. *Child Development*, **41**, 138–144.

Csikszentmihalyi, M. (1975). *Beyond Boredom and Anxiety.* San Francisco: Jossey-Bass.

Dansky, J. L. (1976). Cognitive functions of sociodramatic play: a training study. Unpublished Doctoral Dissertation, Ohio Dominican College. (Also paper read to American Psychological Association, Washington, D. C., 1976.)

Dansky, J. L., and Silverman, I. W. (1973). Effects of play on associative fluency in preschool-aged children. *Developmental Psychology*, **9**, 38–43.

Dansky, J. L., and Silverman, I. W. (1975). Play: a general facilitator of associative fluency. *Developmental Psychology*, **11**, 104.

Ekman, P., and Friesen, W. (1975). *Unmasking the Face.* Englewood Cliffs, New Jersey: Prentice-Hall.

Ekman, P., Friesen, W., and Ellsworth, P. (1971). *Emotions in the Human Face: Guidelines for Research and a Review of Findings.* New York: Pergamon Press.

Ellis, M. (1973). *Why People Play.* Englewood Cliffs, New Jersey: Prentice-Hall.

Erikson, E. H. (1940). Studies in the interpretation of play. *Genetic Psychology Monographs*, **22**, 557–671.

Fein, G. (1975). A transformational analysis of pretending. *Developmental Psychology*, **11**, 291–296.

Feitelson, D. (1972). Developing imaginative play in preschool children as a possible approach to fostering creativity. *Early Child Development and Care*, **1**, 181–195.

Feitelson, D. (1978). Cross-cultural studies of representational play. In B. Tizard and D. Harvey, (Eds.), *Biology of Play*, in press.

Forisha, B. (1975). Mental imagery, verbal processes: a developmental study. *Developmental Psychology*, **11**, 259–267.

Franklin, D. (1975). Block play modeling and its relationship to imaginativeness, impulsivity-reflection and internal-external control. Unpublished predissertation research, Yale University.

Friedlander, B. Z., Wetstone, H. S., and Scott, C. S. (1974). Suburban preschool children's comprehension of an age appropriate informational television program. *Child Development*, **45**, 561–565.

Friedrich, L., and Stein, A. (1975). Prosocial television and young children: the effects of verbal labeling and role playing on learning and behavior. *Child Development*, **46**, 27–38.

Freyberg, J. (1973). Increasing the imaginative play of urban disadvantaged kindergarten children through systematic training. In J. L. Singer, (Ed.), *Child's World of Make-Believe*. New York: Academic Press.

Gardner, R. (1971). *Therapeutic Communication with Children: The Mutual Story-Telling Technique*. New York: Science House.

Getzels, J. W., and Jackson, P. W. (1970). The highly intelligent and the highly creative adolescent. In P. E. Vernon, (Ed.), *Creativity: Selected Readings*. Harmondsworth, England: Penguin Books. Also in C. W. Taylor and F. Barron (Eds.), 1963, *Scientific Creativity: Its Recognition and Development*. New York: Wiley.

Golumb, C., and Cornelius, C. (1977). Symbolic play and its cognitive significance. *Developmental Psychology*, **13**, 246–252.

Gould, R. (1972). *Child Studies Through Fantasy*. New York: Quadrangle Books.

Gump, P., and Sutton-Smith, B. (1971). Activity-setting and social interaction: a field study. In R. E. Heron and B. Sutton-Smith, (Eds.), *Child's Play*. New York: Wiley. Reprinted from 1955, *American Journal of Orthopsychiatry*, **25**, 755–760.

Halverson, C., and Waldrop, M. (1974). Relations between preschool barrier behaviors and early school-age measures of coping, imagination and verbal development. *Developmental Psychology*, **10**, 716–720.

Harlow, H. (1949). The formation of learning sets. *Psychological Review*, **56**, 51–65.

Heron, R. E., and Sutton-Smith, B. (1971). *Child's Play*. New York: Wiley.

Homme, L., C'de Baca, P., Cottingham, L., and Homme, A. 1968. What behavioral engineering is. *Psychological Record*, **18**, 425–434.

Huba, G., Segal, B., and Singer, J. L. (1977). The consistency of daydreaming styles across samples of college male and female drug and alcohol users. *Journal of Abnormal Psychology*, **86**, 99–102.

Hutt, C. (1970). Specific and diversive exploration. In H. W. Reese and L. P. Lipsitt (Eds.), *Advances in Child Development and Behavior*, Vol. 5. New York: Academic Press.

Hutt, C. (1977). The taxonomy of play. *Pediatric roundtable on play and learning*. Johnson and Johnson Baby Products Company Symposium. New Orleans.

Izard, C. (1971). *The Face of Emotion*. New York: Appleton-Century-Crofts.

Izard, C. (1972). *Patterns of Emotions*. New York: Academic Press.

Izard, C. (1977). *Human Emotions*. New York: Plenum Press.

Kendler, T. (1963). Development of mediating responses in children. In J. C. Wright and J. Kagan (Eds.), *Basic Cognitive Processes in Children. Society for Research in Child Development Monograph*, **28**, 33–47.

Klinger, E. (1971). *Structure and Functions of Fantasy*. New York: Wiley.

Kogan, N. (1976). *Cognitive Styles in Infancy and Early Childhood.* Hillsdale, New Jersey: Erlbaum. .

Kritzberg, N. (1975). *Structured Therapeutic Game Method of (Child) Analytic Therapy.* New York: Grune and Stratton.

Lazarus, A., and Abramovitz, A. (1962). The use of 'emotive imagery' in the treatment of children's phobias. *Journal of Mental Science*, **108**, 191–195.

Lazarus, A., Davison, G., and Polefka, D. (1965). Classical and operant factors in the treatment of school phobia. *Journal of Abnormal Psychology*, **70**, 225–229.

Levin, H., and Wardwell, E. (1962). The research uses of doll play. *Psychological Bulletin*, **59**, 27–56.

Lewis, M. (1977). Mother–child and peer–peer relations as play and as competence. *Pediatric roundtable on play and learning.* Johnson and Johnson Baby Products Company Symposium. New Orleans.

Lewis, R. H. (1973). The relationship of sociodramatic play to various cognitive abilities in kindergarten children. Unpublished Doctoral Dissertation, Ohio State University.

Lieberman, J. N. (1965). Playfulness and divergent thinking: an investigation of their relationship at the kindergarten level. *Journal of Genetic Psychology*, **107**, 219–224.

Lieberman, J. N. (1977). *Playfulness.* New York: Academic Press.

Lovinger, S. (1974). Socio-dramatic play and language development in preschool disadvantaged children. *Psychology in the Schools*, **11**, 313–320.

Lyle, J., and Hoffman, H. (1972a). Explorations in patterns of television viewing by preschool-age children. In *Television and Social Behavior*, Vol. 4. Washington, D. C.: U.S. Government Printing Office.

Lyle, J., and Hoffman, H. (1972b). Children's use of television and other media. In *Television and Social Behavior*, Vol. 4. Washington, D.C.: U.S. Government Printing Office.

MacKinnon, D. (1967). The study of creative persons: A method and some results. In J. Kagan (Ed.), *Creativity and Learning.* Boston: Beacon Press.

MacKinnon, D. (1970). The personality correlates of creativity: a study of American architects. In P. E. Vernon (Ed.), *Creativity: Selected Readings.* Harmondsworth, England: Penguin Books.

McGhee, P. E. (1971). Development of the humor response: a review of the literature. *Psychological Bulletin*, **76**, 328–348.

Manosevitz, M., Prentice, N., and Wilson, F. (1973). Individual and family correlates of imaginary companions in preschool children. *Developmental Psychology*, **8**, 72–79.

Marshall, H., and Hahn, S. (1967). Experimental modification of dramatic play. *Journal of Personality and Social Psychology*, **5**, 119–122.

Maw, W., and Maw, E. (1970). Self-concepts of high and low curiosity boys. *Child Development*, **41**, 123–129.

Meichenbaum, D. (1971). Training impulsive children to talk to themselves. *Journal of Abnormal Psychology*, **77**, 215–226.

Meichenbaum, D. (1976). *Cognitive-Behavior Modification Newsletter*, No. 2. Waterloo, Canada: University of Waterloo.

Meichenbaum, D. (1977). Clinical implications of modifying what clients say to themselves. In R. Jurjevich, (Ed.), *Direct Psychotherapy*, Vol. 3. Coral Gables, Florida: University of Miami Press.

Meltzoff, A., and Moore, M. (1977). Imitation of facial and manual gestures by human neonates. *Science*, **198**, 75–78.

Messer, S. (1976). Reflection-impulsivity: a review. *Psychological Bulletin*, **83**, 1026–1052.

Millar, S. (1968). *The Psychology of Play.* Harmondsworth, England: Penguin Books.

Moore, B., Clyburn, A., and Underwood, B. (1976). The role of affect in delay of gratification. *Child Development*, **47**, 273–276.

Moore, B., Underwood, B., and Rosenhan, D. (1973). Affect and altruism. *Developmental Psychology*, **8**, 88–104.

Mowbray, C., and Luria, Z. (1973). Effects of labeling on children's visual imagery. *Developmental Psychology*, **9**, 1–8.

Nahme-Huang, L., Singer, D. G., Singer, J. L., and Wheaton, A. (1977). Imaginative play and perceptual-motor intervention methods with emotionally-disturbed, hospitalized children: an evaluation study. *Journal of Orthopsychiatry*, **47**, 238–249.

Noble, G. (1970). Concepts of order and balance in a children's TV program. *Journalism Quarterly*, **47**, 101–108.

Parten, N. (1971). Social play among preschool children. In R. E. Heron and B. Sutton-Smith (Eds.), *Child's Play*. New York: Wiley. Reprinted from 1933, *Journal of Abnormal and Social Psychology*, **28**, 136–147.

Pavenstadt, E., (Ed.) (1967). *The Drifters*. Boston: Little-Brown.

Peller, L. W. (1971). Models of children's play. In R. E. Heron and B. Sutton-Smith (Eds.), *Child's Play*. New York: Wiley. Reprinted from 1952, *Mental Hygiene*, **36**, 66–83.

Perlmutter, M., and Myers, N. (1975). Young children's coding and storage of visual and verbal material. *Child Development*, **46**, 215–219.

Piaget, J. (1960). *Psychology of Intelligence*. New York: Littlefield, Adams.

Piaget, J. (1962). *Play, Dreams and Imitation in Childhood*. New York: Norton.

Piaget, J. and Inhelder, B. (1971). *Mental Imagery in the Child*. New York: Basic Books.

Pulaski, M. (1971). *Understanding Piaget*. New York: Harper and Row.

Pulaski, M. (1973). Toys and imaginative play. In J. L. Singer (Ed.), *Child's World of Make-Believe*. New York: Academic Press.

Reese, H. W. (1975). Verbal effects in children's visual recognition memory. *Child Development*, **46**, 400–407.

Rose, S. (1975). *The Conscious Brain*. New York: Vantage Books.

Rubin, K., Maioni, T., and Hornung, M. (1976). Free play in middle- and lower-class preschoolers: Parten and Piaget revisited. *Child Development*, **47**, 414–419.

Saltz, E. (1976). Training for thematic-fantasy play in culturally-disadvantaged children. Annual Report to the Spencer Foundation, Wayne State University.

Schank, R., and Abelson, R. (1977). *Scripts, Plans, Goals and Understanding*. New York: Halstead.

Schwartz, G., Fair, P., Greenberg, P., Freedman, M., and Klerman, J. (1974). Facial electromyography in the assessment of emotion. *Psychophysiology*, **11**, 237.

Schwartz, G., Fair, P., Salt, P., Mandel, N., Klerman, J. (1976). Facial muscle patterning to affective imagery in depressed and non-depressed subjects. *Science*, **192**, 489–491.

Shmukler, D. (1978). The origins and concomitants of imaginative play in young children. Unpublished Doctoral Dissertation, University of Witwatersrand, South Africa.

Singer, D. G., Caldeira, J., and Singer, J. L. (1977). The effects of television-viewing and predisposition to imagination on the language of preschool children. Paper presented to the Annual Convention of the Eastern Psychological Association, Boston.

Singer, D. G., and Singer, J. L. (1976). Family television viewing habits and the spontaneous play of preschool children. *American Journal of Orthopsychiatry*, **46**, 496–502.

Singer, D. G., and Singer, J. L. (1977). *Partners in Play*. New York: Harper and Row.

Singer, J. L. (1961). Imagination and waiting ability in young children. *Journal of Personality*, **29**, 396–413.

Singer, J. L. (1966). *Daydreaming*. New York: Random House.

Singer, J. L. (1973). *The Child's World of Make-Believe.* New York: Academic Press.

Singer, J. L. (1974). *Imagery and Daydream Methods in Psychotherapy and Behavior Modification.* New York: Academic Press.

Singer, J. L. (1975). *The Inner World of Daydreaming.* New York: Harper and Row.

Singer, J. L. (1977). Television, imaginative play and cognitive development: some problems and possibilities. Paper presented as an invited address to the American Psychological Association, Annual Convention, San Francisco.

Singer, J. L. (1978). The powers and limitations of television: a cognitive-affective analysis. In P. Tannebaum and R. Abeles (Eds.), *Television as Entertainment.* Report of an SSRC Conference. New York: Erlbaum.

Singer, J. L., and Brown, S. L. (1977). The experience-type: some behavioral correlates and theoretical implications. In M. A. Rickers-Ovsiankina (Ed.), *Rorschach Psychology*, 2nd Edn., Huntington, New York: Krieger.

Singer, J. L., and Singer, D. G. (1976a). Imaginative play and pretending in early childhood. In A. Davids (Ed.), *Child Personality and Psychopathology*, Vol. 3. New York: Wiley.

Singer, J. L., and Singer, D. G. (1976b). Fostering imaginative play in preschool children: television and live model effects. *Journal of Communication*, **26**, 74–80.

Singer, J. L., and Singer, D. G. (1977). Television viewing and imaginative play in preschoolers. National Science Foundation Grant Progress Report. New Haven, Connecticut.

Smilansky, S. (1968). *The Effects of Sociodramatic Play on Disadvantaged Preschool Children.* New York: Wiley.

Sroufe, L., and Waters, E. (1976). The ontogenesis of smiling and laughter: a perspective on the organization of development in infancy. *Psychological Review*, **83**, 173–189.

Starker, S. (1977). Daydreaming styles and nocturnal dreaming: further observations. *Perceptual and Motor Skills*, **45**, 411–416.

Stein, A. and Friedrich, L. (1975). The effects of television content on young children. In A. D. Pick (Ed.), *Minnesota Symposium on Child Psychology*, Vol. 9. Minneapolis, Minnesota: University of Minnesota Press.

Stein, A., Friedrich, L., and Vondracek. (1972). Television content and young children's behavior. In *Television and Social Behavior*, Vol. 2. Washington, D.C.: US Government Printing Office.

Stone, G. P. (1971). The play of little children. In R. E. Heron and B. Sutton-Smith (Eds.), *Child's Play.* New York: Wiley. Reprinted from 1965, *Quest*, **4**, 23–31.

Sutton-Smith, B. (1971). Boundaries. In R, E. Heron and B. Sutton-Smith (Eds.), *Child's Play.* New York: Wiley.

Sutton-Smith, B., Abrams, D., Botvin, G., Caring, M., Gildesgame, D., and Stevens, T. (1975). The importance of the story-taker: an investigation of the imaginative life. *Urban Review*, **8**, 82–95.

Taylor, C., and Ellison, R. (1964). Prediction of creativity with the biographical inventory. In C. Taylor, (Ed.), *Widening Horizons in Creativity.* New York: Wiley.

Thomas, A., Chess, S., and Birch, H. (1968). *Temperament and Behavior Disorders in Children.* New York: New York University Press.

Tomkins, S. (1962, 1963). *Affect, imagery, consciousness.* (Vols. 1 and 2). New York: Springer.

Tomkins, S. (1977). Personal communication.

Tower, R., Singer, D., Singer, J., and Biggs, A. (1978). Differential effects of television programming on preschoolers' cognition and play. In preparation.

Tucker, J. (1975). The role of fantasy in cognitive-affective functioning: Does reality make a difference? Unpublished Doctoral Dissertation, Columbia University.

Tversky, B. (1973). Pictorial and verbal encoding in preschool children. *Developmental Psychology*, **8**, 149–153.

Underwood, B., Moore, B., and Rosenhan, D. (1973). Affect and self-gratification. *Developmental Psychology*, **8**, 209–214.

Vanty, D., and Vaillant, S. (1975). Affect and self-gratification. *Journal of Educational Research*, **69**, 122–124.

Wallach, M., and Kogan, M. (1965). *Modes of Thinking in Young Children.* New York: Holt, Rinehart, and Winston.

Walters, R., Leat, M., and Mezei, L. (1963). Inhibition and disinhibition of responses through empathetic learning. *Canadian Journal of Psychology*, **17**, 235–243.

Weisler, A., and McCall, R. (1976). Exploration and play: resumé and redirection. *American Psychologist*, **31**, 492–508.

Wetstone, H., and Friedlander, B. (1974). The effect of live TV and audio story narration on primary grade children's listening comprehension. *Journal of Educational Research*, **68**, 32–35.

Wexler, D. (1974). Self-actualization and cognitive processes. *Journal of Consulting and Clinical Psychology*, **42**, 47–53.

Wilgosh, L. (1975). Effects of labels on memory for pictures in four-year-old children. *Journal of Educational Psychology*, **67**, 375–379.

Witelson, S. (1975). Sex and the single hemisphere: specialization of the right hemisphere for spatial processing. *Science*, **193**, 425–527.

Children's Humour
Edited by P. McGhee and A. Chapman.
© 1980, John Wiley & Sons, Ltd.

CHAPTER 3

The Development of Linguistic Humour in Children: Incongruity through Rule Violation

THOMAS R. SHULTZ
and
JUDITH ROBILLARD

As the present volume attests, children express humour within many different media. Jokes may be conveyed through physical behaviours, drawings, cartoons, facial expressions, and even covert ideation (thinking to oneself). Yet it would seem that among these language is the most eminently suitable vehicle for creating, relaying, and enjoying humour. There would appear to be a number of reasons for the pre-eminence of linguistically based humour. One of the foremost is that language is at each of its several levels a rule-based system. And humour, as is demonstrated more clearly below, thrives on the violation of rules. In addition, language is a highly differentiated system, capable of refining and combining the most subtle of ideas. It is furthermore the most natural mode of human expression and social communication. Finally, language enables ideas to be communicated in a convenient, economical fashion which largely transcends time, space, and object. It is often not true that 'You had to be there to appreciate it'. The joke can effectively be related by even a moderately skilled raconteur.

It is the purpose of this chapter to analyse the development of linguistic humour in children. The overall thesis of the chapter is that linguistic humour is based on the child's developing metalinguistic knowledge; that is, awareness of language *qua* language. The incredible surge of psycholinguistic research over the last twenty years has made it increasingly clear that language is essentially a rule-governed system. Language is commonly conceptualized at a number of different levels: phonology, morphology, semantics, syntax, and pragmatics. At every one of these levels, there appears to be a set of rules which any accomplished speaker/listener eventually masters. As these rules develop the speaker/listener may in addition become at least vaguely or intuitively aware of the rules. It is this implicit awareness of rule systems which is referred to as *metalinguistics*—the capacity to reflect on one's language. Such awareness rarely attains the sophistication of an explicitly detailed analysis by, say, a professional linguist. But everyone does seem to develop at least a modicum of metalinguistic knowledge. This may be revealed even in young children through such events as spontaneous correction of language errors, concern over appropriate language usage, and judgments about language constructions (Clark, 1977).

Recent research has established the utility of conceptualizing the structure of humour in terms of *incongruity* and *resolution* (e.g. Shultz, 1976). The concept of incongruity refers to the notion that something unexpected happens in a joke which serves to arouse, surprise, or mystify the listener. The concept of resolution refers to the notion that the incongruity can be explained or rendered sensible. These structural properties have been found to characterize the humour of various cultures including both literate and non-literate (Shultz, 1977). Evidence has also been adduced indicating that young children show an early enjoyment of humorous incongruity but only later develop an appreciation of resolution in humour (Shultz, 1976). Many of the resolutions in verbal jokes have been found to be based on various types of linguistic ambiguity (phonological, lexical, and syntactic); and the child's understanding and appreciation of joke resolutions appear to depend on the ability to detect the hidden meanings of these ambiguities (Shultz, 1974; Shultz and Horibe, 1974). It is argued here that the various rule systems of language provide rich and varied opportunities for the construction of incongruities through rule violation.

Linguistic rules, like all other rules, are meant to be followed. They emerge during the course of development and they come to govern the way people discriminate and combine sounds, form words, derive and convey meaning, combine words into phrases and sentences, and conduct monologues or conversations. The tendency for speakers and listeners to conform to linguistic rules is so strong and pervasive that, when violations of the rules occur, it is indeed incongruous. In this chapter, we examine the rule systems inherent within each of the major levels of language, the development and use of such rules, the child's emerging awareness of the rules, and the possibilities that such awareness affords for humorous incongruity. For the time being, we ignore the issue of whether and to what extent such incongruities may be resolved. In this connection it is important to note that incongruity by itself seems to be humorous both to younger and older children, that is, before and after the emergence of resolvable humour (Shultz, 1972; Shultz and Horibe, 1974). Unlike the notion of linguistic devices for resolution in humour, the idea that humorous incongruity may have a linguistic basis has not been empirically researched. Consequently, much of our present treatment is anecdotal and exploratory. It is meant to stimulate rather than to report research on linguistic humour. We begin at the level of sounds and finish at the level of conversations.

PHONOLOGY

Phonology concerns the study of the sound system of language. It deals with the systematic use of sounds in making meaningful contrasts and with the combination of these meaningful sounds into syllables. Sound segments which are used for contrasting meanings are termed *phonemes*. For example, the initial consonants /p/ and /b/ in the English words *pin* and *bin* function to differentiate the meanings of the two words and hence constitute phonemes. When a speaker attempts to repeat a particular sound, the production necessarily varies across repetitions since no two utterances are exactly alike. If these variations are not used to contrast meaning, they are considered to be *allophones* of the same phoneme rather than separate phonemes. For every phoneme, a set of articulatory/acoustic features (known as *distinctive features*) can be specified which provide a unique description of that phoneme (Jakobson, Fant, and Halle, 1963). In this particular example, the phonemes /p/ and /b/ share an identical distinctive feature matrix with the single exception of the feature known as *voicing*. (See Table 3.1 for the distinctive features of English consonants and Table 3.2 for the distinctive features of English vowels.) The distinctive feature of *voicing* refers to the presence or absence of vocal cord vibrations. Its acoustic correlate is the presence or absence of periodic low-frequency excitation. The interested reader may refer to Hyman (1975) for a comprehensive description of the articulatory and acoustic characteristics of each of the features listed in Tables 3.1 and 3.2.

In addition to providing a structural description of how sounds are differentiated and classified into phonemes, phonology deals with rule structures for the combination of phonemes into syllables. One such system for combining English phonemes was provided by Whorf (1956). This system specifies, for example, that /dr/ as in drain is a permissible combination whereas /dl/ in the first syllable of a word is not a permissible combination.

Rule use

Our discussion of the development of the use of phonological rules covers the acquisition of phonemes, rules for substitution of phonemes, and rules for

Table 3.1 Distinctive features of English consonants

Consonants and examples

Distinctive features	p	b	f	v	m	t	d	θ thin	ð then	s	z	n	tʃ church	dʒ judge	ʃ ship	ʒ garage	k	g	ŋ sing	l	r	w	j yellow	h
Consonantal	+	+	+	+	+	+	+	+	+	+	+	+	+	+	+	+	+	+	+	+	+	−	−	−
Vocalic	−	−	−	−	−	−	−	−	−	−	−	−	−	−	−	−	−	−	−	+	+	−	−	−
Diffuse	+	+	+	+	+	+	+	+	+	+	+	+	−	−	−	−	−	−	−	+	+	+	+	−
Grave	+	+	+	+	+	−	−	−	−	−	−	−	−	−	−	−	+	+	+	−	−	+	−	+
Flat	−	−	−	−	−	−	−	−	−	−	−	−	−	−	−	−	−	−	−	−	−	+	−	−
Voice	−	+	−	+	+	−	+	−	+	−	+	+	−	+	−	+	−	+	+	+	+	+	+	−
Continuant	−	−	+	+	−	−	−	+	+	+	+	−	−	−	+	+	−	−	−	+	+	+	+	+
Strident	−	−	+	+	−	−	−	−	−	+	+	−	+	+	+	+	−	−	−	−	−	−	−	−
Nasal	−	−	−	−	+	−	−	−	−	−	−	+	−	−	−	−	−	−	+	−	−	−	−	−
Compact	−	−	−	−	−	−	−	−	−	−	−	−	+	+	+	+	+	+	+	−	−	−	−	−

NOTE: Adapted from Halle (1964); Hyman (1975); Jakobson, Fant, and Halle (1963); and Jakobson and Halle (1956). The phonemes /l/, /r/, /w/, and /j/ are not, technically, considered true consonants; /l/ and /r/ are termed *liquids*, and /w/ and /j/ are termed *glides*.

Table 3.2 Distinctive features of English vowels

Distinctive features	heat i	late e	debt ɛ	bad æ	shoot u	boat o	tall ɔ	father a
				Vowels and examples				
Consonantal	−	−	−	−	−	−	−	−
Vocalic	+	+	+	+	+	+	+	+
Diffuse	+	−	−	−	+	−	−	−
Compact	−	−	−	+	−	−	+	+
Grave	−	−	−	−	+	+	+	+
Flat	−	−	−	−	+	+	+	−
Tense	+	+	−	−	+	+	−	−
Voice	+	+	+	+	+	+	+	+
Continuant	+	+	+	+	+	+	+	+
Strident	−	−	−	−	−	−	−	−
Nasal	−	−	−	−	−	−	−	−

NOTE Adapted from Halle (1962); Hyman (1975); Jakobson, Fant, and Halle (1963); and Jakobson and Halle (1956).

combining phonemes. The most explicit and influential theory of the development of phonemic contrasts was proposed by Jakobson (1968). He specified that the earliest phonemic contrasts to emerge are those which are universal among world languages. According to Jakobson, there are three such universal contrasts: (a) oral-nasal /b/ versus /m/, (b) labial-dental /p/ versus /t/, and (c) stop-fricative /p/ versus /f/. The first of these oppositions is equivalent to the distinctive feature ± *nasal*; the second is equivalent to ± *grave*; and the third is characterized by two features ± *continuant* and ± *strident* (see Table 3.1.). Subsequent to these three initial contrasts, phonemic development is considered by Jakobson to correspond both to phonemic asymmetries and to phonemic frequencies in world languages. As an example of asymmetry, there are no world languages possessing back consonants such as /k/ and /g/ without also having front consonants such as /p/ and /b/. Similarly, in individual development, back consonants are assumed to presuppose front consonants. In other words, front consonants should develop before back consonants. An example of frequency is the phoneme /æ/ (as in bad) which, although often used in English, is infrequent in world languages in general. Therefore Jakobson predicts /æ/ to emerge relatively late in the speech of children, whether acquiring English or any other language. Data from case studies of the acquisition of phonemic contrasts have been generally consistent with Jakobson's theory (Ervin-Tripp, 1966). This evidence indicates that the phonemic contrasts discussed as examples here are typically present by three to four years of age.

A number of investigators have adopted a less theoretical approach and have charted the normative development of English phonemes (Poole, 1934; Sander, 1972; Templin, 1957; Wellman, Case, Mengert, and Bradbury, 1931). Most of these studies have emphasized acquisition of consonants rather than vowels since vowels are known to emerge very early (Winitz, 1969). Acquisition of consonants has generally been studied in either a spontaneous picture-naming task or through word imitation. The focus of this research has been on correct production of phonemes rather than the use of phonemes to contrast meaning. Representative results, in terms of ages of correct production of English consonants, are presented in Table 3.3 for four different studies using criteria ranging from fifty to one hundred per cent correct. The data indicate that children acquiring English master the production of consonants between the ages of eighteen months and eight years.

Table 3.3 Ages of correct production of English consonants

Consonants and examples		Study and percentage correct				
		Sander (1972) 50%	Sander (1972) 90%	Templin (1957) 75%	Wellman et al. (1931) 75%	Poole (1934) 100%
p		1.5	3.0	3.0	4.0	3.5
m		1.5	3.0	3.0	3.0	3.5
h		1.5	3.0	3.0	3.0	3.5
n		1.5	3.0	3.0	3.0	4.5
w		1.5	3.0	3.0	3.0	3.5
b		1.5	3.0	4.0	3.0	3.5
k		2.0	4.0	4.0	4.0	4.5
g		2.0	4.0	4.0	4.0	4.5
d		2.0	4.0	4.0	5.0	4.5
t		2.0	6.0	6.0	5.0	4.5
ŋ	ring	2.0	6.0	3.0	—	4.5
f		2.5	4.0	3.0	3.0	5.5
j	yes	2.5	4.0	3.5	4.0	4.5
r		3.0	6.0	4.0	5.0	7.5
l		3.0	6.0	6.0	4.0	6.5
s		3.0	8.0	4.5	5.0	7.5
tʃ	child	3.0	7.0	4.5	5.0	—
ʃ	share	3.0	7.0	4.5	—	6.5
z		3.5	8.0	7.0	5.0	7.5
dʒ	jam	4.0	7.0	7.0	6.0	—
v		4.0	8.0	6.0	5.0	6.5
θ	think	4.5	7.0	6.0	—	7.5
ð	that	5.0	8.0	7.0	—	6.5
ʒ	rouge	6.0	8.5	7.0	—	6.5

NOTE Adapted from Sander (1972) and Templin (1957).

A more recent orientation is to examine the development of the distinctive features which presumably underlie sound production. Menyuk (1968), for example, has presented evidence that children learning either Japanese or English acquire the +specification of six features in the following rank order—*nasal, grave, voice, diffuse, continuant*, and *strident*. Her developmental data are based on correct production of sounds characterized by these features in spontaneously generated sentences. The Japanese sample apparently acquired these six features between the ages of one and three years while the American sample started and finished somewhat later (two-and-a-half to five years). The distinctive feature analysis has also proved to be useful in characterizing deviant articulation in children. It appears that large numbers of deviant phonemes can be described in terms of a small number of distinctive feature errors (Compton, 1970; Costello and Onstine, 1976; McReynolds and Huston, 1971; Pollack and Rees, 1972). Moreover, training a particular feature in one phonetic context generalizes to some extent to untrained phonemes in a variety of phonetic contexts (Costello and Onstine, 1976; McReynolds and Bennett, 1972).

All of the foregoing indicates that phonemes are not produced by the neonate but rather develop with age. An interesting question arises as to what the child does when he needs to produce a phoneme which he does not yet possess. According to a good deal of clinical evidence (e.g. Van Riper and Irwin, 1958), the child in this situation may substitute a phoneme already in his repertoire for a target phoneme which he has not yet acquired. Those English phonemes which are most frequently misarticulated are presented in the left-hand column of Table 3.4. There are two interesting observations about this set of phonemes. First, a scanning of Table 3.3 shows that these difficult to produce phonemes emerge relatively late in development. Second, each of these phonemes contains the features +*continuant* and/or +*strident* (see Table 3.1). This corroborates Menyuk's (1968) conclusion that these two features develop rather late.

The substitutions that the child makes for target phonemes are not random or haphazard. Some of the most common substitutions for each target are presented in the right-hand column of Table 3.4. It is striking that nearly all of these common substitutions differ from the target phoneme in only a single distinctive feature. The number of such distinctive feature differences, calculated via Table 3.1, is shown in Table 3.4 in parentheses after each substitution. It appears that the general tendency is to substitute the closest feature matrix that the child has in his repertoire. Thus, not only is the emergence of phonemes and their underlying distinctive features rule-governed, but so is the process of substituting acquired for inaccessible phonemes.

The reader will notice in Table 3.4 a small number of exceptions to this general principle. There are three common substitutions that differ from their target phoneme by two distinctive features (e.g. /t/ for /s/ and /b/ for /v/), one that differs by three distinctive features (/j/ for /1/), and two that differ by five distinctive features (e.g. /w/ for /r/). Even these discrepancies from the 'minimal

Table 3.4 Frequently misarticulated English phonemes and some common substitutions

Misarticulated phonemes and examples	Some common substitutions and examples
/s/ soon	/θ/ thoon (1); /ʃ/ shoon (1); /t/ toon (2)
/z/ zebra	/ð/ thebra (1); /ʒ/ gebra (as in garage) (1); /s/ sebra (1)
/r/ road	/w/ woad (5)
/θ/ think	/t/ tink (1)
/ð/ then	/d/ den (1)
/ʃ/ shut	/tʃ/ chut (1)
/ʒ/ rouge	/dʒ/ rouj (as in judge) (1); /ʃ/ roush (1)
/tʃ/ chair	/ʃ/ shair (1); /t/ tair (2)
/dʒ/ jam	/tʃ/ cham (1); /d/ dam (2)
/v/ vase	/f/ fase (1); /b/ base (2)
/l/ lady	/w/ wady (5); /j/ yady (as in yellow) (3)

NOTE Adapted from Van Riper and Irwin (1958) and Winitz (1969) and also arising from the clinical experience of the second author. Numbers in parentheses represent distinctive feature differences between the substitution and the target.

distinctive feature difference' principle appear to be rule-governed. The so-called *gliding* rule specifies that *glides* (/w/ and /j/) may be substituted for *liquids* (/l/ and /r/) (Dale, 1976; Ingram, 1976). *Glides* and *liquids* are named for their manner of production and are often classified as being somewhere between consonants and vowels (Dale, 1976). Substitutions for /r/ and for /l/ in Table 3.4 can be characterized in terms of the *gliding* rule. The so-called *stopping* rule specifies that *stops* (/p/, /t/, /k/, /b/, /d/, /g/) may be substituted for *fricatives* (/f/, /θ/, /s/, /ʃ/, /v/, /ð/, /z/, /ʒ/) or affricates (/tʃ/, /dʒ/) (Dale, 1976; Ingram, 1976). The terms *stop*, *fricative*, and *affricate* refer to particular manners of production (Heffner, 1950). Substitutions for /s/, /tʃ/, /dʒ/ and /v/ in Table 3.4 can be characterized in terms of the *stopping* rule. In summary, most of the common phoneme substitutions are encompassed by the minimal distinctive feature difference principle; those few which are not can be described in terms of other well-known rules having to do with particular manners of production.

Gliding and *stopping* are but two of several substitution rules which have been identified in the speech of young children. Others listed by Dale (1976) and Ingram (1976), for example, include *fronting* and *assimilation*. *Fronting* refers to the substitution of front consonants for back consonants (e.g. /p/ for /k/) where front and back refer to place of articulation. *Assimilation* refers to the modification of a sound to make it more similar to neighbouring sounds. For example, in substituting *namb* for *lamb*, the child assimilates the target phoneme /l/ to the nasality of /m/ while maintaining the original place of production, thereby producing /n/ (Dale, 1976).

In addition to the rules for phonemic acquisition and substitution already discussed, the child also develops rules for combining phonemes into syllables. Three different studies indicate that the child learning English may have such combination rules well in hand by three to four years of age. Menyuk (1968) presented permissible (e.g. *trut*) and non-permissible (e.g. *tsut*) combinations to four-and-a-half to eight-year-old English speakers. She found that reproducing the non-permissible sequences was more difficult and took longer than reproducing the permissible sequences at all age levels. Most of the phonetic substitutions which occurred resulted in a permissible phonological combination. In a similar study, Morehead (1971) assessed sequences which varied in their approximation to English combination rules. Subjects ranged between four and twenty years of age. The number of changes in reproduction increased with the degree of deviation from the combination rules and the combination rules were consistently followed in producing such changes. Relevant to our previous discussion of substitution rules, it may be noted that these changes never differed from the original sequence by more than two distinctive features. Finally, Messer (1967) employed Whorf's (1956) combination system to construct permissible and non-permissible phoneme combinations. In some cases, only one consonant cluster was non-permissible (e.g. *dlek* versus *klek*) whereas in other cases both the opening and closing consonant clusters were non-permissible (e.g. *tlidk* versus *trisk*). His three- to four-year-old subjects mispronounced the non-permissible items more frequently than the permissible ones. Regarding substitution rules, it was found that their mispronunciations usually represented no more than one distinctive feature change. The fact that children of even three- and four-years-old in these studies had more difficulty with non-permissible than permissible sequences indicates that they had already acquired rules for combining English phonemes. The additional fact that errors of pronounciation conformed to combination rules in the studies by Menyuk (1968) and Morehead (1971) further strengthens this conclusion.

In summary, developmental studies of the use of phonological rules in English indicate that: (a) the acquisition of phonemes and their underlying distinctive features is completed between one-and-a-half and eight years of age, (b) before phonemic acquisition is completed children substitute, in a very systematic fashion, phonemes which they do have for phonemes they have not yet acquired, and (c) systems for combining phonemes into syllables emerge by three to four years of age.

Rule awareness

Our treatment of the child's developing awareness of phonological rules focuses on the three rule systems just discussed and also on some phonological aspects of poetics. Turning first to the child's awareness of phonemes, a variety of anecdotes suggests that such awareness may even precede phoneme production. These anecdotes indicate that the young child may know that a phoneme has been incorrectly produced, either by himself or by someone else, even though he does not yet correctly produce that phoneme. A clear example of such awareness of another's speech is cited by Berko and Brown (1960). They spoke with a child who referred to his inflated plastic fish as *fis*. 'In imitation of the child's pronunciation, the observer said, "That is your *fis*?" "No", said the child, "my *fis*". He continued to reject the adult's imitation until he was told, "That is your *fish*." "Yes," he said, "my *fis*" ' (Berko and Brown, 1960, p. 531). Jesperson (1964) presented a similar example from a French-speaking girl who said *tosson* for *garçon* (boy) and *cochon* (pig) but consistently protested when other people used *tosson* in the same ways. Knowledge of incorrect production in the child's own speech is exemplified by Smith (1973) who tried to get his young son to say *ship*, the son replying, 'No, I can only say *sip*' (p. 137). Awareness also seems to accompany the child's acquisition of correct phonemic productions. Smith (1973) reported that his son would often spontaneously comment on his own newly-acquired pronunciations. For example, after nearly a year of pronouncing *quick* as *kip* he declared, 'Daddy, I can say quick' (p. 10).

An innovative study by Read (1977) provides evidence that children as young as five years are aware of the major principle of phoneme substitution, that of minimal distinctive feature difference. The children were introduced to a puppet named Ed who liked to find words which sounded like *Ed* such as *Ted, Jed, fled*, and *sled*. The experimenter then mentioned some word pairs which did not sound exactly like *Ed* and the child had to guess the word in each pair that Ed would like. For example, 'Would Ed like *aid* or *owed*? Would Ed like *showed* or *shade*?' (pp. 13–14). Read's findings indicated that five-year-olds consistently chose the word in each pair that had the fewest differences from *Ed* in distinctive features. For example, they would choose *aid* over *owed* and *shade* over *showed*. The reader may consult Table 3.2 to discover that the vowel /e/ in *shade* differs from /ɛ/ in *Ed* by only one distinctive feature (*tense*) whereas the vowel /o/ in *showed* differs from /ɛ/ by three distinctive features (*tense, grave,* and *flat*). It should be noted that our interpretation of these findings differs from Read's which emphasizes the child's knowledge of spelling patterns.

Messer's (1967) study of children's use of combination rules (discussed above) also has implications for rule awareness. In addition to attempting to pronounce the monosyllabic items, Messer's three-and-a-half-year-old subjects were asked to identify which ones were 'possible' and which were 'impossible'. In this task they had little difficulty distinguishing those items which violated the Whorfian formula from those that did not. Thus, children as young as three-and-a-half years of age learning to speak English not only use rules for combining phonemes, but are to some extent aware of these combination rules.

Although it is well beyond the scope of this paper to provide a full treatment of the development of poetic language, the possible relevance of this topic to the study of metalinguistic awareness should at least be mentioned. In normal discourse, meaning is generally 'foregrounded' whereas phonology is typically 'backgrounded'. To some extent, poetic language alters this relationship by making the phonology quite opaque or explicit. Alliteration and rhyme are two of the principal phonological features which are employed in poetry and each has been found to characterize language play in children of a variety of ages (Abrams and Sutton-Smith, 1977; Chukovsky, 1965; Opie and Opie, 1959; Sanches and Kirshenblatt-Gimblett, 1976; Slobin, 1977; Weir, 1962). Although it may not be possible to affirm a child's awareness of various phonological devices from a particular utterance, regular and systematic use of such devices may indeed suggest some metalinguistic awareness. An investigation by Jusczyk (1977) indicates that children as young as six years are able to appreciate, identify and produce poetic rhyme and alliteration. Further discussion of poetics in the present chapter is confined to an analysis of humorous poems.

Humour

Among the most common forms of humorous incongruity based on violations of phonological rules are distorted articulations, immature articulations, and tongue twisters. As will become clear below, these classes of humour are based primarily on deviant phoneme production but the deviations involved, at least with respect to immature articulations and tongue twisters, are quite consistent with both patterns of phonemic development and rules for phoneme substitution. In principle, it should be possible as well to create humorous incongruities based on violations of rules for combining phonemes. Violations of combination rules would create unpronounceable sequences of phonemes which may be perceived as humorous when presented graphically as was done occasionally in Al Capp's *L'il Abner* comic strip. However, this type of humour appears to be extremely rare and hence does not warrant further discussion. Following our treatment of distorted articulations, immature articulations, and tongue twisters, we also discuss humorous verse which is based on phonological devices such as alliteration and rhyme.

Distorted articulation may be produced through physical interference with the articulatory system such as spreading the lips apart laterally. Such techniques will systematically distort standard phonemes, and Garvey (1977) has reported that this was used spontaneously to good humorous effect by nursery-school children in a play situation.

Immature articulation may also enter children's play as a comic device, but it was brought to international prominence by Warner Brother's cartoon characters such as *Tweety Bird* and *Elmer Fudd*. These two members of the *Bugs Bunny* troupe are well known to children of a variety of countries and languages around the world through frequent appearances in comic books, films, and television programmes. Both characters are easily recognized by their distinctive patterns of immature phoneme production. *Tweety Bird* was perhaps immortalized by the line he utters on encountering his nemesis, *Sylvester* the cat, 'I tought I taw a putty tat'. His particular articulation disorder consists of substituting /t/ for a variety of other phonemes such as /θ/, /s/, and /k/. We know from data presented in Table 3.3 that /θ/ and /s/ emerge relatively late among English-speaking children. We also know from data presented in Table 3.4 that /t/ is a very common substitution for the phonemes /θ/ and /s/. The phoneme /t/ differs from the phoneme /θ/ by a single distinctive feature (*continuant*; see Table 3.1) thus supporting the minimal distinctive feature difference principle. This substitution is also consistent with the *stopping* rule which specifies that a *stop* may be substituted for a corresponding *fricative* or *affricate*. The phonemes /t/ and /s/ differ by two distinctive features (see Table 3.1), but the substitution of /t/ for /s/ can also be explained by the *stopping* rule. According to data presented in Table 3.3, /k/ may emerge earlier than /t/ and, according to Table 3.1, these two phonemes differ by two distinctive features. However, the systematic substitution of /t/ for /k/ is not uncommon in young children and can be accounted for by the *fronting* rule which states that a forward-articulated consonant may be substituted for a back consonant. In summary, the humour in such utterances derives from incongruous but rule-governed violations of standard phoneme production.

When confronted with his nemesis *Bugs Bunny*, *Elmer Fudd* has been heard to exclaim, 'Oh, oh! What's that wabbit wascal up to . . .?'. His deviant articulation consists of substituting /w/ for /r/. We know that /r/ develops relatively late (see Table 3.3), is frequently misarticulated (see Table 3.4), and is most commonly substituted for by /w/ (see Table 3.4). Although these two phonemes differ by five distinctive features (see Table 3.1), this substitution conforms to the *gliding* rule which states that *glides* may replace *liquids*. As in the previous example, this case of humorous immature articulation is based on systematic deviations from standard phonemes.

It is clear that this kind of humour is not confined to commercial media but also occurs in naturalistic situations, particularly those involving interactions between older and younger children. In many such instances, the older child is amused by the younger one's misarticulations. This amusement is often expressed through mimicry and teasing as in an example cited by Maccoby and Bee (1965, p. 67): ' . . . a child asked if he could come along on a trip to the "mewwy-go-wound". An older child, teasing him, said "David wants to go to the mewwy-go-wound".' That the younger child responded with 'No, you don't say it wight' undoubtedly enhanced the humour and confirms our earlier point that the young child may be aware of incorrect phoneme productions in others even though he does not yet correctly produce that phoneme himself.

A somewhat more ritualized technique for producing humorous phonological incongruities practised by North American children is the so-called 'tongue twister'. This consists of a difficult-to-pronounce utterance which a speaker is supposed to repeat over and over again, at a faster and faster rate. Here are four representative examples which the reader is encouraged to try:

(1) Rubber baby-buggy bumpers.
(2) Bring a broad-backed black bath brush.
(3) She sold sea shells at the seashore.
(4) Peggy Babcock.

The reader will by now have noticed that he or she has made a number of phonological errors, most of which are probably accounted for by the principle of *assimilation*. This is the substitution process wherein one phoneme is made to sound more like a neighbouring phoneme. In (1), *rubber* is often assimilated to *buggy* and pronounced as *rugger; baby* assimilated to *buggy* and pronounced as *bagy; buggy* assimilated to *bumpers* and pronounced as *bunky*; and *bumpers* assimilated to *rubber* and pronounced as *bubbers*. In (2), *backed* and *bath* are often assimilated to *black* and pronounced as *blacked* and *blath*, respectively. In (3), *sea shells* may become *shea sells* and *seashore* may become *sheasore*. In these cases, a sort of reciprocal assimilation apparently occurs between two syllables in a single word. And (4) is frequently rendered as *Pebby Bagcock*, apparently reflecting a reciprocal assimilation between consonants in two separate words.

Many of these errors of assimilation seem to involve the minimal distinctive feature difference principle (refer to Table 3.1). In (1), /b/ and /g/ differ by a single distinctive feature (*diffuse*), as do /g/ and / ŋ / (*nasality*), /g/ and /k/ (*voicing*), /b/ and /m/ (*nasality*), and /b/ and /p/ (*voicing*). Similarly in (3), the phonemes /s/ and / ʃ / differ by one feature (*diffuse*), as do /g/ and /b/ in (4). Notice that the example of assimilative error in (2) does not involve the minimal distinctive feature principle since it consists of adding a phoneme where none was present.

The tongue twisters themselves appear to have been designed to maximize assimilatory errors by: (a) repetition of the same consonant sound in several different contexts, (b) use of different consonant sounds which differ minimally in distinctive features, and (c) recitation at a faster and faster rate. This last characteristic obviously produces a general increase in errors and is not of much theoretical interest. Circular repetition of the same consonant in several different phonemic contexts undoubtedly serves to confuse these contexts and increase the probability of producing a context with that consonant at an inappropriate instant. For example, in (1) /b/ is followed by the vowel contexts / ɚ /as in rubber, /c/, /i/, and /ʌ/ as in bumpers. In (2) /br/ is followed by the vowel contexts /ɪ/ as in bring, / ŋ /, and / ʌ/; and /b/ is followed by the contexts /r/, /æ/, and /l/. In (3) /s/ is followed by the vowel contexts /ɛ/ and /i/; and / ʃ / is followed by the vowel contexts /i/, / ɛ/, and /o/. When consonants vary rather than repeat, the tongue twister has them differ only minimally in distinctive features thereby enhancing the probability of assimilative substitutions based on the minimal distinctive feature difference principle. In each of our four tongue twister examples, there are a number of consonants which differ by only a single distinctive feature (refer to Table 3.1): (1) /b/ versus /p/ (*voicing*), /b/ versus /g/ (*diffuse*), and /b/ versus /m/ (*nasality*); (2) /d/ versus /t/ as in back<u>ed</u> (*voicing*); (3) /s/ versus / ʃ / (*diffuse*); (4) /p/ versus /b/ (*voicing*), /g/ versus /k/ (*voicing*), /p/ versus /k/ (*diffuse*), and /b/ versus /g/ (*diffuse*). The astute reader may have noticed that the /r/ and /l/ used in (2) differ by no feature in this system (see Table 3.1). It should be pointed out that such anomalies are not unusual in distinctive feature systems and they do represent limitations for these systems. Nonetheless, it would not be amiss to conclude that /r/ and /l/ must be very similar in underlying distinctive features.

Humorous verse does not violate phonological rules as do the above types of humour, but rather, like serious poetry, it functions to make phonology opaque or explicit. It is perhaps best described as an incongruous wedding of poetic form with tendentious content. It trivializes a valid artistic form while simultaneously dignifying a crude, silly, or naughty idea. Here are five representative examples of humorous verse by and for children, each dealing with the highly relevant topic of school (Keller, 1973):

Now I lay me down to rest,
I pray to pass tomorrow's test;
If I should die before I wake,
That's one less test I'll have to take.

God made the bees,
The bees make honey;
We do the work
And teacher makes the money.

Birds on the mountain,
Fish in the sea;
How you ever passed
Is a mystery to me.

An eagle flew from North to South
And caught our teacher in the mouth.
When he saw she was a fool
He dropped her here to teach our school.

Roses are red,
Violets are blue,
I copied your paper
And I flunked too.

These poems obviously express a cynical and somewhat hostile attitude towards school, sentiments which are often exhibited in non-poetic fashion. What makes them funny, and even partly acceptable, is the fact that they are here expressed in standard poetic format. That they possess alliteration and rhyme, both based on phonological devices, is also obvious. What may be somewhat less evident to the uninitiated is the standard rhythm or metre which characterizes each of these five poems. Technically, it is referred to as *trochaic tetrameter*, trochaic meaning that a strong stressed syllable is followed by an unstressed syllable and tetrameter referring to four strong stresses per line. It is noteworthy that trochaic tetrameter is common to nursery rhymes in several languages (Burling, 1966), to spontaneous language play of infants (Abrams and Sutton-Smith, 1977), and to other humorous and non-humorous rhymes of children (Opie and Opie, 1959). The hypothesis that humour in humorous verse results from an incongruous fusion of tendentious content and poetic form could be readily tested by creating altered versions of such poems through the deletion of either the tendentious content or the poetic form. Our prediction is that children would find the altered versions decidedly less funny that the original.

MORPHOLOGY

One level up from phonology is morphology, the study of the smallest meaningful language units—words and their inflections. Like the level of sounds, this level too appears to be rule-governed and, as children become implicitly aware of these rules, the rules can be exploited for humorous purposes. As with the phonological level, our analysis here focuses first on rule use, then on rule awareness, and finally on humour.

Rule use

Psychological studies of the development of morphological rules in children have so far been confined to a limited aspect of morphology, the so-called *grammatical morphemes* or *inflections*. These inflections have two purposes: (a) to modify the meaning of major content words, like nouns and verbs, by adding such features as plurality or tense, or (b) to indicate the precise relations among such content words as in possession. The most extensive study in this area was conducted by Brown (1973) on the development of fourteen English inflections. Brown studied the child's use of these inflections in what are called 'obligatory contexts' which were defined separately for each morpheme. For example the context 'three chair—' requires the addition of the plural morpheme s. Similarly, the context 'yesterday he sat, today he is sit___' specifies the present progressive inflection ing applied to the verb sit. Brown considered that a child had mastered a particular grammatical morpheme when the child provided it in at least ninety per cent of obligatory contexts. The order of acquisition of these English inflections appeared to be extremely regular and was found to be related both to the grammatical and the semantic complexity of the inflections. Brown's evidence further suggests that children acquiring English master this set of morphemic inflections between about two and four years of age.

One of the more striking aspects of the development of morphological rules is the phenomenon of over-regularization. English, of course, provides many exceptions to morphological rules such as those dealing with tense or plurality. But the young child, as he begins to construct a rule, vastly over-extends it, ignoring the exceptions (Cazden, 1968; Ervin, 1964). For example, the child might say *mouses* for *mice* and *goed* for *went*. Eventually though, the child learns when to apply the rule and when to use the exceptions.

Rule awareness

Unfortunately, because of a lack of systematic studies of awareness of morphological rules, our discussion of rule awareness is restricted to anecdotal evidence. The most revealing set of anecdotes was collected by Slobin (1977) from observations of his young daughter. Each of these observations involves the young girl analysing or judging the appropriateness of some morphological construction. Here are a few examples. 'On the TV news she (at 4; 9) hears the word *persons* and mulls over it for sometime, since she had recently discovered that *people* is the normal plural of *person*' (p. 6). At 4; 2 she refused to accept irregular past tenses (e.g. *came*) instead insisting on her own customary over-regularizations (e.g. *comed*). About a month later she became able to judge some morphological forms correctly and Slobin notes that this occurred even before she used the forms correctly in her own speech. Slobin would present her with a problem of the following sort: 'Suppose you were eating something yesterday. Which is right to say: *Yesterday I ate something*? or *Yesterday I eated something*?' (p. 10). Presumably she would choose the irregular form *ate* even though she would use the over-regularized form *eated* in her own spontaneous speech. This continued over the next month when she, for example, offered *knowed* but accepted *knew*; and offered *winned*, rejected *wan*, and accepted *won*.

Humour

The primary form of humour based on deviant morphological rules involves 'play languages'. According to Sherzer (1976), these play languages are created through a linguistic code derived from an ordinary language by certain definable rules. Play languages are used by children in many different cultures and appear to have two primary functions: secrecy and fun. Some cultures appear to cultivate play languages. For example, Sherzer (1976) has counted no fewer than five Cuna play languages and seven Javanese play languages. They are ordinarily formed by one or two simple rules which operate on a particular utterance, altering the sounds and thereby producing a new and difficult-to-recognize form. This is done with great efficiency because the rules of the standard language are left very much intact. The play language uses the standard language as a base adding to it a few new morphological rules of its own.

Sherzer (1976) has identified four different types of morphological rules used to create play languages: addition, subtraction, reversal, and substitution. An example of an addition rule is provided by a Javanese play language in which every vowel of a word is followed by a syllable which consists of /f/ plus a repetition of the vowel. *Aku arep tuku klambi* (I want to buy a dress) in ordinary Javanese becomes *Afakufu afarefep tufukufu klafambifi* in this particular play language (Sherzer, 1976, p. 27). Still another Javanese play language is based on a subtraction rule. In this case every syllable of every word except the initial one is deleted. Also, every syllable is closed by retaining the initial consonant of the second syllable of the word if this is needed. For example, *Aku arep lungo* (I am going to go) in ordinary Javanese becomes *Ak ar lung* in this play language (Sherzer, 1976, p. 28). A good example of a play language based on reversal is French backwards talk, *langage à l'envers*. One variant of this play language involves a switching of syllables. For example, *l'envers* (backwards) becomes *verlen; mari* (husband) becomes *rima; copains* (friends) becomes *painsco*; and *cul* (ass) becomes *luc* (Sherzer, 1976, p. 25). A substitution rule is illustrated by a Cuna language in which every vowel becomes /i/. In this play language *pia* (where) becomes *pii*, *pe* (you) becomes *pi*, *tanikki* (he's coming) becomes *tinikki*, *nuka* (name) becomes *niki*, and *iki* (how) remains as *iki* (Sherzer, 1976, p. 24).

Among North American children, the principal play language is *Pig Latin* which involves both reversal and addition rules. It is based on two rules to be applied in a particular order and on one definition. The first rule is to take the first consonant cluster in a word, unless it is the last consonant cluster, and shift it and all prior phonemes to the end of the word. In this context, a consonant cluster can be defined as a single consonant or a string of consonants. The second rule is to add /e/ as in pay to the end of the newly formed word. (Hence: eakingspay igpay atinlay ancay ebay eryvay umoroushay eedinday.)

There would appear to be two psycholinguistic prerequisites to facility in a play language such as *Pig Latin*. One of these is segmentation, the ability to separate words into their constituent phonemes. A study by Fox and Routh (1975) indicates that children can, with great accuracy, segment sentences into words and words into syllables by the age of four years and segment syllables into sounds by the age of six years. The other prerequisite is the ability to consider the word as the primary unit of analysis and systematically apply rules in the formation of words. Studies in morphological rule use which we reviewed above suggest that this latter ability is well within the grasp of the four- to five-year-old child. Consequently, one would expect Pig Latin and other such languages to emerge no earlier than about six years of age.

SEMANTICS

Semantics deals not with the formation of words but rather with the meaning of words and the rules for constructing meaningful combinations of words. It is generally acknowledged that there is at present no essentially adequate theory of semantics and semantic development. Various theories of semantics have been proposed, however, and one of the currently most popular is the 'semantic feature' theory (Katz and Fodor, 1963). Just as it has proved useful to characterize speech sounds in terms of underlying distinctive features, so it has been proposed that word meanings can be analysed in terms of underlying semantic features. According to semantic feature theory, the meaning of a word consists of two parts: (a) a set of semantic features each of which expresses a dimension or part of the meaning, and (b) selection restrictions on possible combinations of words. Selection restrictions are, in turn, based on values of the semantic features. For example, the word *bachelor* contains at least the three semantic features *+ human, + male*, and *− married*. And because of these features, certain possible combinations of *bachelor* with other words are ruled out. The expression *bachelor's wife*, for instance, violates the selection restrictions since *bachelor* possesses the feature *− married* and *wife* possesses the feature *+ married*. It is perhaps needless to say that this formulation still has a number of serious problems (see Bolinger, 1965, and Weinreich, 1971, for a general theoretical critique). Not the least of these is the formidable task of constructing a coherent set of features which could efficiently characterize and discriminate the vast number of word meanings that the competent speaker/listener eventually masters. More recent approaches have stressed that meaning is more complex than a set of semantic features and that, consequently, it is necessary to consider additional semantic structures. Some have emphasized the importance of a concept core, that there exists a best instance (Rosch, 1973) or a best feature (Rips, Shoben, and Smith, 1973) in the meaning of a word. Others have stressed the importance of relational information in analysing word meaning, that any given word has a specified set of relations with other concepts (Norman and Rumelhart, 1975). In spite of its controversial status, the basic insights of semantic feature theory are generally regarded as providing one of the more promising avenues of approach to the problem of linguistic meaning.

Rule use

Most of the research on semantic development has in fact been guided by a particular version of semantic feature theory set forth by Clark (1973). According to her theory, the child acquires the meanings of words by sequentially adding semantic features. Because the child is presumed to start with only a few semantic features, Clark predicts that the child's first words will be inappropriately over-extended. For example, the word *horse* might be initially applied to all four-legged animals. Clark also hypothesizes that the first semantic features are based on static perceptual attributes such as size and shape which can be applied to many words. Much of the empirical research stimulated by Clark's version of semantic feature theory has concerned the child's acquisition of polar or antonymic adjectives such as *long* versus *short* and *more* versus *less*. The results of this line of research have not been in total agreement with Clark's analysis (see Dale, 1976, for a review). Clark's theory has also been criticized for emphasizing the wrong features. Nelson (1974), for example, has presented evidence indicating that the child's first words are based on function or action rather than on static perceptual features. And a number of investigators have presented evidence of under-extension in the child's first words suggesting that, at least in some cases, the child may begin with a surfeit of features some of which are gradually eliminated (Bowerman, 1976; Schlesinger, 1974). None of this mitigates against semantic feature theory *per se* but rather suggests problems with specific characterization of the nature and development of these features. We anticipate that future research and theoretical work will serve to clarify some of these important issues on semantic development.

Empirical research on language development has established that semantics is, from the very beginning, basic to language. Development obviously occurs in the area of semantics, but the child's language is never meaningless. Even the very first single-word utterances seem to convey semantic ideas. Nelson (1973) examined the first fifty words acquired by eighteen children and found not only considerable uniformity across children but that the first fifty words constituted a highly selective set of possibilities. What seemed to be crucial in determining whether a word was acquired was that the child could actively engage the referent. The child's first words, then, referred to things which were most directly meaningful to him or her. Similarly, a number of studies have indicated that the child's first two-word utterances express a variety of semantic relations such as action, recurrence, attribution, possession, and question (Bowerman, 1976; Bloom, Lightbown, and Hood, 1975; Brown, 1973; Slobin, 1970). These semantic relations are inferred, with some degree of reliability, from the context in which the child is speaking and from consistent word order. It is also clear that the child's early words are not hopelessly fused with their referent. From the beginning of language the child is capable of mastering arbitrary and conventional relations between words and their referents. Linguistic reality is rarely confused with empirical reality. For example, a child talking about tigers behaves quite differently from a child interacting with tigers (Markman, 1976).

Rule awareness

Our treatment of awareness of semantics focuses on word meanings, selection restrictions, and relations between word and referent. Unfortunately, we could find no evidence regarding awareness of semantic features *per se*. The evidence on awareness of word meaning is strictly anecdotal. Slobin's (1977) observations on his young daughter are quite representative. At 2; 9 she began to use the word *mean* for foreign words which she was trying to learn, for example 'What does *bread* mean in German?' (p. 2). As early as 3; 3 she was able to accept correct paraphases and reject incorrect ones, and from 3; 6 she could offer appropriate paraphrases. At 4; 7 she began offering spontaneous definitions for words; for example, 'Today I learned what *super* means. It means *really, really, really* something!' (p. 4).

In contrast, awareness of selection restrictions has been the focus of several systematic studies. De Villiers and de Villiers (1972) asked two- and three-year-olds to judge whether each of several sentences was right or wrong. Some of the sentences were semantically anomalous in the sense that they violated selection restrictions (e.g. *Throw the sky*) whereas others were semantically sound (e.g. *Throw the stone*). If the sentence was judged to be wrong, the child was asked to correct it. It was found that six out of the eight children tested judged anomalous sentences to be wrong on at least seventy-five per cent of the occasions and that most of these children could correct the anomalies. In a similar investigation by James and Miller (1973), five- and seven-year-olds were asked to identify anomalous or meaningful sentences as being 'silly' or 'okay' and to convert the anomalous sentences into meaningful ones. The semantic features $\pm$ *human* and $\pm$ *animate* were used to construct sentences which involved subject-verb or noun-adjective constituents. In the anomalous sentences, a semantic feature of the noun was contradicted by a semantic feature of the adjective or verb. For example, in *The large rock walked down the hill*, the word *rock* possesses the feature $-$ *animate* and the word *walk* possesses the feature $+$ *animate*. The results indicated that both five- and seven-year-olds could accurately distinguish anomalous from meaningful sentences and that seven-year-olds were better than five-year-olds at correcting the anomalies. The general nature of these results was corroborated in another study by Glass, Holyoak, and Kossan (1977) with six-, eight- and ten-year-olds. They presented the children with meaningful or semantically anomalous (e.g. *Some kings are queens* or *Some kings are chairs*) sentences which the child was to judge as being true or false. Children of all ages could easily identify the anomalous sentences as false and performance was virtually perfect even among the six-year-olds.

Although observations of early language use suggest that the child has no difficulty in accepting the arbitrary relation between words and their referents, several recent studies report that until about five years of age the child still has some difficulty conceptualizing these arbitrary relations. Young children sometimes believe that changing the name of an object also involves changing physical properties of the object (e.g. if a cat is relabelled *dog* then it would bark), that words possess properties of their referents (e.g. the word *rain* is itself wet), and that if a referent disappears the word also will disappear or at least lose some of its meaning (e.g. if all giraffes were gone we could not still have the word *giraffe*) (Markman, 1976; Osherson and Markman, 1975; Papandropoulou and

Sinclair, 1974). The methodological problems inherent in this line of research are considerable in that the young child may not share the experimenter's notion of *word*. If this is so, the child may easily misinterpret the question he is being asked and thus not reveal his actual level of awareness of word-referent relations.

To summarize the research on semantic rule awareness, it appears that children as young as three-years-old focus explicitly on word meanings and are able to identify violations of selection restrictions. Certainly by the age of six children identify these violations with nearly complete accuracy at least for familiar words. Until about six years of age they may still have some difficulty conceptualizing the arbitrary and conventional nature of the relations between words and their referents.

Humour

Our treatment of humour based on semantic violations employs the same organizational scheme used in our presentation of semantic rule use and semantic awareness. Semantically based humour can be produced by the absence of word meaning, violation of selection restrictions, and the use of inappropriate names. Probably the archetypal example of humour based on lack of word meaning in the English language is the Lewis Carroll poem, *Jabberwocky*, the opening and closing stanzas of which go as follows (Gardner, 1963, pp. 191 and 197):

> Twas brillig, and the slithy toves
>> Did gyre and gimble in the wabe:
> All mimsy were the borogroves,
>> And the mome raths outgrabe.

The major content words in this selection are completely void of semantic content in the usual sense although Carroll himself does provide his own idiosyncratic interpretations. Even though lacking in meaning, the poem remains phonologically and syntactically valid, aided by the use of standard English function words and a few strong verbs. The humorousness of such semantically void material for children remains somewhat of a controversy. Gardner (1963) claims that the *Jabberwocky* poem was immensely popular among nineteenth-century English schoolboys. But Sanches and Kirshenblatt-Gimblett (1976) report finding no examples of Jabberwocky-like material in their rather large corpus of children's speech play. However, Garvey (1977) claims that the creation of meaningless common nouns was one of the most productive processes for making humorous nonsense in nursery-school dyads. Unfortunately, she presents no examples in her 1977 paper.

Humour based on violation of semantic selection restrictions appears to be much more pervasive in children. First of all, it should be noted that many of the semantically anomalous sentences used in the experiments on awareness of selection restrictions are in fact quite funny. This is well illustrated in the de Villiers' (1973) film *Out of the Mouths of Babes* which shows virtually every accurate identification of an anomalous sentence to be accompanied by smiling or laughing on the part of the child. The use of nonsensical or impossible-to-carry-out instructions in the hazing of initiates to children's groups is also based on violation of selection restrictions. The unfortunate initiate, for example, may be asked to retrieve a *sky hook* or some *polka-dot paint*. Another example of children's humour based on violated selection restrictions is 'tangletalk'. Opie and Opie (1959) have collected a large number of instances of tangletalk from British children. The oldest and best known instance is the following (p. 25):

> One fine day in the middle of the night,
> Two dead men got up to fight,
> Back to back they faced each other,
> Drew their swords and shot each other.
> A paralysed donkey passing by
> Kicked a blind man in the eye,
> Knocked him through a nine inch wall
> Into a dry ditch and drowned them all.

A similar form occurs in Russian children's folklore which Chukovsky (1965) has termed 'topsy-turvies'. A favourite example among Russian children is the following (p. 96):

> The blind man gazes
> The deaf man listens
> The cripple runs a race
> The mute cries: 'Help'.

In all of these examples, humorous incongruity derives from the use of non-permissible combinations of semantic features.

Name-calling or name-switching is based on the awareness that the assignment of names to people is essentially arbitrary and hence can easily be changed in play. According to Garvey's (1977) observations of pre-schoolers, children in non-play situations were quite insistent that they be called by their correct names and that their names be correctly pronounced. However, in a play situation, names were rather freely invented, exchanged, and assigned often with very humorous results (e.g. *dingba, poopaw, fool-around, Mrs. Poop, silly face, Mrs. Fingernail, and dumbhead*). The following represents a playful exchange of this type (p. 39):

F(5; 7)   F(5; 1)
[Both children are using telephones to call friends]
1. Mommy, mommy, I got new
    friends called Dool,
    Sol, Ta.
                                    2. Dool, Sue, and Ta?
        [both laugh]
3. Those are funny names,
    aren't they?
                                    4. No, it's Poopoo, Daigi,
                                        and Dia . . . Diarrhea.
        [both laugh]

The use of such humour perhaps reveals a more sophisticated awareness of the arbitrary nature of word-referent relations among five-year-olds than suggested by the question and answer format used in studies reviewed above. It may be that humorous use of language occasionally provides a more natural index of metalinguistic awareness than does the more conventional problem-solving sort of paradigm.

SYNTAX

Syntax is the aspect of language which specifies logical relations among words in a sentence such as predication and object complementation. In English, unlike highly inflected languages such as Latin or Russian, this type of information is conveyed primarily through word order—subjects precede verbs, verbs precede objects, and so on. Alternate word orders are sometimes used in English, as in questions or passives, but their construction is strictly governed by various transformational rules.

Rule use

Developmental investigations of syntax indicate that deviations from adult word order rarely occur in the speech of children acquiring English, even in the earliest stages (Brown, 1973). This appears to be true not only of children's spontaneous utterances but also of their imitations of adult speech. For example, when asked to imitate such sentences as *I showed you the book*, responses such as *I show book* were commonly given (Brown and Fraser, 1964). In both spontaneous and imitative speech, young English-speaking children typically delete inflections and preserve the adult word order. There is evidence that children learning more highly inflected languages with freer word order are somewhat more variable in their own use of word order (Dale, 1976).

Rule awareness

Two recent experiments suggest that the child's awareness of word order violations emerges rather later than his or her use of correct word order. Gleitman, Gleitman, and Shipley (1972) presented two-and-a-half-year-old girls with a set of imperative sentences which they were asked to judge as 'good' or 'silly'. The sentences were either well-formed in contour (e.g. *Bring me the ball, Ball me the bring*) or telegraphic (e.g. *Bring ball, Ball bring*). And the word order was either correct (e.g. *Bring me the ball, Bring ball*) or reversed (e.g. *Ball me the bring, Ball bring*). Although there was an overall tendency for their three subjects to judge correct order sentences, but not reversed order sentences, as 'good', performance was far from perfect. Furthermore, the girls did not often achieve a correct word order in their attempts to fix the 'silly' sentences.

In a similar study, de Villiers and de Villiers (1972) asked two- and three-year-olds to judge a series of sentences as 'right' or 'wrong'. Some of these sentences (discussed above under *semantics*) varied in semantic acceptability, whereas others represented correct (e.g. *Brush your teeth*) versus reversed (e.g. *Teeth your brush*) word order. It was found that only two of the eight children tested identified the reversed sentences as 'wrong' more than seventy-five per cent of the time. Only one of these two children was successful at correcting the reversed order sentence (e.g. *Cake the eat* to *Eat the cake*). This performance on syntactic anomalies was considerably worse than on the semantic anomalies discussed above. Such a finding is consistent with the growing body of literature which suggests the psychological primacy of semantics over syntax (cf. Shultz and Pilon, 1973).

Humour

This may partly explain why humour based on deviations from syntactic rules is so rare. In fact, we are not able to report a single instance of such humour in all of the material available to us. The lack of humour based on syntactic incongruities parallels the relative rarity of syntactic resolution devices in humour (Shultz, 1976). But this should not be taken to imply that violations of syntactic rules are not humorous. On the contrary, anecdotal evidence from the two experiments on awareness of such violations suggests that children find syntactic anomalies quite humorous indeed. Gleitman, Gleitman, and Shipley (1972) presented an interview with a seven-year-old child who considered the task of identifying syntactic anomalies to be 'plain fun' and sometimes downright funny. Experimenter: 'How about this one: Clair and Eleanor is a sister'. Claire: '[laugh] Claire and Eleanor are sisters' (p. 149). Similarly, younger children in the de Villiers' (1973) film of their experiment can be observed to smile or laugh as they detect syntactic violations. This form of humour may be largely un-known, but it undoubtedly has potential.

PRAGMATICS

Pragmatics concerns rules governing the use of language in social context. Context in this sense is considered to be part of the structure of language itself. Linguistic meaning is conveyed and interpreted through mapping of sentences on to events in social settings. One of the principal structures in pragmatics is the conversational postulate. In general, these postulates describe the assumptions which underlie conversation. Among the conversational postulates outlined by Bates (1976b) are the assumptions that people who enter into a conversation will: (a) be co-operative, (b) tell each other the truth, (c) offer only new and relevant information, and (d) request only information that is sincerely wanted. These postulates may not always be used in conversations, but when violations occur it is assumed that they will be recognized as such and used to interpret what is said.

Rule use

Virtually all of the developmental research on conversational postulates deals only with one limited aspect of pragmatics, namely, forms of request. Ervin-Tripp (1977) hypothesized that children's use of forms of request progresses from direct imperatives (e.g. *Gimme cookies!*) to indirect requests based on conversational postulates (e.g. Those look good!). Recent empirical studies on the use of request forms have generally confirmed this prediction, although children seem to do better at comprehending than producing indirect requests. The results of two studies suggest that children as young as two-years-old can respond to a variety of subtle request forms. Bates (1976b) analysed video-taped conversations between mothers and their children of two, three and four years of age. She found that children at each of these ages were just as likely to comply with indirect requests as with direct commands. A similar study by Shatz (reported in Bates, 1976a) examined two-year-olds' responses to direct and indirect requests from their mothers. She, too, found no difference in the likelihood of compliance to direct versus indirect requests. Although it was the case that question directives (e.g. *Can you shut the door?*) were sometimes misinterpreted as literal questions. It may be that the young children in these studies did interpret indirect requests correctly on the basis of the context in which they were uttered. Alternatively, however, it is possible that they were relying on non-verbal cues from the mother or on parts of the request only (e.g. interpreting *Can you shut the door?* as *Shut the door*).

Bates (1976b) also examined the production of request forms by two- to four-year-olds interacting with their mothers. She found that virtually all such requests by children were either conventional commands, *Can I have?* requests, or statements of desire (e.g. *I want that*). In a longitudinal study of two Italian children, Bates (1976a) found that indirect requests based on conversational postulates do not appear until at least three-and-a-half to four years of age. Thus,

Bates concludes that comprehension use of indirect requests precedes production use of these requests.

In a more systematic study of the production of requests, Bates (1976a) had three- to seven-year-old Italian pre-schoolers, sixty in number, each ask a hand puppet for a piece of candy. After the child's first request, the experimenter urged the child to ask more politely. This technique, of course, yielded data not only on spontaneous requests but also on the ability to increase indirectness of request. She reports that three-year-olds were rarely capable of altering their original requests. Older children adopted a variety of strategies when asked to increase the politeness of their requests, including the adding of *please*, the use of softer intonation, asking for less candy, and shifting from imperative to interrogative forms.

Rule awareness

In the same study, Bates added a procedure to assess the child's awareness of indirect forms of requests based on conversational postulates. Here the child played the role of the individual who doles out the candy. Two identical puppets in turn requested candy from the child. Thus, the child heard a series of paired requests reflecting soft versus harsh intonation, presence versus absence of formal versus informal forms of address, interrogative versus imperative constructions, and conditional versus declarative constructions (e.g. *I would like a piece of candy* versus *I want a piece of candy*). The child then had to say which puppet was nicer and to explain what it was he said that was nicer. In this task, three-year-olds correctly discriminated two kinds of items in terms of politeness: the presence versus absence of *please* and soft versus harsh intonation. Five-and-a-half- to six-year-old children were able correctly to discriminate some of the more complex forms such as conditionals versus declaratives and formal versus informal modes of address. The differential politeness of the interrogative versus imperative construction was not discriminated by children tested at any age level. In general, children had a good deal more trouble in justifying their choices. Three-year-olds could not justify their choices at all. Although four- to five-year-old children would often choose the conditional (e.g. *I would like*) as being more polite, their justifications would often transform it to an imperative (e.g. *Because he said, 'gimme some candy'*). Sometimes the child would justify a correct choice by saying that the puppet said *please* even though *please* was not used in either alternative.

Summing up the developmental evidence on this one aspect of pragmatics, it appears that indirect request forms based on conversational postulates are comprehended as young as two years, produced by four years, and made objects of the child's awareness by about six years.

Humour

The violation of pragmatic rules appears to be a rich natural source of incongruity humour. Our discussion focuses on two types of humour, one that violates the general notion of pragmatics and another that violates specific conversational postulates. Violations of the more general type could well be characterized in terms of 'over-literality'. The person seems deliberately to ignore the essential context, making instead a literal interpretation of the utterance. This can easily be exploited for humorous purposes in answering requests for information (e.g. *Do you know where Royal Street is? Yes; Do you know what time it is? Yes, I do.*); in responding to conversational invitations (e.g. *I hear you had an interesting vacation. Yes; Have you been talking to Margaret lately? Yes, I have*); or in interpretations of indirect forms of request (e.g. *Can you close the door? Of course I can; Can you hand me the newspaper? Yes*). It should be noted that, in the latter two examples, the request is not actually carried out. In each of these cases, the respondent's overly brief reply is acceptable in a literal sense but is in fact incongruous since it disregards the ordinary contextual variables which provide the original question with its full meaning. This technique is used by children with devastating effect to confound their disciplinarians and occasionally each other as when they act out the literal interpretations of instructions to *Hold your tongue, Watch your step*, and even *Drop dead.*

However, the acknowledged master of over-literality is almost certainly Lewis Carroll, as the following examples drawn from *Alice's Adventures in Wonderland* attest. At the Mad Hatter's Tea-Party, the March Hare urges Alice to 'Take some more tea'. ' "I've had nothing yet", Alice replied in an offended tone: "so I can't take more". "You mean you can't take *less*", said the Hatter: "It's very easy to take *more* than nothing" ' (Gardner, 1963, p. 101). During the trial of the Knave of Hearts, the King terminated the Mad Hatter's testimony by saying 'If that's all you know about it, you may stand down'. ' "I can't go no lower", said the Hatter: "I'm on the floor, as it is" ' (Gardner, 1963, p. 150). It is perhaps worth noting that the technique of over-literality is just the opposite of metaphor. In metaphor, the literal interpretation is deliberately ignored and the utterance is instead interpreted in terms of the context (see H. Gardner, Chapter 4, this volume). It is likely that both metaphor and humorous over-literality could profitably be studied to asses the child's developing awareness of pragmatic structures.

Humour can also be based on the violation of specific conversational postulates. Garvey (1977) presents two examples with pre-school children in which the assumption that participants in a conversation tell the truth is playfully violated. One of these concerns an interaction between Garvey, a two-year-old girl, and the girl's five-year-old brother: 'Susie started to show me parts of her face, pointing to her eye, saying *Eye*, then her nose, saying *Nose*, and then her mouth. Her somewhat neglected brother, who had been watching, moved in and pointed to his forehead and said, quite dramatically, *Here's my mouth*. David and I laughed then, but Susie was not amused' (Garvey, 1977, p. 40). The other concerns a five-year-old girl who was asked by a five-year-old boy whom she would rather play with, Mary Ann or Lisa : 'She looked at him reflectively and replied, *Um. I think . . . um . . . Lisa, because she's a boy.* Then she giggled and her partner laughed and said, *No, she's a girl. You silly'* (Garvey, 1977, p. 41).

A more serious (and, at the same time, more humorous) undermining of the entire notion of a conversation was achieved by Humpty Dumpty in Carroll's *Through the Looking Glass*. Humpty Dumpty has the maddening tendency to treat a conversation as if it were a riddle contest. ' "Why do you sit out here all alone?" said Alice, not wishing to begin an argument. "Why, because there's nobody with me!" cried Humpty Dumpty. "Did you think I didn't know the answer to *that*? Ask another". "Don't you think you'd be safer down on the ground?" Alice went on, not with any idea of making another riddle, but simply in her good-natured anxiety for the queer creature. "That wall is so *very* narrow!" "What tremendously easy riddles you ask!" Humpty Dumpty growled out. "Of course I don't think so!" ' (Gardner,1963, p. 263). Later, he continues, ' "So here's a question for you. How old did you say you were?" Alice made a short calculation, and said "Seven years and six months". "Wrong!" Humpty Dumpty exclaimed triumphantly. "You never said a word like it!" "I thought you meant How old *are* you?" Alice explained. "If I'd meant that, I'd have said it", said Humpty Dumpty' (Gardner, 1963, p. 265).

SUMMARY

In this chapter an attempt has been made to analyse the possibilities inherent within each of the major rule systems of language for creating humorous incongruities. Literature has been reviewed on the development of phonological, morphological, semantic, syntactic, and pragmatic rule structures and on the child's emerging awareness of these rules. Numerous examples have been provided of how rule violations could be used to generate incongruity humour. In closing, though, it should be emphasized that we have glimpsed only the tip of the iceberg on all of these issues. Research in both psycholinguistics and the psychology of humour is still in its infancy. We need to know considerably more about what linguistic rule structures develop at what particular stages and when (and how deeply) the child becomes aware of these structures. The psycholinguistic research we reviewed here is rather limited in scope, based on theoretical concepts which undoubtedly will be refined or replaced, and empirically rather thin. The corresponding humour research is practically non-existent. We know very little about how children of various ages respond to and/or create the types of humour discussed here. It is our hope that the chapter might serve to stimulate research of this nature.

REFERENCES

Abrams, D. M., and Sutton-Smith, B. (1977). The play and poetry of early word play: a re-analysis of Ruth Weir's 'Language in the crib'. Paper presented at the meeting of the Society for Research in Child Development, New Orleans, March.

Bates, E. (1976a). *Language and Context: The Acquisition of Pragmatics.* New York: Academic Press.

Bates, E. (1976b). Pragmatics and sociolinguistics in child language. In D. M. Morehead and A. E. Morehead (Eds.), *Normal and Deficient Child Language.* Baltimore: University Park Press.

Berko, J., and Brown, R. (1960). Psycholinguistic research methods. In P. H. Mussen (Ed.), *Handbook of Research Methods in Child Development.* New York: Wiley.

Bloom, L., Lightbown, P., and Hood, L. (1975). Structure and variation in child language. *Monographs of the Society for Research in Child Development, 40,* (2, Serial Number 160).

Bolinger, D. (1965). The atomization of meaning. *Language, 41,* 555–573.

Bowerman, M. (1976). Semantic factors in the acquisition of rules for word use and sentence construction. In D. M. Morehead and A. E. Morehead (Eds.), *Normal and Deficient Child Language.* Baltimore: University Park Press.

Brown, R. (1973). *A First Language: The Early Stages.* Cambridge, Massachusetts: Harvard University Press.

Brown, R., and Fraser, C. (1964). The acquisition of syntax. In U. Bellugi and R. Brown (Eds.), The acquisition of language. *Monographs of the Society for Research in Child Development, 29,* (1, Serial Number 92), 43–79.

Burling, R. (1966). The metrics of children's verse: a cross-linguistic study. *American Anthropologist, 68,* 1418–1441.

Cazden, C. (1968). The acquisition of noun and verb inflections. *Child Development, 39,* 433–438.

Chukovsky, K. (1965). *From Two to Five.* Berkeley: University of California Press.

Clark, E. V. (1973). What's in a word? On the child's acquisition of semantics in his first language. In T. E. Moore (Ed.), *Cognitive Development and the Acquisition of Language.* New York: Academic Press.

Clark, E. V. (1977). Awareness of language: some evidence from what children say and do. Paper presented at the meeting on The Child's Conception of Language, Nijmegen, The Netherlands, May.

Compton, A. J. (1970). Generative studies of children's phonological disorders. *Journal of Speech and Hearing Disorders, 35,* 315–339.

Costello, J., and Onstine, J. (1976). The modification of multiple articulation errors based on distinctive feature theory. *Journal of Speech and Hearing Disorders, 41,* 199–215.

Dale, P. S. (1976). *Language Development: Structure and Function.* (Second Edn.). New York: Holt, Rinehart, and Winston.

de Villiers, P. A., and de Villiers, J. G. (1972). Early judgments of semantic and syntactic acceptability by children. *Journal of Psycholinguistic Research, 1,* 299–310.

de Villiers, P. A., and de Villiers, J. G. (1973). *Out of the Mouths of Babes.* Toronto: Canadian Broadcasting Corporation, (Film).

Ervin, S. (1964). Imitation and structural change in children's language. In E. H. Lenneberg (Ed.), *New Directions in the Study of Language.* Cambridge, Massachusetts: M.I.T. Press.

Ervin-Tripp, S. (1966). Language development. In L. W. Hoffman, and M. L. Hoffman (Eds.), *Review of Child Development Research.* Volume 2. New York: Russell Sage Foundation.

Ervin-Tripp, S. (1977). Wait for me, roller-skate. In C. Mitchell-Kernan, and S. Ervin-Tripp (Eds.), *Child Discourse*. New York: Academic Press.

Fox, B., and Routh, D. K. (1975). Analyzing spoken language into words, syllables, and phonemes: a developmental study. *Journal of Psycholinguistic Research*, **4**, 331–342.

Gardner, M. (1963). *The Annotated Alice: Alice's Adventures in Wonderland and Through the Looking Glass*. New York: Meridian.

Garvey, C. (1977). Play with language and speech. In C. Mitchell-Kernan and S. Ervin-Tripp (Eds.), *Child Discourse*. New York: Academic Press.

Glass, A. L., Holyoak, K. J., and Kossan, N. E. (1977). Children's ability to detect semantic contradictions. *Child Development*, **48**, 279–283.

Gleitman, L. R., Gleitman, H., and Shipley, E. F. (1972). The emergence of the child as grammarian. *Cognition*, **1**, 137–164.

Halle, M. (1962). Phonology in generative grammar. *Word*, **18**, 54–72.

Halle, M. (1964). On the basis of phonology. In J. A. Fodor and J. J. Katz (Eds.), *The Structure of Language: Readings in the Philosophy of Language*. Englewood Cliffs, New Jersey: Prentice-Hall.

Heffner, R-M. S. (1950). *General Phonetics*. Madison, Wisconsin: University of Wisconsin Press.

Hyman, L. M. (1975). *Phonology: Theory and Analysis*. New York: Holt, Rinehart, and Winston.

Ingram, D. (1976). *Phonological Disability in Children*. London: Edward Arnold.

Jakobson, R. (1968). *Child Language, Aphasia, and Phonological Universals*. The Hague: Mouton.

Jakobson, R., Fant, G., and Halle, M. (1963). *Preliminaries to Speech Analysis*. Cambridge, Massachusetts: M.I.T. Press.

Jakobson, R., and Halle, M. (1956). *Fundamentals of Language*. The Hague: Mouton.

James, S. L., and Miller, J. F. (1973). Children's awareness of semantic constraints in sentences. *Child Development*, **44**, 69–76.

Jesperson, O. (1964). *Language: Its Nature, Development, and Origin*. New York: Norton.

Jusczyk, P. W. (1977). Rhymes and reasons: some aspects of the child's appreciation of poetic form. *Developmental Psychology*, **13**, 599–607.

Katz, J. J., and Fodor, J. A. (1963). The structure of a semantic theory. *Language*, **39**, 170–210.

Keller, C. (1973). *Ballpoint Bananas and Other Jokes for Kids*. Englewood Cliffs, New Jersey: Prentice-Hall.

Maccoby, E. E., and Bee, H. L. (1965). Some speculations concerning the lag between perceiving and performing. *Child Development*, **36**, 367–377.

Markman, E. M. (1976). Children's difficulty with word-referent differentiation. *Child Development*, **47**, 742–749.

McReynolds, L. V., and Bennett, S. (1972). Distinctive feature generalization in articulation training. *Journal of Speech and Hearing Disorders*, **37**, 462–470.

McReynolds, L. V., and Huston, K. (1971). A distinctive feature analysis of children's misarticulations. *Journal of Speech and Hearing Disorders*, **36**, 155–166.

Menyuk, P. (1968). Children's learning and reproduction of grammatical and nongrammatical phonological sequences. *Child Development*, **39**, 849–859.

Messer, S. (1967). Implicit phonology in children. *Journal of Verbal Learning and Verbal Behavior*, **6**, 609–613.

Morehead, D. M. (1971). Processing of phonological sequences by young children and adults. *Child Development*, **42**, 279–289.

Nelson, K. (1973). Structure and strategy in learning to talk. *Monographs of the Society for Research in Child Development*, **38**, (1–2, Serial Number 149).

Nelson, K. (1974). Concept, word, and sentence: interrelations in acquisition and development. *Psychological Review*, **81**, 267–285.

Norman, D. A., and Rumelhart, D. E. (1975). *Explorations in Cognition*. San Francisco: Freeman.

Opie, I., and Opie, P. (1959). *The Lore and Language of Schoolchildren*. Oxford: Clarendon Press.

Osherson, D., and Markman, E. (1975). Language and the ability to evaluate contradictions and tautologies. *Cognition*, **3**, 213–226.

Papandropoulou, I., and Sinclair, H. (1974). What is a word? Experimental study of children's ideas on grammar. *Human Development*, **17**, 241–258.

Pollack, E., and Rees, N. (1972). Disorders of articulation: Some clinical applications of distinctive feature theory. *Journal of Speech and Hearing Disorders*, **37**, 451–461.

Poole, I. (1934). Genetic development of articulation of consonant sounds in speech. *Elementary English Review*, **11**, 159–161.

Read, C. (1977). Children's awareness of linguistic structure, with special emphasis on the sound systems of language. Paper presented at the meeting on The Child's Conception of Language, Nijmegen, The Netherlands, May.

Rips, L. J., Shoben, E. J., and Smith, E. E. (1973). Semantic distance and the verification of semantic relations. *Journal of Verbal Learning and Verbal Behavior*, **12**, 1–20.

Rosch, E. H. (1973). On the internal structure of perceptual and semantic categories. In T. E. Moore (Ed.), *Cognitive Development and the Acquisition of Language*. New York: Academic Press.

Sanches, M., and Kirshenblatt-Gimblett, B. (1976). Children's traditional speech play and child language. In B. Kirshenblatt-Gimblett (Ed.), *Speech Play: Research and Resources for Studying Linguistic Creativity*. Philadelphia: University of Pennsylvania Press.

Sander, E. K. (1972). When are speech sounds learned? *Journal of Speech and Hearing Disorders*, **37**, 55–63.

Schlesinger, I. M. (1974). Relational concepts underlying language. In R. L. Schiefelbusch and L. L. Lloyd (Eds.), *Language Perspectives—Acquisition, Retardation and Intervention*. Baltimore: University Park Press.

Sherzer, J. (1976). Play languages: implications for (socio) linguistics. In B. Kirshenblatt-Gimblett (Ed.), *Speech Play: Research and Resources for Studying Linguistic Creativity*. Philadelphia: University of Pennsylvania Press.

Shultz, T. R. (1972). The role of incongruity and resolution in children's appreciation of cartoon humor. *Journal of Experimental Child Psychology*, **13**, 456–477.

Shultz, T. R. (1974). Development of the appreciation of riddles. *Child Development*, **45**, 100–105.

Shultz, T. R. (1976). A cognitive-developmental analysis of humour. In A. J. Chapman, and H. C. Foot (Eds.), *Humour and Laughter: Theory, Research, and Applications*. Chichester: Wiley.

Shultz, T. R. (1977). A cross-cultural study of the structure of humour. In A. J. Chapman, and H. C. Foot (Eds.), *It's a Funny Thing, Humour*. Oxford: Pergamon Press.

Shultz, T. R., and Horibe, F. (1974). Development of the appreciation of verbal jokes. *Developmental Psychology*, **10**, 13–20.

Shultz, T. R., and Pilon, R. (1973). Development of the ability to detect linguistic ambiguity. *Child Development*, **44**, 728–733.

Slobin, D. I. (1970). Universals of grammatical development in children. In G. B. Flores d'Arcais, and W. J. M. Levelt (Eds.), *Advances in Psycholinguistics.* New York: American Elsevier.

Slobin, D. I. (1977). A case study of early language awareness. Paper presented at the meeting on The Child's Conception of Language, Nijmegen, The Netherlands, May.

Smith, N. V. (1973). *The Acquisition of Phonology: A Case Study.* Cambridge: Cambridge University Press.

Templin, M. C. (1957). *Certain Language Skills in Children.* Minneapolis: The University of Minnesota Press.

Van Riper, C., and Irwin, J. V. (1958). *Voice and Articulation.* Englewood Cliffs, New Jersey: Prentice-Hall.

Weinreich, U. (1971). Explorations in semantic theory. In D. D. Steinberg and L. A. Jakabovits (Eds.), *Semantics: An Interdisciplinary Reader in Philosophy, Linguistics, and Psychology.* Cambridge: Cambridge University Press.

Weir, R. (1962). *Language in the Crib.* The Hague: Mouton.

Wellman, B. L., Case, I. M., Mengert, I. G., and Bradbury, D. E. (1931). Speech sounds of young children. *University of Iowa Studies in Child Welfare,* **5**, (Serial Number 2).

Whorf, B. (1956). *Language, Thought and Reality.* New York: Wiley.

Winitz, H. (1969). *Articulatory Acquisition and Behavior.* New York: Appleton-Century-Crofts.

CHAPTER 4

Children's Literary Development: The Realms of Metaphors and Stories

HOWARD E. GARDNER

with the collaboration of

Robin Bechhofer,
Jane Hanenberg,
S. William Ives, Laurence
Meringoff, Shelley Rubin,
Jen Silverman, Ellen
Winner, and Dennie Wolf

INTRODUCTION: THE LINKS BETWEEN JOKES AND LITERARY ART

Jokes, along with other invitations to humour, may be considered within a number of psychological traditions. The psychoanalytically trained observer discerns themes of aggression and sexuality; the student of cognition looks for incongruities and for transformations of logical relations; social psychologists stress the solidarity and scapegoating functions of wit. In calling attention to such themes, jokes have naturally illustrated the chief concerns of psychologists during the past half-century: thus it is not surprising that jokes have seldom been considered in the light of concerns minimized by psychologists, such as the nature of artistic activity.

Flaunting tradition, though hopefully not good sense, we will in this chapter consider jokes as an instance of verbal or literary art. By reviewing what is known about children's literary development—and by focusing particularly on two instances of literary competence—we hope to provide a fresh perspective on jokes and other forms of humour. In what follows we consider in some detail the ways in which children achieve competence in the realms of metaphor and storytelling. As such, we touch but indirectly on the domain of humour. Yet, because metaphors and stories provide two endpoints which, in both length and linguistic form, bracket the joke, such a discussion may in fact help to fix the nature of verbal humour and suggest some of the mechanisms by which it operates. To be sure, the research described here has not directly addressed the relationship between literary development and verbal humour. Yet the connections which emerge between the domains, and the suggestiveness of this literary perspective, are sufficiently compelling to evoke, in the concluding pages of this chapter, some speculations on the relations between metaphors, stories, and jokes.

The concerns confronted by students of literary development may be conveyed by a few simple examples. Consider the statement 'Johnny is a rat'. Such an equation of Johnny and a rat can be taken in any number of ways: as literally true statement (if Johnny happens to be the name of a rat); a taunt, an anomalous statement, an ironic comment. If, however, the speaker intends to make a substantive point about a fellow named Johnny, then he is likely to be speaking metaphorically. He begins by assuming the existence of two categories usually considered separate (human beings and animals); then, overriding the usual gulf between these categories, he suggests an equation—for certain purposes—between one member of *homo sapiens* and the contrasting species of *rattus*. The appropriateness of this metaphor depends upon the aptness of the comparison: if Johnny is sneaky, if he fails to honour his commitments, if he revels in dirt, has a pointed nose, or scampers about quickly, then the comparison has some justification and the 'metaphor' works. If, on the other hand, the comparison seems strained, if it clashes with either Johnny's general personality, appearance, or the particular situation in which he finds himself, then the statement is an inappropriate metaphor or perhaps simply an anomalous characterization.

The equation of Johnny and a rat exemplifies a *paradigmatic* use of language in which instances of the same category can serve the same function or occur in the same 'slot' (Jakobson and Halle, 1956). A contrasting use of language, called *metonymy, combination, or the expression of syntagmatic relations*, involves the juxtaposition (rather than equation) of terms drawn from different linguistic categories. As we continue with our hapless Johnny, consider the following brief vignette:

Returning from play in the woods, Johnny wanted to rest in the barn. However, there was a rat there whom he greatly feared. Johnny decided to make sure that he would not be bothered by the rat. So he accumulated a large amount of garbage and put it behind the gate. Sure enough, the rat spied the garbage, ran behind the gate, and Johnny shut it securely. Now he could safely go to the barn.

In this instance, we are again reading about Johnny and a rat but this time, in lieu of an equation of the two elements, we are instead confronted with their juxtaposition in the form of a problem: how to thwart the rat. Johnny succeeds in doing so, thereby achieving his goal—and, at the same time, providing us with a story: a series of events, featuring two characters, in which the protagonist poses and eventually solves a dilemma. The concatenation of 'Johnny' and 'rat' in the same work here illustrates a *syntagmatic* relation.

We have then two poles of language and two literary forms: the metaphor and the story. As phrased above, neither merits nomination as an instance of humour. Yet one can readily transform these tropes to make them funny, at least for a relevant audience—in the present case, school-age children. If Johnny has applied some whiskers to himself, and a friend yells out 'Look, Johnny is a rat', this remark is likely to evoke laughter from peers. Or if, in a baseball game, Johnny is always stealing second base, the nickname of the 'Rat' may be considered funny. Rather than the form of the metaphor having changed, it is the occasion: in certain contexts (about which we permit ourselves some speculations later on), the equation of the person and the animal successfully evokes the responses of humour.

Analogous considerations can convert the simple vignette about Johnny into a joke. Suppose that Johnny, an untidy boy, has just finished playing with mudpies in the woods. He may still want to get rid of the rat: but should the above vignette achieve its climax with the rat's running away as soon as he beholds the squalid Johnny, this 'O'Henry-esque' ending will confer 'joke' status on a once 'straight narrative'. The juxtapositions featured in stories and jokes are similar: once more it is the context in which they are related, and the means employed—in this case, an unexpected reversal of roles—which determine whether a particular story will double as a joke.

Far from being a species unto itself, then, the joke can be rather readily assimilated to some familiar instances of literary language. Nor is this envelopment restricted to metaphors and stories: other literary forms, ranging from puns and poems to similes and sagas, can each at times enter the charmed circle of humour. And so, while jokes have not until now been considered by psychologists as instances of the literary domain, their association with two principal forms of literature (reflecting the two primary poles of language) seems a reasonable point of departure for an inquiry into the nature of verbal art.

Before returning to the realm of humour, we now consider in some detail current knowledge about children's competence in the realms of metaphor and storytelling. In each case we initially sketch an 'end-state' of competence touching on the realms of both production and comprehension. Such a delineation of an 'end-state' provides a point of departure for any developmental analysis; moreover, it doubles to introduce the kinds of materials and examples which empirical studies have usually featured.

Following the delineation of an end-state we then review synoptically the major lines of research relevant to the development of competence in metaphor and storytelling. While these reviews incorporate a range of references, they are not intended as exhaustive surveys (cf. Applebee, 1978; Billow, 1977; Gardner, Winner, Bechhofer, and Wolf, 1978; Mandler and Johnson, 1977; Ortony, 1977; Thorndyke, 1977). Nor do they focus on general studies of language development, most of which have been strictly confined to literal language. Rather, the aim of the surveys is to identify the major strands of research, the problems posed and solved, the major areas of inquiry which remain to be confronted. In each case we also report on the current status of our own research. In conclusion, we offer some speculations on the relation between jokes and other forms of literary art.

THE DEVELOPMENT OF METAPHORIC COMPETENCE

End state

Within literary analysis, metaphor is defined as a figure of speech that transports a word from its customary context to another which, although novel, proves in given circumstances to be appropriate (cf. Black, 1962; Richards, 1936). Specifically, two elements—from domains of experience usually considered disparate—are linked in such a way that their similarities are illuminated: an unusual juxtaposition or comparison is formed which prompts a novel view of the elements in question. For example, in Shakespeare's play, Juliet is referred to as 'the sun'. Here, a topic, 'Juliet' is compared with, and illuminated by a second term 'sun' which is called the vehicle. The underlying links between the animate and inanimate subjects—such qualities as brilliance, warmth, the sustenance of life, the cynosure of Romeo's universe—are termed the *ground* of the metaphor.

While the apprehension of the phrase 'Juliet is the sun' poses little problem for the educated adult, a variety of competences are necessary for a full appreciation of this trope. To begin with, awareness of the fact that instances of different categories are being compared forms a necessary prerequisite for apprehension of the metaphor: if an individual thinks that Juliet actually is the sun, if no 'tension' is felt between star and girl, if there is no awareness that two usually incompatible terms have been thrown together, then the metaphor cannot be said to be operating appropriately (cf. Carmichael, 1966).

Once the basic 'stretch' or 'tension' involved in the comparison has been experienced, the task of decoding can begin in earnest. Here, the variety of levels at which a metaphor can be apprehended becomes pertinent. If an individual—for instance, a young schoolchild—sees the equation as involving only a single, physically manifest property, such as the redness of Juliet's hair and the brightness of the sun, then a purely physical comparison has been effected. To be sure, an incipient appreciation of the metaphor has occurred, but many of its implications have been missed. A qualitatively higher degree of understanding occurs when an individual is aware of expressive or psychological similarities between the topic and vehicle—for example, the radiance and warmth of both objects. A still more sophisticated degree of comprehension has emerged with an awareness of multiple similarities and differences, accompanied by the capacity to explicate the reasons for the metaphor's appropriateness; the abilities in fact represent an acceptable end-state for the comprehension of metaphor.

Defining an end-state for competence in the realm of metaphoric production proves a delicate matter, for the issue of intentionality must be confronted. Adopting a purely behaviouristic approach, one might consider as metaphorically competent anyone who had ever produced a verbal figure that had been judged as effective by the surrounding community. The risk here—one which most literary critics and psychologists are understandably loath to run—is that nearly every normal child (and perhaps even a language-learning chimpanzee at a typewriter) will, in the course of development, produce a raft of linguistic equations, at least some of which will strike observers as apt, appropriate, and perhaps even metaphoric.

To avoid conceding metaphoric competence to anyone who happens to have uttered—by accident or design—an apt equation, it proves necessary to add some qualifications. As in the case of metaphoric comprehension, one may posit the need for awareness that some traditional category boundaries have been overridden. One might add the further requirements of some intention on the part of the speaker to produce a comparison that is interesting or illuminating, and/or some ability to offer a verbal account of what has been accomplished. Side-stepping the problematic philosophical issue of intentionality, one may instead devise a task (e.g. a sentence-completion exercise) and maintain that anyone who performs at a certain level is competent in the production of metaphors. Yet even this prudent scientific step entails difficulties in interpretation.

For our purposes, we can avoid setting a specific criterion for competence in the realm of metaphoric production. Instead, we will speak of the capacity to produce, upon request, and in a reasonably consistent manner, figures of speech: these figures must be viewed by members of the community as entailing a comparison of elements from disparate domains which, in the requested context, have been appropriately juxtaposed. By adopting this approach, we allow the possibility that there may be several types and levels of metaphor. On this account, certain forms of metaphoric production, such as those based upon perceptual similarities, prove within the ken of young children. Others, for instance those which involve comparisons between physical and psychological domains, or which entail the production of a figure which 'works' on several levels, appear to be within the purview of competent adults, and, especially, of poets.

The traditional view of metaphor development and the paradox of early production

The initial and seminal study of the development of metaphoric competence was published in 1960 by Solomon Asch and Harriet Nerlove. These investigators chose a particular metaphoric form—so-called dual-function adjectives—which have both a physical and a psychological meaning (e.g. *sweet, cold*). They presented to children ranging in age from three years to twelve a series of such words and asked the children to explain the meanings. Subjects were then asked 'Are people cold? Do you know any cold people? How do you know that they are cold?' Similar probes were employed for each of the dual-function words.

Asch and Nerlove found that children first learn the physical meanings of the words and do not become sensitive to the psychological meanings until middle childhood. Moreover, children continue for some time to believe that the physical and the psychological meanings are unrelated. Only the oldest subjects could recognize the connecting grounds, indicating for example, that 'hard things and hard people are both unmanageable'. And even these subjects often required prompting before they acknowledged the dual property of the adjectives.

In view of this path-breaking study, and a number of treatments which followed later (e.g. Elkind, 1969; Lesser and Drouin, 1975), the development of metaphoric competence came to be regarded as a rather late-emerging capacity, one possibly dormant until the years just prior to adolescence. And, indeed, adequate paraphrases and explications of the rationale for metaphors are rarely secured from children before this time. Yet the withholding of metaphoric competence from young children proves difficult to justify in view of contrary findings, well documented in studies of children's early language (e.g. Billow, 1977; Carlson and Anisfeld, 1969; Chukovsky, 1968; Gardner, 1973). If one examines the verbal output of pre-schoolchildren, one finds many figures of speech which are striking, and which on the above definition qualify as metaphorically appropriate. For instance, one finds a three-year-old calling a series of interweaving lines 'scrambled eggs'; a four-year-old sees skywriting in the sky and comments 'The sky has a scar in it'; a three-and-a-half-year-old picks up a potato chip that is folded over on itself and declares it a 'cowboy hat'; and a one-and-a-half-year-old, who has just begun to talk, notices his toe sticking out of a sock and labels it 'a turtle'.

It thus appears that, contrary to the situation typically found in linguistic development, children exhibit a competence in the productive realm which they do not yet evince in the realm of comprehension of metaphor. Subsequent research in the realm of metaphor has in fact entailed an effort to resolve, or at least understand more precisely, this apparent paradox.

The development of productive capacities

In a study which sought to duplicate inside the laboratory this phenomenon of early metaphoric competence, children were encouraged to complete in an appropriate and pleasing manner unfinished similes such as: 'Things don't have to be huge in size to look that way. Look at that boy standing over there. He looks as gigantic as . . . ' (Gardner, Kircher, Winner, and Perkins, 1975). At no age was there a high incidence of acceptable figurative language; most subjects at each age produced comparisons judged to be conventional (e.g. as gigantic as 'a skyscraper', 'a tree', 'a giant'). The two exceptions to this result came at the opposite ends of the age spectrum. College students and pre-schoolchildren proved more likely than elementary schoolchildren to produce endings which were judged imaginative; indeed the pre-schoolers produced a number higher than that found among any other age group. Among the figures created spontaneously by these youngsters were 'sad as a pimple', 'quiet as a magic marker', 'stupid as a stony person', and 'weather as boiling as your head popping open'. In sharp contrast, children in the early-grade school years showed a distinct distaste for such violations of conventional usage; subjects at this 'literal stage' not only failed to produce metaphors but also rejected as improper or unacceptable those figures offered to them by experimenters.

The surprisingly metaphoric bent of the pre-schoolers was the most striking result in this study. But their behaviour had another telling dimension to it as well. Pre-schoolers were more likely than any other group to produce endings which were unusual but apparently devoid of sense (e.g. 'weather as cold as the Indian', 'a boy as gigantic as a light switch'). This finding raises the possibility that the appropriate metaphors cited above may just have been accidental; scattered bits of gold dust amidst the dross of childhood over-extensions, generalizations, and imprecise grasp of word meaning. Yet it is equally possible that the pre-schoolers may have a heightened capacity to exploit linguistic resources, without a concomitant 'blue-pencilling' ability with which to reject those figures unlikely to be appreciated by others (cf. Billow, 1977). The egocentrism of young children may prevent them from sifting out those figures which, on purely idiosyncratic grounds, make sense to them from those likely to be understood by others.

Determining which of these alternatives in fact obtains is by no means an easy task. Nor do we yet understand the relationship between the propensity of pre-schoolers to produce arresting figures of speech and the reluctance of somewhat older schoolchildren to abandon literal language. Does this 'literal stage' mark a lamentable end of childhood spontaneity and creativity, or is it a necessary step in the consolidation of word meaning, a step upon which genuinely metaphoric activity needs to be constructed?

We are currently investigating this vexing issue. Our efforts include the examination of metaphors produced by pre-schoolchildren in the course of everyday conversation, as well as metaphors elicited in the course of various forms of symbolic play. By assessing a child's lexical knowledge, observing the child's reactions to his own figures of speech, and tracing his use of a single word over time, we hope to pinpoint the kind of knowledge involved in children's early metaphor as well as the child's own motivation for producing such figures and his evaluation of their effectiveness. We are still uncertain whether children's early metaphors bear an integral relationship to the figures of speech produced by competent adults, or whether they are better viewed as qualitatively distinct entities. Yet the fact that children's early metaphors appear to follow a regular developmental course (cf. Gardner *et al.*, 1978; Gardner and Winner, 1978), the ability of these children to distinguish explicitly between 'real' and 'pretend' names, and the apparent delight exhibited by many children as they violate normal lexical markers, suggests that these figures are more than simple aberrations: these factors indicate instead a freshness of outlook and an easy access to linguistic resources which must somehow be retained throughout the literal period if the youthful producer of metaphors is eventually to become a master of figurative language.

The development of metaphoric understanding

In one sense, the investigation of children's understanding of metaphors has proved a less troublesome undertaking than the study of production. There is little suggestion of a U-shaped curve of development (Strause, 1977); investigators seem agreed that, with age, children become better able to interpret metaphors.

Despite this agreement, however, controversies abound. To mention but a few, one encounters disputes about the proper tasks with which to assess metaphoric understanding; the age at which metaphoric understanding comes about; the obstacles thwarting (or obscuring) metaphoric understanding; and the types of metaphor upon which an empirical investigation should centre.

The classic study by Asch and Nerlove, mentioned earlier, has stimulated these several controversies. Recall that these investigators questioned the existence of genuine metaphoric understanding until the period of adolescence, at which point dual-function terms could be defined and the connections between them appreciated. Critics have suggested, however, that children's understanding may already have emerged at around the age of seven or eight years, at the time when they recognize that a 'sweet person' is a nice or kind person; the later-evolving capacity to indicate the relationship between two forms of *sweet* seems better viewed as a form of metalinguistic analysis, one not central to metaphoric competence *per se*. Commentators also noted that appreciation of the meaning of the term *sweet* involves an understanding of the psychological domain, including features of character, personality, and the like: children's difficulty in addressing such relatively abstract psychological issues, rather than any deficiency in metaphoric processes *per se*, may lie at the core of that problem. Asch and Nerlove can be criticized, finally, for the contrived conditions of their study; metaphors are usually encountered in a meaningful context (e.g. in a story, or in daily conversation); presumably these figures should much more readily be understood under those circumstances than in the stark 'dictionary-entry' interview utilized by the original team of researchers.

Stimulated by issues raised in the pioneering Asch and Nerlove study, a number of investigators have probed the limits of the child's metaphoric understanding (Billow, 1975; Gardner, 1974; Kogan, 1975; Lesser and Drouin, 1975; Ortony, 1977; Winner and Gardner, 1977; Winner, Rosenstiel, and Gardner, 1976). These investigators have documented the relative ease of decoding metaphors which capture perceptual similarities (Billow, 1975; Winner and Gardner, 1977); the greater difficulty experienced by children in dealing with psychological metaphors (Winner *et al.*, 1976); the special demands posed by metalinguistic explication, as contrasted with the relative ease of tasks requiring only multiple choices or matching (Gardner *et al.*, 1978).

Indeed, using simple tasks of mapping, where the child must simply relate one domain of experience (e.g., sounds) to another domain (e.g. abstract line configurations), a number of investigators have secured evidence for a form of metaphoric understanding as early as the pre-school years (Bond and Stevens, 1969; Gardner, 1974; Gentner, 1977; Werner and Kaplan, 1963). Such findings have stimulated some commentators to argue that the obstacles to metaphoric understanding reported in earlier studies reflect the contrivances of an experimenter rather than the incapacity of their subjects. Such critics contend that the capacity to appreciate metaphoric relations is an extremely primitive human mental ability, one present in the first years of life, one upon which much of learning and development must in fact be based (cf. Arnheim, 1969; Ortony, 1975, 1977; Verbrugge, 1974; Verbrugge and McCarrell, 1977).

Beyond doubt, if the task demands are modest enough and the items readily accessible, some evidence for early metaphoric understanding can indeed be adduced. Yet, as in the investigation of metaphoric production, the question arises about the significance of this early phenomenon, and its precise relationship to the more mature forms of metaphoric understanding—of the sort on which appreciation of poetry or comprehension of scientific models might in fact be based. The appreciation of perceptual similarities, between the letter S and a snake, for example, may not require that overriding of tension, that suspension of normal categories of classification, which confers potency upon poetic metaphor. Nor is there evidence, in these early forms of metaphoric comprehension, that the subject would on his own have appreciated the connections between the realms: all that has been shown is that, given a forced choice, some capacity for appropriate mapping can be demonstrated.

Probing of metaphoric understanding at a somewhat more sophisticated level is thus desirable. Toward this end, Winner *et al.* (1976) asked schoolchildren to paraphrase metaphors which involved an intersection between the psychological and the physical domain. A typical item for paraphrase was this: 'After many years of working at the jail, the prison guard had become a hard rock that could not be moved'. To comprehend this metaphor subjects had to recognize that the relationship between two physical entities—the guard and the rock—could not be merely perceptual or concrete; rather a psychological property of the guard shared certain features (or had a common ground) with the physical properties of a rock.

Subjects in fact issued an instructive variety of paraphrases. Six-year-olds often failed to recognize that the metaphors were intended non-literally. Accepting the sentences at face value, they contrived a pretend-world in which natural laws did not apply: for example, 'The king had a magic rock and he turned the guard into another rock'. A second strategy favoured by young children was to alter the relation between the elements of the metaphor: the stated relationship of identity (guard equals rock) was transformed to one of contiguity (the guard is associated with the rock). For example, subjects indicated that the guard worked in a prison with rocky walls.

Eight-year-old subjects often realized that a direct comparison between the terms was called for but were unable to view the links as entailing the psychological realm. Instead subjects interpreted both terms of the metaphor as belonging to the physical domain: for example, 'The guard had hard, tough muscles'. Only at the age of ten or so could children regularly appreciate the ways in which the single dual-function term *hard* could capture both psychological and physical connotations. At this age, they became able to paraphrase the figure, concluding, for example, that 'the guard was mean and did not care about the prisoners'.

Here, then, in a task where a genuine gap between domains had to be bridged, one encounters again the phenomenon first noted by Asch and Nerlove: the relatively late emergence of the ability to comprehend metaphor. Moreover, efforts to document the comprehension of such psychological-physical metaphors at a significantly earlier age have not so far been successful. There arises a question of pivotal developmental consequence: which factors might in fact preclude appreciation of such metaphors until the middle years of childhood?

We have recently initiated a set of studies designed to uncover the obstacles to understanding of such psychological-physical metaphors, and, in the process, to illuminate the general factors which mediate metaphoric competence. Though this programme of research is not yet near completion, we are already beginning to discern the broad outlines of those abilities prerequisite to metaphoric understanding. We have, on the one hand, isolated certain factors which do not appear to be crucial: precise and explicit knowledge of the 'core meaning' of a word like *hard* (that meaning which cuts across both the psychological and physical projections of the term) appears unnecessary for adequate metaphoric understanding. By the same token, an ability to pick out which features of a word apply to a term in one context, and which apply in another, also seems relatively independent of metaphoric understanding (Winner and Gardner, 1977). Such findings suggest that precise lexical knowledge of the meanings of words is not a necessary prerequisite to metaphoric understanding (cf. Verbrugge, 1974).

Other factors can, however, materially aid in the decoding of metaphors. A linguistic context, in which is laid the groundwork for a 'target metaphor', or a pictorial context, in which the topic of the metaphor is clearly designated, can elicit signs of metaphoric understanding at a somewhat earlier age. The form in which the metaphor is presented is also a factor: the same topic-vehicle relation, garbed in riddle or analogy form, seems more easily 'solved'. Furthermore, information has been gained about some of the difficulties attending the decoding of metaphors drawn from the psychological domain. Children apparently appreciate that a psychological meaning is intended before they become cognizant of *which* psychological meaning is intended. Thus, returning to our prison-guard example, children in the primary grades may realize that a negative aspect of the guard's personality is being described, while remaining unclear for a time about whether the guard's stupidity, nastiness, stubbornness, or anger makes him a 'hard rock'.

At the very least, the lines of investigation described above have cracked the issue of metaphoric understanding into certain of its component parts. It is now clear that one's conclusion about the trajectory of metaphoric understanding will reflect one's definition of metaphor, choice of task, and criteria for understanding. Equally, the factors prerequisite to metaphoric understanding are undergoing increasing scrutiny even as the roles of contributory linguistic, classificatory, and contextual cues are being sorted out (Billow, 1975; Cometa and Eson, 1977).

As the broad lines of metaphoric comprehension and production begin to be discerned, certain affinities between these two competences can be observed. In both cases, awareness of the usual domain of a word—the boundaries of the categories to which it belongs—appear to be crucial. In the pre-school years, aspects of metaphoric competence can already be observed; but they require, in the case of metaphoric production, an assumption that the child appreciate the boundaries that are being overridden: and they require, in the case of metaphoric comprehension, the deployment of domains familiar to children, the use of simple mapping tasks, and, again, some faith that such mapping in fact entails the overriding of tension.

A further parallel obtains during the years of early schooling, where one finds a clear decline in children's proclivity towards metaphor. Children tend to produce fewer metaphors, to reject obvious violations of category boundaries, and to offer paraphrases which either take the metaphor literally or convert it into a metonymic statement. Only after the customary usages of words have been firmly consolidated does it once again become permissible to violate category boundaries; and only then can children fashion adequate paraphrases of those figures of speech created by others.

A recognition of these general parallels need not imply that the same processes are at work. For instance, as regards metaphoric understanding, the child may be seeking any cue which will aid him in making sense of a metaphor; in the absence of a useful cue, he will simply confabulate a response. Conversely, in the instance of early metaphoric production, the young child may be seeking to convey what is on his mind, with metaphors simply an incidental symptom of an impoverished lexicon. Finally, ultimate success in metaphor understanding may reflect the child's growing appreciation of *which* category boundaries can be transcended, while the ultimate resurgence in metaphoric language may reflect motivational factors, patterns of social reward, or vocational or avocational inclinations.

Despite these candidate differences, one intriguing link unquestionably obtains between metaphoric comprehension and production, that link forged in the pre-school years. There seems little question that, at the age of three years or so, children gain the ability to map on to one another a variety of domains. Possibly because they have now explored with some initial thoroughness the structure of specific domains, they become able—and even eager—to map these domains with reference to one another. No one knows what brings about consensus in these mappings—the respective roles of neural circuitry, parental modelling, and aesthetic elegance, remain to be sorted out. But this tendency to align domains and to discover their appropriate links seems central to the often intriguing figures of speech produced by young children as well as to the incipient signs of comprehension in simple mapping tasks. To be sure, subtler forms of expressiveness, as well as sensitivity to the psychological realm, remain for later mastery; but the fundamental delight and gaiety in effecting connections has clearly emerged.

THE DEVELOPMENT OF COMPETENCE WITH STORIES

Few cultural elements have achieved such centrality in the lives of children the world over as have stories. Many cultural practices are passed on by means of narratives. Much of children's entertainment comes from stories. Education in subject matters, ranging from history and geography to the sciences and even mathematics, relies frequently on storytelling methods. Individuals (including children) relate much of what has happened to them through the informal means of storytelling.

Given the undisputed significance of storytelling and understanding in the lives of young children, it is surprising that so little systematic psychological research has been undertaken on the nature of the story, the mechanisms by which it is constructed and apprehended, and its psychological effects upon individuals. It may be that the full importance of stories was not realized—and, given the history of American psychology during the past century, perhaps could not be realized—until quite recently. If, as some now think (e.g. Bower, 1976), stories can provide a 'royal road' to the mind, they were, like dreams before Freud's time, relegated to the trivial, little appreciated except as curiosities or leisure-time pursuits.

In any case, if this gap in our knowledge is to be filled, some picture of the abilities involved in story competence needs to be sketched. As in the case of metaphor, a variety of levels of story competence can be defined. Thus even the average three-year-old in our culture can, when asked for a story, produce a sequence of sentences beginning with 'once upon a time', include a few pieced-together events, and conclude with 'the end'. He may also be able to distinguish a story from a non-story (Leondar, 1977). Giving weight to these factors, one might want to award incipient storytelling competence to such youthful narrators. On the other hand, the ability to provide acceptable instances of a genre—for example, a fairy tale or a shaggy dog story—is a much later occurrence, one which, to the extent it occurs at all, waits upon adolescence. And the supreme heights of storytelling—whether found among Russian novelists or masters of oral verse in the Serbian hills—are achieved by only the most gifted producers of language.

Even as a variety of levels of storytelling competence can be identified, stories can be comprehended at varying degrees of sophistication. Not long after they are capable of understanding simple sentences, children will already be listening assiduously to stories. And, particularly with the aid of an accompanying set of pictures, the tone of voice of a narrator, and frequent repetitions, the young child seems capable of securing at least some meaning from a rendition of *Goldilocks* or the story of *Santa Claus*. Yet, once the complexity of the story itself increases, and once comprehension expands beyond a simple understanding of key events to include an appreciation of underlying struggles, tensions, character moti-vation, and the like, much greater cognitive sophistication seems necessary before adequate understanding can occur.

Outlining the full range of capacities needed to appreciate stories is a massive job, one which cannot be undertaken in a review, and one which, indeed, might require attention to all of the individual's intellectual, emotional, and moti-vational capacities. In fact, much of the initial round of research in storytelling has focused simply on an identification of the capacities which are indeed the most central in story understanding. Nonetheless, a few general principles can be stated, ones which should aid in motivating our review of studies of competence in the literary realm.

One fundamental prerequisite for engagement with stories involves some recognition of what in fact qualified as a story. (Note the parallel to awareness of what is a metaphor.) Even literary critics disagree on the defining attributes of a story, but, at the least, one can include the positing of a character and a setting, the introduction of some situation or problem which confronts the character, and her efforts to overcome or circumvent the problem. Most stories transcend this skeleton—in the complexity of setting, the number of characters and incidents, the statements of goals, intentions, and the like; accordingly the perceiver's abilities to categorize and store a body of information are called into play. But the crux of a story does seem to inhere in the capacity of a character to recognize and to negotiate her way around some kind of an obstacle. In fact, young children are in accord with critics: literary instances which lack this nexus of character-problem-solution fail to qualify as stories.

Once one exceeds this skeleton definition, two other vital ingredients come into play. On the one hand, a range of real-world knowledge—often now called knowledge of schemas or frames—must be invoked in understanding a story. Thus a story about gypsies is unlikely to be understood unless the subject knows something about the way of life, and the customary behaviours and motivations of this population. Complementing such 'real world knowledge' is some acquaintance with literary genres in which stories are generally garbed. One cannot fully appreciate a fairy-tale unless one has gained familiarity with the stock characters, kinds of events, tensions between characters, range of possible, magical, and impossible events which typify the collection of tales by the brothers Grimm. We are able to maintain our literary bearings amidst the wide range of texts—mysteries, science fiction works, romances, myths, and jokes—because we have developed a well-articulated set of schemes which tell us what stories in this area are generally like. Not that the instances of this genre must always follow the text to the letter: indeed, certain effects—including those of parody and satire—gain their power precisely by their deviation from the ideal. But again, unless the customary features and modes of these genres have been internalized, neither paradigmatic instances, nor variations upon these genres, can be assimilated.

This sketch of the essentials of stories should help fix the task of the producer and the comprehender. The producer must either conform to the general principles of a story and operate within a genre, create and 'sell' her own new genre, or risk banishment from the hall of the storyteller. And the consumer must have general expectations of what a story is like, knowledge of how certain genres work, and sufficient acquaintance with the real world so that the details, as well as the overall organization of the narrative, can be appropriately apprehended.

Lines of investigation

Interest among 'story' researchers has traditionally been of three sorts. To begin with, some investigators have offered descriptive accounts of children's storytelling capacities (Ames, 1966; Pitcher and Prelinger, 1963); the interest here has been in factual characterizations of children's stories, specifying their average length, favourite themes, or mean number of characters. A second line of research has examined children's stories (and their preferences among stories) as clues to children's personality and motivation (cf. Gould, 1972; Greenacre,

1959). While this line of research has produced useful information about individual youngsters, it has rarely illuminated the structure of stories *per se*. A final, well-entrenched line of study has utilized stories to illuminate some aspects of children's mental or problem-solving capacities (Fitzhenry-Coor, 1977; Kohlberg, 1969; Piaget, 1963); from such studies has come valuable information about children's moral, social, or cognitive growth but only incidental insights into their literary competence.

Only in the past decade or so have researchers looked more directly at the development of storytelling capacities (Abrams and Sutton-Smith, 1977; Botvin and Sutton-Smith, 1977; Gardner, 1973; John, Horner, and Berney, 1970; Leondar, 1977; Maranda and Maranda, 1970). Collecting large samples of children's stories, usually obtained under naturalistic conditions, such investigators have proposed 'stages of literary development', which incorporate aspects of standard literary analysis, and take into account the child's level of conceptual development. Looking at stories from different cultural settings, for example, Maranda and Maranda (1970) have identified four discrete developmental stages: (a) a primitive level, at which children make no effort to mediate the conflict or threat posed in a story; (b) a second state in which the attempt to mediate the conflict proves unsuccessful; (c) a third stage, during which the protagonist is now able to negotiate the threat; and (d) a fourth, highest level, where the initial situation can be so transformed that the threat is permanently nullified, and the protagonist accordingly gains in status.

Such accounts have considerably advanced our understanding of story competence, in part by merging it into the mainstream of developmental analysis. Yet the wide variety of descriptions emanating from these typically atheoretical accounts bespeaks a fundamental problem: given a finite number of stories, one can conjure up a host of possible stage-sequences—possibly as many as there are willing analysts. Clearly a more precise way to characterize children's stories is desirable.

Drawing on insights from linguistics, artificial intelligence, and experimental psychology, a number of researchers have in fact offered more precise descriptions: they have proposed various grammars, or formal schemata, which characterize the 'well-developed' or 'grammatical' story; then they have examined various stories to indicate the ways in which they exemplify—or deviate from—such ideal-type descriptions (cf. Bower, 1976; Charniak, 1975; Mandler and Johnson, 1977; Rumelhart, 1975; Rumelhart and Ortony, 1976; Stein, 1976, 1978; Stein and Glenn, 1977a,b; Thorndyke, 1977). Though even a brief sketch of the various grammars exceeds the scope of this chapter, a few characteristics of this approach should be indicated (cf. Gardner, 1978). To begin with, analysts have taken from transformational linguists the notion of a hierarchy of component elements, with logical relations obtaining among them, from which the story is generated. Thus, in its broadest outline, a story consists of a setting and an episode, but episodes can be embedded within one another and broken down into sub-categories of increasing specificity. Proceeding further from the linguistics model, analysts have tended to list a set of features of a story—for instance, initiating event, internal response, plan, attempt, consequence, goal, concluding event—and then observed which of these features emerges as most important for the individual bent on generating, comprehending, or recalling a story. From work in artificial intelligence, the investigators have adopted the practice of laying out in precise detail each of the steps involved in generating or understanding a story; and they have also adopted the recent preoccupation with interpretative schemata or frames—those bodies of knowledge (or data bases) about real world experience upon which an individual normally draws in understanding a story about, say, a doctor ministering to a patient, or a person entering a restaurant (cf. Minsky, 1975; Rumelhart, 1975; Schank, 1975). Indeed, one goal of this group has been to create programmes fully stocked with information about frames and with the general procedures governing story generation that they can 'understand' or at least answer a series of questions about a story (Charniak, 1975). Finally, drawing upon the tradition of experimental psychology, researchers have tended to rely on tasks of paraphrase, recall, or completion in order to gain a reliable measure of their subject's apprehension of stories.

The 'grammarian' approach has been applied to the study of children's story competence (Mandler and Johnson, 1977; Stein, 1976, 1978; Stein and Glenn, 1977a,b,c; Trabasso, Nicholas, Omanson, and Johnson, 1977). Having established that children have a general story schema by first grade (six years of age), such investigators have then tested the robustness of the schema through various manipulations, for example, deleting certain episodes or rearranging elements of the story. With impressive regularity, these researchers have reported the same effects of these manipulations across various stories and various populations.

The implications of this line of research for students of literary development (as well as researchers concerned with humour) are considerable. For the first time, a powerful method for describing stories has been demonstrated in psychological research. Certain findings, such as the shift from an exclusive appreciation of the physical events in a story, to an alertness to psychological features such as motivation and planning, have been well documented. Moreover, in reading these accounts, one gets the distinct—and bracing—feeling, that the story works in a manner reminiscent of a biological entity. Stories have robust forms, which can be distended to a certain extent without disruption. But once this critical point of tolerance has been exceeded, the overall coherence of the structure breaks down. Furthermore, like an equilibrating organism, the system is dynamic. A stress on one portion—for example, a deletion or transformation—induces an effect on others. Nor are these effects inviolate with age; rather one finds an intriguing and instructive interaction between the age (or stage) of the subject and the way in which s/he responds to such transformation.

A critique and some new directions for study

Beyond doubt, this 'grammatical approach' is well served by its rigorous methods. One encounters little of the allusiveness and sloppiness rampant in certain descriptive accounts. Yet if our understanding of literary development has advanced a quantum leap, this precision and control is captured at a price, and one that may be relatively expensive in the realm of literary development (Garnder, 1978).

To begin with, the grammars are rather Procrustean. Stories must fit into them and those which do not fit are not subjected to further analysis. Similarly, the stories are denuded of aesthetic components: there is little style, figurative language, dialogue—the very aroma of literature has largely evaporated. And, to complicate matters further affectively-charged events do not populate these stories; for whatever reasons, the grammarians prefer works which are remarkably (and even disquietingly) calm. Such omissions are not only disappointing from an aesthetic point of view: they may also call into question empirical results. For instance, some of our own studies report quite different results when such figurative aspects as refrains (Ives, 1977), and such affective components as emotional descriptions (Silverman, 1977), are once again incorporated into a story framework.

Three other omissions are worth pondering. First of all, individual differences in story aptitude and preferences have been almost entirely neglected. Second of all, the medium in which the story is presented—oral, pictorial, written—has not been systematically investigated. Finally, and perhaps most crucially, the grammarians have by-passed entirely the issue of literary value, although, in the last analysis, the evocativeness and merit of a story may determine its significance for children. Paradoxically, and especially for a seasoned listener, just those stories which violates the grammar may exert the deepest and most lasting appeal.

In sum, then, the 'grammar' approach represents a significant advance; but the questions raised above need to be tackled before it can proceed beyond an analysis of verbal comprehension and recall, to an adequate treatment of the more complex issue of literary development. In the remainder of this review, we consider briefly a number of our own recent attempts to approach stories in a way that perhaps remains more faithful to their pivotal literary status.

Children's grasp of the fairy-tale genre. One way to remain faithful to the literary origins of the story is to consider a genre whose status within the world of storytelling is unimpeachable. The fairy-tale genre—with its roots in myth—has been with us for centuries and has demonstrated its hold—both cognitive and affective—on numerous generations. In addition, there exists a definite fairy-tale *frame*—a series of stock characters, emotions, and events—which is eventually assimilated by normal individuals. These factors constitute an open invitation to developmental psychologists to examine the mastery of a well-entrenched form.

Recalling our analysis of the characteristics of a story, we may note that a fairy-tale features a network of characters who find themselves facing a set of problems. Often two focal characters are opposed: a powerful evil character *vis-à-vis* an initially powerless good character, whose status will be heightened at the end of the tale, frequently with the aid of magical intervention. And there will be a series of associated motivating affects and incentives; ones intrinsic to the characters, which combine to yield a series of increasingly dramatic episodes and an inevitably climactic *dénouement*.

How can one glimpse children's emerging apprehension of this intricate form? In a preliminary exploration of a number of facets of this issue, Shelley Rubin, Jane Hanenberg, and I devised a new fairy-tale. We asked children to contrive an ending appropriate for the story, and then tested recall for the story three days later (cf. Rubin and Gardner, 1977). To gain information on the extent to which the fairy-tale genre had become entrenched in the course of the children's earlier development, the story was presented to subjects under one of two conditions. Either the subjects heard a 'motivation included' version of the story, which featured ample motivation for each of the characters; or they heard a 'motivation deleted' version, one identical in all essentials but completely deprived of any character traits or motivational states. For instance, in the 'included' condition, the bad queen's hostile attitude toward her good stepdaughter was spelled out completely and the motivation underlying each of her capricious actions against the stepdaughter was delineated. In the 'deleted' version, the queen and princess were simply identified as such and the queen proceeded to pose to her hapless stepdaughter (without rhyme or reason) a series of increasingly difficult and ultimately impossible tasks.

We anticipated mastery of the fairy-tale during the first few years of school. Accordingly, we hypothesized that the youngest subjects—first graders (six-year-olds)—would be unable to use the motivational information because they had only acquired the rudiments of the fairy-tale genre, while the oldest subjects—sixth graders (twelve-year-olds)—could on their own supply this motivation which they would simply 'transfer' from tales that they had already heard. Intermediate age subjects—third graders (nine-year-olds)—would benefit most from this 'motivation included' condition for, while already familiar with the outlines of the fairy-tale, they had not sufficiently mastered motivation to supply it on their own.

Roughly speaking, these expectations were confirmed. The youngest subjects were actually hindered by motivation. The 'motivation-included' version featured so many details that young subjects found it difficult to process, complete, and remember them. This group also exhibited relatively little mastery of the fairy-tale genre: at most they knew something about the kinds of titles appropriate for fairy-tales, exhibited an incipient sense of which characters were good and bad, and showed some familiarity with magical events. Though no one would deny the powerful hold that fairy-tales exert over this young population, the contention that they have already mastered this genre is not supported by our findings (cf. Bettelheim, 1976; Gardner, 1977).

In sharp contrast, sixth graders gave numerous indications that they had mastered the genre of fairy-tales. They exhibited firm knowledge and expectations about characters, plot lines, episodes, and outcomes: indeed, so confident were some sixth graders that they even transcended the genre, parodying it and consciously mixing-in features from other genres. In further contrast to the first graders, these subjects were also helped by motivation; their endings were better, their recall sharper, their control of the stories' resources more complete. Confirming their hypothesized ability to supplement an impoverished version in the 'motivation-deleted' condition, youngsters actually included *more* motivation in their retellings *after a three-day interval*—they, and they alone, had so well assimilated the fairy-tale genre that on their own they proved capable of reintroducing needed (but missing) motivation into their delayed retellings.

Pros and cons of a story rich in motivation came across dramatically in the performance of the third graders. Subjects in the 'motivation-included' condition produced stories which were in certain respects more effective: their endings entailed greater integration of strands of the narrative, more genuine interaction among the characters, and better solution to one specific problem posed in the story: how the princess was to fulfil a difficult task posed by her evil stepmother.

In other respects, however, the inclusion of motivation actually hindered the subjects. They proved less able to deal with the major general problem posed by the story—what to do in the end with the queen; they were less likely to afford the king an active role in solving this looming problem; they were unable to include retributive justice in their endings (where the queen gets her come-uppance). We hypothesized that, in its fully motivated garb, the story built up the power of the queen to such an extent and at such length that these youngsters, not yet fully in control of the story's resources, were simply overwhelmed. Rather than honouring fairy-tale practices, where the powerful but mean queen is suitably disposed of, these youngsters succumbed to the queen's power, failed to allow the king any initiative, and produced a story devoid of retributive justice. Conversely, those third graders who heard the motivation-deleted condition were not so hindered: instead, already privy to some principles of fairy-tales and not overpowered in the present instance by the malignantly-motivated monarch, they proved better able to handle the queen and to produce a story which satisfied certain basic demands of the genre.

First steps in storytelling. So described, the performances of schoolchildren seem relatively primitive; we are struck by the several steps through which they must still pass before they gain control of the genre of fairy-tales. Yet, as often noted in the course of this review, the competence of an individual in the literary realm depends critically upon one's perspective. If, from the point of view of the adult, the schoolchild seems deficient in his story-apprehending capacities, he has already, from the perspective of the student of early development, made remarkable strides.

The significance of the schoolchild's accomplishment can best be appreciated if one looks back much farther, to the child's first efforts at storytelling during the second through to the fifth years of life (cf. Rubin and Gardner, 1977; Shotwell, Wolf, and Gardner, 1977; Wolf and Gardner, 1978). One line of information has come from observation of the child at play. Selected story-like behaviours are observed in the realm of symbolic play where, during the second and third years of life, the child re-enacts familiar patterns of behaviour from everyday life. When the child begins to accompany this play with language, aspects of narration become evident: for instance, the child will describe a goal that a character is trying to achieve, or depict interaction between characters. Yet, until the child is three or four years of age, voices of narrator and character are typically confused, the sequence of events is often illogical, and, most frequently, no problem is posed for subsequent solution. Only by the age of four or so, does the child produce stories exclusively in the linguistic mode; and only at this time does s/he display the capacity to pose a problem within the constraints of the story genre.

Through posing stories—with problems in them—and through observing children's attempted 'solutions', we have secured particularly revealing evidence regarding the narrative competence of pre-schoolers. A number of tentative conclusions have emerged. To begin with, the three-year-old will sometimes miss the problem altogether. More frequently, s/he will simply propose a physical solution to the problem—for example, lifting up and 'rescuing' a doll in trouble. Sometimes s/he will simply declare that the problem has been solved, or deny that the problem exists at all. At best, the child will suggest but a single ending to the story—the possibility of multiple solutions seems foreign. Still, in nearly all of these instances, there is at least an implicit recognition that a problem has in fact been posed.

By the age of three-and-a-half, or so, the child first becomes able to solve the problem within the story frame. As an example, consider the tale about a large bear who always teases a small mouse. One day, in search of some honey, the bear eats too much and gets caught in a tree. Afraid that the bees will return, the bear calls to the mouse for help. Hearing this incomplete saga, Kim, near her fourth birthday, picks up the mouse, says for it in a high voice 'I'll get you out' and has the mouse yank the bear out of the hold. The problem has been solved within the narrative. But note that the solution proposed by the child is completely physical. Ignoring the irony of the big bear who has always made fun of a little mouse, the child falls back on a mechanical solution even when (to an adult) the plot clearly demands something more.

In other exercises, other limitations have emerged. For example, the child rarely draws in his or her solution upon traits of the characters; by the same token, s/he rarely if ever takes steps to see that the problem will not recur. And in case an appropriate solution does not readily suggest itself, s/he often resorts to an affectively comforting but essentially *ad hoc* ending: the character returns home, has supper, and goes to bed. Indeed, so often is this ending favoured that it sometimes appears the child has but a single story frame.

Nonetheless, as the child approaches the age of four, the first glimmerings of specific frames can be discerned. With respect to the child's own spontaneous stories, the major frame to emerge initially might be termed a 'monster frame'. Featured here is a dominant and frightening personage, an aggressive human or animal that threatens other characters, and as often as not, destroys or defeats the others (cf. Sutton-Smith, 1975). Populating such stories are the words 'good' or 'bad', used to assess and characterize all protagonists: moreover, all personages tend to be defined in relationship to the evil central character. The point of the story seems to be to get rid of the fearful character, but this is typically done at the price of getting rid of all characters. The reforming of the miscreant or the possibility of his permanent banishment seems beyond the ken of this age group.

By this age, most children have already had some contact with the fairy-tale frame. Rarely do they fashion fairy-tales on their own. Nonetheless, given a task in which their knowledge is called for, children do show some awareness of typical characters (king, queen, castle) as well as certain other staples (a moat, a dark forest). But, there is little exploitation of the rich potential of the fairy-tale genre. Instead, the fairy-tale stock characters are simply used as a pretext to act out favourite themes, such as being lost, going home, and going to bed. This 'conservative' behaviour is not unexpected since, as we have seen, the ability to mobilize the features of a fairy-tale, and on one's own to formulate an adequate tale or ending, does not flower until the years preceding adolescence.

'A story' presented in two media. So far, our discussion of 'story research' has focused exclusively on content—the child's grasp of information contained in plots, his command of genres, his ability to manipulate the various features of a story. Such research is based on the assumption—usually unexamined—that a story has an existence apart from the particular medium in which it happens to be presented. From one perspective, this positing of a 'pure and unmediated' story seems permissible. Yet the possibility that a child's apprehension of a story may be materially affected by the medium in which it has been presented deserves serious examination.

To secure preliminary information on the effects of medium of presentation, we located an African folk-tale—entitled, as it happens, *A Story A Story* (Haley, 1970)—which was available in both book and video-tape form. One group of primary school subjects encountered *A Story A Story* as a picture book read in a natural setting; the other group viewed it as an animated tape, one having a sound-track identical to the 'story-book' version (Meringoff, 1977).

Preliminary analysis of the data indicated a number of effects of medium. Video-presentation resulted in greater salience in responses of visualized information, especially the actions of characters. In the making of inferences, 'video' children also relied more upon the actions actually viewed; thus, asked to evaluate how difficult it was to tie up a leopard on a tree, these subjects drew upon information about the way in which the hanging action was visually depicted. In contrast, presentation in an oral form resulted in a higher degree of recall of peripheral verbal content (e.g. phonetic refrains). And, in making inferences, children were more likely to rely upon other information contained within the story, or to draw on their own 'general knowledge' of the world.

While roughly equivalent 'bits' of information were derived from the two conditions of presentation, the overall way in which the story was assimilated, represented mentally and drawn upon for subsequent recall, proved substantially different. And, of particular note for our topic, the kinds of associations and inferences made by subjects, and the degree of attention to ornaments of language and visual depiction, was closely correlated with the medium of presentation. Beyond question, further attention to the conditions in which a story is encountered is indicated.

Concluding note

Conducting research on children's apprehension of stories turns out to be a complex yet promising undertaking. Powerful new techniques for analysing stories, when coupled with careful attention to their literary aspects, should yield considerable information about how children apprehend stories of various types. Only further research can specify the links between the developmental trajectories describing the production and comprehension of stories. Yet it already seems clear that several years are necessary before the child is aware, either in his own stories or in those related by others, of the problems posed in narrative and the means available for solving them. Moreover, full mastery of a genre, including sensitivity to psychological content, and that meta-genre ability to parody or irony, rarely appears before adolescence and may in fact flower only in youngsters with pronounced literary inclinations.

CLOSING THOUGHTS: EXPLORING THE RELATION BETWEEN THE REALMS OF HUMOUR AND LITERARY ACCOMPLISHMENT

Clearly, the story (and the metaphor) of the child's literary development remains to be elaborated. The present effort represents, at best, some scattered notes toward this endeavour. Given that any synthesis is premature, we can at most note some broad characteristics of these syntagmatic and paradigmatic approaches to language: the general shift from a preoccupation with concrete and surface facets to an appreciation of, and concern with, psychological dimensions; an increasing trend, in middle childhood, toward the adoption of rules, the recognition of genres, the fixing of boundaries, and feelings of discomfort in violating them; a freer, more spontaneous approach toward language in early childhood, which may be recaptured near the time of adolescence, when once again one dares to transcend conventional categories; a special flair for structuring events or for perceiving similarities, which characterizes that minority of the population which eventually achieves literary artistry.

But while we can postpone positing a panorama of literary development, we should at least offer a few observations about the relation between the domains under exploration here—stories and metaphors—and the topic of the remainder of this volume—those contrivances, often linguistic, which elicit laughter and other indices of humour. Lamentably, there exist virtually no empirical data on what renders certain figures of literary language—selected metaphors and selected stories—as humorous. Nor do we know whether these features are peculiar to metaphors and stories, or whether they are simply general factors eliciting mirth. Thus we are restricted to speculations, ones which need not, however, be idle.

There seems to be little *a priori* reason to deem certain metaphors and stories as funny, others as unconducive to humour. Metaphors, we have argued, are figures which join two domains customarily viewed as separate—but this formula characterizes many jokes as well. To call Juliet 'the sun' is not to produce humour: and yet if Juliet has just dyed her hair bright yellow, the same remark might well provoke laughter. Stories relate to attempts on the part of characters to solve problems—but many jokes address the same challenge. To relate Johnny's efforts to avoid the rat is not funny; and yet, if it is the rat who elects to avoid Johnny, then the same story line is likely to elicit a humorous response.

Even these (deliberately) homely examples caution against any sharp effort to separate humorous from non-humorous language on principled grounds; and yet they begin to suggest a few of the ways in which a given figure may be pushed toward (or away) from the realm of humour. We would tentatively suggest that those literary figures which evoke humour are more likely to possess at least some of the following characteristics—and that the most humorous of literary figures may well exhibit in tandem several of these.

(1) A set, or context, in which something funny is expected or desired (e.g. an introduction 'there was this rat who', or a toast at a convivial party).

(2) A situation in which the roles generally attributed to individuals are reversed or otherwise altered (a mighty individual is seen in a trivial circumstance; an ignoble person is suddenly raised to new heights) thus, if Shakespeare's exalted Juliet is suddenly compared to the 'Avon Lady', the classic heroine might well be seen as funny.

(3) The inclusion of sexual aggressive themes about which people have strong,

and sometimes ambivalent feelings—which can be more safely expressed in humour.

(4) The creation of pictures, images, or situations which are in themselves incongruous to contemplate. For example, the novelist Arthur Koestler refers to a group of intellectuals who travel from one conference to another as *Call Girls*. Taken as a characterization of the motives and standards of travelling intellectuals, this remark may be seen as an insightful metaphor. If, on the other hand, some of these same intellectuals are seen dressed up in gaudy clothes, sasshaying up Park Avenue in a provocative manner, the same characterization becomes funny.

(5) In the case of a story, the explicit violation of an expectancy spawned by the introduction. If, for example, one expects Johnny somehow to outwit the rat, and instead the *rat* solves Johnny's problem, this unexpected twist is likely to titillate.

(6) In the case of metaphor, a manipulation of the usual relationship between topic and vehicle. Contrary to ordinary practice, one may illuminate a topic whose features are intrinsic to it through a vehicle whose features are incidental (e.g. 'The suitcases tumbling down the baggage chute resembled an avalanche coming down the mountain' is less likely to evoke smiles than the seemingly symmetrical comparison 'The avalanche coming down the mountain resembled suitcases tumbling down the baggage chute'.).

It would be easy to extend this list, even as it would be possible—though hopefully not quite so easy—to collect counter-examples. Yet we hope that the spirit of this exercise—to indicate that several factors may, individually or jointly, modulate the humorous impact of a literary figure—has been vindicated. Armed with such hypotheses, it should be possible to take candidate figures and, by performing the appropriate operation or devising the suitable context, increase or decrease the likelihood that they will be found humorous by, and elicit humour from, a relevant target audience. Only such manipulations will enable us to establish with some confidence just what relations, if any, obtain between the realms of humour and literary accomplishment.

Whatever the fate of this fledging attempt to bridge the literary and humorous products, we have yet to confront a most fundamental issue—the *reason* for the appeals of literary efforts—whether they be the first metaphoric incongruities, the monster stories fashioned by the child, or the more complex efforts by literary artists and humorists.

It seems reasonable to propose that a certain affective appeal—an arousal jag, an *aha* experience, the arousal and resolution of tension—has permitted these various domains to endure, to compel interest, and to pull new individuals each generation into their ranks (cf. Berlyne, 1971). Yet, solving the riddle of how—and why—certain literary specimens stimulate effects of pleasure mixed with humour, while others arouse effects of pleasure tinged with admiration, awe, or insight may well require the juxtaposition of models and the uniting of domains of understanding which until now have remained as separate from one another as two episodes in a tale told by a three-year-old child.

ACKNOWLEDGEMENTS

The research reported in this chapter has been supported by grants from the National Science Foundation (BNS 77–13699), the National Institute of Education (G–00–3–0169 and G78–0031), the John and Mary R. Markle Foundation, and the Spencer Foundation. We are indebted to each of these agencies for allowing us to mount a multi-pronged attack on the complex issue of children's literary development.

REFERENCES

Abrams, D. M., and Sutton-Smith, B. (1977). The development of the trickster in children's narrative. *Journal of American Folklore*, **90**, 29–47.

Ames, L. B. (1966). Children's stories. *Genetic Psychology Monographs*, **23**, 337–396.

Applebee, A. (1978). *The Child's Concept of Story: Ages Two to Seventeen*. Chicago: University of Chicago Press.

Arnheim, R. (1969). *Visual Thinking*. Berkeley, California: University of California Press.

Asch, S. E., and Nerlove, H. (1960). The development of double-function terms in children: An exploratory investigation. In B. Kaplan and S. Wapner (Eds.), *Perspectives in Psychological Theory: Essays in Honor of Heinz Werner*. New York: International Universities Press.

Berlyne, D. E. (1971). *Aesthetics and Psychobiology*. New York: Appleton-Century-Crofts.

Bettelheim, B. (1976). *The Uses of Enchantment: The Meaning and Importance of Fairy Tales*. New York: Knopf.

Billow, R. (1975). A cognitive developmental study of metaphor comprehension. *Developmental Psychology*, **11**, 415–423.

Billow, R. (1977). Metaphor: a review of the psychological literature. *Psychological Bulletin*, **84**, 81–92.

Black, M. (1962). *Models and Metaphors: Studies in Language and Philosophy*. Ithaca, New York: Cornell University Press.

Bond, B., and Stevens, S. S. (1969). Cross-modal matching of brightness to loudness by five-year-olds. *Perception and Psychophysics*, **6**, 337–339.

Botvin, G., and Sutton-Smith, B. (1977). The development of structural complexity in children's fantasy narratives. *Developmental Psychology*, **13**, 377–388.

Bower, G. (1976). Comprehending and recalling stories. APA Division 3 Presidential Address, Washington, D.C., September.

Carlson, P., and Anisfeld, M. (1969). Some observations on the linguistic competence of a two-year-old child. *Child Development*, **40**, 565–575.

Carmichael, D. (1966). Irony: a cognitive-developmental study. Unpublished Doctoral Dissertation, University of California at Berkeley.

Charniak, E. (1975). Organization and inference in a frame-like system of common sense knowledge. Working paper, Institute for Semantic and Cognitive Studies, Castagnola, Switzerland.

Chukovsky, K. (1968). *From Two to Five*. Berkeley, California: University of California Press.

Cometa, M. S., and Eson, M. E. (1977). Logical operations and metaphor interpretation. Unpublished paper, Bradford College, Radford, Virginia.

Elkind, D. (1969). Piagetian and psychometric conceptions of intelligence. *Harvard Educational Review*, **39**, 319–337.

Fitzhenry-Coor, I. (1977). Children's comprehension and inference in stories of intentionality. Paper presented at the Society for Research in Child Development, New Orleans, March.

Gardner, H. (1973). *The Arts and Human Development*. New York: Wiley.

Gardner, H. (1974). Metaphors and modalities: how children project polar adjectives onto diverse domains. *Child Development*, **45**, 84–91.

Gardner, H. (1977). A brief on behalf of fairy tales. Review of B. Bettelheim, *The Uses of Enchantment: The Meaning and Importance of Fairy Tales. Semiotica*, **21**, 363–380.

Gardner, H. (1978). From Melvin to Melville: on the relevance to aesthetics of recent research on stories. In S. Madeja (Ed.), *The Arts, Cognition, and Basic Skills*. St. Louis: CEMREL.

Gardner, H., Kircher, M., Winner, E., and Perkins, D. (1975). Children's metaphoric productions and preferences. *Journal of Child Language*, **2**, 125–141.

Gardner, H., and Winner, E. (1978). The development of metaphoric competence. Paper presented at the Conference on Metaphor: The Conceptual Leap. University of Chicago, February. To be published in *Critical Inquiry*.

Gardner, H., Winner, E., Bechofer, R., and Wolf, D. (1978). The development of figurative language. In K. Nelson (Ed.), *Children's Language*. New York: Gardner Press.

Gentner, D. (1977). Children's performance on a spatial analogies task. *Child Development*, **48**, 1034–1039.

Gould, R. (1972). *Child Studies Through Fantasy*. New York: Quadrangle Books.

Greenacre, P. (1959). Play in relation to the creative imagination. In *Psychoanalytic Study of the Child*. Vol. 14. New York: International Universities Press.

Haley, G. (1970). *A Story A Story*. New York: Atheneum.

Ives, S. W. (1977). Unpublished research on story comprehension. Harvard Project Zero: Harvard University.

Jakobson, R., and Halle, M. (1956). *Fundamentals of Language*. The Hague: Mouton.

John, V. P., Horner, V. M., and Berney, T. D. (1970). Story retelling: A study of sequential speech in young children. In H. Levin and J. Williams (Eds.), *Basic Studies in Reading*. New York: Basic Books.

Kogan, N. (1975). Metaphoric thinking in children: developmental and individual-difference aspects. Paper presented at the Society for Research in Child Development, Denver, Colorado.

Kohlberg, L. (1969). Stage and sequence: the cognitive-developmental approach to socialization. In D. Goslin (Ed.), *Handbook of Socialization*. New York: Rand McNally.

Leondar, B. (1977). Hatching plots: Genesis of storymaking. In D. Perkins and B. Leondar (Eds.), *The Arts and Cognition*. Baltimore: Johns Hopkins University Press.

Lesser, H., and Drouin, C. (1975). Training in the use of double-fuction terms. *Journal of Psycholinguistic Research*, **4**, 285–302.

Mandler, J. M., and Johnson, N. S. (1977). Remembrance of things passed: Story structure and recall. *Cognitive Psychology*, **9**, 111–151.

Maranda, P., and Maranda, E. L. (1970). *Structural Models in Folklore and Transformational Essays*. The Hague: Mouton.

Meringoff, L. (1977). The influence of the medium on children's apprehension of stories. Unpublished paper, Harvard Project Zero: Harvard University.

Minsky, M. (1975). A framework for representing knowledge. In P. Winston (Ed.), *The Psychology for Computer Vision.* New Orleans: McGraw-Hill.

Ortony, A. (1975). Why metaphors are necessary and not just nice. *Educational Theory,* **25,** 45–53.

Ortony, A. (1977). Psychological processes in the comprehension of metaphor. Presentation at the Conference on Metaphor and Thought, Urbana, Illinois.

Piaget, J. (1963). *The Language and Thought of the Child.* Cleveland: Meridian.

Pitcher, E., and Prelinger, E. (1963). *Children Tell Stories.* New York: International Universities Press.

Pollio, M., and Pollio, H. (1974). The development of figurative language in children. *Journal of Psycholinguistic Research,* **3,** 185–201.

Richards, I. A. (1936). *Rhetoric.* New York: Oxford University Press.

Rubin, S., and Gardner, H. (1977). The development of sensitivity to story structure. Paper presented to the Conference on Researching Responses to Literature and the Teaching of Literature, Buffalo, New York, October. To be published in *Proceedings.*

Rumelhart, D. E. (1975). Notes on a scheme for stories. In D. G. Brown and A. Collins (Eds.), *Representation and Understanding: Studies in Cognitive Science.* New York: Academic Press.

Rumelhart, D. E., and Ortony, A. (1976). The representation of knowledge in memory. In R. C. Anderson, R. J. Spiro, and W. E. Montague (Eds.), *Schooling and the Acquisition of Knowledge.* Hillsdale, New Jersey: Lawrence Erlbaum.

Schank, R. C. (1975). *SAM A Story Understander.* New Haven: Yale University Department of Computer Science.

Shotwell, J., Wolf, D., and Gardner, H. (1977). Exploring early symbolization: Styles of achievement. Paper presented at the Wenner-Gren Symposium on the Fundamentals of Symbolization, Burg-Wartenstein, Austria.

Silverman, J. (1977). Unpublished research on story comprehension. Harvard Project Zero: Harvard University.

Stein, N. L. (1976). The effects of increasing temporal disorganization on children's recall of stories. Paper presented at the Psychonomic Society Meeting, St. Louis, November.

Stein, N. L. (1978). The development of appreciation of stories as an art form. In S. Madeja (Ed.), *The Arts, Cognition, and Basic Skills.* St. Louis: CEMREL.

Stein, N. L., and Glenn, C. G. (1977a). An analysis of story comprehension in elementary school children. In R. Freedle (Ed.), *Multidisciplinary Approaches to Discourse Comprehension.* Hillsdale, New Jersey: Ablex, Inc.

Stein, N. L., and Glenn, C. G. (1977b). The role of structural variation in children's recall of simple stories. Paper presented at the Society for Research in Child Development, New Orleans, March.

Stein, N. L., and Glenn, C. G. (1977c). A developmental study of children's construction of stories. Paper presented at the Society for Research in Child Development, New Orleans, March.

Strauss, S. (1977). Educational implication of U-shaped development. Paper prepared for the Ford Foundation.

Sutton-Smith, B. (1975). The importance of the storytaker: an investigation of the imaginative life. *The Urban Review,* **8,** 82–95.

Thorndyke, P. W. (1977). Cognitive structures in comprehension and memory of narrative discourse. *Cognitive Psychology,* **9,** 77–110.

Trabasso, T., Nicholas, D. A., Omanson, R., and Johnson, L. (1977). Inferences and story comprehension. Paper presented at the Society for Research in Child Development, New Orleans, March.

Verbrugge, R. (1974). The comprehension of analogy. Unpublished Doctoral Dissertation, University of Minnesota.
Verbrugge, R., and McCarrell, N. S. (1977). Metaphoric comprehension: studies in reminding and remembering. *Cognitive Psychology*, **9**, 494–533.
Werner, H., and Kaplan, B. (1963). *Symbol Formation*. New York: Wiley.
Winner, E., and Gardner, H. (1977). What does it take to understand a metaphor? Paper presented at the Society for Research in Child Development, New Orleans, March.
Winner, E., Rosenstiel, A. K., and Gardner, H. (1976). The development of metaphoric understanding. *Developmental Psychology*, **12**, 289–297.
Wolf, D., and Gardner, H. (1978). Style and sequence in early symbolic play. In M. Franklin and N. Smith (Eds.), *Early Symbolization*. Hillsdale, New Jersey: Lawrence Erlbaum.

Children's Humour
Edited by P. McGhee and A. Chapman.
© 1980, John Wiley & Sons, Ltd.

CHAPTER 5

Development of the Creative Aspects of Humour

PAUL E. McGHEE

Investigations of the creative aspects of children's humour have been rare. The resurgence of interest in children's humour (and humour generally) in the past decade has focused almost exclusively upon reactions to pre-arranged cartoons, jokes, films, and so forth. Our understanding of humour development, then, is mainly based on observations of the kinds of events children smile and laugh at, and their statements indicating both how funny they think a particular stimulus event is and why they think it is funny. This approach is essential to the ultimate achievement of a full understanding of humour and its development, but there can be no assurance that it will produce an accurate picture of the kinds of humour children themselves produce at different age levels. It is time for humour researchers to pay closer theoretical and empirical attention to the productive and creative aspects of children's humour, so that a fuller understanding of humour development can be achieved. In this chapter, we first consider humour as a creative act, relating it to creativity in a broader sense, and we then discuss factors related to age changes in spontaneously produced humour.

CREATIVITY AND HUMOUR DEVELOPMENT

It is beyond the scope of this chapter to review thoroughly the vast theoretical and research literature dealing with creativity. Accordingly, we discuss only those aspects of this literature which have a direct bearing on the relationship between humour and creativity.

Tests of creativity

There continues to be controversy regarding both the nature of creativity and how to measure it. One of the most persistent problems has been that of separating the influence of general intelligence from performance on tests of creativity. Wallach (1970, 1971) and others have noted that some creativity tests actually tap convergent thought processes (Guilford, 1959) similar to those required by standard intelligence tests. Tests which clearly measure divergent thinking capacities (assumed to characterize creative thought) point to the importance of two basic dimensions: highly productive and unique ideational content. In short, the highly creative individual is typically considered to be the child or adult who has a lot of associations to events or ideas, many of which are very novel (at least, more novel than those of people in general).

The cognitive nature of creativity

We have already noted Guilford's (1959) view that creative insights are characterized by divergent thinking. 'In divergent thinking operations we think in different directions, sometimes searching, sometimes seeking variety.' According to Koestler (1964, 1967), all forms of creativity are based on a common mental process, which he calls 'bisociation'. The bisociative act involves 'the perceiving of a situation or idea . . . in two self-consistent but habitually incompatible frames of reference . . .' (1964, p. 35). Through bisociation, two domains of thought which have never previously been considered to have any meaningful relationship are suddenly seen to have certain key commonalities.

> The creative act does not create something out of nothing . . . it combines, reshuffles and relates already existing but hitherto separate ideas, facts, frames of perception, associative contexts. This act of cross-fertilization . . . . . seems to be the essence of creativity . . . . (1967, *The Ghost in the Machine.* Extract in Bruner, Jolly, and Sylva, 1976, p. 645)

A bisociative insight is then relatively more creative than others when the perceived relationship is not easy to see, but is obviously appropriate once it is seen. The creative individual, within this view, is one who has such insights more often than other people. Guilford's divergent thinking would appear to be a prerequisite for the kinds of bisociative thought patterns Koestler describes.

Creative thinking in children. Most views of creative thinking are based on adult intellectual capacities. We simply do not know at this point how creativity is manifest in the earliest childhood years. Only longitudinal studies will clarify the forms of thinking which have some continuity with the creative thinking of adulthood. At issue here is whether underlying cognitive or other developmental changes provide for different forms of thinking, all of which might be labelled 'creative'. Most investigators assume that something akin to divergent thinking is central to creative thought, regardless of age level (e.g. Getzels and Jackson, 1962; Wallach and Kogan, 1965). Even with children, then, abundant and unique ideational associations usually constitute the operational measure of creativity.

Singer (1973) has suggested a promising addition to conceptualizing creativity along these lines in young children. In his view:

> Make-believe play in childhood is probably best regarded as one aspect of the general capacity for divergent production . . . In this sense it has clear links to what later emerges as creativity in the young adult . . . . To the extent that considerable make-believe activities are part of the growing child's repertory, these form links to a general attitude of 'as if' or control over one's products at least in the imaginary sphere. Such predispositions may next become the basis also for an artistic or scientific creative orientation in many young people. (1973, p. 255)

The creative older child or adult, then, may be a person who, during the pre-school years, spent considerable amounts of time in the production of interesting and novel fantasy events (see Feitelson, 1972, for a related view). Consistent with Singer's view, Johnson (1976) found measures of divergent thinking in pre-schoolers to be a stronger predictor of engagement in fantasy play than were measures of convergent thinking. Schaefer (1969) found that high-school students who produced more creative literary works reported a greater incidence of imaginary companions in childhood. Similarly, Helson (1965) found that among college women, artistically more creative individuals tended to spend more time daydreaming in childhood. At this point, conceptualizing the very young child's creativity in terms of highly imaginative fantasy play seems to be the most promising candidate for providing continuity between early and later forms of creativity.

Creating humour

In Koestler's (1964, 1967) view, the cognitive processes involved in creating humour do not differ from those involved in scientific, artistic, literary, or other forms of creative insight. In the case of jokes, and other forms of humour in which the recognition of some second-order meaning is required to get the point of the depicted humour, the bisociative (or divergent) thinker should have the advantage, since s/he tends to bring a much broader range of ideas and associations to bear on any stimulus event being considered. But the task of gaining the initial insight into the key bisociative relationship composing a given humorous event is clearly more demanding than accomplishing the same insight relative to a joke or cartoon made up by someone else. In the latter case, normally disparate ideas have already been brought into close juxtaposition with one another, greatly facilitating the perception of their relatedness. As with all great discoveries, then, a higher level of creativity should be required to create a joke, cartoon, or other humour situation, than simply to understand the same event when it is initiated by another person.

While the general qualities of bisociative thinking are considered to be the same in humorous and other forms of creative insight, Koestler (1964, 1967) does specify two ways in which humour differs. In non-humorous forms of bisociative insight, the individual sees a connection between two events, ideas, or concepts previously thought to have no meaningful link. In humour, this connection makes sense or is logical within one frame of reference, but not within another (the one which is likely to be brought to bear on the situation initially). To make sense out of the situation and appreciate the humour involved, some unexpected principle or logic must be perceived to apply (see Suls, 1972, for a related view). In specifying a peculiar logic to humour, Koestler's position is nearly identical to that advanced some thirty years earlier by Maier (1932) who explained humour in terms of Gestalt principles.

The intensity of the humour reaction, once the basis for humour is understood through bisociation, is considered by Koestler (1964) to depend on the amount of emotional tension present. He has suggested that every humour situation 'must contain one ingredient whose presence is indispensable: an impulse, however faint, of aggression or apprehension'. It is this 'aggressive-defensive' element which produces the emotional arousal released through laughter. Once our intellect has achieved the insight necessary to understand the humour of a joke, cartoon, etcetera, our emotions are left in an aroused state. Laughter serves the necessary function of removing this redundant tension 'along physiological channels of least resistance', enabling the laugher to return to a normal more relaxed state.

Several psychoanalytic theorists (e.g. Freud, 1960; Grotjahn, 1957; Kris, 1938; Levine, 1977; Wolfenstein, 1954) have drawn attention to the importance of cognitive mastery for the creation of humour by children. In a strictly cognitive sense, the child must achieve a sense of confidence about knowing how a relationship or event should occur before s/he can derive humour from distorting it in some way. Children are also believed by these writers to use humour to help cope with sources of anxiety and distress. McGhee (1972, 1974a, 1977, 1979) also stressed the importance of cognitive mastery in children's humour, suggesting that as successively higher orders of mastery are achieved in the child's understanding of the world (as a result of underlying cognitive developmental changes), they both create and respond maximally to humour consistent with that new level of mastery. He also emphasized the fantasy nature of children's humour, noting that whether a given incongruity or violation of expectancy is perceived to occur in reality or only in fantasy has a pivotal effect on whether it is seen as humorous. Because of the young child's limited level of mastery in understanding the environment, s/he is highly dependent on external cues (such as a smile, a cartoon format, or a statement like 'I'm only pretending') in order to be certain that a fantasy interpretation of the event is appropriate. Since it is much easier to be confident of the fantasy nature of an incongruous event if it is created by oneself, this suggests that the majority of the very young child's humour is self-created. This emphasis on the fantasy properties of young children's humour, in combination with Singer's (1973) view that early signs of creativity may be evident in their fantasy and make-believe activities, suggests a further basis for predicting a link between humour and creativity measures.

Empirical studies linking humour to creativity

A number of studies have been completed which suggest that both the creation and comprehension of humour, as well as other forms of playful or fantasy behaviour, are closely linked to children's creative abilities.

Relationship between creativity and playfulness. Many researchers studying creativity have suggested that a close link exists between play (or playfulness) and creativity (e.g. Jackson and Messick, 1965; Klinger, 1969; Lieberman, 1965, 1977; Wallach and Kogan, 1965), but only limited supporting data have been obtained. Torrance (1961) was the first to demonstrate a positive relationship between measures of play and creativity among elementary schoolchildren. Getzels and Jackson (1962) reported that their highly creative adolescents enjoyed playing with ideas for their own sake, and such ideational play tended to show up in a wide range of situations. Lieberman (1965, 1977) found creative five-year-olds to be more spontaneous and playful than less creative ones. Singer and Rummo (1973) found that highly creative four-and-a-half to six-and-a-half-year-old boys were rated by teachers as possessing more of a humorous, playful attitude than less creative boys. Finally, Wallach and Kogan (1965) found that high-creative/low-IQ fifth graders had a generally playful and imaginative approach to their behaviour, and were willing to tolerate unconventional ways of thinking about the world. They were willing to risk a 'crazy idea', without being preoccupied with people's reaction to it or being in error. They were described as having a playful contemplation of the possible. High-IQ/low-creative children, on the other hand, tended to be 'intolerant of unlikely, unconventional types of hypothesizing about the world'. Sutton-Smith (1967) concluded, on the basis of such findings, that it seems to make sense that the variations in response which constitute playful exercise should be similar to the required variations in response to creativity tests. In other words, these two variables appear to be structurally similar.

When a child plays with particular objects, varying his responses to them playfully, he increases the range of his associations for those particular objects. In addition, he discovers many more uses for those objects than he would otherwise. Some of these usages may be unique to himself and many will be 'imaginative', 'fantastic', 'absurd', and perhaps 'serendipitous' . . . it is also probable that this activity increases the child's repertory of responses and cognitions so that if he is asked a 'creativity' question involving similar objects and associations, he is more likely to be able to make a unique (that is, creative) response. (p. 365)

Relationship between creativity and ability to create humour. Again, there have only been a few studies which have related performance on creativity tests to the ability to create humour on demand. There are several bases, however, for predicting a positive relationship. We have already noted that divergent or bisociative thinking appears to characterize both humorous and non-humorous forms of creativity. If there is a particular cognitive style which differentiates between more and less creative children, then there is every reason to expect it to manifest itself in the area of humour. Also the close relationship believed by many to hold between play and humour (e.g. Bateson 1956; Fry, 1963; Lieberman, 1977; McGhee, 1979) has a clear parallel with the relationships we have just noted between playfulness and creativity. In most cases, a playful frame of mind is seen as a prerequisite for either initiating humour or appreciating it fully when it is initiated by others. The highly creative adolescents studied by Getzels and Jackson (1962) attached higher value than their less creative peers to having a 'good sense of humour', and were also more likely actually to use humour in relating to others. Apart from any other considerations, this combination of greater interest in, and experience with, humour should result in better performance on any test of their capacity to create humour. The early success of high-creative children in using humour is evident in Hauck and Thomas's (1972) finding that even their peers see them as having a better sense of humour.

One of the key characteristics of the creative child is a strong general curiosity about the world (Singer and Rummo, 1973). Piaget (1952) has made us very aware of the fact that infants and children are intrigued by novel and incongruous events, and commonly seek them out (see McCall and McGhee, 1977, for supporting evidence). Some children, though, seem to be more preoccupied than others with the maintenance of new and varied forms of stimulation in order to keep their environment interesting. That is, some children display a greater sense of curiosity about the new and unknown than others. It seems likely that the ongoing nurturance of this curiosity over a period of years constitutes one of the most important influences on the development of creativity in a child. Singer (1973) and McGhee (1979) have argued that this interest in maintaining an optimally varied and interesting environment may be one source of many children's engagement in different forms of fantasy activity (including humorous fantasies). Fantasy creations are especially well-suited to this purpose, since the child always remains in control over the nature of stimulation received. Thus, the following sequence of events may be responsible for the development of a positive relationship between measures of creativity and humour. Children with higher levels of curiosity and greater interest in novelty become more interested in fantasy creations than do their peers because of the endless variations of novel and incongruous events that are possible. Many of these make-believe creations are experienced as humorous to the child because of their acknowledged incompatibility with the child's understanding of the real world. Continued experience with new and unusual events in fantasy, and the pleasure experienced in connection with them, lead to both increased skill at divergent forms of thought and increased appreciation of the fruits of such thinking. Since humour is only one of the outcomes of the creation of novel or incongruous fantasies, such skill and appreciation should extend beyond humour to a broad range of areas of creative insight. The child with a high level of curiosity is sometimes in a serious frame of mind, and sometimes in a playful frame of mind. Unless one frame of mind greatly predominates over the other, these early germs of creative thinking should be broad, rather than narrow in focus.

Only a few investigators have actually correlated children's scores on creativity tests to their ability to understand or create humour. Weisberg and Springer (1961) found that highly creative fourth graders showed greater appreciation of the humour stimuli presented than less creative ones. Getzels and Jackson (1962) found that high-creative/low-IQ adolescents were more likely than high-IQ/low-creative ones to insert humour into their fantasy productions, and to use it in their drawings. Gidynsky (1972) found greater comprehension and appreciation of humour among highly creative than among less creative pre-adolescent boys.

These data are admittedly limited, but their validity is supported by comparable findings for adult samples. Creativity in adults has been found to be significantly positively related to level of comprehension of humour (Rouff, 1975), number of cartoon captions produced (Babad, 1974), funniness of captions produced (Brodzinsky and Rubien, 1977; Treadwell, 1970), and number of funny captions produced (Day and Langevin, 1969).

A longitudinal study of creativity is required to determine whether children who give evidence of being highly creative during the early years are more likely to be the initiators or creators of humour at later points in childhood. I was recently able to obtain such data in the context of a larger study of the antecedents of children's humour production and appreciation (see McGhee, 1976, and Chapter 8 of this volume for methodological details, reliabilities, and so on). As part of the Fels Research Institute's regular data-gathering procedures (for a brief period of time) for their ongoing longitudinal study of human development, a regular Fels Observer rated a number of dimensions of child behaviour during the semi-annual visit of pre-schoolers to the Fels Nursery School, and the annual visit of six- to eleven-year-olds to the Fels Day Camp. Among the twenty child behaviours rated was an evaluation of the overall amount of creativity shown by the child during the two or three weeks of the nursery school or day camp session. A child's creativity rating was based on using materials in original ways, showing flexibility and originality in language and when solving intellectual or social problems, and finding innovative approaches during dramatic play and fine and gross motor activities. At the present writer's request, the day camp teacher and the regular Fels Observer provided additional ratings of a number of humour-related behaviours, following a recent day camp session (see Chapter 8). Two measures of spontaneously created humour were included among the latter: frequency of verbal and of behavioural attempts to initiate humour. Verbal humour included the distortion of familiar sounds, puns, riddles, jokes, 'bathroom' words or jokes, incongruous or meaningless word combinations, calling objects by the wrong name, playful verbal teasing, and so forth. Behavioural humour included silly or clowning behaviour, arranging objects in incongruous positions or causing them to be engaged in incongruous activities, teasing through gestures, and so forth.

Table 5.1 shows the correlations obtained between each of the two humour measures for the six- to eleven-year-old day camp sample and prior ratings of their creativity. The 3–6 row of correlations is based on each child's average

Table 5.1 Correlations between frequency of day camp subjects' verbal and behavioural attempts to initiate humour and ratings of creativity at earlier ages

	Age period	Verbal humour	Behavioural humour
Males	3–6[a]	0.41	0.08
	6 +[b]	0.48*	0.64*
Females	3–6[c]	0.42	0.33
	6 +[b]	0.62*	0.59*

[a] $n = 12$ * $p < 0.05$
[b] $n = 16$
[c] $n = 11$

creativity rating for all nursery school sessions attended between the ages of three and six years. The 6 + row is based on the average day camp creativity score for all day camp sessions attended between the age of six and the current session (on which humour ratings were based). Table 5.1 shows that for both males and females, ratings of creativity during the pre-school years were not predictive of either form of humour initiation in middle childhood. Creativity ratings were positively predictive of humour initiation, however, after the age of six. These findings suggest that either creativity is highly unstable during the pre-school and early elementary school years, or that the criteria used for creativity were inappropriate for pre-school children. The latter interpretation is in line with Singer's (1973) view that early creativity may be more clearly manifest in the child's make-believe activities.

Relationship between amount of fantasy play and humour. A recent session of the Fels Nursery School was used to obtain data on the relationship among three- to five-year-olds between frequency of engagement in make-believe or fantasy activity and both amount of humour responsiveness and frequency of initiation of different forms of humour. Both fantasy and humour ratings were based on a seven-point scale, and were completed at the end of the nursery school session by two research assistants (Spearman-Brown reliabilities ranged from 0.80 to 0.98). It was found that frequency of pre-schoolers' engagement in fantasy activity was not significantly related to either frequency of verbal or behavioural initiation of humour, or to the degree of hostility evident in the child's humour, but it was positively related to the amount of laughter shown in response to the humour attempts of other children ($r = 0.53$, $p < 0.05$). If those children who spend large amounts of time engaged in imaginative activities are the children who are subsequently considered to be highly creative, then the young creative child does not appear to show more frequent initiation of either behavioural or verbal forms of humour. Of course, these data indicate nothing about these children's capacities to create these forms of humour; they suggest only that they do not make the effort to initiate such humour in social play. The findings are puzzling, but if these high-fantasy children are the kinds of children who subsequently are highly initiating of humour (and are creative, generally) the antecedent data presented in the next section suggest that they may not have had the kind of relationship with their peers which would provide support for such attempts at humour. The finding that high-fantasy children showed more laughter than low-fantasy children at other humour events does provide some evidence that they had begun to develop a special interest in humour by the pre-school years. It is not clear at this point why such interest would not carry over into the production of humour.

Antecedents of high-fantasy play. Antecedent maternal and child behavioural data were available in the permanent Fels files for the nursery school sample described in the previous section. Thus, it was possible to relate amount of current fantasy behaviour to earlier characteristics of the child's own behaviour, and to the mother's behaviour toward the child. Table 5.2 lists the nineteen child behaviours for which ratings were available from nursery school sessions between the age of three and the current session, and their relationship to the amount of fantasy activity shown during this session. The findings indicate that

Table 5.2 Correlations between frequency of engagement in fantasy behaviour among nursery school children (sexes combined) and antecedents in the child's own behaviour during the period between the age of three and the child's present age

Child behaviour[a]		Child behaviour	
Unprovoked physical aggression, same-sex peers	0.39^+	Effort on mastery of fine motor skills	-0.37^+
Unprovoked verbal aggression same-sex peers	0.41^+	Effort on mastery of gross motor skills	0.41^+
Retaliation to physical or verbal aggression from peers	0.40^+	Effort on mastery in intellectual activities	0.10
Dominance of same-sex peers	0.55^*	Parallel play	0.75^{**}
Quantity of speech	0.72^{**}	Associative play	0.14
Imitation of peers	0.56^*	Restless activity	0.08
Instrumental help seeking from adults	-0.18	Conformity to adult demands	0.30
Affection and emotional support seeking from adults	0.05	Body co-ordination	0.32
		Quality of language	0.21
Recognition seeking for achievement from adults	0.31	Amount of masculinity versus femininity (traditionally defined; masculinity = high)	0.66^{**}

[a] $n = 16$ in all cases
$^+ p < 0.10$ $^* p < .05$ $^{**} p < 0.01$

the high-fantasy three- to five-and-a-half-year-olds tended to be (in the year or two preceding the current session) both physically and verbally aggressive toward peers, generally talkative, and dominating in interactions with same-sex peers. These relationships also account for the positive relationship obtained between the amount of fantasy and the degree of masculinity evident in the child's behaviour. The tendency of the high-fantasy child to have been especially imitative of peers' behaviour is surprising, both in the light of their assertiveness toward peers and the previously described high level of curiosity presumed to characterize the highly creative child. However, since other children are not likely to react positively to a dominating and aggressive child—which might account for the high-fantasy child's greater engagement in parallel play rather than associative play—imitativeness may have evolved as a means of improving social relationships and bringing about more rewarding forms of social play. The positive relationship obtained for effort to master gross motor skills might be interpreted to mean that gross motor activity is especially effective for acting out the make-believe episodes of the high-fantasy child, while fine motor skills are not very effective in doing so.

In the previous section, we noted that for this same sample of children, high-fantasy children did not make more attempts to initiate humour than their low-fantasy peers, although they did show more laughter at others' humour. We also noted earlier that early ratings of creativity do not become predictive of frequency of socially initiated humour until after the age of six. This is just about the age at which most children begin to understand double meanings which form the basis for most riddles, 'moron' jokes, and so forth, of the type that are popular among elementary schoolchildren. It may be only at this point, then, that the high-fantasy child begins to take an active interest in initiating humour in social interaction. Humour provides an ideal means for such children to extend their aggressive, dominating, and talkative qualities in a socially-favoured direction.

Methodological considerations. In future investigations along these lines, control should be exercised over the varieties of humour children are asked to produce. Just as a child might show a bent toward creativity in one area (e.g. artistic, literary, physical skills, or scientific), but not another, s/he might be good at creating certain forms of humour, but not others. For example, Singer and Berkowitz (1972) found that wit (humour based on verbal communications, usually involving double meanings) and clowning (humour based on body language or movement, and facial expression) among college students were discrete creative skills. Thus, even within the category of verbal humour, an individual may be very good at creating original puns, but be unable to produce jokes, riddles, anecdotes, or other types of humour. As research on the creative aspects of humour proceeds, we will have to refine our measures of created humour.

The methodological problems confronting the investigator of the creative aspects of humour do not differ from those confronting the investigator of general creativity. Since discussions of these are available elsewhere, we will not consider them here (see Taylor, 1964; Wallach and Kogan, 1965). The major issue to be dealt with concerns a child's (or adult's) ability to create humour under laboratory conditions. Wallach and Kogan (1965) and others have stressed the importance of not instilling in children a task or test orientation when measuring creative abilities. Thus, a child's ability to create punchlines or cartoon captions upon request may not be a valid index of such abilities in the more relaxed conditions of spontaneous social interaction. So, it is essential to approximate the natural social environment as much as possible in testing for the capacity to create humour. In addition to maintaining a relaxed, spontaneous, and non-evaluative atmosphere, providing ample time to come up with a humorous response may be an especially important prerequisite for the bisociative forms of thinking required to produce humour. A sense of time 'pressure' is bound to lower humour creativity scores. It may prove useful to have a 'warm up' period prior to testing for humour creativity. That is, providing the child with a series of jokes, cartoons, films, etcetera, might produce the kind of atmosphere which is conducive to creating humour in the laboratory. Support for this view is provided by Ziv's (1976) finding that tenth graders who listened to a humorous record prior to taking a creativity test obtained higher creativity scores than those who did not hear the record before taking the test.

Finally, caution should be exercised in interpreting a finding that more creative children or adults are more successful at creating funny captions or punchlines. We have noted that more creative children are more intrigued than their peers by humour. Thus, they have probably had considerably more experience in listening to and thinking about humour than low-creative children. It may be this greater experience with humour which produces funnier captions or punchlines, and not creative abilities *per se*. To rule out this factor, it should be fruitful to build in comparable levels of experience with the kind of humour to be tested. By presenting several examples to the child, and drawing his/her attention to the structure of the humour involved, prior differences in experience with such humour can at least be reduced, if not removed (see McGhee, 1974b).

AGE-RELATED CHANGES IN CREATED HUMOUR

Only two published studies have investigated age changes in children's ability to create humour. Wolfenstein (1953) presented children between six and seventeen years of age with examples of joking and non-joking answers to riddles, and then asked them to create their own humorous answers to additional riddle questions. She did not analyse her data statistically, but did report that very few children at any age level were successful at this task. Children's skill at creating a joking answer seemed to depend more on interest in jokes and prior experience with them than on age, so that seven-year-olds sometimes performed better than seventeen-year-olds. She noted that children are typically able to discriminate joking from non-joking answers before they can make up a joking answer of their own.

McGhee (1974b) conducted a similar study, but in a more systematic fashion. Humorous and non-humorous examples of word play (based on double meanings) and absurdity (based on an elephant doing something impossible, because of its size or other physical characteristics) riddles were presented to boys and girls in grades one, two, four, and six in order to familiarize them with the structural nature of the riddles, and reduce experimental differences with comparable jokes in the past. It was predicted that children would have better success both at discriminating between humorous and non-humorous and at creating their own humorous answers to absurdity than to word-play riddles, since only the former involve perceptual violations of past experience (see McGhee, 1971a). The more abstract level of humour in riddles based on different forms of linguistic ambiguity (see Chapter 3) should make both the comprehension and production of such humour more difficult. Like Wolfenstein (1953), McGhee found that children at all age levels were more successful at discriminating a joking from a non-joking answer than they were at creating their own joking answer. Most children could identify the joking answer to absurdity riddles by grade two, but choices were still near chance level among second graders for word-play riddles, confirming the greater difficulty of the latter. As expected, the ability to create humorous answers to both types of riddles increased significantly with age (for both sexes). Consistent with the discrimination data, a greater number of humorous answers were produced for absurdity than for word-play riddles at all age levels. The ability to make a general statement about the prerequisites for humour in a given type of riddle increased across the age levels studied for absurdity riddles, but such general statements regarding word-play humour were rare at all levels. Finally, the ability to make such a general statement was not found to be necessary to create examples of a given form of humour.

These findings should not be interpreted to mean that it is only at the age of six or so that children begin to be able to create their own humour. Just as a child's developmental level is closely associated with the kinds of humour that are understood and appreciated, it determines the form of humour the child is capable of creating. It is not clear at this point, however, whether children become capable of creating a given form of humour as soon as (or soon after) they are able to understand it. McGhee's (1974b) data suggest that this is true for at least some children. It may be that while underlying cognitive and experiential factors determine the age at which a child can comprehend and appreciate externally initiated humour, interest in joking and frequency of previous attempts at producing that form of humour play the crucial roles (as suggested by Wolfenstein, 1953, 1954) in determining the skill at creating it upon demand.

Children's use of metaphor and simile

Chapter 4 of this volume documents the recent surge of research interest in children's use and comprehension of figurative language. While metaphors and similes are not funny in most cases, the structural similarity to certain forms of humour is readily apparent. In using a metaphor, the child describes one object or idea in terms of another. The metaphor is understood and appreciated when the common property is realized. It would seem, then, that the same bisociative or divergent processes we have described here for humour must also be involved in gaining the kinds of insight required to produce metaphors and similes. Even the developmental model of metaphoric thinking advanced by Gardner, Winner, Bechhofer, and Wolf (1977) bears considerable similarity to the developmental model of incongruity humour set forth by McGhee (1977, 1979). Additional similarities between humour and various non-humorous figurative uses of language may be seen; just as an incongruous event may produce a range of reactions, such as curiosity and interest, puzzlement, fear or anxiety, or humour, so metaphors and similes may be clever, interesting, or puzzling in some cases, but funny in others. It would behoove any investigator of the creative aspects of children's humour, then, to take into account research findings on the development of figurative uses of language before planning studies of children's humour production.

Cognitive development as a source of age differences

The fact that children were neither able to discriminate humorous from non-humorous riddle answers nor to create their own humour based on word play until at least the second grade, led McGhee (1974b) to suggest that concrete operational thinking must be mediating the capacity both to understand and create this form of humour. Shultz has also found the first or second grade to mark an important transition point in children's humour appreciation, and has similarly concluded that concrete operational thinking might account for the changes occurring during this period (Shultz 1972, 1974; Shultz and Horibe, 1974). While these findings do suggest such a relationship, no attempt has yet been made to relate children's ability to create different forms of humour to the acquisition of specific Piagetian cognitive skills. If it can be assumed that children must be able to understand a given form of humour before they can initiate it on their own, however, studies of children's reactions to humour should provide suggestions as to the kinds of outcomes we might expect if studies relating cognitive level to creative capacities were to be completed. The acquisition of concrete operational thinking in seven- and eight-year-olds has been found to be positively related to the ability to detect hidden meanings (Shultz and Bloom, 1974), comprehension and appreciation of riddles based on homonyms (e.g. pear versus pair) (Whitt and Prentice, 1977), comprehension of behavioural incongruities (in the absence of perceptual incongruities) (McGhee, 1971a), and comprehension of sequential cartoons (McGhee, 1971b). Two additional studies have demonstrated that developmental changes in children's level of moral functioning (which parallel the acquisition of operational thinking) lead to sharp differences in humour appreciation (McGhee, 1974c; Zillmann and Bryant, 1975). Any studies along similar lines of children's spontaneous or laboratory-produced humour should yield comparable differences.

The origins issue: self-constructed or reactive humour?

It is only in the past few years that humour researchers have begun to discuss issues related to the earliest appearance of humour in infants. Just as different theoretical views suggest opposing ages at which humour makes its initial appearance, they also differ with respect to their stance on the issue of whether those initial humour perceptions result from self-created incongruities or externally encountered ones. McGhee (1974a, 1977) argued that the earliest form of humour results from directing 'inappropriate' actions toward a given object (e.g. using a piece of wood as one would normally use a glass or comb). Thus, the child *creates* the earliest opportunities for humour by *acting toward one object as if it were another*. The onset of such behaviour depends on: (a) the development of primitive symbolic capacities early in the second year; (b) the possession of a well-developed memory or expectation regarding the various properties of the object; (c) a playful set or frame of mind, such that the child's attention is more strongly directed toward the inappropriateness of this particular action than to satisfying a sense of curiosity regarding the outcome of the act; and (d) a high level of confidence that the action is not consistent with a 'reality-oriented' mode of adaptation to the environment; this confidence enables the child to derive maximal enjoyment of the incongruous event at the fantasy or pretend level.

Shultz (1976) also proposed that the earliest form of incongruity humour centres around self-constructed incongruities which begin to appear following the onset of symbolic play early in the second year. In his view, though, other more primitive forms of humour occur in the first year. For example, the smiling and occasional mild laughter that infants show following successful, effortful (i.e. requiring some accommodation of existing schemas) assimilation of discrepant events is seen as an early form of humour based on 'pleasure in mastery'. McGhee (1977, 1979) has criticized this view arguing that, while this activity does appear to be intrinsically pleasurable, and while it also appears to enhance the funniness of an otherwise humorous event, it does not follow that such bases for pleasure constitute a source of humour in their own right. Shultz also argues that other forms of humour in the first year occur in connection with tickling, peek-a-boo, chasing, and other 'games'. The laughter and smiling which usually accompany these activities are considered to reflect early forms of humour because they share the biphasic sequence of arousal increase followed by a decrease which characterizes the identification and resolution of incongruities by older children and adults. While the occurrence of a common pattern of arousal fluctuation does not provide a satisfactory basis for designating these activities as humorous, in the present writer's view, the important point for our present concerns is that these events appear to be of a reactive rather than a self-constructed nature.

Pien and Rothbart have taken the position in Chapter 1 of this volume that symbolic capacities are not required in order to experience humour. They conclude that humour must be experienced as early as the fourth month, since infants of this age demonstrate the capacity to (a) assimilate events in a playful or ludic fashion, and (b) detect incongruities. This early humour, however, is considered to be a reactive rather than a created form of humour.

To some extent, of course, the issue of whether infants experience humour in the first year is a definitional one. Different conclusions about the onset of the capacity either to create or perceive external sources of humour follow from the selection of such factors as patterns of arousal fluctuation, demonstration of smiling or laughter, detection of discrepant or incongruous relationships, demonstration of symbolic capacities, or the ability to interpret a discrepant event in either a serious or playful fashion as being the essential earmarks of humour. There can be no doubt about the fact that children begin to demonstrate a new form of behaviour when they acquire the capacity to represent their world in terms of image-symbols. Fantasy and pretend behaviour simply do not occur prior to this point. It seems equally clear that the human nervous system is equipped (as are many infrahuman systems) to seek out and pay maximal attention to events which have an optimal moderate degree of similarity/difference in relation to previously encoded information (McCall and McGhee, 1977). Finally, the playfulness both of infants in the first year (Piaget, 1962) and of animals (Aldis, 1975) is well documented. If the ability to detect discrepant events and the capacity for playfulness are the only prerequisites for humour, then many other species in addition to man must also be capable of experiencing humour. This would appear to be a difficult position to defend. The importance of each of these components for humour is difficult to question. The issue is whether they are sufficient in themselves to produce humour perceptions.

The present writer has suggested elsewhere (McGhee, 1979) that humour might best be conceptualized as a form of intellectual play. Several lower species show playful forms of overt behaviour, but they do not provide any evidence of more purely intellectual forms of play. The most primitive form of evidence of such intellectualized play involves the treating (i.e. pretending) of one object as if it were another. Even chimpanzees and gorillas do not give evidence of this form of behaviour in the wild (see McGhee, 1979, for related evidence). Apes which have learned to use sign language, however, do show this form of play behaviour, along with other forms of playful incongruity-production using the signing system. It is the provision of these animals with a ready-made gestural communication system which transforms them from playful animals who take pleasure in viewing incongruous events (as do human infants) into animals who take pleasure in the symbolic and playful manipulation of ideas. These animals have the capacity for the ready manipulation of abstract symbols, even though they have not developed complex representational communication systems on their own (they have developed non-representational communication systems). Providing apes with a ready-made representational system which they can learn leads to the same transformation in behaviour shown by human infants early in the second year. In the present view, it is this transition which marks the onset of humour capacities for each species. This initial humour is of a self-constructed nature; it is only later that incongruities created by others are viewed as humorous.

DEVELOPMENT OF THE HUMORIST

Once underlying cognitive and other developmental changes have provided for the capacity to produce or appreciate particular forms of humour, some children become more preoccupied with them than others. Generally speaking, the child who becomes more interested in different forms of humour should tend to initiate humour more often, and should also be better than others at being funny. We know very little at this point, however, about how this interest develops in the early years. A number of studies have been completed upon comedians' and comedy writers' early childhood experiences (e.g. Fry and Allen, 1975, 1976; Janus, 1975; Wilde, 1968), but each of these studies was based on recall data drawn from adult interviews. Moreover, these data apply only for a select group of individuals who subsequently became professionals within the world of comedy.

Chapter 8 of this volume reports the findings of the only longitudinal study to be completed thus far on the early childhood of individuals who later became frequent initiators of humour. The reader will discover in that chapter that the antecedents of heightened levels of humour production and responsiveness are similar to those reported here with respect to high amounts of fantasy play. This overlap adds support to the writer's view that fantasy processes play a central role in the humour of young children.

CONCLUDING REMARKS

It was suggested here that the basic cognitive processes involved in creating humour do not differ appreciably from those involved in understanding and appreciating humour initiated by others. Gaining the initial insight into relationships involved in a humorous episode, however, is considerably more difficult than merely recognizing those relationships when encountered through some external source. In this sense, humour is similar to other areas of thought. That is, great discoveries and innovative ideas are easily understood once they are organized and developed, but the difficulty lies in the initial development of those ideas. It is here that the truly creative individual stands out. Few individuals seem to have the capacity to break through traditional or commonplace ways of conceptualizing events in order to establish new and meaningful relationships. Regardless of whether it occurs in the arena of science, literature, art or humour, those individuals who demonstrate a capacity to re-order meaningfully our thinking about the world are given a special place in our society. Where would we be without the creative talents of humorists in literature, theatre, television and other mass media?

The limited data available support the view that an increased ability to create humour is associated with heightened creative abilities generally. More creative children initiate behavioural and verbal forms of humour more often than their less creative peers, attach greater value to possessing a good sense of humour, and are generally more playful in interactions with others. There is also some evidence suggesting that more creative children and adults show greater understanding and appreciation of humour created by others.

More creative children appear to have a stronger sense of curiosity about their world, and are more likely to enjoy and seek out novel and incongruous forms of stimulation. It is undoubtedly these characteristics which initially foster increased levels of creativity. Such children are drawn toward a special interest in fantasy events both because of the infinite possibilities for generating novel and incongruous relationships, and because they can control such events at will. Whether or not such fantasy creations are experienced as humorous or ('merely') interesting or exciting should depend on whether the child is in a serious or more playful frame of mind. If it can be assumed that most children fluctuate between these frames of mind, and if Singer (1973) is correct in suggesting that early fantasy play fosters creativity, then increased creativity in humorous and non-humorous areas is the logical developmental outcome. Increased creativity in a specific area (such as humour, art, woodworking, writing, and so forth) may develop simply because the child becomes especially interested in that area.

REFERENCES

Aldis, O. (1975). *Play Fighting*. New York: Academic Press.
Babad, E. Y. (1974). A multi-method approach to the assessment of humor: a critical look at humor tests. *Journal of Personality*, **42**, 618–631.
Bateson, G. (1956). The message 'This is Play'. In B. Schaffner (Ed.), *Group Processes* (2nd conference). New York: Josiah Macy Jr. Foundation.
Brodzinsky, D. M., and Rubien, J. (1977). Humor production as a function of sex of

subject, creativity, and cartoon content. *Journal of Consulting and Clinical Psychology*, **44**, 597–600.

Bruner, J. S., Jolly, A., and Sylva, K. (1976). *Play: Its Role in Development and Evolution*. New York: Basic Books.

Day, H. L., and Langevin, R. (1969). Curiosity and intelligence: two necessary conditions for a high level of creativity. *Journal of Special Education*, **3**, 263–268.

Feitelson, D. (1972). Developing imaginative play in preschool children as a possible approach to fostering creativity. *Early Child Development Care*, **1**, 181–195.

Freud, S. (1960). *Jokes and Their Relation to The Unconscious*. New York: Norton.

Fry, W. F. (1963). *Sweet Madness: A Study of Humor*. Palo Alto: Pacific.

Fry, W. F., and Allen, M. (1975). *Make 'Em Laugh*. Palo Alto: Science and Behavior Books.

Fry, W. F., and Allen, M. (1976). Humour and creativity. In A. J. Chapman and H. C. Foot (Eds.), *Humour and Laughter: Theory, Research, and Applications*. Chichester: Wiley.

Gardner, H., Winner, E., Bechhofer, R., and Wolf, D. (1977). The development of figurative language. In K. Nelson (Ed.), *Children's Language*. New York: Gardner Press.

Getzels, J. W., and Jackson, P. W. (1962). *Creativity and Intelligence*. New York: Wiley.

Gidynsky, C. G. (1972). Associative shift, peer rejection and humor response in children: an exploratory study. Unpublished Doctoral Dissertation, Columbia University.

Grotjahn, M. (1957). *Beyond Laughter*. New York: McGraw-Hill.

Guilford, J. P. (1959). Three faces of intellect. *American Psychologist*, **71**, 164–174.

Hauck, W. E., and Thomas, J. W. (1972). The relationship of humor to intelligence, creativity, and intentional and incidental learning. *Journal of Experimental Education*, **40**, 52–55.

Helson, R. (1965). Childhood interest clusters related to creativity in women. *Journal of Consulting Psychology*, **29**, 353–361.

Jackson, P. W., and Messick, S. (1965). The person, the product, and the response: conceptual problems in the assessment of creativity. *Journal of Personality*, **33**, 309–329.

Janus, S. S. (1975). The great comedians: personality and other factors. *American Journal of Psychoanalysis*, **35**, 169–174.

Johnson, J. E. (1976). Relations of divergent thinking and intelligence test scores with social and nonsocial make-believe play of preschool children. *Child Development*, **47**, 1200–1203.

Klinger, E. (1969). Development of imaginative behavior: implications of play for a theory of fantasy. *Psychological Bulletin*, **72**, 277–298.

Koestler, A. (1964). *The Act of Creation*. New York: Dell.

Koestler, A. (1967). *The Ghost in The Machine*. New York: Hutchinson.

Kris, E. (1938). Ego development and the comic. *International Journal of Psychoanalysis*, **19**, 77–90.

Lieberman, J. N. (1965). The relationship between playfulness and divergent thinking at the kindergarten level. *Journal of Genetic Psychology*, **107**, 219–224.

Lieberman, J. N. (1977). *Playfulness: Its relationship to Imagination and Creativity*. New York: Academic Press.

Levine, J. (1977). Humour as a form of therapy: introduction to symposium. In A. J. Chapman and H. C. Foot (Eds.), *It's a Funny Thing, Humour*. Oxford: Pergamon Press.

Maier, N. R. F. (1932). A gestalt theory of humour. *British Journal of Psychology*, **23**, 69–74.

McCall, R. B., and McGhee, P. E. (1977). The discrepancy hypothesis of attention and affect in infants. In I. C. Uzgiris and F. Weizmann (Eds.), *The Structuring of Experience*. New York: Plenum.

McGhee, P. E. (1971a). Cognitive development and children's comprehension of humor. *Child Development*, **42**, 123–138.

McGhee, P. E. (1971b). The role of operational thinking in children's comprehension and appreciation of humor. *Child Development*, **42**, 733–744.

McGhee, P. E. (1972). On the cognitive origins of incongruity humor: fantasy assimilation versus reality assimilation. In J. H. Goldstein and P. E. McGhee (Eds.), *The Psychology of Humor: Theoretical Perspectives and Empirical Issues*. New York: Academic Press.

McGhee, P. E. (1974a). Cognitive mastery and children's humor. *Psychological Bulletin*, **81**, 721–730.

McGhee, P. E. (1974b). Development of children's ability to create the joking relationship. *Child Development*, **45**, 552–556.

McGhee, P. E. (1974c). Moral development and children's appreciation of humor. *Developmental Psychology*, **10**, 514–525.

McGhee, P. E. (1976). Sex differences in children's humor. *Journal of Communication*, **26**, 176–189.

McGhee, P. E. (1977). A model of the origins and early development of incongruity-based humour. In A. J. Chapman and H. C. Foot (Eds.), *It's a Funny Thing, Humour*. Oxford: Pergamon Press.

McGhee, P. E. (1979). *Humor: Its Origin and Development*. San Francisco: Freeman.

Piaget, J. (1952). *The Origins of Intelligence in Children*. New York: International Universities Press.

Piaget, J. (1962). *Play, Dreams and Imitation in Childhood*. New York: Norton.

Rouff, L. L. (1975). Creativity and sense of humor. *Psychological Reports*, **37**, 1022.

Schaefer, C. E. (1969). The self-concept of creative adolescents. *Journal of Psychology*, **72**, 233–242.

Shultz, T. R. (1972). The role of incongruity and resolution in children's appreciation of cartoon humor. *Journal of Experimental Child Psychology*, **13**, 456–477.

Shultz, T. R. (1974). Development of the appreciation of riddles. *Child Development*, **45**, 100–105.

Shultz, T. R. (1976). A cognitive-developmental analysis of humour. In A. J. Chapman and H. C. Foot (Eds.), *Humour and Laughter: Theory, Research and Applications*. Chichester: Wiley.

Shultz, T. R., and Bloom, L. (1974). Concrete operational thought and appreciation of verbal jokes. Unpublished manuscript, cited in Shultz (1976).

Shultz, T. R., and Horibe, F. (1974). Development of the appreciation of verbal jokes. *Developmental Psychology*, **10**, 13–20.

Singer, D. L., and Berkowitz, L. (1972). Differing 'creativities' in the wit and the clown. *Perceptual and Motor Skills*, **35**, 3–6.

Singer, D. L., and Rummo, J. (1973). Ideational creativity and behavioral style in kindergarten age children. *Developmental Psychology*, **8**, 154–161.

Singer, J. L. (1973). *The Child's World of Make-Believe: Experimental Studies of Imaginative Play*. New York: Academic Press.

Suls, J. M. (1972). A two-stage model for the appreciation of jokes and cartoons: an information-processing analysis. In J. H. Goldstein and P. E. McGhee (Eds.), *The Psychology of Humor: Theoretical Perspectives and Empirical Issues*. New York: Academic Press.

Sutton-Smith, B. (1967). The role of play in cognitive development. *Young Children*, **22**, 361–370.

Taylor, C. (Ed.) (1964). *Widening Horizons in Creativity*. New York: Wiley.

Torrance, E. P. (1961). Priming creative thinking in the primary grades. *Elementary School Journal*, **62**, 139–145.

Treadwell, Y. (1970). Humor and creativity. *Psychological Reports*, **26**, 55–58.

Wallach, M. A. (1970). Creativity. In P. H. Mussen (Ed.), *Manual of Child Psychology*. (3rd edn.) New York: Wiley.

Wallach, M. A. (1971). *The Intelligence Creativity Distinction*. New York: General Learning Press.

Wallach, M. A., and Kogan, N. (1965). *Modes of Thinking in Young Children*. New York: Holt, Rinehart, and Winston.

Weisberg, P. S., and Springer, K. J. (1961). Environmental factors in creative function. *Archives of General Psychiatry*, **5**, 64–74.

Whitt, J. K., and Prentice, N. M. (1977). Cognitive processes in the development of children's enjoyment and comprehension of joking riddles. *Developmental Psychology*, **13**, 129–136.

Wilde, L. (1968). *The Great Comedians*. Secaucus, New Jersey: Citadel Press.

Wolfenstein, M. (1953). Children's understanding of jokes. *The Psychoanalytic Study of the Child*, **9**, 162–173.

Wolfenstein, M. (1954). *Children's Humor*. Glencoe, Illinois: Free Press.

Zillmann, D., and Bryant, J. (1975). Viewer's moral sanction of retribution in the appreciation of dramatic presentations. *Journal of Experimental Social Psychology*, **11**, 572–582.

Ziv, A. (1976). Facilitating effects of humor on creativity. *Journal of Educational Psychology*, **68**, 318–322.

CHAPTER 6

Humour, Laughter, and Social Interaction

ANTONY J. CHAPMAN,
JEAN R. SMITH,
and
HUGH C. FOOT

In discourses throughout history various scholars have intimated that humour and laughter are influenced significantly by social factors (cf. Bergler, 1956; Hertzler, 1970; Lauter, 1964; Piddington, 1933). Amongst modern-day psychologists one can readily discern a widespread consensus that creating humour, initiating humour and reacting to humour are each, in part, social-psychologically determined; and amongst humour researchers there is some evidence of a general belief that, whatever the principal focus of a humour study, social parameters should receive consideration (McGhee, 1976). Regrettably, social psychologists can claim to have contributed only minimally to our understanding of these parameters and to our awareness of their pervasiveness and salience. As a result, there is a paucity of objective data concerning the social dimensions of humour. Indeed humour and laughter have received only cursory attention from social psychologists and they are conspicuous lacunae within the subject matter of social psychology.

Children's humour has been particularly neglected by social psychologists; out of necessity, therefore, this chapter refers more than others to the adult humour literature. The first of three main sections sketches out some theoretical and empirical advances appertaining principally to the social psychology of adult humour. The second section includes a review of the relatively few studies, other than those of the present authors, which relate to social aspects of children's humour. The third section overviews the authors' own social interaction research on responsiveness in humour situations: a new series of child studies is set against a background of experiments already reported.

ADULT ANALYSES: PROCESSES AND FUNCTIONS

A caveat should be sounded loudly at the start of this section. An obvious theoretical and practical constraint, and one of paramount importance, is the necessity to exercise extreme caution in attempting to generalize along the chronological scale between adults and children. Within humour research there are scarcely any developmental data upon which to draw in order to assess the validity of proposed or implied generalizations from adults to adolescents, or even from adults to quite young children; but, in the absence of at least some rudiments of corroborative research, everyday observations of differences between adult and child humour would appear to militate against propagating or countenancing thoughts of universalities. Outside the domain of humour research there is no deficit of data affirming common-sensical views that the social worlds of children are radically different from those of adults and that social behaviours and complexity of relationships develop gradually throughout childhood (cf. Foot, Chapman, and Smith, 1980; McGurk, 1978; Richards, 1974; Schaffer, 1971). However, at the very minimum, selected humour studies of adult subjects are of value in delineating areas of heuristic potential *vis-à-vis* research with children; and, although it may transpire that their findings have restricted generality with respect to other populations of subjects, they are certainly rich sources for preliminary models and hypotheses.

In surveys of humour research published in the first and second editions of the *Handbook of Social Psychology*, only small portions of the total available space were allotted to evaluating social aspects of humour (cf. Berlyne, 1969; Flugel, 1954). One can surmise that there were several interrelated reasons why the authors deemed that, even in a social psychology text, no more space was warranted: for example, studies were comparatively sparse, they tended to be of the 'one-off' variety, and no single area had been developed to any substantial degree. Taken as a whole, studies bearing on the social psychology of humour are disparate conceptually as well as methodologically, and they tap a diverse range of issues relating both to content and function. A preponderance of studies have centred either upon the individual or upon the group, but there are some which have addressed humour at the level of society (e.g. Matusewicz, 1976; Powell, 1977) and there are others which have made cross-cultural comparisons (cf. Goldstein, 1977). Since the early days of psychological analyses (cf. Feibleman, 1939; Hayworth, 1928; Wallis, 1922), and at each of the levels of analysis, a basic premise underlying a high proportion of studies has been that above all else humour and laughter are linked to communication: in some studies this has been made explicit, while in others it has remained tacit.

A central tenet of this chapter is that humour has to do with communication, particularly at the group level where it is especially important in social interaction. In contrast to most other chapters in this volume the emphasis here is on research relating to humour processes and functions, rather than to content and structure. Like our own research with children, some of the works cited in this section have in fact been directed towards broadening our knowledge of social behaviour, social development and group processes generally, rather more than towards exploring the dynamics of humour *per se*.

Groups are of course dynamic entities, and generic transitions regularly occur in small-group processes. While no humour researcher has systematically looked for evidence of changes in the salient functions of humour concomitant with temporal changes in group processes, Wolosin (1975) has noted briefly that different phases in the life of the group are characterized by a differential propensity to laugh. In this context he cites a review paper by Tuckman (1965) in which it is proposed that the adult group develops through four stages, and these Tuckman labels 'testing-dependence', 'conflict', 'cohesion', and 'functional roles'. There is no equivalent developmental analysis of children's groups but our informal observations suggest that, as young as seven or eight years of age, children do sometimes use humour to test out the current status of their relationships and to assist the passage of the group from one stage to the next.

Empirical appraisals of humour in interpersonal encounters and in the mass media attest to there being a myriad of communicative functions served by humour both within and between small and large groups (cf. Gruner, 1976; Taylor, 1977; Zillmann, 1977). Turning briefly to large groups in the first instance, research is beginning to show that humour has wide implications for intergroup relations and intragroup interactions. These implications have been debated in reviews elsewhere, notably by Martineau (1972), Zillmann and Cantor (1976), and La Fave (1977).

Martineau concentrated on the sociological and anthropological literature, and observed that first and foremost humour operates as a social mechanism: sometimes it 'lubricates' interactions and sometimes it acts as an 'abrasive' to instigate or augment interpersonal friction. Based upon an argument that humour serves definite social functions, he proffered a theoretical model identifying the social impact of humour according to structural variations in social settings. Through providing typologies of situations in which humour is manifested, analyses such as Martineau's are of special value in giving emphasis to the complex and ubiquitous social character of humour.

Common experience suggests that instances of humour can simultaneously serve a number of functions for the individual and these can differ according to the social context; jokes and other forms of humour may have multiple and variegated effects on their initiators, targets, and bystander recipients. A joke which appears innocuous to an outsider may perhaps increase morale and consolidate one particular group whilst sustaining or intensifying hostility towards another group; it may also encourage the reciprocation of aggression from that other group. The effects of humour on recipients must inevitably be mediated in part by the perceived motives, values, and intentions of the initiators (cf. Bourhis, Gadfield, Giles, and Tajfel, 1977; Husband, 1977), and the effects on initiators must in turn be mediated to some extent by the perceived reactions of the recipients (cf. Fry and Allen, 1975); however such complex interactive aspects of efficacy, appreciation, and enjoyment remain virtually unexplored for adults, let alone children.

One benefit which accrues from analyses of the depicted relationships between protagonists in humour is that attention is drawn to the multi-dimensional nature of affective dispositions harboured towards the disparaged agents. The work of Zillmann and his colleagues has been especially valuable in this respect. From retaliatory-equity principles, Zillmann and Cantor have advanced a disposition model of mirth which has broad predictive as well as explanatory power (Zillmann and Cantor, 1976). They have argued persuasively that all 'ethnic humour' findings known at the time of their writing were explicable within their model. The model has not passed unchallenged (cf. La Fave, 1977), but it is of interest to note that hypotheses derived from it have been firmly upheld in at least one subsequent experimental study of young children. In the United Kingdom (Wales), the present authors demonstrated in four-, five-, and six-year-olds that ethnic allegiances found expression through responsiveness to humour with English/Welsh butts (Chapman, Smith, and Foot, 1977). The results are consonant also with Martineau's sociological analysis: they render some support for his position that particular types of humour can help to sustain intergroup relations. However, it remains to be established at what period children begin to attain sufficient mastery over techniques of humour to enable them to foster any tangible growth in group differences and/or intragroup ethos. The indications from the experiment just mentioned are consistent with our informal observations, namely, that by six years of age, and perhaps before then, children are capable of generating increments and decrements in group esteem through regulating humour content and humour responses.

A critique by Kane, Suls, and Tedeschi (1977) is also fundamentally related to group processes but, in common with most other social psychological critiques of humour, it converges on the individual within the group rather than on the group itself. Also, it focuses on the causes and functions of humour initiation rather than on responses. In other words, it addresses questions about the circumstances under which various brands of humour are initiated and it attempts to expose why humour should be invoked at all. The authors note in passing that Martineau's analysis fails to explain why direct praise or criticism should not operate just as well as humour to further a group's aims and objectives. But it behoves us to interpose here that most of the so-called 'theories' associated with the humour and laughter literature are little more than statements of function or statements of properties; and comments akin to those of Kane *et al.* could, with equal entitlement, be levelled against most other models and theories.

Kane *et al.*'s own analysis is couched in terms of the social functions served for the source of humour. It overtly disregards the target or audience and it is therefore incomplete with respect to social interaction; however, the authors disclose that a comprehensive treatise is forthcoming. Whenever possible their preliminary critique is reinforced through objective data but, because of the dearth of empirical studies, it is inescapable that they should draw heavily upon anecdotal information and personal impressions. They summarize their proposals as follows:

> ... the source's use of humour serves as a rather safe way of self-disclosing taboo interests or values and to probe the values, intentions, and/or motives of others, is a decommitment tactic allowing the source to dissociate himself from responsibility for performing a prior action, is a face-saving device that helps preserve a person's identity after an embarrassing incident, is an unmasking tactic that reveals the hypocrisy and pretensions of persons, groups, institutions, and nations, provides a basis for forming positive and long-standing relationships with others, and allows for safe practice of ingratiation of powerful others. In each instance, laughter can be used to initiate a cognitive transformation of a situation into a non-serious one or it may indicate acceptance of the meanings conveyed by a source of humour ... (p. 16)

La Gaipa (1977) is also concerned with the social functions of humour for the individual, but his research strategy contrasts with that of Kane *et al.* and most others. Following Bateson (1953), La Gaipa's formal aim is first to identify observable, empirically-objective indicators of socially-functioning humour. In empirical research, he has begun to meet that aim: specifically, he has evidence that tempo of interaction is both a sensitive and a reliable index of responses to humour. He has found that whether humour facilitates or impairs the flow of conversation depends on such stimulus properties as kind of humour (e.g. 'cognitive wit' versus 'hostile wit') and target of humour.

Of all humour models currently available, the one most patently geared to social interaction is that of Giles and his associates (Giles, Bourhis, Gadfield, Davies, and Davies, 1976). It is a dynamic model and it was inspired by Rothbart's (1973, 1976) 'arousal-safety' model of children's laughter. Rothbart gave some consideration to those incongruous stimuli, such as masks (cf. Scarr and Salapatek, 1970), which have varying success in eliciting laughter, to the extent that they sometimes induce distress and crying. In like vein, Giles *et al.* have given consideration to the immediate cognitive and social repercussions for the individual of not comprehending or appreciating stimuli which a fellow interactant intended as funny; and, again like Rothbart, Giles *et al.* advocate an arousal formulation. Their model is, on the one hand, expansive and psychologically corporate in that it attempts to encompass not just the personal attributes and cognitions of the source of the humour and recipients, but the social factors impinging upon them too. On the other hand, the model confines itself to an individual-social level of analysis and to dyadic interchanges in which language is a prominent feature. Reflecting the authors' underlying socio-linguistic interests, the source and recipient of the humour are designated 'encoder' and 'decoder' respectively. Four major functions are then distinguished for the encoder of humour: to create and maintain in-group solidarity; to attack another individual, and thereby kindle feelings of superiority; to satisfy a need for approval by causing the decoder to laugh, and thereby dispose him/her to evaluate the encoder's character and viewpoints more favourably than otherwise; and to divert attention from actions, or to disguise actions, which might be evaluated unfavourably by the decoder.

Components of the social context of the interaction are envisaged by Giles *et al.* as playing crucial roles at various points in the humour process, particularly in decisions about how to encode the humour linguistically. The structure of humour is said to be dependent upon why humour is to be introduced and, related to that, how the encoder perceives the potential audience. The principal dimensions of variation in a 'humorous message' (e.g. a joke) are said by Giles *et al.* to be linguistic content, semantic-thematic content, and cognitive content. In discussing the decoding of humour, Giles *et al.* again pay special attention to sociolinguistic factors.

The models of Martineau, Kane *et al.*, and Giles *et al.* have yet to be subjected to empirical scrutiny. Consequently their merits and validity remain largely to be determined. Also, it should be borne in mind that all of the social psychological analyses reviewed in this section have been designed with adults in mind and pre-adolescents clearly lack the cognitive abilities required to appreciate a good proportion of adult humour. It is not merely that they lack vocabulary and linguistic expertise, but their level of moral reasoning, for instance, is inadequate for a full understanding of many jokes. Indeed, setting aside obvious content differences, the structural features of children's preferred jokes are known to change radically through childhood. Bryant and Meyer (1977), for example, have reported that the provocation-retaliation formula—which Zillmann (1977) testifies is common in adult humour—seldom features in the jokes of children aged between five and ten years. Then again, Zillmann states that in children's humour especially the consequences of brutal actions are highly tri-vialized:

Tom and Jerry, or all the other cartoon heroes and villains, can be cut up to slices, burned to death, or crushed to mush—in the next moment they will, of course, pop up alive and well . . . . Hostility, brutality, and cruelty, ultimately have no apparent ill-effects. (Zillmann, 1977, p. 299)

Since the time that Freud (1905) expressed the view that hostile wit can function as a valid and displaced form of attack, there has ensued a string of studies examining humour and aggression. Without exception, however, adults have served as subjects in these studies, and attempts to unravel relationships between aggression and humour appreciation have largely yielded inconclusive findings. One set of experiments purports to have shown that humour produces a purging, cathartic effect (e.g. Dworkin and Efran, 1967; Lamb, 1968); a second set has suggested the converse, namely, that hostile humour reinforces aggressiveness (e.g. Baron, 1978b; Berkowitz, 1970); a third set has been unsuccessful in attempting to unearth any relationship (e.g. Byrne, 1961); and then the work of Zillmann and colleagues points to the existence of factors other than provocation which have a major effect upon the enjoyment of aggressive humour (e.g. Zillmann, Bryant, and Cantor, 1974). There is, however, some consistency emerging from studies which have examined the effects of exposure to *non*-hostile humour on previously angered adults: such humour appears to attenuate aggression (Baron, 1978a; Baron and Ball, 1974; Landy and Mettee, 1969; Mueller and Donnerstein, 1977).

Although the materials and procedures giving rise to these findings call into question their generalizability to children, there is little reason to suppose that psychological mechanisms invoked by way of explanation should not also be apposite to adolescents and perhaps younger children. Studies showing a diminution of aggression have been interpreted as indicating that humour responses divert attention from annoyance and/or that they are incompatible with anger, while the increased aggression observed in other humour studies has been attributed to modelling and to the impact of aggressive cues.

Other specific functions of adult humour have been separately isolated in a diverse collection of small-group studies (e.g. Bradney, 1957; Coser, 1959, 1960; Goodrich, Henry, and Goodrich, 1954; Klapp, 1950; Miller, 1967; Radcliffe-Brown, 1940; Sykes, 1966; Zenner, 1970); and a series of studies by Goodchilds and Smith has focused upon antecedents of wittiness (Goodchilds, 1959, 1972; Goodchilds and Smith, 1964; Smith and Goodchilds, 1959, 1963). All these studies have analysed the causes and consequences of humour as it has eventuated in its various guises during social interactions. Such studies have not tended to regard groups as on-going entities. Instead, groups are usually regarded as *ad hoc* assemblies of people, and Fine (1977b) notes critically that this approach to research inevitably overlooks the history and cultures of groups: thus vital factors underlying the traditions of humour initiation and humour responsiveness pass unnoticed.

Further studies on adults have related humour appreciation to a host of additional variables which might be considered to be social psychological or to have social psychological connotations: for example, attitudes, dissonance, suggestibility, conformity, feelings of inadequacy, embarrassment, manifest anxiety, ethnocentrism, conservatism, authoritarianism, political affiliations, and socio-professional background. Generally speaking, such studies have involved verbal humour introduced outside the context of social interaction: typically, subjects have been invited to rate a short series of jokes or single-frame cartoons for funniness, and the subsequent ratings have been compared, for example, with scores derived from questionnaire responses. No equivalent studies on young children or adolescents have been published and, in any event, the value of such research with children is open to question. There is not in young children the requisite stability between key psychological factors to attract research along these lines: children's personalities, self-concepts and attitudes can undergo substantial change in short spaces of time, and their moods may fluctuate dramatically within the duration of their involvement in an experiment.

Thus far we have made no attempt to separate *humour* and *laughter* in this discussion, but of course they do sometimes occur one without the other (cf. Chapman and Foot, 1976). Accentuating that point, the analysis of La Gaipa (1977) concludes with a four-fold classification of models: laughter models that exclude humour; laughter models that include humour; humour models that exclude laughter; and humour models that include laughter. No modern-day psychologist has attempted to provide a comprehensive taxonomy of laughter-evoking stimuli but Giles and Oxford (1970), in discussing the causes and implications of laughter, maintained that there are at least six kinds of laughter, other than humorous laughter:

> *A priori*, it would appear that laughter principally occurs under seven mutually exclusive conditions, giving rise to the following forms of laughter: humorous, social, ignorance, anxiety, derision and apologetic laughters and the phenomenon of tickling. (p. 97)

Although social cues were viewed by Giles and Oxford as crucial in helping to generate many incidents of laughter, inherent in their account is the proposition that many instances of laughter materialize independently of social factors. We have come to believe that almost all instances of laughter are to some extent governed by interpersonal factors—social signals and processes associated with the psychological presence of others (cf. Chapman, Foot, and Smith, 1977). Our own empirical research, for example, has established that so-called 'humorous laughter' is to a large degree dependent upon companion variables (Chapman, 1976; Foot and Chapman, 1976), and in 'psychological presence' effects we include those which can arise when companions are not physically present (Chapman, 1974). In recent times, Giles *et al.* have revealed at least part agreement with our position as regards humorous laughter: 'The magnitude of . . . humorous laughter', they say, 'can be influenced by factors in the social situation . . .' (1976, p. 144).

Looking globally at the sparse adult literature on social aspects of humour and laughter, one is bound to conclude that psychologists have hardly begun to scratch the surface. Regarding connections between adults' interactions and their use of humour and laughter our knowledge has been advanced only slightly through psychological analyses. Research examining humour experiences as a function of interrelationships between verbal content and style of presentation is all but non-existent. Paralinguistic features of oral humour (e.g. timing and voice inflection) have been totally ignored, as have accompanying non-verbal behaviours. This is a lamentable state of affairs. The proverbial man-in-the-street can tell us that never is humour merely a matter of words. Considering the individual, a single joke no doubt varies in its perceived funniness according to his/her group membership, the surrounding company, the jokester, and other factors too. One can no more evaluate the potency of the 'group wit' by content-analysing a verbatim transcript of a conversation or meeting, than one can judge the popularity of a comedian by reading his scripts. Consider also the 'catch-phrases' of certain well-known television and radio comics: discharged on cue time and again, they always bring forth peals of laughter from studio audiences. Laughing at well-worn witticisms is surely in essence a social psychological phenomenon. It cannot be explained credibly in terms of instinct, superiority, incongruity, surprise or any of the other concepts upon which a plethora of theories is founded (cf. Keith-Spiegel, 1972)—traditional theories are uniform to the extent that at most they pay only lip-service to social facets of humour. In peroration, we restate our conviction that social psychologists with interests in adult interaction will need to become informed about the social dimensions of humour and laughter before they can achieve a sound understanding of everyday communications; and still more will humour researchers have to take account of those dimensions and embrace them within their models.

SOCIAL ASPECTS OF CHILDREN'S HUMOUR

In order to spotlight essential differences between humour and laughter in children and adults, let us take a moment to spell out some fundamental truisms, all of which have a special bearing on our subject. It would be rather too pedantic to enter into an exhaustive definition of 'childhood'; however, it is surely beyond dispute that, in comparison to adults, schoolchildren are less mature socially, emotionally, conatively and cognitively. Although we would not wish to imply that children may be regarded as 'partly-formed' adults (cf. Konner, 1972), it is obviously true to say that with time they become more adult-like in all aspects of their psychological make-up. With regard to humour and laughter in young school-children, it is particularly important to recognize that they lack certain skills and abilities which place severe constraints upon the potential of their verbal and non-verbal interactions. For example, they lack fluency and articulateness in speech, and they have only gross control over their interpersonal styles. Such factors, coupled with their general inexperience of life, render them ill-equipped to inject germane humour into social interaction as a deliberate ploy.

For many adults, on the other hand, humour is a crucial tool in their social armoury, conscripted for both defence and attack across a wide range of everyday encounters. Children can of course engage in various forms of comic activity but, without a firm command over verbal humour, they are disadvantaged in social exchanges. They cannot, for instance, readily precipitate an absorbing and pacifying digression; they cannot, without rebuke, defuse the threats of others by engendering a debilitative discomfort; and they cannot easily make light (or pretend to make light) of their own predicaments and misfortunes. All these factors seriously affect the nature and quality of same-age interactions, and their consequences are inevitably still greater for mixed-age and adult-child interactions.

The contrast between children and adults is stark when one contemplates interactions and relationships. Children's interactions with adults and with friends lack refinement relative to adult interactions (cf. Foot, Chapman, and Smith, 1978, 1980), and they are typically more spontaneous. Children's social relations rarely incorporate any subtle instrumental elements, and expediency appears to be alien to them. Their goals tend to be ephemeral but, when frustrated, it is primarily our acceptance of their social immaturity that sanctions the emission of their 'temperamental' behaviours—those behaviours which if displayed by adults would normally be found upsetting and would be judged socially inept or improper: for example, becoming 'shy' or acutely withdrawn, sulking, running away, stamping feet, shouting and screaming, or crying. Unable to use humour deftly as a manipulative tool, children regularly circumvent difficult social situations, or extricate themselves from them, by recourse to one or more of those less gracious and more unbecoming modes of behaviour.

In recent times, there have been extensive examinations of the phylogenetic and ontogenetic development of smiling, laughter, and humour (e.g. Fry, 1977; Lockard, Fahrenbruch, Smith, and Morgan, 1977; McGhee, 1977, 1979; Sroufe and Waters, 1976; van Hooff, 1972), and nowhere has it been postulated that humour develops from foot-stamping or temper tantrums! But we are suggesting that if young children, like most adults, had ready access to the power and finesse of humour then they would with greater comfort and success parry those stressful altercations which otherwise prompt their more extravagant and inelegant posturing. In this sense, then, such behaviours may be viewed as precursors of sophisticated forms of humour initiation and humorous laughter and smiling.

Throughout this section we are unspecific about ages and this is unavoidable because there is something approaching a void on age differences in the empirical data. It remains to be ascertained at what ages the various social functions identified in adult humour begin to be manifested in children's humour. However, in addition to those of our hypotheses reported in the next section, we have naturally formed a number of impressions, so far untested, about the social functioning of humour in young schoolchildren. Some of these impressions accord well with objective data from adults and therefore encourage us to treat the adult literature as a plausible medium for gaining insights and testable notions concerning the social development of humour in children. On the basis of our ten years of continuous research with children aged between four and nine, we are reasonably confident about the following observations: (a) by seven or eight years of age 'peck orders' have begun to emerge in children's use of humour in classroom groups—academic, physical, and sporting prowess largely determine hierarchies, and the functions of humour within children's 'peck orders' tend not to be dissimilar to those reported by Coser (1960) for the humour of psychiatric staff; (b) by seven years of age the classroom 'clown' or 'fool' has achieved popularity, but generally he is not taken to be viable as a group leader, either by teachers or by children, for tasks which matter to the children—this ties in with some work on adults by Goodchilds (1959) and Klapp (1950); (c) instances of humour and laughter in the classroom seem to be integral components of some children's coping strategies in ways similar to those documented for adults (Coser, 1959; Mechanic, 1962; Milgram, 1965); and (d) 'cognitive similarity' of group members as young as five years of age appears to be a significant determinant of the amount of laughter arising from a group—just as it has shown to be for university students (Wolosin, 1975).

Many regard tickling as a reliable stand-by for winning-over children and making them laugh, and it is disappointing then to find that only a handful of empirical studies have been published on the topic (Claxton, 1975; Justin, 1932; Leuba, 1941; Washburn, 1929; Weiskrantz, Elliott, and Darlington, 1971). No one, for example, has published developmental investigations outside the first year of life. Partly as a consequence perhaps, it seems to be widely held that tickling is a low-level activity, relying for affect almost solely on the strength of physical sensations (see Rickwood, 1978, for a review). Social and cognitive considerations have been relegated to the point of near banishment by psychologists and laymen alike. This seems to us quite unsatisfactory since the social significance of tickling appears, for example, to alter radically during late childhood. In time research may confirm our view by demonstrating, for instance, that in adolescents tickling has sexual overtones, whereas in the pre-adolescent child it is more of an hedonic endurance test. Regarding tickling as an acceptable form of task or challenge is peculiar to children. In some respects it is analogous to determining who can stare at the sun for longest (cf. Callois, 1961), but the desire to 'win' is not continuous in tickling: until the child is satiated, there is a vacillation between begging for the tickling to be terminated and pleading for it to commence again. Assuming that there are developmental changes in its social significance, tickling serves to illustrate that it is foolish to take for granted identity of systems of behaviour across ages (cf. Lewis, 1967). Sroufe and Waters (1976) have synthesized a substantial literature indicating that there are changes in the functions of laughter and smiling during infancy, and it would be unwise with older children to expect developmental invariance in the functions of the smile, or of the laugh, or of humour-related behaviours in general.

As mentioned in the previous section, Giles and Oxford (1970) maintained that in addition to humorous laughter there are at least six other kinds. Their analysis relates implicitly to adult behaviour and it omits reference to children. Yet everyday observations lead us to suspect that as one passes through childhood so the proportion of laughter episodes preceded by humour increases substantially. McGhee (1971) notes for children that although their laughter frequently signifies humour appreciation, it can sometimes be an expression of heightened pleasure experienced in the absence of humour. Pleasurable, non-humorous laughter has been highlighted in Sherman's (1975, 1977) ecological studies of pre-school children; he terms it 'gleeful laughter'. Such laughter is witnessed rarely in adults but Sherman finds it to be not uncommon in the free-play of nursery schoolchildren. Otherwise, there are few objective data throwing light upon which stimuli can trigger laughter in the absence of humour. Indeed, apart from investigations of laughter in clinical patients, virtually all studies of laughter report responses to *humour* stimuli. Moreover, in the great majority of cases, stimuli have been presented to adults by an experimenter—usually on slides or paper, and occasionally on audio- or visual-recordings.

Those few empirical studies of children, other than the present authors' in the next section, which have made pronouncements about social aspects of humour and laughter have by and large recorded laughter as it occurs during free-play and routine activities. Almost without exception they were observational studies completed about fifty years ago; characteristic of research on children's humour, the child subjects were six years of age or younger. The exceptions are four in number, two of which are cited in the following section: one is a paper by Prerost (1977) on crowding, and the other is by Leventhal and Mace (1970) on facilitation of expressive and evaluative responses. The other exceptions are Fine (1977b) and Ransohoff (1975). Through participant and non-participant observations, respectively, they have analysed the various types of humour occurring spontaneously in the interactions of nine- to twelve-year-old boys (Fine) and twelve- to fourteen-year-old girls (Ransohoff). The strengths and limitations of the techniques employed in these studies have been well documented by Fine (1977a) himself. In our view, however, the three principal weaknesses of their research are as follows: (a) it is not known to what extent the researcher's presence affects the data available; (b) the analyses are *post hoc*; and (c) it is not known to what degree the findings are specific to the small sample of children under scrutiny.

Gregg, Miller, and Linton (1929) took as the starting point for their pioneering studies the hypothesis that laughter is an indication of social awareness; and some of their data have been taken as supporting that all-embracing hypothesis. However, in this study and its contemporaries, the absence of control and the looseness of definitions could provide fuel for inexhaustible contention about the meaning of the conclusions, let alone their generality. No doubt both the lack of definitive data and the atheoretical nature of the studies contributed to the decline of interest in this area of research. Although the early studies have had minimal influence on present-day research they did constitute an unusually cohesive group to the extent that none disputed the vital role of the social situation in determining laughter. Indeed, most of them were unified in emphasizing the social nature of laughter: 'Laughing was found to be highly social' (Brackett, 1933, p. 125; Brackett, 1934, p. 89); children 'seldom laughed when with adults or alone' (Enders, 1927, p. 353); 'Out of the 223 situations in which laughter was noted, only 14 . . occurred when the child was alone' (Kenerdine, 1931, p. 229). Additionally, both Kenerdine (1931) and Bridges (1932) reported that the only evidence of humour appreciation in two-year-olds was that derived from incongruities and from the enjoyment of socially unaccepted situations. Then again, several of the studies from that early period noted that children's laughter is often associated with gross motor activity (e.g. Ding and Jersild, 1932; Enders, 1927; Gregg et al., 1929; Kenerdine, 1931; Wilson, 1931); but such activity invariably arose when children were playing together and hence this observation is almost certainly attributable to cognitive and social factors rather than to kinaesthesis per se. Several studies also included some preliminary accounts of individual differences (e.g. Washburn, 1929), including sex differences (e.g. Justin, 1932).

Until the nineteen-seventies, there were no traces of any resurgence of empirical interest in social aspects of children's humour and laughter. The first modern-day study was that of Leventhal and Mace (1970) mentioned above. However, there has been no revival of social-developmental studies, and there is still little or no objective evidence through which one may appraise Jacobson's (1947) thesis that laughter grows as a social response during childhood.

CHILDREN'S RESPONSIVENESS IN HUMOUR SITUATIONS

This section of the chapter is primarily directed towards overviewing a three-year research programme recently completed (see Acknowledgements, p. 173). The purpose of the research was to investigate experimentally the influence of the social environment upon children's responsiveness to one another in humour situations. It followed on theoretically and methodologically from experimental studies already reported (for reviews see Chapman, 1976, and Foot and Chapman, 1976). Our experiments have generally been framed in the context of social facilitation theory, social intimacy theory, and laughter theory; and the experiments have been conducted in schools using a mobile laboratory specially designed for observing children. The subjects have been drawn from a broad cross-section of lower- and middle-class home backgrounds, and their ages have ranged between four and nine years. Typically they have been video-taped in dyads or small groups while watching comedy cartoon films.

Previous research

Preliminary work leading up to the new research programme is summarized in Chapman (1976),

> . . . some of the important features of the companion's presence and responsiveness [are]: the amount of time he spends laughing; the amount he engages in humorous smiling; the amount he looks at the subject's face; whether he is an 'audience' and therefore unable to hear the [aurally presented] humour, or whether he listens to humour (though it does not matter whether it is the same humour); how close he sits to the subject; his seating orientation relative to that of the subject; and whether or not he encroaches upon the subject's psychological body space while laughing. The mere addition of a second companion is not sufficient to enhance laughter and smiling, but the degree to which two companions look at one another can be an important determinant of responsiveness to humour. (p. 181)

Additionally, it has been found that 'a two-year age/status difference between seven-year-old subjects and nine-year-old confederates has no effect on laughter and smiling, and that knowledge of (being viewed through) a one-way screen suppresses laughter severely whilst augmenting smiling and eye-contact' (p. 181). Taken together these studies have led us to infer that laughter serves as a 'safety valve' and that it helps diminish various forms of motivational arousal:

> . . . 'social arousal', which is built up through the psychological presence of others and through social signals and a variety of interpersonal factors, can reach uncomfortable proportions during everyday encounters. However, the injection of humour into interactions invariably prompts laughter and this permits the withdrawal of attention from the companion; the momentary reduction of the companion's presence in the subject's psychological environment alleviates social arousal. (p. 182)

Without doubt there are other functions of laughter superimposed upon that just mentioned: for example, laughter often conveys information and it can serve to attract attention. Various aspects of a companion's presence and behaviour have been highlighted in accounting for social increments in humorous laughter:

> Some of the behavioural effects are explicable in terms of the sharing of social situations and the companion's variable psychological presence; other effects are explicable in terms of reflexive, disinhibitory, motivational and perceptual models of social facilitation; and other effects may be the result of social conformity and social desirability processes. (p. 181)

Sex differences

We have only recently begun to observe boys and girls in mixed-sex groups (Foot, Chapman, and Smith, 1977; Foot, Smith, and Chapman, 1977, 1978). Most of our studies have investigated sex as a separate factor, but within same-sex dyads. This is because research by us and by others had hinted at interesting sex differences in laughter and smiling within same-sex groups. While results are not unequivocal (see Chapter 7), our own research (since Chapman, 1975b) has repeatedly suggested that boys are more responsive than girls to humour stimuli while girls are more responsive to companions. In the studies incorporating mixed-sex as well as same-sex pairs, we have found that girls prefer higher levels of social intimacy than boys (e.g. Foot, Chapman, and Smith, 1977) and that they are more affected by the sex of their companion than boys are (e.g. Foot and Chapman, 1976). Nevertheless, boys—like girls—are more responsive to humour when with a companion of their own sex (e.g. Foot, Smith, and Chapman, 1978). These conclusions are based upon various gross and molecular indices of humour and social responsiveness, including measures of laughter, smiling, looking behaviour, proximity, talking, and touching. Generally boys have tended to laugh more and to smile less than girls, but these trends have often failed to reach two-tailed statistical significance and on rare occasions they have even been reversed.

Although sex differences in children's laughter and smiling have emerged with some regularity, we have not been able to replicate the major finding of Leventhal and his colleagues (e.g. Leventhal and Cupchik, 1975; Leventhal and Mace, 1970). They have reported that for females—children and adults—there is a direct relationship between funniness ratings and expressive responses (i.e. laughter and smiling), whereas in males the two measures are rather more independent. Results along these lines have been interpreted as indicating that there is a sex difference underlying the way information is processed: it is assumed that 'the judgments of cartoons made by female subjects are based upon a subjective, emotional feeling, while the judgments made by male subjects are based upon the perceived properties of the external stimulus' (Leventhal and Cupchik, 1975, p. 364). However, only one child study (viz Leventhal and Mace, 1970) has produced sex differences consonant with that view and not one of our own' attempts to supplement the supportive evidence has met with success. In other words, in our research the subjective ratings of funniness from boys have been as closely matched to their expressive responses as they have been for girls. So consistent has this been that it obviates the need to refer to ratings in this chapter.

General methodology

Our mobile laboratory has been fully described elsewhere (e.g. Foot and Chapman, 1976). Essentially, it is an extremely comfortable and pleasant children's playroom with an adjoining room housing the experimenters and the recording equipment. The video apparatus includes several concealed microphones (with mixer unit) and cameras; two of the cameras have silicon tubes for filming at low levels of illumination as children watch cartoons. Amongst items of equipment in the experimenters' room are four monitors plus a video mixer and effects unit (used for 'split-screen' filming). Independent of the recording apparatus, a colour video-cassette-recorder is installed for presenting cartoons and other material; the associated 'television set' is the single piece of electronics visible in the playroom.

The cartoon films have included *Tom and Jerry, Bugs Bunny, Deputy Dawg*, and *Dastardly and Mutley*. Some studies have involved the use of non-cartoon comedy (e.g. *Charlie Chaplin*), non-humorous control films, single-frame cartoons, and aural comedy material. As far as we can tell, no child has ever been aware that s/he was being observed; and, similarly, we have no reason to suspect that any child has known of our interest in humour and laughter. Children who asked about the purpose of their involvement were informed that we were interested in finding out what kinds of films children most liked. This justification always proved entirely adequate and it usually elicited spontaneous and useful verbal information about their reactions to the humour material; nevertheless, subjective reports are not discussed in this chapter.

Through this sophisticated laboratory arrangement, recordings were obtained of laughter and smiling as they occurred naturalistically during social interaction and humour presentation. The video-tapes were always transcribed at the completion of individual studies. We worked simultaneously on an event-recorder system, each of us accepting separate responsibility for extracting two or three dependent measures; whenever feasible we operated without knowledge as to which experimental condition the observed children were assigned. Hence frequencies and cumulative durations of a number of behaviours were obtained (from counters), plus information about the temporal patterning of these behaviours (from chart paper); also, a selection of combined measures was derived, such as mutual laughter and laughing while looking at a companion. However, for our purposes here, we can largely confine our remarks to duration measures of 'laughter' (operationally defined as reiterated *ha ha* sounds) and 'smiling' (upward stretching of the mouth without vocal sound); sometimes we refer to 'looking' (at the companion's face) and/or to 'eye-contact' (mutual looking in the region of the eyes). The experiments were usually multi-factorial in their designs, and data were subjected to conventional statistical analyses. Within the constraints of the experimental designs and subject availability, boys and girls were selected on the basis of age alone, and they were randomly allocated to treatment conditions such that there were usually five boys and five girls in each condition. From the same population of children additional boys and girls were recruited to serve as companions.

It is safe to say that after children had once spent a few minutes in the laboratory they eagerly awaited further visits. It was our policy to refrain from any formal testing in schools until the children were well acquainted with the experimenter(s) and with the laboratory. They became familiar with the principal experimenter (JRS) and with the laboratory through several 'warm-up' visits prior to the start of the experiments: as a consequence, no child ever displayed any noticeable apprehension. Once in the playroom for a test session, it was usually the case that children sat on chairs facing the screen and, after a few moments of casual conversation, the experimenter would leave so that they watched the film on their own. Most sessions were of about six minutes' duration.

Theoretical bases in brief

Social facilitation theory Research on social facilitation processes has been dogged by the mere-presence/evaluation-apprehension controversy: Zajonc (1965) has suggested that the mere presence of a companion is sufficient to arouse drive and hence facilitate the emission of dominant responses and impair the emission of non-dominant responses; others have argued that these effects are not brought about by presence as such but by evaluation apprehension (cf. Chapman, 1973, 1974; Geen and Gange, 1977). Virtually no research has satisfactorily isolated the contaminating influence of evaluation apprehension (cf. Weaver, 1978). The study of mirth, however, provides an ideal vehicle for minimizing evaluation apprehension effects. Expressive behaviours like laughter and smiling are normally spontaneous and, given a naturalistic, familiar environment, it is unlikely that such behaviours are subject either to apprehension or experimenter effects—particularly when, as in our research, the task situation is totally undemanding.

Laughter theory The merits of studying social processes through laughter stem not only from early research evidence that laughter is enhanced by the presence of others, but also from its status as an almost entirely social and sociable behaviour: it cannot be over-emphasized that laughter rarely occurs except in the company of others. Facilitative effects appear to be much more closely associated with the sharing of a social situation than with the sharing of humour *per se* (Chapman, 1975b). More important still, from a theoretical standpoint, work by Berlyne (1969), Chapman (1976) and Rothbart (1973, 1976) has established laughter not merely as a malleable facilitative response but also as a functional behaviour which serves to relieve tension in a wide range of situations, whether or not humour is an intrinsic aspect of those situations. Berlyne saw laughter as completing an arousal-relief sequence when the punchline to a joke suddenly dissipates the build-up of tension associated with an unfulfilled expectation. As outlined above, we see it in more general terms as operating as a safety-valve against excessive social arousal. Some psychophysiological evidence supports the view that laughter is contingent upon changes in arousal (cf. Chapman, 1976).

Social intimacy theory In addition to its arousal-relief function, laughter is a non-verbal behaviour reflecting in part the intimacy of an interaction. Chapman (1975a), for example, found that laughter tends to covary with other intimacy behaviours such as smiling, eye-contact, and proximity. These results provided evidence in opposition to the underlying assumption of Argyle and Dean's (1965) model: theirs is an equilibrium model founded upon the assumption that there is a static level of intimacy for any given social encounter such that an increase in intimacy behaviour by one interactant is compensated by a decrease in intimacy behaviour(s) by the other. There appears to be no obvious justification for the view that the level of intimacy remains unvarying; and, during the course of our research programme, Patterson (1976) published an arousal model to account for the discrepancies existing between the various studies which had tested the equilibrium model. Patterson proposed that in a two-person interaction, sufficient changes in the intimacy behaviours of one person (A) produce arousal changes in the other person (B). The arousal changes in (B) can be of negative or positive emotional value depending, for example, upon the nature of the interaction. A negative change generates compensatory responses which reduce intimacy to its previous level; a positive change generates reciprocated, matching responses and these lead to a new level of intimacy acceptable to both (A) and (B).

Social facilitation of children's reactions to humour

Experimenter versus child companion and some demand characteristics in humour research Our research suggests that a problem confronting all who investigate children's humour concerns the demand characteristics of their research, particularly demand characteristics associated with their own presence in the testing environment. Their presence *per se* and their activities can dramatically confound the children's evaluations of humour, as well as their behavioural reactions to it and their overall experience of it. Unfortunately, the effects arising during the course of any one study are difficult to control and they are not easy to assess.

We found that two researchers, when watching a cartoon with pairs of seven-year-olds, were unable to achieve a satisfactory standard of uniformity with respect to their modes of interaction and 'mirth' behaviours (Foot and Chapman, 1976). They were of course thoroughly briefed and practised; they had access to video-feedback between sessions; and they were highly experienced at communicating with children. Yet the tendency of one experimenter over twenty test sessions was to enhance the children's responsiveness (especially smiling), while the other inhibited responsiveness (especially laughter). Moreover, informal observation suggested that they varied their own interactive styles across sessions: there were signs that they were influenced by prior interactions with children and by the latter's humour responsiveness and attentiveness during sessions. However presumably, if they had not been socially perceptive and sensitive in these ways, and if this had not been revealed in their behaviours, both of them would have exerted powerful inhibitory influences.

There can be no doubt, then, that the amount anyone engages in humorous laughter is a complex function of a variety of factors. Naturally, the quality of the humour is one of those factors (multi-dimensional in nature), but our research demonstrates that it is often the social factors which are dominant, rather than the humour itself (Chapman, Foot, and Smith, 1977). As indicated earlier, we know that responsiveness to humour can be greatly reduced if a child is aware that it is possible to see him/her through a one-way viewing screen (Chapman, 1976). In humour research generally, therefore, demand characteristics would appear to be potentially acute and problematic. In particular, it is more than likely that awareness of being observed, the presence of the researcher, and the behaviour of the researcher have all produced major artifacts in results.

It has intrigued us to find for children that, with another child as companion, laughter and smiling are augmented even when that companion reacts blankly to the humour and ignores the subject's presence (e.g. Chapman and Wright, 1976): this is a vivid testimony to the social facilitation of laughter. In adults, on the other hand, detrimental effects can be extremely pronounced when companions are unresponsive (Osborne and Chapman, 1977). One explanation for this might be that, as individuals, we become socially more skilled during adolescence and we learn, for instance, to modulate responses when those of our companions do not accord with our own. This explanation may hold intuitive appeal but its validity is called into question by the study just mentioned (Foot and Chapman, 1976) in which social-inhibition effects were induced by one of the experimenters. It is also called into question by objective data not before reported. Two new experiments offer tentative evidence that, when the companion is an adult (Experimenter), the responses of a child are suppressed—as for an adult subject—whenever that companion is dour or simply straightfaced.

In one experiment, independent groups of seven-year-old boys ($n = 19$) and girls ($n = 15$) were observed watching a cartoon (a) alone, (b) with an unresponsive experimenter, or (c) with an experimenter who laughed for about one second on ten separate occasions. No significant differences emerged for laughter or smiling across conditions, largely due to there being very low response levels in all conditions. However, not one child laughed on the occasion that s/he was with the unresponsive experimenter.

A follow-up study embodied some substantial modifications. A repeated measures, 5×2 design was adopted, the two factors again being social conditions and sex. After the customary warm-up sessions, the boys ($n = 10$) and girls ($n = 10$), aged eight-and-a-half to nine-and-a-half years, visited the laboratory on five occasions, so that all twenty subjects were tested in each of the five social conditions. They watched *Tom and Jerry* films lasting approximately six minutes: order of films and order of conditions were counterbalanced across subjects. The five social conditions are apparent from Table 6.1. Subjects were tested individually with a further twenty boys and twenty girls serving as same-sex companions in two conditions.

This time there was a significant social-conditions effect on laughter and smiling and, in numerical terms, there was, overall, less laughter and smiling in the condition where the experimenter was present but unresponsive: statistically, the trend for smiling was highly significant while the trend for laughter was close to being significant (two-tailed $p < 0.08$). This study provided some evidence, therefore, that children's responses to humour, like adults', can be both facilitated and reduced by an adult's presence. We are confident that the adult experimenter could have induced almost total suppression of overt mirth if s/he had responded negatively to the films, rather than just impassively.

Taking into account all available data, it is evident that the age/status of a companion can be a major determinant of laughter. As far as children are concerned, companions of approximately their own age invariably facilitate humour responsiveness, but an adult companion (at least, an Experimenter) can readily facilitate or inhibit responses by fairly subtle changes in his/her non-verbal behaviours.

Facilitation of humorous laughter as a function of age and group size As suggested by inspection of Table 6.1, children laughed significantly more when in the triadic condition than when in a dyad or alone. Previous

Table 6.1 Mean laughter and smiling scores in seconds

		Alone	With responsive experimenter	With unresponsive experimenter	With same-sex companion	With same-sex companion and responsive experimenter
				SOCIAL CONDITIONS		
Laughter	Boys	3.3	3.4	1.2	5.9	9.5
	Girls	1.5	13.3	2.5	12.9	16.4
Smiling	Boys	82.0	224.3	72.7	69.6	221.8
	Girls	66.7	215.3	45.6	55.2	154.9

comparisons between levels of responses in dyads and triads had not yielded any corresponding group-size differences (e.g. Chapman, 1975b). However, in another study, children who watched films in groups of just over fifty were found to laugh considerably more than children in dyads (Smith, Chapman, and Foot, 1975). Seven large groups corresponded to different years (grades) in a primary school, with five-year-olds as the youngest and eleven-year-olds as the eldest. All groups were shown a twenty-five minute sequence of *Tom and Jerry* and *Charlie Chaplin* films, and the 'film-shows' were presented in one of the school's classrooms.

The statistics available to test for age effects were severely restricted: this was due to the limited number of large groups which could be formed from the one school population (i.e. seven in total). Visual scrutiny of scores derived from the video-tapes and the sound spectrographs indicated that there were no gross differences between the age groups in overall durations of laughter, but there were clear age differences with respect to the comic incidents evoking most laughter. Additionally, comparing this study with others, it was noticeable that of the passages which did evoke loud and vigorous laughter across all the large groups, many tended to be received with relatively little enthusiasm by children in small groups. Indeed, even the opening credits/music for the *Tom and Jerry* films—which were well-known to most of the children—always elicited laughter (and applause!) from children in large groups, whereas they have rarely, if ever, elicited laughter from members of dyads.

Another major difference between small and large groups of children appears to be that, with repeated presentation, humour becomes stale and unfunny to small groups but, by contrast, it becomes more enjoyable to large groups. Our preliminary research has demonstrated unambiguously that successive presentations of humour recordings to children in small groups or alone produces a sharp decline in laughter and smiling. Then, in a subsequent study, no 'warm-up' effects were found in pairs of children when two different *Tom and Jerry* films were projected in quick succession (Foot and Chapman, 1976). On the other hand, warm-up effects were abundantly clear in the large groups of over fifty; although, in that study, the order of films was not counterbalanced.

Warm-up effects in large groups were also evident in another of the recent studies. On three occasions during the course of a single morning, a class of thirty-four nine-year-olds was video-recorded while watching a twenty-minute set of three cartoons (*Tom and Jerry, Deputy Dawg*, and *Asterix the Gaul*): at the beginning of the morning the children had been shown a fourth ('familiarization') film. Through the usual procedures various measures were subsequently extracted from video-tapes for individual children. Unfortunately, the laughter data were not considered to be reliable and they were not analysed statistically. The problem was essentially one of transcriptional difficulties (i.e. in attributing laughter sounds to individuals) but, in any case, visual insepction of the scores which were obtained suggested no gross differences across films. On successive showings, children increasingly glanced away from the screen and they talked progressively more. Nevertheless, at the final showing of the three films the children, on average, were looking at the screen approximately ninety-five per cent of the time. Unfortunately, the video-recordings did not permit an accurate matching of responses to humour stimuli; but our impression was that, on successive occasions, the children detected fresh aspects of the films which were intended as funny and which had previously escaped their attention. At the same time, the most slapstick of incidents were eagerly awaited and many prompted mirth when they did arrive: evidently it was these stimuli which were the prime vehicle for the growth in social facilitation. In fact, there was less laughter than we had originally expected: this we attributed to the children being in their own classroom and to the consequent low social density (cf. Prerost, 1977). Although the study was not sophisticated methodologically, there can be little doubt that the significant increases in smiling and in attentiveness to companions observed through the morning's films were attributable to increased enjoyment of the humour.

Largely because of practical necessity, the subsequent research was confined to detailed studies of small groups. In a preliminary fashion two experiments examined age effects and a third examined size of small group: they were run in separate schools. The first two compared children in their final year in infants school (aged six, approximately) and children in their first year at the adjoining junior school (aged seven, approximately). The experiments differed in ways which are not of direct consequence here: *viz* one incorporated mixed-sex as well as same-sex pairings, and it also required subjects to involve themselves in a drawing exercise immediately prior to the film (in these respects it was a precursor to Foot, Chapman, and Smith, 1977). Most subjects were observed in dyads (thirty-six of each sex in one experiment; twenty-four girls and twenty-two boys in the other experiment), but some children were observed in alone conditions ($n = 24$ and 9) to provide the baseline scores against which to gauge facilitation effects. The stimulus material was the same in both experiments—a *Tom and Jerry* film. As in all previous social facilitation studies the differences in both laughter and smiling scores from children in dyads and children alone were highly significant. However, of much greater interest was that, in both experiments, the junior schoolchildren laughed significantly more than their younger counterparts. A trend for smiling was non-significant in the first experiment and highly significant in the second: again the older children were the more expressive. There were no corresponding age differences for solitary subjects, and the experiments thus point to a developmental trend in social facilitation processes: the older subjects were more affected by the presence of a companion.

The experiment on group size was of an independent groups, 5×2 design. Girls ($n = 72$) and boys ($n = 78$), aged between eight years and nine-and-a-half years, were allocated randomly to same-sex groupings of two, four, and six children. Statistical calculations were based on just one child from each group, and these 'subject-children' were defined beforehand on the basis of seating positions. This process yielded cell numbers of at least six in each sex/group-size condition, and all children watched a *Dastardly and Mutley* cartoon. As expected, subjects in groups of four laughed significantly more than those in dyads, and subjects both in the groups of six and the groups of four smiled more than did those in dyads. There were also trends which ran contrary to expectations, but they were non-significant. Boys in groups of six tended to be *less* responsive, in both laughter and smiling, than boys in groups of four. Girls likewise tended to laugh more in the four-person groups but, consistent with expectations, they did smile significantly more in the six-person than in the four-person group.

Above all, this part of the research programme has continually impressed upon us the immensely complex social nature of humour responsiveness. The experimental and observational approaches have helped us both to disentangle various key variables and to appreciate how they interact. Some of the studies have reinforced evidence, already strong, that the most striking facilitation effects arise when a solitary child is given a partner. However, although the addition of a companion-child invariably enhances laughter and smiling enormously,we have seen that the same is not necessarily the case if the child's companion is an adult: hence attention is drawn to cognitive factors associated with the construing of the companion's presence and behaviour. But, as yet, subjective reports and ratings relating to the factors remain to be analysed in detail. Also, there is a strong suggestion that, as far as humorous laughter is concerned, susceptibility to social influences may develop with age: certainly enhancement effects were stronger in junior school seven-year-olds than in six-year-old infant schoolchildren. This is one reason why we have tended to concentrate on the slightly older children.

Increasing group size (of junior schoolchildren) from two to four promoted higher levels of responsiveness; but there were no additional increases when two more companions were added. However, in large groups—groups the size of teaching-classes and larger—facilitation effects were much greater than any previously recorded. They were also somewhat different in character, and it appears that members of small and large groups sometimes enjoy different humorous incidents within the same film. Also, with (three) successive presentations of the same humour stimuli, laughter and smiling increased in large groups, while in dyads a rapid diminution has been observed under similar circumstances. It seems that in large groups some events which are found funny first time round are appreciated more on the second and third occasions, while other incidents remain unnoticed initially or are not thought funny until presentation is repeated.

Social intimacy, friendship, and sex differences in laughter and smiling

Our research on sharing and social intimacy has emanated in part from a demonstration by Chapman (1975b) that rather than sharing humour, it is the sharing of the social situation *per se* which is important in the facilitation of children's laughter. Chapman's study required pairs of confederates to laugh, to smile, and to engage in patterns of gaze in a pre-determined manner. The follow-up research did not employ confederates, and it was generally more naturalistic. Two experiments were concerned with the effects of the exclusion of one child from an otherwise shared situation in which two other children watched a cartoon (*Tom and Jerry*). The basic aim was thus to investigate humour responsiveness in a triad where two shared a common pleasurable activity which a third was denied.

The first of the two experiments involved children, aged seven to eight years, who were known (from four prior visits to the laboratory) to be relatively responsive to humour. Boys ($n = 70$) and girls ($n = 70$) were assigned in equal numbers, but otherwise at random, to one of five treatment groups. The 'shared' task consisted of watching a *Tom and Jerry* cartoon. The 'exclusion' task involved a piece of reaction-time apparatus, and the subject was required to press a button every time a light went on. The light occurred randomly, within a ten-second period, and it remained on until the subject responded. The apparatus was located in a far corner of the children's playroom, behind and to one side of the viewing screen, enabling all subjects to see each other, but making it impossible for the excluded child to see the screen. The treatment groups were as follows. *Condition A* Same-sex triad—the two children performing the shared task were drawn from the same class; the child performing the exclusion task was from a different class. *Condition B* Mixed-sex triad—the children were similarly drawn from the same or different classes; triads consisted of either two boys sharing and one girl excluded, or two girls sharing and one boy excluded. *Control Condition 1* Same-sex dyad—two children from the same class performed the shared task; there was no excluded child. *Control Condition 2* Solitary 'exclusion'—a single child (boy or girl) performed the exclusion task, while the film was projected without an audience. *Control Condition 3* Solitary 'sharing'—a single child (boy or girl) performed the shared task, with no child performing the exclusion task. The triads and dyads were not comprised of friends, and the children were all given a short questionnaire after the test session. The excluded children were shown the film on later occasions.

The main sources of interest in the data were the differences in responsiveness of the subjects engaged upon the shared task, by virtue of the presence of the excluded child, and the effect upon the excluded child of two companions engaged upon a shared task. Various significant differences were obtained from the data, some of which were as follows: children performing the shared task laughed more when an excluded child was present than when s/he was absent;

excluded girls were more responsive with respect to smiling than excluded boys, both in mixed-sex triads and in same-sex triads; and the excluded girls from mixed-sex triads tended also to be more responsive when watching the film immediately after the test session with companions.

The second experiment embodied a partial replication of the first, and it was designed particularly to follow-up the sex differences. To this end, attention was given to the prior bond existing between the children watching the film, and hence to the relative exclusion of the third child. Thus *friendship* was introduced as an independent variable. A great deal of thought was given to the operational definition of friendship and to how friendship pairs should be determined for research purposes (cf. Chapman, Smith, Foot, and Pritchard, 1979; Foot, Smith, and Chapman, 1979). In this instance, friendship pairs (ten pairs of boys and ten pairs of girls) were based upon sociometric choices. Using a repeated measures design, each child was tested on two separate occasions, once with a third mutual same-sex friend (from the same class), and once with a same-sex non-friend (from a different class). On each occasion the friendship pair (performing the shared task) saw a different cartoon film; order of testing and order of film presentation were counterbalanced. The third, excluded subject performed the same reaction-time task as in the first of the two experiments.

A number of statistically significant effects were obtained, of which the most striking were those bearing on sex differences. Girls displayed more interest in the excluded companions and were generally more responsive when those companions were non-friends: that is, they then laughed and smiled more and they looked more at the excluded child. With boys, the pattern of results for laughter and for smiling was reversed: they were more responsive with friends. For both sexes, the level of responsiveness was reciproacted by the excluded child, whether a friend or non-friend. However, pairs of girls tended to be just as attentive and responsive with an excluded friend as were boys. The major sex difference that arose, therefore, was with respect to reactions to excluded *non*-friends: relative to their responsiveness with an excluded friend, girls' responsiveness was higher while boys' was lower. Trends were consistent for measures, and two-tailed statistical interactions (sex of triad *versus* friend/non-friend as exluded child) were highly significant for smiling and looking at excluded child; the corresponding laughter interaction was not significant ($p < 0.10$). Consistent with previous results, it was found that girls engaged in considerably more looking at their companions than did boys; but an unusual trend (non-significant) was that girls tended to laugh more than boys.

A parsimonious interpretation of the sex differences arising from these two experiments is one which has been proposed in the context of the previous research and to which brief reference was made earlier. When humour is presented to a small group, boys tend to concentrate more on the humour itself than girls do, while girls tend instead to concentrate more on the social interaction and sharing of the social situation. Two earlier experiments on children of the same age (i.e. seven-and eight-year-olds) had given support to the related notion that girls normally prefer higher levels of social intimacy than boys do (Foot, Chapman, and Smith, 1977). In the first of these experiments, the effects of intimacy were examined through contrasting the interactions of friends (high intimacy) and strangers (low intimacy) in same-sex and mixed-sex pairs. In the other experiment, intimacy was manipulated by having same-sex pairs of children either draw one another (high intimacy) or colour pictures while sitting out of sight of one another (low intimacy): the paper-and-pencil tasks were of five minutes' duration, and immediately afterwards subjects sat together to watch a *Tom and Jerry* cartoon. When intimacy was low at the start of the cartoon it seemed that girls used laughter and smiling to gain and maintain the attention of companions.

> . . . it is our view that laughter reflects tension within the individual. However, the context in which the laughter occurs is important. The inference is that the high-intimacy condition is experienced as relatively too intimate for the comfort of boys, and the low-intimacy condition is not sufficiently intimate for girls. If this is so, then laughter may be bifunctional in its arousal-reducing properties: It serves to gain or maintain the companion's attention in situations that are experienced as too low in intimacy and to break attention in situations that are experienced as too high in intimacy. These can both be regarded as restorative functions designed to reestablish the preferred level of intimacy. In relation to laughter's attention-avoiding function, . . . laughing (allows withdrawal of attention) from the partner and hence (permits the reduction of) his or her psychological presence at times when the level of social arousal is uncomfortably high. These two functions of laughter may not be qualitatively differentiated, but our informal observations lead us to speculate that the accompanying behaviors may be crucial: Laughter may be accompanied by upraised head and averted gaze aimed at breaking contact momentarily with the partner, or it may be accompanied by direct looking at the companion. (Foot, Chapman, and Smith, 1977, p. 409)

In the second of the experiments examining the effects of an excluded child, the pairs of girls appeared to make a greater effort to share the social situation with the excluded child when that child was a non-friend. If they had not done so, the prevailing low level of intimacy, according to the above view, would have caused them to feel uncomfortable. Their laughter may thus have operated as a psychological tool in the cause of promoting intimacy. Boys, on the other hand, seemed content to experience a relatively low level of intimacy, perhaps in the interest of enjoying humour to the full: low intimacy concomitant with a non-friend usually implied that there was less to distract them from watching the film.

The fact that, in the latter part of this account, *friendship* has been mentioned on several occasions is an indication that it became a major focus of our humour research. Three experiments have been outlined above and others are detailed elsewhere (e.g. Foot, Smith, and Chapman, 1977, 1979; Foot, Chapman, and Smith, 1980; Smith, Foot, and Chapman, 1977a). The common underlying objective has been to help delineate the various social functions of humour, laughter, and smiling by examining their occurrence under different levels of intimacy. Together they provide strong support for Patterson's (1976) arousal model which was sketched out earlier. It would appear that through laughter and smiling the children can produce major changes in intimacy; but level of intimacy also affects humour responsiveness—the one feeds on the other. Additional experiments in this phase have confirmed the complex interrelationships between intimacy and humour responsiveness. For example: 'At low levels of intimacy, increments have very little effect upon responsiveness, but at high levels of intimacy a slight increase (e.g., through adopting a more intimate front-on seating orientation) can have a marked boosting effect until a ceiling is attained for laughter and smiling' (Smith, Foot, and Chapman, 1977a, p. 420).

We have argued that laughter—while promoting a gradual growth in interpersonal intimacy—can reflect the individual's degree of tension or unpleasant social arousal. Smiling, on the other hand, usually seems to be indicative of the congeniality or 'felt comfort' of the social/humour situation (cf. Foot, Chapman, and Smith, 1977). Of course 'comfort' and 'tension' are closely related concepts and it would be unrealistic to expect sharp distinctions in the functioning of laughter and smiling. Often, for example, smiling may substitute for laughter, particularly as a low-level or reserved form of mirth response: one gross effect of companionship is to convert or boost 'humorous smiles' into laughs (Chapman, 1976). However, except in solitary children, it was observed that laughter and smiling behaviour frequently seemed detached from the comic incidents in cartoons—to such an extent that it was difficult to envisage that there could be any causal connection. From previous comments, it is evident that this observation applied particularly to girls since it was their behaviour which had the appearance of being the more sociable.

In line with these and previous observations, sex differences in measures of laughter and smiling were predicted in an experiment where an eight-minute *non*-humour film (*African Animal Hunt*) was presented to seven- and eight-year-olds. Members of girl dyads ($n = 30$) were found to smile more than members of boy dyads ($n = 30$), and this is consistent with the view that girls' smiling typically has a larger 'sociable' component than boys' and a smaller 'mirth' component: in fact, boys smiled less than half as much as girls and this clearly indicates that, in the humour experiments (in which the sex difference is invariably of a smaller magnitude), a greater proportion of the boys' smiling was elicited by the humour itself. As also expected, girls engaged in more looking at the companion and more smiling while looking; but a corresponding trend for laughter was non-significant. Not surprisingly levels of laughter were low in all test sessions.

The investigation of sex differences in functions of laughter and smiling has also been approached through the use of *discrete* humour stimuli. One experiment examined the facilitative influences of a friend/non-friend of the same/opposite sex. Pairs of boys ($n = 30$) and girls ($n = 30$), aged seven and eight years, were presented with a series of thirty-eight single-frame cartoon slides. Each slide was illustrated by a play-on-words or riddle spoken by the experimenter through a microphone from the adjoining room (e.g. *Question:* How do you know the ocean is friendly? *Answer* [with slide]: Because it waves!). A 2 × 3 factorial design was employed with friendship (friends/non-friends) and sex (boy–boy, girl–girl, boy–girl) as the independent variables. Mirth scores were derived from video-tapes on a five-point scale by three independent judges: they scored the maximum level of response occurring between stimuli.

The results for friendship conformed to predictions and were unequivocal. There was not one of the thirty-eight jokes in which the non-friend subjects obtained a higher average mirth score than did friend subjects. Sex differences were also marked. Boys responded with considerably more mirth, and there were large differences in the responsiveness of boys and girls according to the sex of their companion. For not one joke did boys with a girl companion exceed the mean level of mirth achieved by boys with a boy companion. For girls, on the other hand, the sex of the companion appears to have been relatively immaterial. Sex differences also emerged after the slide series when children were encouraged to tell jokes to the experimenter (until they had exhausted their supply). This was regarded as a pilot exercise and the prior session would clearly have had a contaminating influence on the children's joke-telling. Nevertheless, the data pointed to boys being more affected than girls by whether their companion was a friend or not: this became a focus of a separate study (below). The lack of sex-of-companion effects for girls in the main part of the study may be explicable in terms of the test sessions being of unusually high intimacy. The distinct gaps between the humour stimuli, plus the fact that there were no other especially interesting stimuli detracting from the companion's and their own prominence, permitted a comfortable level of interaction for girls, whether with another girl or a boy; otherwise, girls would have been expected to laugh more, especially with a boy. The effects for boys are readily explicable in terms of competition. Our informal observations leave us in no doubt that boys, especially with other boys, often compete to respond first to jokes; sometimes they seem even to compete over laughing loudest or longest, yet on these occasions their laughter is rarely 'forced'. Another factor contributing to the sex differences is that, in this subject population at least, telling jokes is regarded as a male prerogative. It is a routine matter for boys and girls to watch cartoons and television together; but it may have been something of a privilege for a girl to be placed with an opposite sex companion in order to swap jokes.

Effects which were presumed to be due to competition also emerged in the follow-up experiment on children's joke-telling. Boys ($n = 16$) and girls ($n = 14$), aged eight and nine years, were divided into same-sex pairs of friends and non-friends. The pairs were presented with a series of seven riddles selected from the earlier thirty-eight as being the most successful in eliciting mirth; this aspect of the procedure was part of the 'warm-up' and its specific purpose was to stimulate children into producing their own jokes, riddles, or funny stories. The joke-telling sessions continued until one minute elapsed without either child attempting to supply any form of humour. The experimenter was present and reinforced each attempted joke by laughing, but she offered no prompts or evaluative comment. Verbal responses were analysed from the video-recordings and durations of various behaviours were extracted as in all but the previous study. It was found that boys engaged in more mirth (laughter/smiling) with non-friends, and a part explanation for this is immediately obvious: the sessions tended to be longer for boys with non-friends ($p < 0.10$) and there was, therefore, more opportunity for laughter and smiling. However, the trend remained when scores were adjusted appropriately. The length-of-session difference (non-significant) is, in turn, not difficult to explain: friends tended to know one another's jokes more than non-friends did. The trends for girls were the converse in each case, but none of them was close to significance. Informal scrutiny of the video-tapes indicated that competitiveness was most evident in boys who were non-friends, and this we see as the principal reason for the sex differences. On average, non-friend boys told twice as many jokes as any of the other three types of subject pairing, and only they laughed more at their own jokes than at their companion's.

Further research

In this one section of a review chapter it has been possible in relation to our own data merely to outline some of the main trends. Moreover, through concentrating on expressive mirth responses (laughter and smiling), we have inevitably had to omit specific reference to a number of other behavioural measures (e.g. talking and touching), as well as to temporal patterning of behaviours and to subjective evaluations. Nevertheless, the data reviewed have amply demonstrated that a variety of complex social factors influence reactions to humour.

Our research contrasts with other social psychological work on humour in three major methodological features: our subjects have been children; only rarely have subjects generated the humour themselves; and humour *per se* has not been embodied within any of our independent variables. This third point also distinguishes our research from virtually all other research connected with the psychology of children's humour; and this is partly because we have not brought developmental issues to the fore.

Our approach has been to present children with recorded humour and thereby investigate the salient interpersonal factors governing their reactions to humour stimuli. Thus, social variables associated with companionship have been examined systematically in a series of experimental social-child studies. In the account above we have outlined how the experimental approach has opened up and consolidated various lines of interest. We would strongly commend this rigorous approach to researchers aiming either to extend our findings or to test their generalizability (e.g. to children outside the four-to-eleven age range). Our conviction is that this form of detailed analysis, or 'trawling for facts', is essential for the founding of durable theory. At the same time, we are convinced of the need to check laboratory findings against 'field' observations of naturally occurring social encounters. In these comparatively early days of research, it is important to supplement the available data and, in particular, to begin to relate humour responsiveness to other psychological characteristics of the individual.

Recognizing that experimentation is not well-suited to exploring when and why children tell jokes or create humour and comedy, we have recently broadened our methodology in several directions. With experimentation we have combined observational, ethological, sociometric, questionnaire, and interview techniques in a project investigating intensively a relatively small number of children. By turning our attention to the *when* and *why* of humour, we aim to begin building bridges between our own previous research (reviewed above) and the social psychological research of others (reviewed in the earlier sections).

The project involved a single class of thirty-four nine-year-olds (nineteen boys and fifteen girls). During most schooldays over a period of six months, the children were observed systematically in their classroom (JRS recorded behaviours—especially humour-related behaviours—for individual children over thirty-second periods); and occasionally the children were observed in the mobile laboratory and in the playground. Also, information was collected about personality, ability, attainment, popularity, friendships, and family circumstances. At the very least, this form of in-depth analysis is certain to throw more light upon the functions of humour and laughter in children's interactions. More ambitiously, we anticipate that it should be possible through this project to begin synthesizing knowledge about encoding humour and knowledge about decoding and reacting to humour. Social psychological aspects of children's humour and laughter will be poorly understood until some headway has been made on syntheses of this nature.

SUMMARY AND CONCLUSIONS

Explicit in this chapter is our conviction that humour and laughter can often be fundamental in social interaction. Further, we believe that humour researchers in general should be sensitive to those social psychological factors which normally play a part in determining the production and appreciation of humour and which are paramount in the elicitation of laughter. Even in designing and evaluating research which is not specifically social psychological, these factors should be borne in mind; effects due to social desirability and demand characteristics, for example, are not difficult to generate inadvertently.

Traditionally, humour and laughter have been ignored by those in 'mainstream' social psychology, even by those interested in communication or interaction. Amongst humour researchers, however, an awareness of the prevalence and potency of social parameters appears to be growing. Nevertheless, an empirical and theoretical literature is only just beginning to take form. Within this chapter there is a review of the various theoretical models which focus on the social functions of humour and laughter: all of these models have been formulated in the past decade and, without exception, they have been developed with adults in mind rather than children.

Published studies are few in number, and most child studies were reported about fifty years ago: they were based upon direct observations and were largely atheoretical. In this chapter, after examining the empirical work of other researchers, we have given emphasis to our own empirical work on children—especially the most recent work which has not appeared elsewhere.

In considering the literature bearing upon the social psychology of adult humour—which is far more substantial than the corresponding literature on children—it was noted that there are no developmental studies indicating the ages at which adult functions and processes begin to emerge in children. Our own observations in classrooms, which are of an informal nature, have led us to speculate that many of the functions identified for adults have begun to operate by the time children have reached seven or eight years of age. For example, the ways humour is used can sometimes be seen to vary according to the *peck order* within a classroom; the *clown* usually scores high on popularity within the group, but s/he is rarely a leader; humour and comic activity can form an integral part of a child's *coping strategy*; and *cognitive similarity* of group members seems to relate to numbers of attempts at humour creation and to humour responsiveness. Another informal observation is that by this same age children use humour to assess their status within the group as the group itself develops. Also, one of our experimental studies demonstrated that, rather like adults, four-, five- and six-year-olds can use humour responsiveness to express ethnic allegiances: indeed, by the age of six, children seem able to use humour to generate increments and decrements in group esteem.

The theoretical bases for our empirical studies have been outlined in the chapter—they are drawn from laughter theory, social facilitation theory, and social intimacy theory—and attention has been paid to robust, consistent, sex difference data. A parsimonious interpretation of the sex differences in behaviours is that boys are more responsive than girls to humour stimuli while girls tend to concentrate more than boys on social interaction *per se*: girls make more effort to enhance sharing of the social situation. Both boys and girls tend to be more responsive to humour when with a companion of their own sex. A non-humour study, which is methodologically similar to our humour studies and which is reported for the first time in this chapter, has led us to suspect that girls (seven- and eight-year-olds) may tend generally to be more sociable than boys. Other new research using discrete humour stimuli (rather than films or stories), and research where the children themselves generate the humour, indicates that boys *compete* more than girls: they appear to want to respond first and to respond most; occasionally they compete to respond loudest. Also, some data suggest that in our samples telling jokes is regarded as a male prerogative. Contrasting with the findings of others, our results show that for boys as well as girls subjective ratings of funniness closely match expressive responses.

In our early research, detailed elsewhere, subjects were generally paired with confederate children, and social facilitation effects were investigated in a series of factorial experiments. 'Humorous laughter' was found to depend upon the following features of the companion's (confederate's) presence and responsiveness: the amount that s/he laughs; the amount s/he engages in 'humorous smiling'; the amount s/he looks at the subject's face; whether s/he is perceived as an 'audience' or a 'coactor'; how close s/he sits; his/her seating orientation; and whether s/he encroaches upon the subject's body space while laughing. When there are two companions, the amount that they look at one another influences the subject's mirth. In naturalistic pairs, responsiveness is greatly affected by whether or not the dyad members are aware that they can be observed. An age/status difference of two years between seven-year-old subjects and nine-year-old companions has no noticeable effect on the seven-year-old's laughter and smiling. Throughout the series of experiments it was observed that when the companion is another child of approximately the same age as the subject, then that subject's humorous laughter and smiling is enhanced relative to baseline levels of solitary children; that is the case even when the companion ignores the subject and reacts blankly to the humour. However, our more recent studies demonstrate that if the companion is an adult (Experimenter) then the child's responses are suppressed (as they are for an adult subject) if the companion is not responsive.

The newer studies, previously unpublished, follow directly from the earlier ones, but they tend to be more naturalistic: for instance, none of them employs confederates. A number of interesting findings have emerged. For example, we now have some hints that susceptibility to social influence is amplified with age, at least between infants and junior schoolchildren (five- to eight-year-olds): as far as humour is concerned, the social facilitation of laughter and smiling becomes more marked across this age range. Also, there is evidence that facilitation effects become greater when a small group is increased in size (from two to four members). There seem to be qualitative and quantitative differences in social facilitation effects for small and large groups: for example, within a single film, particular humour events elicit a good deal of mirth from members of large groups but relatively little from members of small groups. Overall, individuals in large groups of about fifty children exhibit considerably more laughter than their counterparts in small groups; and the converse holds for other humour events. Also, with repeated film presentations to large groups, warm-up effects become evident. For solitary children and for members of small groups, successive presentations of films generally produce a decline in overt mirth. Members of large groups appear to detect humorous incidents which had previously passed unnoticed, and they eagerly anticipate the more slapstick and obvious stimuli.

Our experiments on friendship, sharing, and social intimacy have pointed to 'humorous laughter' having two distinct arousal-reducing functions in social interaction. In circumstances experienced as too low in social intimacy, it is used to gain or maintain a companion's attention. In circumstances experienced as too high in intimacy, it is used as a 'safety valve' to break attention and reduce the companion's psychological presence. Laughter appears sometimes to be indicative of the extent to which an individual is experiencing unpleasant social arousal, while smiling appears usually to reflect the congeniality or 'felt comfort' of the social situation. (Clearly, laughter and smiling have other functions too, and some of these have been mentioned in the chapter.) The 'friendship' studies have indicated that there are complex interrelationships between humour and social intimacy: humour and laughter can give rise to changes in intimacy, and so too can changes in intimacy affect humour responsiveness.

Our studies, combined with others, serve to emphasize the social nature of humour and laughter. At the very least, the chapter pinpoints salient 'social' variables to which humour researchers in general should attend when planning and conducting their studies. More than that, however, it is shown, first, that children's responses to humour are largely governed by social psychological factors and, second, that humour can play a prominent role in children's social interactions.

ACKNOWLEDGEMENTS

The research was sponsored in the UK by the Social Science Research Council (Grant HR 3043). For their kindness and co-operation we thank warmly the headteachers, the staffs and the pupils of the following junior and infant schools in Cardiff: Bryntaf (Mr. T. Evans), Lakeside (Miss I. M. Roberts and Mr. E. G. Dawkins), Llanedeyrn (Mr. E. E. Powell and Mrs. M. C. M. Taylor), Marlborough (Mrs. K. Jones), and Springwood (Mr. D. Rees and Mrs. M. L. Lewis).

REFERENCES

Argyle, M., and Dean, J. (1965). Eye-contact, distance and affiliation. *Sociometry*, **28**, 289–304.

Baron, R. A. (1978a). Aggression-inhibiting influence of sexual humor. *Journal of Personality and Social Psychology*, **36**, 189–197.

Baron, R. A. (1978b). The influence of hostile and nonhostile humor upon physical aggression. *Personality and Social Psychology Bulletin*, **4**, 77–80.

Baron, R. A., and Ball, R. L. (1974). The aggression-inhibiting influence of nonhostile humor. *Journal of Experimental Social Psychology*, **10**, 23–33.

Bateson, G. (1953). The role of humor in human communication. In H. von Foerster (Ed.), *Cybernetics*. New York: Macy Foundation.

Bergler, E. (1956). *Laughter and the Sense of Humor*. New York: Intercontinental Medical Book Corporation.

Berkowitz, L. (1970). Aggressive humor as a stimulus to aggressive responses. *Journal of Personality and Social Psychology*, **16**, 710–717.

Berlyne, D. E. (1969). Laughter, humor and play. In G. Lindzey and E. Aronson (Eds.), *Handbook of Social Psychology*. Vol. 3. Reading, Massachusetts: Addison-Wesley.

Bourhis, R. Y., Gadfield, N. J., Giles, H., and Tajfel, H. (1977). Context and ethnic humour in intergroup relations. In A. J. Chapman and H. C. Foot (Eds.), *It's a Funny Thing, Humour*. Oxford: Pergamon Press.

Brackett, C. W. (1933). Laughing and crying of preschool children. *Journal of Experimental Education*, **2**, 119–126.

Brackett, C. W. (1934). Laughing and crying of preschool children. *Child Development Monographs*, No. 14, 119–126.

Bradney, P. (1957). The joking relationship in industry. *Human Relations*, **10**, 179–187.

Bridges, K. M. (1932). Emotional development in early infancy. *Child Development*, **3**, 324–341.

Bryant, J., and Meyer, T. P. (1977). A developmental analysis of children's favourite jokes. In A. J. Chapman and H. C. Foot (Eds.), *It's a Funny Thing, Humour*. Oxford: Pergamon Press.

Byrne, D. (1961). Some inconsistencies in the effect of motivation arousal on humor preferences. *Journal of Abnormal and Social Psychology*, **62**, 158–160.

Callois, R. (1961). *Man, Play and Games*. Glencoe, Illinois: The Free Press.

Chapman, A. J. (1973). Social facilitation of laughter in children. *Journal of Experimental Social Psychology*, **9**, 528–541.

Chapman, A. J. (1974). An electromyographic study of social facilitation: a test of the 'mere presence' hypothesis. *British Journal of Psychology*, **65**, 123–128.

Chapman, A. J. (1975a). Eye-contact, physical proximity and laughter: a re-examination of the equilibrium model of social intimacy. *Social Behavior and Personality*, **3**, 143–156.

Chapman, A. J. (1975b). Humorous laughter in children. *Journal of Personality and Social Psychology*, **31**, 42–49.

Chapman, A. J. (1976). Social aspects of humorous laughter. In A. J. Chapman and H. C. Foot (Eds.), *Humour and Laughter: Theory, Research and Applications*. Chichester: Wiley.

Chapman, A. J., and Foot, H. C. (1976). Introduction. In A. J. Chapman and H. C. Foot (Eds.), *Humour and Laughter: Theory, Research and Applications*. Chichester: Wiley.

Chapman, A. J., Foot, H. C., and Smith, J. R. (1977). Laughter: a social psychological phenomenon, irrelevant to the study of humor? *Humor Research Newsletter*, **2**, 4–5. (Albany: State University of New York).

Chapman, A. J., Smith, J. R., and Foot, H. C. (1977). Language, humour and intergroup relations. In H. Giles (Ed.), *Language, Ethnicity and Intergroup Relations*. London: Academic Press.

Chapman, A. J., Smith, J. R., Foot, H. C., and Pritchard, E. (1979). Behavioural and sociometric indices of friendship in children. In M. Cook and G. D. Wilson (Eds.), *Love and Attraction*. Oxford: Pergamon Press.

Chapman, A. J., and Speck, L. J. M. (1977). Humorous laughter and relief of anxiety in first-born children. *Journal of Individual Psychology*, **33**, 37–41.

Chapman, A. J., and Wright, D. S. (1976). Social enhancement of laughter: an experimental analysis of some companion variables. *Journal of Experimental Child Psychology*, **21**, 201–218.

Claxton, G. (1975). Why can't we tickle ourselves? *Perceptual and Motor Skills*, **41**, 335–338.

Coser, R. L. (1959). Some social functions of laughter: a study of humor in a hospital setting. *Human Relations*, **12**, 171–182.

Coser, R. L. (1960). Laughter among colleagues: a study of the social functions of humor among the staff of a mental hospital. *Psychiatry*, **23**, 81–95.

Ding, G. F., and Jersild, A. T. (1932). A study of the laughing and smiling of preschool children. *Journal of Genetic Psychology*, **40**, 452–472.

Dworkin, E. S., and Efran, J. S. (1967). The angered: their susceptibility to varieties of humor. *Journal of Personality and Social Psychology*, **6**, 233–236.

Enders, A. C. (1927). A study of the laughter of the pre-school child in the Merrill-Palmer Nursery School. *Papers of the Michigan Academy of Science, Arts and Letters*, **8**, 341–356.

Feibleman, J. K. (1939). *In Praise of Comedy*. New York: Macmillan.

Fine, G. A. (1977a). Humour and communication: discussion. In A. J. Chapman and H. C. Foot (Eds.), *It's a Funny Thing, Humour*. Oxford: Pergamon Press.

Fine, G. A. (1977b). Humour in situ: the role of humour in small group culture. In A. J. Chapman and H. C. Foot (Eds.), *It's a Funny Thing, Humour*. Oxford: Pergamon Press.

Flugel, J. C. (1954). Humor and laughter. In G. Lindzey (Ed.), *Handbook of Social Psychology*. First Edn. Reading, Massachusetts: Addison-Wesley.

Foot, H. C., and Chapman, A. J. (1976). The social responsiveness of young children in humorous situations. In A. J. Chapman and H. C. Foot (Eds.), *Humour and Laughter: Theory, Research and Applications*. Chichester: Wiley.

Foot, H. C., Chapman, A. J., and Smith, J. R. (1977). Friendship and social responsiveness in boys and girls. *Journal of Personality and Social Psychology*, **35**, 401–411.

Foot, H. C., Chapman, A. J., and Smith, J. R. (1978). Why making friends is vital for your child. *Psychology Today* (UK), **4**, 14–18.

Foot, H. C., Chapman, A. J., and Smith, J. R. (1980). *Friendship and Social Relations in Children*. Chichester: Wiley.

Foot, H. C., Smith, J. R., and Chapman, A. J. (1977). Sex differences in children's responses to humour. In A. J. Chapman and H. C. Foot (Eds.), *It's a Funny Thing, Humour*. Oxford: Pergamon Press.

Foot, H. C., Smith, J. R., and Chapman, A. J. (1979). Nonverbal expressions of intimacy in children. In M. Cook and G. D. Wilson (Eds.), *Love and Attraction*. Oxford: Pergamon Press.

Freud, S. (1905). *Der Witz und seine Beziehung zum Unbewussten*. Leipzig and Vienna: Deuticke.

Fry, W. F. Jr. (1977). The appeasement function of mirthful laughter. In A. J. Chapman and H. C. Foot (Eds.), *It's a Funny Thing, Humour*. Oxford: Pergamon Press.

Fry, W. F. Jr., and Allen, M. (1975). *Make 'Em Laugh*. Palo Alto, California: Science and Behavior Books.

Geen, R. G., and Gange, J. J. (1977). Drive theory of social facilitation: twelve years of theory and research. *Psychological Bulletin*, **84**, 1267–1288.

Giles, H., Bourhis, R. Y., Gadfield, N. J., Davies, G. J., and Davies, A. P. (1976). Cognitive aspects of humour in social interaction: a model and some linguistic data. In A. J. Chapman and H. C. Foot (Eds.), *Humour and Laughter: Theory, Research and Applications*. Chichester: Wiley.

Giles, H., and Oxford, G. S. (1970). Towards a multidimensional theory of laughter causation and its social implications. *Bulletin of the British Psychological Society*, **23**, 97–105.

Goldstein, J. H. (1977). Cross-cultural research: humour here and there. In A. J. Chapman and H. C. Foot (Eds.), *It's a Funny Thing, Humour.* Oxford: Pergamon Press.

Goodchilds, J. D. (1959). Effects of being witty on position in the social structure of a small group. *Sociometry,* **22,** 261–272.

Goodchilds, J. D. (1972). On being witty: causes, correlates and consequences. In J. H. Goldstein and P. E. McGhee (Eds.), *The Psychology of Humor: Theoretical Perspectives and Empirical Issues.* New York: Academic Press.

Goodchilds, J. D., and Smith, E. E. (1964). The wit and his group. *Human Relations,* **17,** 23–31.

Goodrich, A. J., Henry, J., and Goodrich, D. W. (1954). Laughter in psychiatric staff conferences: a sociopsychiatric analysis. *American Journal of Orthopsychiatry,* **24,** 175–184.

Gregg, A., Miller, M., and Linton, E. (1929). Laughter situations as an indication of social responsiveness in young children. In D. S. Thomas (Ed.), *Some New Techniques for Studying Social Behavior.* New York: Teachers' College.

Gruner, C. R. (1976). Wit and humour in mass communication. In A. J. Chapman and H. C. Foot (Eds.), *Humour and Laughter: Theory, Research and Applications.* Chichester: Wiley.

Hayworth, D. (1928). The social origin and function of laughter. *Psychological Review,* **35,** 367–384.

Hertzler, J. O. (1970). *Laughter: A Socio-Scientific Analysis.* New York: Exposition Press.

Hooff, J. A. R. A. M. van, (1972). A comparative approach to the phylogeny of laughter and smiling. In R. A. Hinde (Ed.), *Non-Verbal Communication.* Cambridge University Press.

Husband, C. (1977). The mass media and the functions of ethnic humour in a racist society. In A. J. Chapman and H. C. Foot (Eds.), *It's a Funny Thing, Humour.* Oxford: Pergamon Press.

Jacobson, E. (1947). The child's laughter. *The Psychoanalytic Study of the Child,* **2,** 39–60.

Justin, F. (1932). A genetic study of laughter provoking stimuli. *Child Development,* **3,** 114–136.

Kane, T. R., Suls, J. M., and Tedeschi, J. (1977). Humour as a tool of social interaction. In A. J. Chapman and H. C. Foot (Eds.), *It's a Funny Thing, Humour.* Oxford: Pergamon Press.

Keith-Spiegel, P. (1972). Early conceptions of humor: varieties and issues. In J. H. Goldstein and P. E. McGhee (Eds.), *The Psychology of Humor: Theoretical Perspectives and Empirical Issues.* New York: Academic Press.

Kenerdine, M. (1931). Laughter in the pre-school child. *Child Development,* **2,** 228–230.

Klapp, O. E. (1950). The fool as a social type. *American Journal of Sociology,* **55,** 157–162.

Konner, M. J. (1972). Aspects of the developmental ethology of a foraging people. In N. Blurton Jones (Ed.), *Ethological Studies of Child Behaviour.* Cambridge: Cambridge University Press.

La Fave, L. (1977). Ethnic humour: from paradoxes towards principles. In A. J. Chapman and H. C. Foot (Ed.), *It's a Funny Thing, Humour.* Oxford: Pergamon Press.

La Gaipa, J. J. (1977). The effects of humour on the flow of social conversation. In A. J. Chapman and H. C. Foot (Eds.), *It's a Funny Thing, Humour.* Oxford: Pergamon Press.

Lamb, C. W. (1968). Personality correlates of humor enjoyment following motivational arousal. *Journal of Personality and Social Psychology,* **9,** 237–241.

Landy, D. and Mettee, D. (1969). Evaluation of an aggressor as a function of exposure to cartoon humor. *Journal of Personality and Social Psychology*, **12**, 66–71.

Lauter, P. (1964). *Theories of Comedy*. New York: Anchor Books.

Leuba, C. (1941). Tickling and laughter: two genetic studies. *Journal of Genetic Psychology*, **58**, 201–209.

Leventhal, H., and Cupchik, G. C. (1975). The informational and facilitative effects of an audience upon expression and evaluation of humorous stimuli. *Journal of Experimental Social Psychology*, **11**, 363–380.

Leventhal, H., and Mace, W. (1970). The effect of laughter on the evaluation of a slapstick movie. *Journal of Personality*, **38**, 16–30.

Lewis, M. (1967). The meaning of a response, or why researchers in infant behaviour should be oriental metaphysicians. *Merrill-Palmer Quarterly*, **13**, 7–18.

Lockard, J. S., Fahrenbruch, C. E., Smith, J. L., and Morgan, C. J. (1977). Smiling and laughter: different phyletic origins? *Bulletin of the Psychonomic Society*, **10**, 183–186.

Martineau, W. H. (1972). A model of the social functions of humor. In J. H. Goldstein and P. E. McGhee (Eds.), *The Psychology of Humor: Theoretical Perspectives and Empirical Issues*. New York: Academic Press.

Matusewicz, C. (1976). *Humor, Dowcip, Wychowanie*. Warsaw: Nasza Ksiengarnia.

McGhee, P. E. (1971). Development of the humor response: a review of the literature. *Psychological Bulletin*, **76**, 328–348.

McGhee, P. E. (1976). The humour questionnaire: an analysis of humour researchers' views of appropriate directions for future research. Paper presented at the British Psychological Society, Welsh Branch, International Conference on Humour and Laughter, Cardiff, July.

McGhee, P. E. (1977). A model of the origins and early development of incongruity-based humour. In A. J. Chapman and H. C. Foot (Eds.), *It's a Funny Thing, Humour*. Oxford: Pergamon Press.

McGhee, P. E. (1979). *Humor: Origins and Development*. San Francisco: Freeman.

McGurk, H. (Ed.). (1978). *Issues in Childhood Social Development*. London: Methuen.

Mechanic, D. (1962). *Students under Stress*. New York: The Free Press of Glencoe.

Milgram, S. (1965). Some conditions of obedience and disobedience to authority. *Human Relations*, **18**, 57–75.

Miller, F. C. (1967). Humor in a Chippewa tribal council. *Ethnology*, **6**, 263–271.

Muller, C., and Donnerstein, E. (1977). The effects of humor-induced arousal upon aggressive behavior. *Journal of Research in Personality*, **11**, 73–82.

Osborne, K. A., and Chapman, A. J. (1977). Suppression of adult laughter; an experimental approach. In A. J. Chapman and H. C. Foot (Eds.), *It's a Funny Thing, Humour*. Oxford: Pergamon Press.

Patterson, M. L. (1976). An arousal model of interpersonal intimacy. *Psychological Review*, **83**, 235–245.

Piddington, R. (1933). *The Psychology of Laughter: A Study in Social Adaptation*. London: Figurehead.

Powell, C. (1977). Humour as a form of social control: a deviance approach. In A. J. Chapman and H. C. Foot (Eds.), *It's a Funny Thing, Humour*. Oxford: Pergamon Press.

Prerost, F. J. (1977). Environmental conditions affecting the humour response: developmental trends. In A. J. Chapman and H. C. Foot (Eds.), *It's a Funny Thing, Humour*. Oxford: Pergamon Press.

Radcliffe-Brown, A. R. (1940). On joking relationships. *Africa*, **13**, 195–210.

Ransohoff, R. (1975). Some observations on humor and laughter in young adolescent girls. *Journal of Youth and Adolescence*, **4**, 155–170.

Richards, M. P. M. (1974). *The Integration of a Child into a Social World.* Cambridge: Cambridge University Press.

Rickwood, L. V. (1978). The arousal mechanism of humour appreciation and its interaction with motivational arousal, muscular tension and stress-related arousal. Unpublished Doctoral Dissertation, University of Manchester.

Rothbart, M. K. (1973). Laughter in young children. *Psychological Bulletin*, **80**, 247–256.

Rothbart, M. K. (1976). Incongruity, problem-solving and laughter. In A. J. Chapman and H. C. Foot (Eds.), *Humour and Laughter: Theory, Research and Applications.* Chichester: Wiley.

Scarr, S., and Salapatek, P. (1970). Patterns of fear development during infancy. *Merrill-Palmer Quarterly*, **16**, 53–87.

Schaffer, H. R. (1971). *The Origins of Human Social Relations.* London: Academic Press.

Sherman, L. W. (1975). An ecological study of glee in small groups of preschool children. *Child Development*, **46**, 53–61.

Sherman, L. W. (1977). Ecological determinants of gleeful behaviours in two nursery school environments. In A. J. Chapman and H. C. Foot (Eds.), *It's a Funny Thing, Humour.* Oxford: Pergamon Press.

Smith, E. E., and Goodchilds, J. D. (1959). Characteristics of the witty group member: the wit as leader. *American Psychologist*, **14**, 375–376.

Smith, E. E., and Goodchilds, J. D. (1963). The wit in large and small established groups. *Psychological Reports*, **13**, 273–274.

Smith, J. R., Chapman, A. J., and Foot, H. C. (1975). Seeing the gag. *New Behaviour*, **2**, 62.

Smith, J. R., Foot, H. C., and Chapman, A. J. (1977a). Nonverbal communication among friends and strangers sharing humour. In A. J. Chapman and H. C. Foot (Eds.), *It's a Funny Thing, Humour.* Oxford: Pergamon Press.

Smith, J. R., Foot, H. C., and Chapman, A. J. (1977b). What makes us laugh? *Psychology Today* (UK), **3**, 18–23.

Sroufe, L. A., and Waters, E. (1976). The ontogenesis of smiling and laughter: a perspective on the organization of development in infancy. *Psychological Review*, **83**, 173–189.

Sykes, A. J. M. (1966). Joking relationships in an industrial setting. *American Anthropologist*, **68**, 188–193.

Taylor, P. (1977). Laughter and joking—the structural axis. In A. J. Chapman and H. C. Foot (Eds.), *It's a Funny Thing, Humour.* Oxford: Pergamon Press.

Tuckman, B. W. (1965). Developmental sequence in small groups. *Psychological Bulletin*, **63**, 384–399.

Wallis, W. D. (1922). Why do we laugh? *Scientific Monthly*, **15**, 343–347.

Washburn, R. W. (1929). A study of the smiling and laughter of infants in the first year of life. *Genetic Psychology Monographs*, **6**, 397–537.

Weaver, S. M. (1978). Mild social stress and human performance: the role of competition, evaluation and the presence of others. Unpublished Doctoral Dissertation, University of Durham.

Weiskrantz, L., Elliott, J., and Darlington, C. (1971). Preliminary observations on tickling oneself. *Nature*, **230**, 598–599.

Wilson, C. O. (1931). A study of laughter situations among young children. Unpublished Doctoral Dissertation, University of Nebraska.

Wolosin, R. J. (1975). Cognitive similarity and group laughter. *Journal of Personality and Social Psychology*, **32**, 503–509.

Zajonc, R. B. (1965). Social facilitation. *Science*, **149**, 269–274.

Zenner, W. (1970). Joking and ethnic stereotyping. *Anthropological Quarterly*, **43**, 93–113.

Zillmann, D. (1977). Humour and communication: introduction. In A. J. Chapman and H. C. Foot (Eds.), *It's a Funny Thing, Humour*. Oxford: Pergamon Press.

Zillmann, D., Bryant, J., and Cantor, J. R. (1974). Brutality of assault in political cartoons affecting humor appreciation. *Journal of Research in Personality*, **7**, 334–345.

Zillmann, D., and Cantor, J. R. (1976). A disposition theory of humour and mirth. In A. J. Chapman and H. C. Foot (Eds.), *Humour and Laughter: Theory, Research and Applications*. Chichester: Wiley.

CHAPTER 7

Individual Differences in Children's Humour Development

DAVID M. BRODZINSKY
and
JONATHAN RIGHTMYER

> The sound is produced by a deep inspiration followed by short, interrupted, spasmodic contractions of the chest, and especially the diaphragm . . . the mouth is open more or less widely, with the corners drawn much backwards, as well as a little upwards; and the upper lip is somewhat raised. (Darwin, 1965, p. 200)

And so we laugh, and that laugh is said to be closely associated with some ludicrous situation. Moreover, that laugh is also said to be uniquely human. Indeed, only humans possess a sense of humour; only humans are given to laughter (Bergson, 1911, 'Man is an animal who laughs').

For centuries man has been contemplating and speculating on the nature of the humour response. Yet for all the scientific observation and experimentation that has been undertaken, we remain relatively ignorant of the basic processes and factors governing this phenomenon. This is particularly true with respect to the issue of individual differences in humour (cf. Leventhal and Safer, 1977).

It is a commonplace observation that people differ considerably in what they find funny. Thus, one individual may be appreciative of risqué humour, while a second individual prefers slapstick humour, and still a third individual is drawn primarily to cognitive humour. Further, it is often the case that two individuals may appreciate an instance of humour equally, but differ in the manner and degree to which their appreciation is expressed. While one individual laughs uproariously at a joke, a companion may simply smile or chuckle. Finally, people also vary in their tendency to create or produce humour. For some individuals joke-telling is a way of life, while for others it is a relatively foreign experience.

These examples of behavioural variability represent the heart of the individual difference question with respect to humour. They also represent the primary focus of the present chapter. In the sections which follow we examine what is currently known about individual differences in children's humour. We begin by presenting a rationale for such an examination, followed by a differentiation of various research strategies. Next, we proceed to review the empirical literature on individual differences in humour development. In concluding, we present several suggestions for future research which may help to answer some of the basic questions in this area.

A RATIONALE FOR STUDYING INDIVIDUAL DIFFERENCES IN CHILDREN'S HUMOUR

Why would someone wish to study individual differences in humour development? For that matter, why study humour at all? The answer to the first question can be found in the answer to the second.

Too often, theoreticians and empirical researchers in psychology have dealt with cognitive, affective, personality, and social processes as if they were truly separate from one another in the functioning human being. Developmental psychologists have been no exception. One need only glance at the index of the third edition of *Carmichael's Manual of Child Psychology* (Mussen, 1970) to appreciate the artificial compartmentalization that plagues our field—one volume primarily concerned with sensory processes, learning, and cognitive development in the traditional sense, and a second volume devoted to topics of socialization. Nowhere is there an attempt to examine the complex interactive nature of human behaviour. In contrast, the area of humour, along with a number of other areas, such as infant attachment, play, and empathy, to name but a few, provides the researcher with a relatively rare opportunity to examine the interplay of cognitive and socioaffective processes within the developing child in a natural and readily observable domain. As such, the study of humour, and the individual difference factors affecting this phenomenon, helps to fill a glaring gap in the current research on human behavioural development.

A second reason for studying humour concerns its role as a vehicle for social communication (see Chapter 6). It is becoming increasingly clear that people often turn to humour as a means of getting across a point to other human beings, particularly when the message involves an area of potential conflict or embarrassment, such as sexuality or interpersonal feelings. Yet our understanding of this process, and the individuals who are likely to use it, as well as the contexts in which it is likely to be used, is quite limited. Furthermore, from a developmental perspective, we have very little information concerning children's awareness of the need for the joke façade. Wolfenstein (1954) has argued that before six years of age, children's inhibitions are quite unstable, and subject to frequent lapses. Consequently, the need for such a façade is mitigated. For older children, however, the joke façade becomes a useful vehicle for overriding more persistent inhibitions. As interesting and potentially enlightening as Wolfenstein's developmental position is, there are no direct empirical data supporting it, nor any other position concerning children's awareness of the joke façade, and individual difference factors affecting its development.

Humour has also been seen as a basic part of the personality structure. Indeed, as far back as Plato, a good sense of humour has been linked to the mature, well-adjusted adult. This is particularly true of contemporary humanistic theorists. To be able to laugh at one's self, and the absurdity inherent in the world, consitutes a fundamental human quality associated with personal adjustment. Investigating humour, therefore, provides the psychologist with insights into differential patterns and mechanisms for psychological adjustment.

This brings us to a fourth reason for studying humor. As Freud (1960) pointed out, humour often serves as a mechanism for dealing with intrapsychic conflicts. Subject areas such as sexuality, aggression, and death are often too anxiety-laden for the individual to deal with directly. Consequently, the individual's thoughts, feelings, wishes, etc. concerning these areas are expressed indirectly through joking. As such, humour can serve as a psychological window through which the clinician may gaze in search of the individual's conflict areas. In fact, clinicians often go a step farther, and use humour as a therapeutic vehicle for exposing patients to their basic conflicts, thus helping them to confront and resolve them (Grossman, 1977; Killinger, 1977; Loewald, 1976).

In the present section we have tried to explain some of the reasons for studying humour, and those individual difference factors associated with its development. Certainly we have not covered all the possible reasons for the renewed interest in humour. Nevertheless, we believe we have offered sufficient justification for its study. Clearly, humour, and the behavioural variability associated with it, is not simply a 'laughing matter'. In fact, the study of humour is quite a serious business, for as we begin to understand this phenomenon, we are that much closer to understanding the human being.

RESEARCH STRATEGIES AND THE QUESTION OF INDIVIDUAL DIFFERENCES

In their quest for understanding human behaviour and development, psychologists have employed a variety of research strategies, of which the three most prominent are the *nomothetic*, the *differential*, and the *idiographic*. The nomothetic approach, which has been the most frequently used strategy in the study of developmental processes, is characterized by a focus on general laws of behaviour applicable to all, or at least very large aggregates of people. While researchers using this approach recognize the existence of within-group variability, they de-emphasize it in favour of generic principles of development. As a result, studies adopting this approach yield global or normative generalizations about the behaviour of the population under study, but very little, if any, information about the determinants of an individual's behaviour, or the determinants of differences among individuals. Indeed, from this perspective, individual differences in behaviour are often 'explained away' as largely due to sampling and/or measurement error (Sigel and Brodzinsky, 1977).

The differential approach, on the other hand, is concerned with individual as well as normative laws of development. This research strategy focuses on the way in which people become assorted into sub-groups characterized by differential status and/or behavioural attributes (Emmerich, 1968). Examples of status attributes include such demographic categories as sex, socioeconomic level, and race, while behavioural attributes include such psychological continua as introversion-extraversion, aggression-passivity, dominance-submissiveness, etc. Concern with normative or generic laws is evident in this approach to the extent that the researcher investigates the variables underlying the basis of differentiation of sub-groups over the course of development. On the other hand, the researcher who adopts this approach may also be interested in individual differences in behaviour. This interest is manifested in the researcher's conceptualization of behavioural variability as stemming from subjects' membership in certain demographic groups and/or their location on some bipolar behavioural dimension.

Finally, the goal of the idiographic or ipsative approach is to discover laws of individual development. Here the emphasis is on individual variability within populations rather than generalizations across populations. As such, the individual is no longer subordinated to the group; that is, normative principles are seen as being meaningless, or at least distorting, when applied to specific individuals. Consequently, the idiographic approach emphasizes intra-individual consistencies and changes in the development of the person (Emmerich, 1968). This most often takes the form of describing and explaining the specific behavioural and psychological attributes that characterize a person over the course of development, including how the attributes are organized, and what influence they have on the individual's psychological growth and adjustment (Korchin, 1976).

As in other areas of psychology, researchers interested in humour development have frequently adopted the nomothetic strategy. Consequently, much of the research on children's humour, to date, has attempted to uncover general laws of humour development. To the extent that researchers have been interested in individual differences in humour, greater emphasis has been given to the differential as opposed to the idiographic approach. Thus, as we shall see in the next section, the issue of individual differences in children's humour has been examined primarily in terms of the influence of such variables as intelligence, cognitive styles, personality traits, atypical patterns of adjustment, and sex of subject.

The focus on the differential approach in contrast to the idiographic approach is understandable given the researcher's traditional concern with empirical generalization. Even in the context of examining individual differences in humour, researchers are usually interested in being able to draw conclusions that go beyond the individual case, thus leading to what McGhee (1972) has termed 'mini-theories' of humour. The idiographic approach, because it is concerned with uncovering the basis of the individual's behaviour and development, is more closely associated with clinical practice and research than with the mainstream empirical research in psychology (Korchin, 1976). To imply that this approach has little to offer the humour researcher (Leventhal and Safer, 1977), however, is greatly to misunderstand this approach and/or underestimate the richness of information that it can generate. We have more to say about this in the concluding section.

EMPIRICAL STUDIES

Research on children's humour dates back to the turn of the century (cf. McGhee, 1971a). Most of the early research, however, was observational or at best, quasi-experimental in nature. It consisted primarily of noting and recording those stimuli and situations that were most successful in eliciting smiling, laughter, and other manifest behaviours associated with humour. Few of these studies were guided by theory and few were concerned with delineating developmental changes in children's humour, or in examining individual difference factors associated with such changes.

In the past ten to fifteen years, however, research on humour in general, and children's humour in particular, has undergone some dramatic changes. In the first place, the amount of systematic work in this area has increased substantially. Secondly, humour has been brought into the laboratory so that appropriate control conditions can be maintained. Humour research has also become more closely tied to theory, although the theories themselves have become more narrowly defined than previous global theories of humour such as those espoused by Freud (1960) and Maier (1932). Finally, greater interest has been shown in investigating developmental changes in children's response to humour stimuli.

In contrast to the above changes, there has been less of an attempt to explore systematically individual differences in humour development. Consequently, our knowledge about this aspect of children's humour is represented by a smattering of loosely related empirical studies which, for the most part, have been unguided by existing humour theory (the research on the cognitive correlates of humour is an exception). In the present section, we attempt to provide some structure to this body of research in the hope that some understanding of individual differences in humour development may emerge. Where possible we differentiate between humour comprehension and humour appreciation processes. Unfortunately, there is almost no research on children's spontaneous production of humour. As a result, little will be said about this aspect of humour development.

Intelligence and humour

It is generally recognized that the enjoyment of humour depends on one's ability to understand what is funny about the humorous event. This realization has led many researchers to speculate that differences in the expression of humour can be understood in terms of individual variation in intellectual competence.

In the past, this speculation was examined by simply correlating IQ with the developing humour response. Unfortunately, the results of a number of studies have yielded a very confusing, and at times, contradictory picture. For example, Kenderdine (1931) noted that nursery schoolchildren whose mean IQ was 141 laughed significantly more often within the observed situations than did children whose mean IQ was 118. On the other hand, both Enders (1927) and Ding and Jersild (1932) failed to find a significant relationship between IQ and laughter for their nursery schoolchildren. Further, Justin (1932) noted that with increasing age, the correlation between IQ and laughter in response to incongruity decreased from 0.40 at three years of age to 0.12 at six years of age.

With respect to somewhat older children, Bird (1925) found a correlation of 0.89 between IQ and success on a humour test for elementary schoolchildren. Williams (1946), utilizing eleven- and twelve-year-olds, also reported that appreciation of cartoons and jokes was significantly related to IQ: that is, the more intelligent the child, the more appreciative s/he was of humorous material which adults rated as being funny. In addition, Wilson (1968) noted that a high sense of humour, as measured by peer ratings, was positively related both to high intelligence and high creativity. In contrast to these findings, Wells (1934), utilizing children in grades seven, nine, eleven, and twelve, found no relationship between mental ability and appreciation of either absurdity, satire, whimsy, or slapstick humour. Similarly, Omwake (1939) also failed to find a significant relation between humour and intelligence with grade schoolchildren. Finally, Cunningham (1962) reported that for children and youths, ten to nineteen years of age, a significant negative correlation was obtained between performance on the Raley Cartoon Test and the Thurstone Test of Mental Abilities.

One cannot help but be impressed by the inconsistency of the empirical findings relating IQ to the development of humour. As McGhee (1971a) has pointed out, the confusion surrounding this question appears to be related to a lack of standardized testing procedures, a lack of clarity in defining humour dimensions, and the frequent failure to distinguish between humour appreciation and humour comprehension processes. Yet several recent studies, which have been more precise and objective in their testing procedures and have obtained both humour appreciation and comprehension responses from their subjects, have not resolved the issue of the relationship between children's IQ and their developing humour. While both Brodzinsky (1977) and Prentice and Fathman (1975) reported no relationship between elementary schoolchildren's intelligence and humour appreciation, significant positive correlations were obtained in each study between intelligence and humour comprehension (the one exception being the correlation between IQ and humour comprehension for third graders in the Prentice and Fathman study). Whitt and Prentice (1977) also reported no relationship between intelligence and humour appreciation. In contrast to the two previous studies, however, they also reported little relationship between intelligence and humour comprehension. Finally, Brodzinsky (1975) found that comprehension of cartoon humour was positively and significantly related to verbal intelligence in six- and eight-year-old reflective children, but not in ten-year-old reflective children, nor in six- to ten-year-old children from the other cognitive style groups studied.

In summary, the relationship between intellectual competence and humour appears to be very complex, and a function of a number of variables including type and complexity of stimuli used, methods of testing and response measures employed, and such organismic factors as the child's developmental level and cognitive style. Furthermore, as we shall presently see, the use of IQ as a measure of intellectual competence is probably too global to capture the subtle relationship that does exist between children's intellectual functioning and humour. This latter realization, plus the recognition of methodological imprecision in past studies, helps to explain the rather confusing picture that has emerged with respect to the relationship between IQ and humour development.

Cognitive development and humour

In the past decade, humour researchers have become dissatisfied with simply documenting age differences in humour comprehension and appreciation. Consequently, a number of investigators have begun to examine individual differences in children's humour as a function of differential level of cognitive development. This approach has given rise to a more circumscribed explanation of children's humour than the general, and relatively diffuse, explanation offered by past theoreticians (e.g. Freud, 1960; Maier, 1932).

The crux of the cognitive developmental theory of humour is that an individual's comprehension and appreciation of ludicrous situations will depend to a great extent (excluding tendentious and social factors) on the match between the individual's existing developmental level and the cognitive demands placed upon him by the humorous event. All things being equal, the individual's appreciation of humour is expected to increase as the cognitive demands placed upon him by the humorous stimulus increase, up to the point where the stimulus becomes too difficult, complex, or novel to be assimilated by the individual's cognitive structures. In other words, humour appreciation requires cognitive work. One must be mentally challenged by the stimulus before one will perceive it as being funny. Joke material which is too readily assimilated because of its cognitive simplicity, or because the individual has heard it many times before, is judged to be trivial, boring, or simply not funny. On the other hand humour which is based upon cognitive principles well beyond the individual's existing developmental level is also likely to lead to decreased appreciation. In this case, however, the lack of enjoyment probably stems from confusion, bewilderment, or possibly even fear.

This mini-theory of humour, known as the 'cognitive congruency principle', was first put forth by Zigler, Levine, and Gould (1966a, 1967). Since then a number of researchers have elaborated and refined the model (e.g. see Kagan, 1971; McGhee, 1974a; Rothbart, 1973; Sroufe and Waters, 1976). Putting aside the differences in the positions of these researchers, there is general agreement that an analysis of subject-object relations is crucial for understanding an individual's response to humour. Moreover, there also seems to be implicit agreement that an explanation of individual variation in humour response also rests on such an analysis. In the present sub-section we examine the empirical research that has been generated by the above positions as it relates to the question of individual differences in humour development.

Working within Piaget's theoretical framework, McGhee (1971b) investigated the importance of concrete operational thought for children's comprehension and appreciation of two distinct forms of humour: (a) novelty humour, in which expectancy violations are manifested in the form of something visually or physically discrepant from the individual's past experience, and (b) incongruity humour, in which expectancy violations are of a more abstract or logical nature. McGhee hypothesized that for seven-year-old children, presumed to be in transition between pre-operational and concrete-operational thought, degree of logical thinking (based on several Piagetian measures) would be positively related to the ability to identify the basis of humour in incongruity, but not novelty, humour. Results completely supported this prediction. For novelty jokes and cartoons, pre-operational and concrete-operational children had equally high humour-comprehension scores, and were just as likely to give interpretive (as opposed to descriptive) explanations for the humour. In contrast, the more cognitively mature seven-year-olds did comprehend incongruity humour to a greater extent than the less mature children. As predicted, none of these relationships held for five- and nine-year-olds, who were well within the pre-operational and concrete-operational periods, respectively. Furthermore, McGhee failed to find a curvilinear relationship between seven-year-olds' cognitive level and humour appreciation (based on subjects' funniness ratings), and consequently concluded that the data did not support the cognitive congruency principle.

More recently, McGhee (1976a) has noted that his earlier design was not really appropriate to test the cognitive congruency principle since it employed a composite measure of operational thought, and did not use humour stimuli which were specifically based upon the cognitive properties being measured in the subjects. In order to overcome these problems, McGhee carried out two experiments. In the first experiment, first-grade conservers and non-conservers of mass, second-grade conservers and non-conservers of weight, fifth-grade conservers of both mass and weight, and college students were presented with conservation of mass and weight jokes, as well as 'filler' jokes. Results indicated a curvilinear relation between subjects' funniness rating of conservation jokes and development of conservation skills. In other words, humour appreciation peaked for first-grade conservers of mass and second-grade non-conservers of weight (who were, however, conservers of mass), and dropped off for the fifth-graders and college students. The second experiment, which used a similar design, also found a curvilinear relation between humour appreciation and degree of logical thought. In this case, funniness ratings for class-inclusion jokes peaked for first-graders who had recently developed the class-inclusion concept, and dropped off for second- and fifth-graders who had attained the concept some time ago. Taken together, these two experiments provide reasonably strong support for the cognitive congruency principle, and indicate that humour appreciation (at least funniness ratings) is greatest when humour stimuli moderately tax the individual's cognitive apparatus. Aside from this general conclusion, however, McGhee's study is also important in that it calls attention to the need to be concerned with the specific structural properties underlying humour as they relate to specific cognitive properties in the subject. If one is concerned with relating humour to individual variation in cognitive or intellectual development, it is important to keep in mind that global measures of cognition (such as IQ, or composite scores from several Piagetian tests) are not likely to be as sensitive predictors of humour as those specific measures of cognition upon which the humour is based.

Of interest is the fact that in both experiments, subjects' smiling and laughter did not show the same curvilinear relationship to logical thought development as was found for funniness ratings. McGhee pointed out that the overall mirth level was quite low, with subjects rarely displaying more than a slight to full smile. He attributed the low expressiveness to the problem-solving nature of the task in which subjects not only responded to the humour on an affective level, but analysed the basis of the humour and explained it to the examiner as well. Whether or not the task orientation of the design interfered with pleasure derived from the challenge of successfully assimilating moderately complex humour is still an open question. What is clear, however, is that the cognitive-congruency principle has yet to be verified for children's public expression of affect using the more stringent type of design employed by McGhee (1976a).

Not every study employing funniness ratings, however, has consistently supported the cognitive congruency principle. McGhee and Johnson (1975) failed to find differences in funniness or mirth ratings to varying stimuli representing violations of weight conservation for third-grade non-conservers and third- and fifth-grade conservers of weight. In explaining their results, McGhee and Johnson pointed out that the acquisition of mass conservation may be sufficient to permit an understanding of conservation-of-weight jokes; that is, children do not seem to differentiate between jokes based upon conservation of mass and weight. The authors speculated that the absence of a main effect for cognitive level for humour appreciation probably stemmed from the fact that even the third-grade non-conservers of weight had already fully attained conservation of mass. Consequently, the stimuli were easily assimilated by all subjects. Yet this explanation appears unconvincing in the light of other findings reported in the study. McGhee and Johnson note that degree of acquisition of weight conservation was significantly related to ratings of surprise concerning the observation of weight conservation violation. In general, third-grade conservers showed the greatest surprise and third-grade non-conservers the least surprise, with fifth-grade conservers in between. Given these findings, the present authors believe that it is difficult to argue that lack of cognitive level differences for funniness and mirth ratings resulted from a relative absence of cognitive challenge for all subjects. If this were the case, one would expect subjects to be equally surprised by the violation of the conservation principle.

In a somewhat similar experiment, Rothbart (1976) examined the hypothesis that five-and-a-half- to six-year-old children, who had attained the concept of conservation of liquid quantity, would see little discrepancy between observed and expected water levels in a water-transfer 'trick', thus showing less smiling and laughter than four-and-a-half- to five-year-old non-conservers whose expectations concerning the water level would be violated. She also hypothesized that older non-conservers would show greater mirth to the 'trick' than younger non-conservers, presumably because they would be more aware of the observed discrepancy as a result of greater experience with the conservation phenomenon. Rothbart's procedure was to give children four humorous tasks (used as a check for overall differences in mirth between conservers and non-conservers), followed by the water-transfer 'trick'. The latter was simply the usual liquid quantity conservation procedure, but in this case labelled as a 'magic trick'. Results indicated that non-conservers laughed more to the initial water-transfer demonstration, showed greater laughter over repeated demonstrations, and asked to have the 'trick' repeated more times than did conservers. Of importance was the fact that there were no differences between the conservers and non-conservers on the four humour tasks preceding the water-transfer task, thus indicating no overall difference in affective responsiveness as a function of cognitive level. In contrast to the first hypothesis, however, no support was found for the hypothesis that older non-conservers would find the discrepancy between observed and expected water levels funnier than younger non-conservers.

Shultz and Bloom (cited in Shultz, 1976) were also interested in examining the relation between concrete operational thought and children's humour. In this case, however, they sought to test the hypothesis that the transition from appreciation of pure incongruity to resolvable incongruity, which Shultz (1974; Shultz and Horibe, 1974) has shown to occur between six and eight years, would be related to the development of logical operations. Results indicated that degree of operational thought in seven- and eight-year-olds (based on a composite measure of class inclusion and length conservation) was not significantly related to preference for resolvable jokes as opposed to jokes containing pure incongruities. On the other hand, concrete-operational children were more successful at comprehending the hidden meanings of the non-transformed jokes than were pre-operational children. Unfortunately, the design used by Shultz and Bloom did not really allow for an adequate test of their original hypothesis. As noted earlier, greater care is needed in matching the structural properties underlying humour and the cognitive operations measured in subjects. Translating this in terms of the purpose of the Shultz and Bloom study, one would need to use original and resolution-removed (pure incongruity) jokes that are based on the specific cognitive principles which differentiate the subjects (e.g. class-inclusion and length-conservation jokes). What we are suggesting here is that the transition from appreciation of pure incongruity to resolvable incongruity may well be related to the development of concrete operations, as Shultz and Bloom hypothesized, but that such a relationship is more likely to be discovered within the type of design employed by McGhee (1976a) than the one used by the authors.

Although McGhee (1974a, 1976a) and the present authors have argued for greater specificity in testing the cognitive congruency principle, at least one recent study (Whitt and Prentice, 1977) has found a more general impact of the acquisition of logical thought for humour development. Working with first, third, and fifth graders, the researchers reported that first-grade conservers of liquid quantity showed greater mirth and funniness ratings and higher comprehension scores for homonymic riddles (based on dual meanings of a single word) than non-conservers. No differences in humour appreciation or comprehension were found between conservers and non-conservers for pre-riddles and more complex riddle forms (based on improbable relationships and riddle parody). Since nearly all third- and fifth-graders were judged to be conservers of liquid quantity, weight, and area, a similar analysis for these children could not be carried out. Whitt and Prentice noted that since none of the homonymic riddles were based on liquid conservation principles, the mediating role played by subjects' cognitive processes was more general than McGhee (1976a) has suggested. While the data reported by Whitt and Prentice are encouraging, it should be recognized that their sample size was extremely small (four non-conservers and seven conservers), and hence additional research is needed to test the robustness of their findings.

In contrast to those studies which have directly measured children's cognitive processes, and related variation in performance to humour development, McGhee (1974b) studied the relationship between children's humour and moral judgments. Drawing on Piaget's (1932) distinction between heteronomous and autonomous stages of morality (where children make judgments about the rightness and wrongness of moral acts on the basis of observed consequences versus intentions, respectively), McGhee asked second-, fourth-, and eighth-grade children, plus college students, to make judgments as to the funniness of stories which varied in terms of amount of damage portrayed, and intentionality of the portrayed act. Generalizing across three experiments that were reported, results indicated that heteronomous subjects preferred stories with highly damaging outcomes more than ones with low damaging outcomes. In contrast, the critical factor for humour appreciation of autonomous subjects was not the amount of damage portrayed, but the intentionality of the damaging act. Only when stories portrayed damage or aggression that was accidental (i.e. unintentional) did autonomous children show increased humour appreciation. It appears, therefore, that the cognitive evaluations underlying heteronomous and autonomous moral orientations are predictive of developmental changes in children's appreciation of humour based on damage or aggression. This is an important finding, since previous research on the cognitive aspects of humour has focused primarily on material containing relatively conflict-free content. Yet it is obvious, even to the casual observer, that much, if not most, of the humour to which we are exposed is based on emotionally charged themes (e.g. hostility, sexuality, death). Any explanation of humour development will eventually have to take into account these forms of humour as well as the more cognitively based humour.

It is interesting to note that concern with individual variation in cognitive development as a factor in humour appreciation and comprehension has not been restricted to children. Schaier and Cicirelli (1976) reported a significant positive correlation between scores on a volume-conservation task and comprehension of volume-conservation jokes, but not of mass- and weight-conservation jokes, for subjects between fifty and seventy-nine years. Further, while the correlation between conservation of volume and joke appreciation was not significant, an interesting age trend emerged. For those subjects who conserved volume, an increase in age was accompanied by a significant increase in appreciation of volume-conservation jokes, while for those subjects who were non-conservers of volume, a non-significant decrease in appreciation of volume-conservation jokes was noted with increasing age. Schaier and Cicirelli suggest that this trend is consistent with the cognitive congruency principle, although they recognize that the number of subjects failing volume conservation was too small for a sensitive test of the principle ($n = 3$ in the 60–69-year-old group; $n = 9$ in the 70–79-year-old group).

Finally, a recent study by Fowles and Glanz (1977), which is unrelated to the bulk of research reviewed so far, provides some insight into the relation between reading ability and verbal riddle comprehension. Children from six to nine years of age were presented with verbal riddles, one at a time, by an adult examiner. After listening to each riddle the child had to retell the riddle and explain it to a second adult. Results indicated that children designated as at or above age level in reading ability were more successful in comprehending the humour material than children below age level in reading ability. Of special interest, however, was the lack of difference between these groups of children in their ability to remember accurately and retell the riddles. As the authors note, the ability to recall a riddle was not predictive of the ability to explain it. This is not surprising, however, given that the procedures used in the study were probably conducive to a rote memory strategy. Had the children been required to listen to all the riddles before retelling each one (instead of retelling the riddle immediately after having heard it), it is more likely that reading ability would also have been predictive of recall performance.

In general, it should be clear that a number of studies have been successful in relating individual differences in humour development to variations in children's cognitive functioning. The results have been more consistent for humour comprehension than appreciation, although as previously suggested the inconsistency with respect to humour appreciation probably stems from inadequate designs. Further, the pattern of results is quite clear in demonstrating the need for careful analysis of the match between specific cognitive demands placed upon the subject by the humour material, and the existing level of cognitive functioning of the individual. The closer the match between subject and object, the more predictive the independent variables will be with respect to the humour response.

Cognitive style and humour

In the past two decades, researchers have differentiated between an individual's *ability* to solve problems and the *manner* or *mode* in which the problems are solved. The former characteristic has been closely tied to intelligence and cognitive development (as represented in the two sub-sections above), while the latter characteristic has been conceptualized in terms of various cognitive styles (Kagan and Kogan, 1970; Kogan, 1976; Sigel and Brodzinsky, 1977).

Cognitive styles represent dispositional variables that mediate the way individuals process information. Further, they are thought to be relatively stable modes of adaptation that represent an interface between cognition and personality (Sigel and Brodzinsky, 1977).

While a number of different cognitive styles have been identified in children (Kagan and Kogan, 1970), only one has been related to children's humour development. In a recent series of studies, Brodzinsky and colleagues (Brodzinsky, 1975, 1977; Brodzinsky, Feuer, and Owens, 1977; Brodzinsky, Tew, and Palkowitz, 1979) have examined the relationship between children's conceptual tempo (also known as reflection-impulsivity) and humour comprehension and appreciation.

The conceptual tempo variable represents a disposition that children adopt in processing task-related information in problem-solving situations involving moderate to high response uncertainty (Messer, 1976). Operationally, this dimension is defined by the child's performance of Kagan's Matching Familiar Figures (MFF) test (Kagan, Rosman, Day, Albert, and Phillips, 1964). The MFF is a match-to-sample task in which the child must choose from six similar variants the one that exactly matches the standard figure. Mean errors and latency to first response are the dependent variables. While some children are quick and cursory in their analysis, and hence are relatively inaccurate (impulsives), other children approach the problem in a cautious, systematic, and detailed manner, and subsequently are more often correct (reflectives). In addition to these two groups, a smaller percentage of children appears to be able to retain a relatively high level of accuracy even though their response is quick (fast-accurates), while other children display both cautiousness in responding and a low level of accuracy (slow-inaccurates).

The rationale for focusing on the relationship between this individual difference dimension and children's humour was the assumption that humour by its very nature poses a type of stimulus ambiguity for the individual in the form of perceptual, linguistic and/or logical incongruities. The level of ambiguity may vary, however, as a function of the degree to which incongruous stimulus features are embedded within the humour context. Thus, humour containing subtle defining characteristics (and hence greater response uncertainty) is more likely to be identified and resolved by children who are cautious and systematic in processing information. In contrast, no differences in humour comprehension are expected among conceptual tempo groups when humour stimuli are based upon very obvious incongruities.

Examination of the results across several studies reveals clear support for a relation between conceptual tempo and children's humour. In the initial study, Brodzinsky (1975) presented six-, eight-, and ten-year-old boys with cartoons varying in cognitive complexity and affective salience. Results indicated that while reflective subjects showed the highest humour comprehension (at six and eight, but not ten years), it was the impulsive subjects who showed the greatest mirth, particularly to cartoons containing aggression themes (as well as to control stimuli). In addition, while humour comprehension decreased for all subjects in response to aggression cartoons, the decrease was significantly less for reflective subjects than for all other children. This suggests that while high levels of cartoon aggression may distract children from fully comprehending humour, the reflective child's cautious and detailed manner of responding overcomes at least part of the distractive potency of aggressive material.

In a second study, which was only tangentially related to humour development, Brodzinsky *et al.* (1977) examined the relationship between conceptual tempo and children's comprehension of linguistic ambiguities. Fourth- and seventh-grade children were asked to paraphrase the meaning of sentences containing either phonological, lexical, surface-structure, or deep-structure ambiguities. In general, reflective children were more successful than impulsive and slow-inaccurate children in spontaneously detecting the multiple meaning of ambiguous sentences (even with IQ controlled). However, when prompted by the examiner to reflect once again upon the meaning of the sentences, the difference among conceptual tempo groups was eliminated.

Arguing that differences in spontaneous detection of linguistic ambiguities may be one factor underlying individual differences in humour response, Brodzinsky (1977) examined humour comprehension and appreciation of linguistically ambiguous jokes in fourth-grade reflective, impulsive, fast-accurate, and slow-inaccurate children. Subjects were presented with jokes containing either phonological, lexical, surface-structure, or deep-structure ambiguities (as well as control stimuli). Measures of spontaneous and prompted comprehension, as well as mirth and funniness ratings were taken. Results indicated that reflective and fast-accurate children spontaneously comprehended the verbal jokes to a greater extent than impulsive and slow-inaccurate children. Once again, however, when subjects were prompted by the examiner to reconsider the meaning of the jokes, comprehension differences among conceptual tempo groups were eliminated. Thus, these findings support the view that humour comprehension differences among conceptual tempo groups reflect differences in style of responding and not cognitive ability.

With respect to humour appreciation, impulsive children showed greater mirth than reflective and fast-accurate children, although this difference was eliminated when children's mirth scores for humorous jokes were covaried for their response to control stimuli. In addition, only reflective children showed differential smiling and laughter as a function of joke complexity. Impulsive and slow-inaccurate children showed equal levels of mirth for all joke types. (Although fast-accurate children also showed a tendency to decrease their mirth for more complex jokes, a floor effect prevented this trend from reaching a significant level.) These findings suggest that affective responding in reflective children is modulated by their cognitive processes to a greater extent than is the case for other children. In other words, while reflective children are more likely to smile and laugh when they understand a joke than when they do not, impulsive and slow-inaccurate children appear just as likely to laugh at a joke when they do not understand it as when they do.

The mirth data from the previous study indicate that impulsive and slow-inaccurate children are more affectively labile than are reflective (and possibily fast-accurate) children. If this is the case, then impulsive and slow-inaccurate children should be more influenced by affective responding in other individuals than reflective or fast-accurate children. To test this hypothesis, Brodzinsky, Tew, and Palkovitz (1979) presented fourth-grade children with video-taped jokes, half of which were followed by a laughing audience and half by a non-laughing audience. (The audience was composed of unfamiliar fourth-graders.) Results generally supported the above speculation. While all subjects showed greater mirth following socially facilitated jokes than non-facilitated jokes, the difference between the two joke conditions was significantly greater for impulsive than for reflective and fast-accurate subjects. In other words, impulsive children were more likely to alter their response in the direction of the audience response than were reflective and fast-accurate children.

To summarize, it is quite clear that the cognitive style known as conceptual tempo is strongly related to children's humour development. Whereas reflective, and possibly fast-accurate, children are more likely to get the point of the joke spontaneously, it is the impulsive and slow-inaccurate children who are most likely to smile and laugh (often at inappropriate times). Interestingly, in all the studies done so far, mirth level, but not funniness ratings, has differentiated the various conceptual tempo groups. This suggests that children who adopt different cognitive styles do not necessarily differ in their appreciation of cartoons and jokes, but only in the way they express their appreciation affectively.

Personality development and humour

As noted earlier in this chapter, a very common assumption concerning humour responsiveness is its association to various personality traits and patterns of psychosocial adjustment. To be sure, this assumption has considerable empirical support in the psychological literature. For example, individual differences in humour have been linked to such traditional personality dimensions as dogmatism (Hunt and Miller, 1968; Rouff, 1974; Smith and Levenson, 1976), authoritarianism (Cleland, 1957), conservatism (Thomas, Shea, and Rigby, 1971), introversion-extraversion (Eysenck, 1942; Koppel and Sechrest, 1970; Verinis, 1970) and internal-external locus of control (Lefcourt, Sordoni, and Sordoni, 1974). Furthermore, a number of studies have related differences in humour appreciation to temporary induced mood states, including aggression and sexual arousal (Dworkin and Efran, 1962; Lamb, 1968; Leak, 1974; Schwartz, 1972; Singer, 1968; Strickland, 1959).

Yet for all the work that has been done in this area, very few studies have included children as subjects. Moreover, those studies that have focused on children's humour, have not examined the developmental relationship between personality and humour. Nor have these studies been based within a programme of research. In fact, they typically have been single-study, atheoretical investigations whose value for understanding the development of humour can be best described as minimal.

For example, Wilson and Patterson (1969) requested high- and low-conservative groups of high-school students (ages fifteen to nineteen years) to rate the funniness of cartoons which varied in tendentious content. Results showed that highly conservative students rated 'safe', formal humour (i.e. cartoons based upon puns or cognitive incongruities) as significantly funnier than tendentious humour (i.e. morbid, sadistic, or sexual cartoons), and preferred the former cartoons more than liberal students, who were more appreciative of the latter stimuli. The authors attributed the results to the conservative group's 'chronically mobilized inhibitions' against sexual and hostile behaviour which, when depicted in cartoons, depressed perceived cartoon funniness. While these results are congruent with humour research using college students (cf. Thomas *et al.*, 1971), they tell us little about the origins of the relationship between conservatism and humour, or about the continuity or discontinuity of the relationship from childhood to adulthood.

Two recent studies have examined the relationship between humour and aspects of the self system in children. McGhee and Grodzitsky (1973) tested the hypothesis that humour based on sex-inappropriate behaviour would be appreciated more by children who had a high as opposed to low level of mastery over their own sex-role identity. Three- to five-year-old boys, whose level of sex-role identity had been measured using the IT scale, were presented with drawings of children engaged in sex-appropriate or inappropriate behaviour, the outcome of which was either positve or negative. Results supported the hypothesis in showing that pre-school boys, high in mastery of sex-role identity, were more appreciative of drawings depicting sex-inappropriate behaviour than were boys low in sex-role mastery. The authors suggested that children who had not yet mastered their sex-role identity were more likely to respond with uncertainty or anxiety rather than with laughter to sex-inappropriate drawings. (This interpretation is similar to one used by Ecker, Levine, and Zigler, 1973, who reported that adult schizophrenics with imparied sex-role identification were less capable than normal subjects in comprehending cartoon humour depicting individuals engaged in ambiguous or sex-inappropriate activities.) LaChance (1972), on the other hand, found only a weak positive relationship between overall self-concept and number of humorous items written by fifth-graders. However, one component of the self system which was strongly related to humour responsiveness was in the area of peer relations. Children with low self-concept in this area were much more likely to produce humour containing hostile themes.

Both Freud (1928) and Mead (1934) have suggested that humour is partially based upon the ability of the individual to empathize with the characters portrayed in the humour stimulus. This suggestion has been verified with adults (Roberts and Johnson, 1957). In order to test this relationship among children, Rightmyer (1976) presented cartoons varying in tendentious content to eight- and nine-year-old boys who had been divided into low, moderate, and high empathy groups based on Rothenberg's (1970) test of 'social sensitivity'. Results indicated a significant positive relationship between empathy and humour comprehension, but no relationship between empathy and funniness ratings or mirth. These results are understandable, however, given that Rothenberg's test is more closely related to the cognitive dimension than to the affective dimension of empathy (Deutsch and Madle, 1975).

The most comprehensive study of patterns of psychosocial adjustment related to humour development was conducted by McGhee (1976b). Drawing on longitudinal data from the Fels Institute files, McGhee related various humour behaviours (amount of laughter, behavioural and verbal initiations of humour, hostile humour) of six- to eleven-year-old children, observed in the naturalistic setting of a summer day camp, to earlier recorded maternal and child behaviours. Interestingly, very few maternal behaviours (including maternal attempts at initiating humour) predicted later humour behaviour in children. In contrast, a large number of predictors of high humour responsiveness were found in antecedents of the children's own behaviour. For example, increased humour responsiveness in later childhood was associated with the following child behaviours during the six-year and above period: increased physical and verbal aggressiveness, and dominance over same-sex peers; frequent imitation of peers; frequent attempts to obtain attention or affection from adults; lack of an effort at mastery of fine motor skills; increased social play; increased restless activity and a lack of body co-ordination; expressive and skillful use of language. (While there were a number of differences in the pattern of responding for boys and girls, a discussion of sex differences in children's humour is reserved for a later subsection.)

Finally, in his study of humour antecedents, McGhee (1976b) suggested that aggressive humour appreciation and initiation may have been an attempt on the children's part to win the recognition of peers who had rejected them due to their aggressive and dominating behaviour. If so, this 'compensatory' use of humour is congruent with the positive relationship obtained by Gidynski (1972) between humour appreciation and peer rejection in pre-adolescent boys. In fact, both of these studies, along with the study by LaChance (1972), are indirectly supportive of Wolfenstein's (1954) position that humour is frequently used by children (and adults) as a means of coping with and regulating stress. These studies, however, have no bearing on the developmental implication of Wolfenstein's position which was mentioned earlier.

Atypical development and humour

Freud's (1960) theory of humour was the first to emphasize the relationship between humour appreciation and production, and the individual's underlying psychic structure. Like dreams and slips of the tongue, one's propensity to appreciate or not appreciate certain types of humour was assumed to be revealing of repressed or suppressed thoughts, feelings, needs, etc. As noted earlier, this assumption has been capitalized upon by clinicians in therapy settings (e.g. Greenwald, 1977; Grossman, 1977; Killinger, 1977; Levine, 1977, Chapter 10 of this volume). It is surprising, however, that few systematic empirical studies have tested Freud's position, particularly with specific atypical populations in which repressed or suppressed motives are thought to be highly salient.

The present authors could find only a handful of studies which focused on the humour of atypical or exceptional children (defined in terms of physical, mental, or emotional disability). Moreover, a number of these studies were simply clinical descriptions of humour as a therapeutic tool and/or of children's joke-telling within therapy settings (Domash, 1975; Loewald, 1976; Tolor, 1966; Wolfenstein, 1954; Yorukoglu, 1974, 1977). These latter reports are instructive, however, in differentiating how humour is used by children characterized by varying degrees of emotional disturbance. Thus, healthier children quite often use the 'pretend' nature of humour to broach their problems in the contexts of therapy, while more disturbed children are more likely to manifest the intrusive force of ongoing problems by rearranging and substituting humorous content, so as to destroy the point of the joke.

One study which did attempt to validate empirically Freud's theory of humour with a group of atypical children was reported by Hetherington (1964). Ten- to twelve-year-old children, suffering from poliomyelitis or cerebral palsy, plus a control group of normal children, were asked to rate the funniness of cartoons whose themes included either motor activity (running, jumping, dancing, etc.) or non-activity (resting, sitting, standing still, etc.). Based upon the assumption that suppressed desires for motor activity in the physically handicapped might be satisfied through humour preferences, it was predicted that handicapped subjects would prefer activity to non-activity cartoons, as well as preferring activity cartoons more than normal subjects. Results partially supported the hypothesis. While normals and the cerebral palsy children showed no preference for activity or non-activity cartoons, the poliomyelitis children did rate activity cartoons significantly higher than non-activity cartoons. They also rated activity cartoons higher than did either the normal or the cerebral palsy children, and non-activity cartoons lower than the cerebral palsy children. No differences in humour ratings were found as a function of age of affliction for poliomyelitis or type of cerebral palsy (i.e. athethoid *versus* spastic forms).

Waterman (1972) studied the humour response of clinically withdrawn and behaviour problem boys, aged nine to eleven years, as well as normal boys, aged seven to twelve years, to film segments of the television show *Laugh In*. The main difference between clinical groups was in their style of responding. Whereas withdrawn boys smiled more than behaviour problem boys, the latter children were more likely to express their appreciation through laughter. These results were interpreted as being congruent with the general behavioural style of the groups. In addition, while all groups of boys preferred aggressive humour more than either incongruity or social embarrassment humour, the hypothesis that behaviour problem children would enjoy the former humour type more than withdrawn or normal children was not conclusively confirmed. On the other hand, normal children did express more appreciation for the social embarrassment humour than the two clinical groups, and a trend was noted for behavioural problem boys to appreciate this humour type more than withdrawn boys. Finally, no difference was noted among groups of children in their response to incongruity humour.

Other researchers have studied humour responsiveness in the retarded child. Zigler, Levine, and Gould (1966b) presented a series of cartoons to groups of normal, non-institutionalized retarded, and institutionalized retarded children matched on MA (mean MA = 10.1, 9.6, and 9.8 years, respectively). As expected, humour comprehension was higher in normal children than in the two groups of retarded children, which did not differ from each other. Further, while no group difference was noted for the number of cartoons liked, both normals and institutionalized retardates displayed greater mirth than non-institutionalized retardates. However, the mirth response of the institutionalized children apparently represented a considerable amount of inappropriate affect as opposed to true humour appreciation. That is, these children were the only ones who failed to show an increase in mirth with increasing humour comprehension. In explaining group differences, Zigler and his colleagues stressed the deleterious effects on cognitive and affective humour behaviours of the restricted range of socializing experiences (both pre-institutional and institutional) that is common among retarded children. Pustel, Sternlicht, and Siegel (1972) also examined humour among the retarded. Specifically, they focused on the central themes represented in the jokes told by mildly retarded institutionalized adolescents (and adults).

They found that the majority of joke themes centred on successful rebellion and on the misfortune of others. Moreover, there was a greater percentage of phallic themes than oral or anal themes. The authors suggested that these themes represented a reaction formation against feelings of inferiority. If this is true, then it is further evidence for Wolfenstein's (1954) position that humour (even among individuals with limited cognitive ability) is used as a means of coping with stress. Finally, in a very interesting study, Cicchetti and Sroufe (1976) examined the early determinants, and course of development, of laughter in Down's syndrome infants. Using a longitudinal design, infants were presented each month (from four months until eighteen months) with a series of laughter-inducing stimuli by their mothers in their own homes, and their reactions were compared with data on normal infants reported by Sroufe and Wunsch (1972). In the first place, Down's syndrome infants lagged far behind normal infants in onset and frequency of laughter. For example, the median age of onset for the retarded infants was ten months, compared to three or four months for normal infants. Down's syndrome infants, being generally hypotonic, also frequently smiled to stimuli which elicited laughter in normal infants. Nevertheless, the order of development of laughter to various categories of stimuli was the same in these retarded infants as in normal infants; that is, both groups of infants laughed first to auditory and tactile stimuli, and only later to more cognitively complex visual and social stimuli. Cicchetti and Sroufe interpreted their data as supporting the role of tension, in addition to cognitive factors, in affective expression (see Sroufe and Waters, 1976).

Sex differences

One of the most frequently researched topics in the area of humour involves sex differences. Unfortunately for our purposes, most of this work has focused on the humour of adults. As McGhee (1976b) noted, studies of children's humour typically have not been concerned with exploring the question of sex differences. However, this is not to say that researchers have totally ignored differences between boys and girls in response to humour. A number of studies have included analyses for sex differences. The problem is that the majority of studies have done so only as secondary analyses (and often only as preliminary analyses in the hope of collapsing data across the sex variable). Such studies are usually not designed to shed appreciable light on the basis of sex differences when, unexpectedly, they do appear. Consequently, researchers have been forced either to ignore the differences or come up with *post hoc* (and usually superficial) interpretations for them. In any case, little headway has been made to date in systematically organizing and explaining patterns of sex differences in humour development. In the present sub-section we make a preliminary effort to do so.

One issue that has been raised occasionally is the degree and type of expressiveness manifested by boys and girls in response to humour. In an early study, Justin (1932) observed that pre-school boys (ages three to six years) laughed more than girls to humorous stimuli, whereas girls smiled more than boys. In contrast, Ding and Jersild (1932) reported the opposite finding. That is, over a wide range of situations, pre-school girls laughed more than boys, while boys smiled more than girls. Still another early study failed to find any sex difference in frequency of laughter during free play activity among nursery schoolchildren (Brackett, 1933). More recently, Kreitler and Kreitler (1970) reported that among Oriental children (aged five and six years), girls smiled and laughed less than boys to incongruity pictures, although no sex difference appeared for a comparable group of European children. Sex differences in nursery schoolchildren's humour also have been observed by Groch (1974a). She noted that girls were more likely than boys to display 'responsive' humour, particularly to the verbal statements of others. In contrast, boys displayed greater 'productive' humour, especially in the form of comic and hostile play.

With older children and adolescents, the majority of studies have reported no difference between boys and girls in smiling and laughter to jokes, cartoons, riddles, etc. (Brodzinsky, 1977; Rothbart, 1976; Shultz, 1972, 1974; Shultz and Horibe, 1974; Zigler *et al.*, 1966a, 1966b, 1967). However, these studies, have utilized relatively structured settings for eliciting children's humour, and as such it is difficult to compare their data with the pre-school data obtained under more natural conditions. One study which did examine older children's humour under naturalistic conditions was reported by McGhee (1976b). For elementary school-age children (six to eleven years), boys were rated higher than girls in all humour categories (frequency of laughter, behavioural and verbal initiations of humour, hostile humour). In addition, for younger, nursery schoolchildren, the only humour category differentiating boys and girls was hostile humour. As expected, boys were rated as more often engaging in this activity. McGhee (1974c) also observed that boys developed the ability to formulate the requirements of a joking relationship in absurdity, but not word play, riddles before girls. Boys were also more successful than girls at creating their own absurdity riddles.

Researchers have also reported on sex differences in children's smiling and laughter under conditions of social facilitation. Generalizing across a number of studies (e.g. Chapman, 1973, 1974, 1975; Chapman and Chapman, 1974; Chapman and Speck, 1977; Chapman and Wright, 1976; Foot and Chapman, 1976; Tew, 1978), it would appear that boys and girls show few differences in response to the smiling and laughter of others. The one tentative trend which does emerge from the data indicates that girls are more interested in sharing the social situation than boys, whereas boys are more interested in the humour stimulus (Chapman, 1973, 1974; Smith, Foot, and Chapman, 1977). McGhee (cited in McGhee, 1976b) has also noted that the humour of elementary school-age girls is more highly affected by social response tendencies than is true for boys. One additional study which found sex differences under varying social conditions was reported by Prerost (1977). Working with adolescents and youths from ten to twenty years of age, Prerost investigated the influence of social and spatial density on humour appreciation. Results indicated that while humour ratings increased under conditions of increasing social density, the effect was significantly stronger for groups of girls than groups of boys. On the other hand, increasing spatial density resulted in a significant decrease in humour appreciation, and more so for boys than girls.

Research by Leventhal and his colleagues indicates that sex differences exist both in children (Leventhal and Mace, 1970) and in adults (Cupchik and Leventhal, 1974; Leventhal and Cupchik, 1975) in the relation between affective and cognitive evaluations of humour. These investigators found that girls (and women) were more likely than boys (and men) to take into account their emotional response to humour when making cognitive judgments about the perceived funniness of the stimuli. On the basis of this finding, it was suggested that for females a relatively high degree of interdependence exists between their emotional (mirth scores) and cognitive (funniness ratings) response to humour, whereas for males, there exists relative independence between these behavioural measures. Although interesting, and certainly provocative, this conclusion has not been consistently supported by empirical research. Recently, Tew (1978), investigating developmental changes in children's response to socially facilitated humour, found significant positive correlations between facilitated mirth scores and facilitated funniness ratings, and between non-facilitated mirth scores and non-facilitated funniness ratings, for both boys and girls. In other words, for both sexes, emotional and cognitive humour responses manifested an interdependent relationship (see also Chapter 6.)

Sex differences in humour expressiveness have also been studied as a function of stimulus content. One assumption behind much of this work is that men and women, because of differences in socialization history, are likely to develop different types of conflicts, which in turn are manifested in appreciation and production of different kinds of humour. Thus, because women are more likely than men to be shielded during development from sexual and aggressive experiences, it is frequently assumed that they will be less comfortable in dealing with these types of humour material. In fact, there is a considerable amount of empirical support for this assumption, at least with adult subjects. Males have been found to prefer sexual humour (Brodzinsky, Barnet, and Aiello, in press; Groch, 1974b; Malpass and Fitzpatrick, 1959) and aggressive humour (Groch, 1974b; Landis and Ross, 1933), while females display greater appreciation of absurd humour (Brodzinsky et al., in press; Groch, 1974b; Landis and Ross, 1933). In addition, males have been reported to be more successful at producing funny captions for sexual and aggressive cartoons, but not for novelty cartoons (Brodzinsky and Rubein, 1976). Perhaps because of the ethical consideration of exposing children to sexual material, no systematic attempts have been made to measure children's response to this type of tendentious humour. However, several studies have reported on sex differences in children's aggressive humour. King and King (1973) observed that four- and five-year-old boys more frequently chose hostile-aggressive endings for humorous drawings than girls. Similarly, Groch (1974a) noted that among nursery schoolboys, but not girls, hostile joking was a very common behaviour. Working with fifth-grade children, LaChance (1972) reported that boys produced more instances of hostility humour than girls, whereas girls produced more instances of 'sophisticated' humour. Further, as noted earlier, McGhee (1976b) found that for elementary school-age children, but not nursery schoolchildren, boys were rated as initiating more hostile humour than girls. Even among retarded adolescents, a greater percentage of jokes told by boys as opposed to girls have been observed to contain hostile themes (Pustel et al., 1972).

While these data are consistent with the sex difference picture that has emerged in the literature on adult humour, other studies with children have failed to replicate this response pattern (Bryant and Meyer, 1977; Prentice and Fathman, 1975; Sinnott and Ross, 1976). To what extent these discrepant findings are a function of procedural differences among the studies is not completely clear. However, given that even among adults, sex differences in response to tendentious humour are not found for all types of stimuli (Brodzinsky *et al.*, in press; Chapman and Gadfield, 1976) or under all social conditions (Brodzinsky, Cundari, and Aiello, 1978), indicates that the stereotype of the female as being too inexperienced or too conflicted to enjoy or produce tendentious humour is simply not valid. Future research, particularly with children, needs to identify the stimulus and social parameters under which sex differences in response to specific humour content are (or are not) likely to appear.

Finally, McGhee (1976b) has reported on sex differences in the antecedents of children's humour. Frequency of laughter, behavioural and verbal initiations of humour, and hostile humour of six- to eleven-year-old children attending the Fels summer day-camp were predicted from earlier recorded maternal and child behaviours. First, although very few maternal behaviours predicted later childhood humour for either sex, it was noted that lack of early maternal babying (from birth to three years) was strongly associated with the amount of laughter and hostile humour among boys, but not girls. Furthermore, a low level of home adjustment in the first three years of life was associated with more frequent behavioural and verbal attempts to initiate humour among girls than boys. McGhee suggests that the latter finding supports the view that females frequently use humour as a means of getting attention or recognition from adults. This position is further supported by data from the children's own behaviour. Instrumental help-seeking and emotional support-seeking from adults by children was more strongly associated with humour initiation in girls than boys. In fact, boys displaying these dependency behaviours tended to show few behavioural attempts at humour, especially hostile humour. High antecedent aggressiveness and dominance over peers, as well as imitation of peers, was also more strongly predictive of humour among girls than boys. In contrast, increased social play, frequent restless activity, a lack of body co-ordination, and greater talkativeness were more highly related to various humour behaviours in boys than girls. Clearly, the pattern of sex differences in the antecedents of children's humour is quite complex. Moreover, these findings are presently without satisfactory explanation. Additional research is needed to test the robustness of these results, as well as explicate their meaning.

CONCLUSIONS AND IMPLICATIONS

The purpose of the present chapter has been to organize some of the literature on children's humour in the hope of providing some insight into the individual differences that are so clearly evident in humour development. It was not our intention to provide a theoretical explanation for these differences. Indeed, it is doubtful that any one theory to date could handle the multitude of differences that exist among children with respect to humour. However, this should not be taken to mean that we are pessimistic about the ability of researchers to formulate testable theoretical accounts of humour variability. Quite the contrary. The work by McGhee, in particular, is a good example of carefully thought out, programmatic, theory-directed research which has been of considerable value for our understanding of children's humour. The problem is that this type of research has been the exception and not the rule. A majority of the humour research reviewed in this chapter has been atheoretical and non-programmatic in nature. The result of this approach has been the accumulation of a great deal of information about children's humour, but little understanding as to its meaning. Thus, one conclusion to be drawn from this review is that we simply do not understand the basis of much, if not most, of the variability in humour development. Moreover, this lack of understanding stems not only from a relative paucity of research into this aspect of humour, but just as important, from the failure of research to be guided by sound, testable theory.

In addition to theory-directed research, continued progress in understanding individual differences in humour will necessitate a more sophisticated approach than has been adopted by most humour researchers in the past. For example, one important point that needs to be recognized is that humour is not something that resides solely in the individual; nor is it something to be found in the environment. On the contrary, it is the Person × Situation interaction that is the spawning ground for what we call humour. This realization has several important implications. First, focusing totally on such organismic factors as cognitive level, cognitve style, personality traits, or sex of subject is unlikely to yield very useful information concerning the manifestation of humour variability. As we have shown in this chapter, children differing in cognitive level or cognitive style show differential response to some types of humour, but not to others. Second, an analysis of humour stimuli *per se* is also unlikely to be helpful for understanding individual differences in humour since not all people respond the same way to specific stimulus dimensions. This brings us to the Person × Situation analysis. Traditionally, the question of individual differences in humour has been investigated as a function of various organismic dimensions in interaction with various stimulus dimensions. While such studies have been successful in furthering our understanding of humour, they have at least one important limitation. That is, the analysis of the situation typically has been restricted to various stimulus dimensions. In contrast, little attention has been given to individual differences in humour as a function of the setting in which the person perceives or creates the humour. In other words, we believe that a more complete understanding of individual variation in humour development necessitates an analysis of Person Variables × Stimulus Variables × Setting Variables. To date, however, humour research has not progressed to this point.

Another major criticism of the literature on individual differences in children's humour is that it has not been truly developmental in nature. In other words, little attention has been given to the continuity or discontinuity of the relationships observed between the various organismic and stimulus/setting variables from early childhood through adulthood. Further, no theoretical or empirical attempt has been made to analyse humour across the entire lifespan. Such analyses are of paramount importance if we are to have a truly comprehensive picture of the individual difference factors influencing humour development.

We also would argue that our relative ignorance of the bases underlying individual variation in children's humour partially stems from a certain methodological myopia. Overconcern with empirical generalization has led many researchers to over-emphasize the value of the nomothetic and differential research strategies, and to downplay the utility of the idiographic approach. While we agree that generalizability is important, and ultimately the goal of any humour theory, we believe quite strongly that in-depth, case-study analyses of humour, which is the core of the idiographic approach, are extremely valuable and deserving of greater attention. If nothing else, they would appear to be a potentially rich source for the generation of testable theoretical ideas. (One should never forget that Freud's unparalleled theory of personality and Piaget's equally impressive theory of cognitive development originated from intensive case studies of a small number of individuals.)

To summarize, the literature on individual differences in children's humour, while growing, is still at a point where only a few clear trends have emerged, and not all of these are completely understood. Thus, one obvious trend that can be seen is that children who are more advanced cognitively are more likely to comprehend the basis of humour than are their less bright counterparts. Similarly, children who adopt a reflective cognitive style also are more likely to get the point of the joke spontaneously than are impulsive children. On the other hand, impulsive and slow-inaccurate children seem to be more affectively responsive to humour (often inappropriately so) than are reflective children. Another trend that has emerged is that humour appreciation (at least for funniness ratings) appears to depend on the match between subject's development level and the cognitive demands placed upon him by the humour stimulus. Humour which is based upon a specific structural property (e.g. violation of weight conservation) is more likely to be appreciated by children who have just developed the cognitive skill necessary to understand the incongruity than by children who have yet to master the skill or by children who have possessed the skill for some time.

In contrast to these trends, little can be said at present about the relationship between children's humour and dimensions of personality and psychosocial adjustment. Similarly, the literature on humour among atypical children is also too sparse to warrant anything but the most general comment; namely, that humour is often used by children as a means of coping with a stress. Finally, few consistent differences have emerged between boys and girls in response to humour. Contrary to McGhee's (1976) conclusion, we can find no basis for the statement that boys are more likely than girls to laugh at humour stimuli, while girls are more likely to smile. Moreover, while there is some evidence to support the view that boys are more likely to appreciate aggressive humour than girls, an equal number of studies have failed to confirm this sex difference.

In conclusion, probably the most definite, yet obvious, statement that can be made is that considerably more research is needed with respect to individual differences in humour development. Specifically, we would suggest that the following topics are in need of further investigation: (a) the influence of cognitive factors in the comprehension and appreciation of tendentious humour; (b) an examination of other cognitive style factors, specifically field-dependence/ independence, in humour development; (c) individual difference factors related to humour production and memory for humour; (d) an investigation of factors associated with the humour/creativity/play relationship; (e) the role of personality and patterns of psychosocial adjustment in humour development; (f) the use, and role, of humour among atypical children; (g) individual difference factors related to the recognition of the need for the joke façade; (h) sex differences in humour; (i) physiological bases of individual differences in humour expressiveness. In addition to these areas, it should be pointed out that researchers must begin to examine the developmental antecedents underlying the relationship between various individual difference dimensions and children's humour. In other words, it is not enough simply to say that impulsive children are more often affectively responsive to humour than reflective children. The establishment of an empirical relationship does not explain the relationship. We need to go beyond this point to examine the socializing practices and general experiences that underlie the empirical relationships observed. It is only at this level of analysis that we will eventually come to understand the bases of individual differences in humour development.

REFERENCES

Bergson, H. (1911). *Laughter: An Essay on The Meaning of The Comic*. New York: Macmillan.

Bird, G. E. (1925). An objective humor test for children. *Psychological Bulletin*, **22**, 137–138.

Brackett, C. W. (1934). Laughter and crying in preschool children. *Child Development Monographs*, **14**, 119–126.

Brodzinsky, D. M. (1975). The role of conceptual tempo and stimulus characteristics in children's humor development. *Developmental Psychology*, **11**, 843–850.

Brodzinsky, D. M. (1977). Children's comprehension and appreciation of verbal jokes in relation to conceptual tempo. *Child Development*, **48**, 960–967.

Brodzinsky, D. M., Barnet, K., and Aiello, J. R. (in press). Sex of subject and gender identity as factors in humor appreciation. *Sex Roles*.

Brodzinsky, D. M., Cundari, L., and Aiello, J. R. (1978). Sex of subject and group composition as factors in humor appreciation. Paper in preparation.

Brodzinsky, D. M., Feuer, V., and Owens, J. (1977). Detection of linguistic ambiguity by reflective, impulsive, fast-accurate, and slow-inaccurate children. *Journal of Educational Psychology*, **69**, 237–243.

Brodzinsky, D. M., and Rubien, J. (1976). Humor production as a function of sex of subject, creativity, and cartoon content. *Journal of Consulting and Clinical Psychology*, **44**, 597–600.

Brodzinsky, D. M., Tew, J. D., and Palkovitz, R. (1979). Control of humorous affect in relation to children's conceptual tempo. *Developmental Psychology*, **15**, 275–279.

Bryant, J., and Meyer, T. P. (1977). A developmental analysis of children's favourite jokes. In A. J. Chapman and H. C. Foot (Eds.), *It's a Funny Thing, Humour*. Oxford: Pergamon Press.

Chapman, A. J. (1973). Social facilitation of laughter in children. *Journal of Experimental Social Psychology*, **9**, 528–541.

Chapman, A. J. (1974). An experimental study of socially facilitated humorous laughter. *Psychological Reports*, **35**, 727–734.

Chapman, A. J. (1975). Humorous laughter in children. *Journal of Personality of Social Psychology*, **31**, 42–49.

Chapman, A. J., and Chapman, W.A. (1974). Responsiveness to humor: its dependency upon a companion's humorous smiling and laughter. *Journal of Psychology*, **88**, 245–252.

Chapman, A. J., and Gadfield, N. J. (1976). Is sexual humor sexist? *Journal of Communication*, **26**, 141–153.

Chapman, A. J., and Speck, L. J. M. (1977). Birth order and humour responsiveness in young children. In A. J. Chapman and H. C. Foot (Eds.), *It's a Funny Thing, Humour*. Oxford: Pergamon Press.

Chapman, A. J., and Wright, D. S. (1976). Social enhancement of laughter: an experimental analysis of some companion variables. *Journal of Experimental Child Psychology*, **21**, 201–218.

Cicchetti, D., and Sroufe, L. A. (1976). The relationship between affective and cognitive development in Down's syndrome infants. *Child Development*, **47**, 920–929.

Cleland, R. (1957). An investigation of the relationship between creative humor and authoritarianism. *Dissertation Abstracts*, **17**, 2005.

Cunningham, A. (1962). Relation of sense of humor to intelligence. *Journal of Social Psychology*, **57**, 143–147.

Cupchik, G. C., and Leventhal, H. (1974). Consistency between expressive behavior and the evaluation of humorous stimuli: the role of sex and self-observation. *Journal of Personality and Social Psychology*, **50**, 429–442.

Darwin, C. (1965). *The Expression of Emotions in Man and Animals*. Chicago: University of Chicago Press (Originally published in 1872).

Deutsch, F., and Madle, R. A. (1975). Empathy: historic and current conceptualizations, measurement, and a cognitive theoretical perspective. *Human Development*, **18**, 267–287.

Ding, G. F., and Jersild, A. T. (1932). A study of the laughing and smiling of preschool children. *Journal of Genetic Psychology*, **40**, 452–472.

Domash, L. (1975). The case of wit and the comic by a borderline psychotic child in psychotherapy. *American Journal of Psychotherapy*, **29**, 261–265.

Dworkin, E., and Efran, J. (1967). The angered: their susceptibility to varieties of humor. *Journal of Personality and Social Psychology*, **6**, 233–236.

Ecker, J., Levine, J., and Zigler, E. (1973). Impared sex-role identification in schizophrenia expressed in the comprehension of humor stimuli. *Journal of Psychology*, **83**, 67–77.

Emmerich, W. (1968). Personality development and concepts of structure. *Child Development*, **39**, 671–690.

Enders, A. C. (1927). A study of the laughter of the preschool child in the Merrill-Palmer nursery school. *Papers of the Michigan Academy of Science, Arts, and Letters,* **8,** 341–356.

Eysenck, H. J. (1942). The appreciation of humour: an experimental and theoretical study. *British Journal of Psychology,* **32,** 295–309.

Foot, H. C., and Chapman, A J. (1976). The social responsiveness of young children in humorous situations. In A. J. Chapman and H. C. Foot (Eds.), *Humour and Laughter: Theory, Research and Applications.* Chichester: Wiley.

Fowles, B., and Glanz, M. E. (1977). Competence and talent in verbal riddle comprehension. *Journal of Child Language,* **4,** 433–452.

Freud, S. (1928). Humor. *International Journal of Psychoanalysis,* **9,** 1–6.

Freud, S. (1960). *Jokes and Their Relation to The Unconscious.* New York: Norton (Originally published in 1905).

Gidynski, C. (1975). Associative shift, peer rejection and humor response in children: an exploratory study. *Dissertation Abstracts,* **36,** 442.

Greenwald, H. (1977). Humour in psychotherapy. In A. J. Chapman and H. C. Foot (Eds.), *It's a Funny Thing, Humour.* Oxford: Pergamon Press.

Groch, A. S. (1974a). Joking and appreciation of humor in nursery school children. *Child Development,* **45,** 1098–1102.

Groch, A. S. (1974b). Generality of response to humor and wit in cartoons, jokes, stories, and photographs. *Psychological Reports,* **35,** 835–838.

Grossman, S. A. (1977). The use of jokes in psychotherapy. In A. J. Chapman and H. C. Foot (Eds.), *It's a Funny Thing, Humour.* Oxford: Pergamon Press.

Hetherington, E. M. (1964). Humor preferences in normal and physically handicapped children. *Journal of Abnormal and Social Psychology,* **69,** 694–696.

Hunt, M. F., and Miller, G. R. (1968). Open- and close-mindedness, belief discrepant behavior, and tolerance for cognitive inconsistency. *Journal of Personality and Social Psychology,* **8,** 35–37.

Justin, F. (1932). A genetic study of laughter provoking stimuli. *Child Development,* **3,** 114–136.

Kagan, J. (1971). *Change and Continuity in Infancy.* New York: Wiley.

Kagan, J., and Kogan, N. (1970). Individual variation in cognitive processes. In P. H. Mussen (Ed.), *Carmichael's Manual of Child Psychology.* Vol. 1. New York: Wiley.

Kagan, J., Rosman, B. L., Day, D., Albert, J., and Phillips, W. (1964). Information processing in the child: significance of analytic and reflective attitudes. *Psychological Monographs,* **78** (1, Whole No. 578).

Kenerdine, M. (1931). Laughter in the preschool child. *Child Development,* **2,** 228–230.

Killinger, B. (1977). The place of humour in adult psychotherapy. In A. J. Chapman and H. C. Foot (Eds.), *It's a Funny Thing, Humour.* Oxford. Pergamon Press.

King, P. V., and King, J. F. (1973). A children's humor test. *Psychological Reports,* **33,** 632.

Kogan, N. (1976). *Cognitive Styles in Infancy and Early Childhood.* New York: Halsted Press.

Koppel, M., and Sechrest, L. (1970). A multitrait-multimethod matrix analysis of sense of humor. *Educational and Psychological Measurement,* **30,** 77–85.

Korchin, S. J. (1976). *Modern Clinical Psychology.* New York: Basic Books.

Kreitler, H., and Kreitler, S. (1970). Dependence of laughter on cognitive strategies. *Merrill-Palmer Quarterly,* **16,** 163–177.

LaChance, A. (1972). A study of the correlation between humor and self-concept in fifth-grade boys and girls. Unpublished Doctoral Dissertation, University of Maryland.

Lamb, C. W. (1968). Personality correlates of humor enjoyment following motivational arousal. *Journal of Personality and Social Psychology*, **9**, 237–241.

Landis, C., and Ross, J. (1933). Humor and its relation to other personality traits. *Journal of Social Psychology*, **4**, 156–175.

Leak, G. (1974). Effects of hostility arousal and aggressive humor on catharsis and humor preference. *Journal of Personality and Social Psychology*, **30**, 736–740.

Lefcourt, H., Sordoni, C., and Sordoni, C. (1974). Locus of control and the expression of humor. *Journal of Personality*, **42**, 130–143.

Leventhal, H., and Cupchik, G. C. (1975). The informational and facilitative effects of an audience upon expression and the evaluation of humorous stimuli. *Journal of Experimental Social Psychology*, **11**, 363–380.

Leventhal, H., and Mace, W. (1970). The effect of laughter on evaluation of a slapstick movie. *Journal of Personality*, **38**, 16–30.

Leventhal, H., and Safer, M. (1977). Individual differences, personality, and humour appreciation: introduction to symposium. In A. J. Chapman and H. C. Foot (Eds.), *It's a Funny Thing, Humour*. Oxford: Pergamon Press.

Levine, J. (1977). Humour as a form of therapy: introduction to symposium. In A. J. Chapman and H. C. Foot (Eds.), *It's a Funny Thing, Humour*. Oxford: Pergamon Press.

Loewald, E. (1976). The development and uses of humour in a four-year-old's treatment. *International Review of Psycho-Analysis*, **3**, 209–221.

Maier, N. R. F. (1932). A gestalt theory of humour. *British Journal of Psychology*, **23**, 69–74.

Malpass, L. F., and Fitzpatrick, E. D. (1959). Social facilitation as a factor in reaction to humor. *Journal of Social Psychology*, **50**, 295–303.

McGhee, P. E. (1971a). The development of the humor response: a review of the literature. *Psychological Bulletin*, **76**, 328–348.

McGhee, P. E. (1971b). Cognitive development and children's comprehension of humor. *Child Development*, **42**, 123–138.

McGhee, P. E. (1972). On the cognitive origins of incongruity humor: fantasy-assimilation versus reality-assimilation. In J. H. Goldstein and P. E. McGhee (Eds.), *The Psychology of Humor: Theoretical Perspectives and Empirical Issues*. New York: Academic Press.

McGhee, P. E. (1974a). Cognitive mastery and children's humor. *Psychological Bulletin*, **81**, 721–730.

McGhee, P. E. (1974b). Moral development and children's appreciation of humor. *Developmental Psychology*, **10**, 514–525.

McGhee, P. E. (1974c). Development of children's ability to create the joking relationship. *Child Development*, **45**, 552–556.

McGhee, P. E. (1976a). Children's appreciation of humor: a test of the cognitive congruency principle. *Child Development*, **47**, 420–426.

McGhee, P. E. (1976b). Sex differences in children's humor. *Journal of Communication*, **26**, 176–189.

McGhee, P. E., and Grodzitsky, P. (1973). Sex-role identification and humor among preschool children. *Journal of Psychology*, **84**, 189–193.

McGhee, P. E., and Johnson, S. F. (1975). The role of fantasy and reality cues in children's appreciation of incongruity. *Merrill-Palmer Quarterly*, **21**, 19–30.

Mead, G. H. (1934). *Mind, Self, and Society*. Chicago: University of Chicago Press.

Messer, S. B. (1976). Reflection-impulsivity: a review. *Psychological Bulletin*, **83**, 1026–1052.

Mussen, P. H. (Ed.). (1970). *Carmichael's Manual of Child Psychology*. New York: Wiley.

Omwake, L. (1939). Factors influencing the sense of humor. *Journal of Social Psychology*, **10**, 95–104.

Piaget, J. (1932). *Moral judgment of the child*. New York: Harcourt, Brace.

Prentice, N. M., and Fathman, R. E. (1975). Joking riddles: a developmental index of children's humor. *Developmental Psychology*, **11**, 210–216.

Prerost, F. J. (1977). Environmental conditions affecting the humour response: developmental trends. In A. J. Chapman and H. C. Foot (Eds.), *It's a Funny Thing, Humour*. Oxford: Pergamon Press.

Pustel, G., Sternlicht, M., and Siegel, L. (1932). The psychodynamics of humor as seen in institutionalized retardates. *Journal of Psychology*, **80**, 69–73.

Rightmyer, J. (1976). Humor appreciation and comprehension among boys as a function of empathy level and cartoon type. Unpublished Masters Thesis, Rutgers University.

Roberts, A., and Johnson, D. (1957). Some factors related to the perception of funniness in humor stimuli. *Journal of Social Psychology*, **46**, 57–63.

Rothbart, M. K. (1973). Laughter in young children. *Psychological Bulletin*, **80**, 247–256.

Rothbart, M. K. (1976). Incongruity, problem-solving, and laughter. In A. J. Chapman and H. C. Foot (Eds.), *Humour and Laughter: Theory, Research and Applications*. Chichester: Wiley.

Rothenberg, B. (1970). Children's social sensitivity and the relationship to interpersonal competence, intrapersonal comfort, and intellectual level. *Developmental Psychology*, **2**, 335–350.

Rouff, L. L. (1974). The relationship of personality and cognitive structure to humor appreciation. *Dissertation Abstracts*, **34**, 5174–5175.

Schaier, A. H., and Cicirelli, V. G. (1976). Age differences in humor comprehension and appreciation in old age. *Journal of Gerontology*, **31**, 577–582.

Schwartz, S. (1972). The effects of arousal on appreciation for varying degrees of sex-relevant humor. *Journal of Experimental Research in Personality*, **6**, 244–247.

Shultz, T. R. (1972). The role of incongruity and resolution in children's appreciation of cartoon humor. *Journal of Experimental Child Psychology*, **13**, 456–477.

Shultz, T. R. (1974). Development of the appreciation of the riddles. *Child Development*, **45**, 100–105.

Shultz, T. R. (1976). A cognitive-developmental analysis of humour. In A. J. Chapman and H. C. Foot (Eds.), *Humour and Laughter: Theory, Research and Applications*. Chichester: Wiley.

Shultz, T. R., and Horibe, F. (1974). Development of the appreciation of verbal jokes. *Developmental Psychology*, **10**, 13–20.

Sigel, I. E., and Brodzinsky, D. M. (1977). Individual differences: a perspective for understanding intellectual development. In H. L. Hom and P. L. Robinson (Eds.), *Psychological Processes in Early Education*. New York: Academic Press.

Singer, D. L. (1968). Aggression arousal, hostile humor, catharsis. *Journal of Personality and Social Psychology*, **8**, 1–14.

Sinnott, J. D., and Ross, B. M. (1976). Comparison of aggression and incongruity as factors in children's judgments of humor. *Journal of Genetic Psychology*, **128**, 241–249.

Smith, D. J., and Levenson, H. (1976). Reactions to humor as a function of reference group and dogmatism. *Journal of Social Psychology*, **99**, 57–61.

Smith, J. R., Foot, H. C., and Chapman, A. J. (1977). Nonverbal communication among friends and strangers sharing humour. In A. J. Chapman and H. C. Foot (Eds.), *It's a Funny Thing, Humour*. Oxford: Pergamon Press.

Sroufe, L. A., and Waters, E. (1976). The ontogenesis of smiling and laughter: a perspective on the organization of development in infancy. *Psychological Review*, **83**, 173–189.

Sroufe, L. A., and Wunsch, J. P. (1972). The development of laughter in the first year of life. *Child Development*, **43**, 1326–1344.

Strickland, J. F. (1959). The effect of motivational arousal on humor preferences. *Journal of Abnormal and Social Psychology*, **59**, 278–281.

Tew, J. D. (1978). Grade level and audience status as factors in the social facilitation of children's humor. Unpublished Masters Thesis, Rutgers University.

Thomas, D. R., Shea, J. D., and Rigby, R. G. (1971). Conservatism and response to sexual humor. *British Journal of Social and Clinical Psychology*, **10**, 185–186.

Tolor, A. (1966). Observations on joke-telling by children in therapy. *Mental Hygiene*, **50**, 295–296.

Verinis, J. (1970). Inhibition of humor enjoyment: effects of sexual content and introversion-extraversion. *Psychological Reports*, **26**, 167–170.

Waterman, R. (1972). Humor in young children: relationship of behavioral styles and age with laughter and smiling. Unpublished Doctoral Dissertation, University of California, Los Angeles.

Wells, R. E. (1934). A study of tastes in humorous literature among pupils of junior and senior high schools. *Journal of Educational Research*, **28**, 81–92.

Whitt, J. K., and Prentice, N. M. (1977). Cognitive processes in the development of children's enjoyment and comprehension of joking riddles. *Developmental Psychology*, **13**, 129–136.

Williams, J. M. (1946). An experimental and theoretical study of humour in children. *British Journal of Educational Psychology*, **16**, 43–44.

Wilson, G. D., and Patterson, J. R. (1969). Conservatism as a predictor of humor preferences. *Journal of Consulting and Clinical Psychology*, **33**, 271–274.

Wilson, M. P. (1968). The relation of sense of humor to creativity, intelligence and achievement. *Dissertation Abstracts*, **29** (4-A), 1142.

Wolfenstein, M. (1954). *Children's Humor*. Glencoe, Illinois: Free Press.

Yorukoglu, A. (1974). Children's favorite jokes and their relation to emotional conflicts. *Journal of the American Academy of Child Psychiatry*, **13**, 677–690.

Yorukoglu, A. (1977). Favourite jokes of children and their dynamic relation to intra-familial conflicts. In A. J. Chapman and H. C. Foot (Eds.), *It's a Funny Thing, Humour*. Oxford: Pergamon Press.

Zigler, E., Levine, J., and Gould, L. (1966a). Cognitive processes in the development of children's appreciation of humor. *Child Development*, **37**, 507–518.

Zigler, E., Levine, J., and Gould, L. (1966b). The humor response of normal, institutionalized retarded, and noninstitutionalized retarded children. *American Journal of Mental Deficiency*, **71**, 472–480.

Zigler, E., Levine, J., and Gould, L. (1967). Cognitive challenge as a factor in children's humor appreciation. *Journal of Personality and Social Psychology*, **6**, 332–336.

Children's Humour
Edited by P. McGhee and A. Chapman.
© 1980, John Wiley & Sons, Ltd.

CHAPTER 8

Development of the Sense of Humour in Childhood: A Longitudinal Study

PAUL E. McGHEE

Much of the recent resurgence of interest in children's humour has focused on the cognitive aspects of humour. This is not surprising, since many of the age-related changes in humour development seem to be closely associated with underlying cognitive developmental changes (McGhee, 1977, 1979; Shultz, 1976). However, Brodzinsky and Rightmyer clearly demonstrated in the previous chapter that widespread individual differences also exist in children's humour-related behaviour as early as the pre-school years. They have noted specific personality and other behavioural dimensions associated with individual differences in humour comprehension, appreciation, and initiation. Furthermore, even casual observation of children is sufficient to suggest that some children are frequent clowns or jokers, while others rarely attempt to make others laugh. Similarly, some children show exaggerated laughter at any humorous incident, while others rarely show vigorous laughter. How are we to account for these differences? Is the funny or highly expressive child born that way? Or do children learn their joking and clowning behaviour from parents and peers? In order to understand fully the differential development of humour initiation and responsiveness among children, a longitudinal investigation of their early developmental histories is required. The present chapter presents data obtained from such a longitudinal study, and identifies precursors of heightened humour initiation and responsiveness in both children's own antecedent behaviour and the prior behaviour of nursery and elementary schoolchildren who were members of the Fels longitudinal sample at Fels Research Institute, Ohio. By making use of the backlog of data relating to early child and maternal behaviour in the permanent Fels files, it was possible to correlate current laughter, joking, and clowning behaviour to early developmental histories.

No previous studies along these lines have been completed. A number of studies of the early childhood experiences of professional comedians and comedy writers have been completed (e.g. Fry and Allen, 1975; Janus, 1975; Wilde, 1968), but these have all been based on recall of early childhood behaviours, home conditions, etc., so that they suffer from the usual methodological weaknesses which characterize this approach (Robbins, 1963; Wenar and Coulter, 1962). In the present study, actual observations of antecedent child and maternal behaviour provided the data on early childhood experiences. Theoretical views pertinent to the development of a heightened sense of humour are not discussed until the final section.

EXPERIMENTAL PROCEDURES

Children within two widely differing age groups within the Fels longitudinal sample served as subjects in this study. The youngest group consisted of twenty-two white pre-school children attending the semi-annual Fels Nursery School. A variety of socioeconomic backgrounds was represented, ranging from Class I through to Class V according to the Hollingshead Two-Factor Index. Children attended nursery school in either of two three-week sessions, with the first session including five girls and three boys between fifty-two and sixty-nine months of age, and the second session including nine boys and three girls between thirty-seven and fifty-two months of age. The age groups and sexes were combined in all analyses reported here.

The older age group consisted of forty-three white children between six and eleven years of age attending the annual Fels summer Day Camp, which lasted for a period of five to eight days. These children attended the day camp on three separate sessions, clustered according to age level. There were twenty-three males and twenty females, again covering the full range of socioeconomic levels.

Two different sets of observers were used to rate humour-related behaviours for the two age groups. For the older day-camp group, the day-camp 'teacher' and the regular Fels observer provided the ratings. Two of the author's research assistants provided them for the nursery-school group. Four behaviours were rated using a seven-point scale on the basis of the child's activity throughout the nursery-school or day-camp session: (a) overall frequency of laughter in social interaction; (b) frequency of behavioural attempts to initiate humour; (c) frequency of verbal attempts to initiate humour; and (d) amount of hostility apparent in the child's laughter or initiated humour. A general rating of the child's sense of humour was obtained by averaging the ratings for the first three humour categories. The reliabilities in rating these variables (Spearman–Brown formula) ranged from 0.72 to 0.89 for the older group and 0.74 to 1.00 for the younger group. Each observer's ratings were converted to standard scores, and a mean score was computed across the two observers' scores for each variable.

In the case of day-camp subjects, a single rating was made by the two observers at the end of the day-camp session. A more systematic set of observational procedures was used, however, with the nursery-school sample. Since it was impossible to observe several children simultaneously, a time-sampling procedure was adopted whereby each child was observed during free play for (the same) eight minutes each day by each observer. Because of the high level of reliability obtained by the observers during the first week, different children were observed during the remaining two weeks using the same time-sampling procedure. The order in which children were observed was randomly determined separately for each observer each day, with the restriction that a child was not observed by both observers at the same time.

Behavioural attempts to initiate humour included silly or clowning activity, arranging objects in incongruous positions or causing them to engage in incongruous activities, teasing through gestures, and so forth. Verbal humour included distortion of familiar word sounds, puns, riddles, 'bathroom' words and jokes, other 'canned' jokes, incongruous or meaningless word combinations, and playful verbal teasing. Amount of hostility in the child's humour was rated on the basis of apparent hostile intent in either the child's laughter (e.g. directed at another child or an event related to that child) or behavioural and verbal attempts to make others laugh. This was usually inferred on the basis of the child's use of humour to attack or threaten other children, name-calling, ridicule, or defiance of others (especially adults).

Antecedent predictor variables

Two types of antecedent data were available in a quantified form in the permanent Fels files. Measures of prior maternal behaviour were based on the Fels Parent Behavior Rating Scales (see Baldwin, Kalhorn, and Breese, 1949, for a detailed description of parent behaviours), and were obtained every six months during the first six years of each child's life by a regular Fels Home Visitor. The ten behaviour ratings used in this study were: (i) general adjustment of the home; (ii) restrictiveness of regulation of the child's behaviour; (iii) severity of penalties for misconduct; (iv) clarity and enforcement of policy on regulation of the child's behaviour; (v) coerciveness of suggestions in attempting to control the child's behaviour; (vi) attempts to accelerate skill development; (vii) general babying; (viii) general protectiveness; (ix) direction of criticism; and (x) affectionateness. A final rating was provided by the Home Visitor at the time of completion of this study. This rating concerned the extent to which joking or other forms of humour were initiated by the child's mother during the years when visits were made; the rating was on a seven-point scale ranging from highly characteristic to highly uncharacteristic. A mean score was obtained for each Parent Behaviour Rating for each child by averaging all available ratings for the zero–three and three–six year periods. These two mean scores were used in all data analyses.

In addition to these measures of maternal behaviour, the Fels Observer rated nineteen dimensions of the child's behaviour during every session of the Fels Nursery School (three- to five-year-olds) and Fels Day Camp (six- to eleven-year-olds). These behaviours included: (i) unprovoked physical aggression toward same-sex peers; (ii) unprovoked verbal aggression toward same-sex peers; (iii) retaliation versus withdrawal from physical or verbal aggression from peers; (iv) instrumental help-seeking from adults; (v) affection-seeking and emotional support-seeking from adults; (vi) recognition-seeking for achievement from adults; (vii) conformity to adult demands; (viii) effort on mastery of fine motor skills; (ix) effort on mastery of gross motor skills; (x) effort on mastery of intellectual activities; (xi) parallel play; (xii) associative play; (xiii) imitation of peers; (xiv) restless activity; (xv) quantity of speech; (xvi) dominance of same-sex peers; (xvii) body co-ordination; (xviii) quality of language; and (xix) amount of masculinity versus femininity.

Interrater reliabilities (based on Pearson product-moment correlations) between two raters on these child behaviours ranged from 0.59 to 0.83. As with the maternal behaviours, a mean score was obtained for each child on all available ratings during the three- to six-year period. Similarly, all available ratings after the age of six (six $^+$) were averaged to determine a mean rating for each child behaviour between six years of age and the child's present age. This mean, of course, was based on a larger number of observations for older than younger day-camp children.

RESULTS AND DISCUSSION OF FINDINGS

Relation between humour measures

Among nursery schoolchildren, the three humour measures were not significantly related (correlations ranged from 0.24 to 0.40). Each of the three components of sense of humour, then, is relatively independent of the others among younger children. However, children initiating high amounts of verbal humour by the pre-school years have begun to display more hostility in their humour $(r = 0.62, p < 0.01)$. The other two humour measures were not significantly related to hostility of humour.

The correlations between humour measures were considerably higher among six- to eleven-year-olds (especially girls) than among pre-schoolers. All of these correlations were highly significant, ranging from 0.71 to 0.77 among boys, and 0.87 to 0.93 among girls. Correlations between the three humour measures and degree of hostility in the child's humour ranged between 0.66 and 0.77 for both sexes ($p < 0.01$ in all cases). It appears, then, that the three components of sense of humour become increasingly interwoven as children advance beyond the pre-school to the elementary school years. Especially in the case of the day-camp sample, then, considerable overlap is to be expected in prediction of the three humour measures from antecedent child and maternal behaviours. Accordingly, we will restrict our discussion of antecedents for this sample to the broader measure of sense of humour and hostility of the child's humour.

Antecedents in early maternal behaviour

Pre-school sample. Table 8.1 shows that a common pattern of prediction of sense of humour by maternal behaviour was obtained both before and after three years of age. Children who showed greater amounts of humour during free play tended to have mothers who were generally warm and approving (direction of criticism), but who also babied and over-protected them. These mothers typically offered their children more help than was needed, such that the child was rarely given the opportunity to solve even minor problems or conflicts. They anticipated discomfort and potential threats to safety so that the child would not be exposed to them (including those which the child is capable of handling). The amount of laughter shown was most strongly predicted by these maternal behaviours during the first three years, becoming less predictive after the age of three. Only behavioural attempts at humour continued to be highly correlated with this pattern of maternal behaviour throughout infancy and the pre-school years.

These findings suggest that development of a heightened sense of humour in pre-school children is fostered by a generally positive and approving maternal relationship, and an early environment free of conflict, danger, and difficult-to-solve problems. Early humour development, then, seems to be associated with positive rather than negative early experiences. There are signs of a change in this relationship, however, by the age of three. Beyond this point, it is children who had more distant and rejecting (although generally approving and uncritical) mothers who showed little affection toward them who showed greater humour development. It is tempting to conclude that children attempted to use their humour to obtain more affectionate reactions from their mothers, but the available data do not permit an evaluation of this interpretation.

The positive relationship between the amount of babying and hostility of children's humour suggests that mothers may have gone too far in helping their children with everyday difficulties. This practice seems incompatible with

Table 8.1 Correlations for the nursery-school sample between humour measures and antecedent maternal behaviour from birth to three-years-old and after three years of age (sexes combined)

| Maternal behaviour | Birth to three years of age[a] | | | | |
	Sense of humour	Hostility of humour	Amount of laughter	Behavioural humour	Verbal humour
General adjustment of home	0.08	0.13	0.06	0.38	0.27
Restrictiveness of regulations	0.31	0.27	0.02	− 0.04	0.39
Severity of penalties for misconduct	− 0.01	0.12	− 0.23	− 0.27	0.14
Clarity and enforcement of policy of regulations	− 0.27	0.29	− 0.21	0.20	0.11
Coerciveness of suggestions in controlling behaviour	− 0.05	0.39	0.15	0.28	0.23
Attempts to accelerate skill development	0.08	0.51**	− 0.02	0.37	0.36
General babying	0.70**	0.48*	0.82**	0.63**	0.28
General protectiveness	0.63**	0.03	0.78**	0.55**	0.31
Direction of criticism (high = approval)	0.68**	0.35	0.71**	0.68**	0.65**
Affectionateness	− 0.19	0.10	− 0.32	− 0.23	0.21

| Maternal behaviour | After the age of three[b] | | | | |
	Sense of humour	Hostility of humour	Amount of laughter	Behavioural humour	Verbal humour
General adjustment of home	0.12	0.02	0.25	0.27	0.23
Restrictiveness of regulations	0.34	0.38	0.14	0.03	0.50*
Severity of penalties for misconduct	0.36	0.46	0.18	− 0.11	0.46
Clarity and enforcement of policy of regulations	− 0.22	0.40	− 0.40	0.36	0.16
Coerciveness of suggestions in controlling behaviour	− 0.26	0.21	0.16	0.01	0.02
Attempts to accelerate skill development	0.03	0.65**	− 0.04	0.47	0.41
General babying	0.73**	0.46	0.49**	0.63**	0.29
General protectiveness	0.64**	− 0.13	0.31	0.54*	0.38
Direction of criticism (high = approval)	0.66**	0.23	0.41	0.61**	0.69**
Affectionateness	− 0.48*	− 0.04	− 0.49*	− 0.48*	0.05

[a] $n = 21$ [b] $n = 16$
*$p < 0.05$ **$p < 0.01$

attempts to accelerate the child's skill development, which were also positively predicitive of hostility of humour. Hostile humour development, then, appears to have resulted from mothers' attempts to accelerate skill development at the same time that they were preventing their sons and daughters from having the kinds of coping and problem-solving experiences which would foster such accelerated development. The frustration produced by this state of affairs may have increased the frequency of aggression apparent in children's laughter and initiated humour.

Elementary-school sample. Correlations between antecedent maternal behaviour and humour measures for the day-camp sample are listed in Table 8.2. The most obvious conclusion to be drawn from this table is that these dimensions of maternal behaviour have little impact on laughter and humour during the elementary-school years, especially in the case of males. Special note should be taken of the fact that the amount of joking and other forms of humorous interaction mothers had with their children was not significantly related to any aspect of either sons' or daughters' later humour behaviour. Thus, a modelling explanation cannot account for subsequent sense of humour development. It may be, however, that fathers provide more important humour models for their children than mothers, since the initiation of humour is generally more characteristic of men than women (Middleton and Moland, 1959; Pollio and Edgerly, 1976; Smith and Goodchilds, 1959). Unfortunately, we could not test this view, since data were not available for fathers.

The only significant predictions obtained for males showed a direction of prediction for maternal babying opposite to that obtained for the pre-school sample. While a heightened sense of humour among pre-schoolers was associated with high amounts of babying in the first three years, it was associated with a lack of babying during this period among elementary-school-aged boys. This reversal may indicate that there is little continuity between humour-related behaviour during the pre-school and elementary-school years. Among six- to eleven-year-olds, humour (especially laughter) is most abundant among boys whose mothers left them alone to solve problems on their own—even when some assistance would have been appropriate. The positive influence of this practice may be seen in the fact that it was also strongly associated with a lack of hostility in boys' humour. This prediction was also obtained for the three- to six-year period, suggesting that it continued to be associated only with more benign forms of humour. No other aspect of maternal behaviour during the first six years was associated with humour development in boys.

Females showed the same reversal of prediction of sense of humour as was shown by males for maternal babying, although only from the three- to six-year period. This maternal behaviour was not, however, significantly related to the amount of hostility shown in girls' humour. Unlike the findings for males, lack of maternal protectiveness during the three-to-six-year period was also associated with a heightened sense of humour among day-camp girls. Thus, it was girls whose mothers exposed them to tough and potentially hazardous situations, at the same time as they were withholding help in problem-solving situations (lack of babying), who were most likely subsequently to demonstrate heightened laughter, joking, and clowning.

The general level of adjustment of the home was the only variable from the

Table 8.2 Correlations for the elementary-school sample between humour measures and antecedent maternal behaviour from birth to three-years-old and from three to six years of age

I *Males*

Maternal behaviour	Sense of humour		Hostility of humour		Amount of laughter		Behavioural humour		Verbal humour	
	0 to 3[a]	3 to 6[a]	0 to 3	3 to 6	0 to 3	3 to 6	0 to 3	3 to 6	0 to 3	3 to 6
General adjustment of home	0.03	0.00	−0.04	−0.19	−0.07	0.03	0.27	0.03	0.05	0.01
Restrictiveness of regulations	0.02	−0.07	0.06	0.00	−0.03	−0.18	0.09	0.01	0.15	0.09
Severity of penalties for misconduct	0.16	0.11	0.23	0.23	0.04	0.04	0.34	0.21	0.17	0.15
Clarity and enforcement of policy of regulations	0.00	0.13	0.03	0.04	−0.17	0.07	0.28	0.19	0.04	0.24
Coerciveness of suggestions in controlling behaviour	0.14	0.00	0.21	0.11	0.01	−0.08	0.31	0.14	0.24	0.09
Attempts to accelerate skill development	0.01	0.06	0.00	0.08	−0.11	0.03	0.26	0.17	0.06	0.13
General babying	−0.41*	−0.31	−0.53**	−0.51**	−0.50**	−0.29	−0.38	−0.36	−0.26	−0.14
General protectiveness	−0.10	−0.25	−0.21	−0.39	−0.16	−0.29	−0.04	−0.22	−0.03	−0.19
Direction of criticism (high = approval)	0.01	0.08	−0.11	−0.10	−0.08	0.00	−0.08	0.02	0.07	−0.03
Affectionateness	−0.07	0.02	−0.09	−0.17	−0.16	0.02	0.01	−0.14	−0.06	−0.11
Amount of maternal humour		0.31		0.25		0.26		0.22		0.17

II *Females*

Maternal behaviour	Sense of humour		Hostility of humour		Amount of laughter		Behavioural humour		Verbal humour	
	0 to 3[b]	3 to 6[c]	0 to 3	3 to 6	0 to 3	3 to 6	0 to 3	3 to 6	0 to 3	3 to 6
General adjustment of home	−0.37	−0.13	−0.46*	−0.36	−0.35	−0.15	−0.37	−0.09	−0.50*	−0.19
Restrictiveness of regulations	−0.03	−0.26	0.36	0.11	−0.06	−0.29	−0.02	−0.25	0.06	−0.11
Severity of penalties for misconduct	0.14	−0.02	0.40	0.17	0.13	−0.03	0.10	−0.10	0.19	0.10
Clarity and enforcement of policy of regulations	−0.18	−0.21	0.12	−0.04	−0.21	−0.21	−0.22	−0.18	−0.09	−0.16
Coerciveness of suggestions in controlling behaviour	0.10	−0.09	0.41	0.22	0.05	−0.13	0.09	−0.06	0.20	0.00
Attempts to accelerate skill development	−0.20	−0.15	−0.19	−0.06	−0.24	−0.16	−0.16	−0.11	−0.18	−0.11
General babying	−0.13	−0.49*	0.04	−0.39	−0.17	−0.47*	−0.14	−0.45*	−0.14	−0.47*
General protectiveness	−0.15	−0.43*	0.02	−0.30	−0.14	−0.41	−0.20	−0.44*	−0.21	−0.43*
Direction of criticism (high = approval)	−0.37	0.03	−0.38	−0.18	−0.36	0.04	−0.33	0.09	−0.27	0.00
Affectionateness	0.19	−0.08	0.03	−0.18	0.18	−0.07	0.23	0.01	0.19	−0.14
Amount of maternal humour		0.24		0.02		0.22		0.30		0.15

[a] $n = 23$ [b] $n = 18$ [c] $n = 20$ *$p < 0.05$ **$p < 0.01$

first three years to be predictive of day-camp girls' humour development. Girls whose homes were characterized during this period by conflict, unpleasantness, repression and insecurity not only initiated more verbal joking, but were very hostile in the process. These findings support the view that humour provides a means of coping with conflict and distress (Bergler, 1937; Freud, 1916; Wolfenstein, 1954). These girls may have used the socially adaptive process of joking in order to achieve a partial release of hostile feelings. The fact that home adjustment in the first three years was not predictive of any humour measure in pre-schoolers may have resulted from the combining of the two sexes in this sample. On the other hand, it may be that joking is not used by girls as a means of coping with home-related distresses until after the pre-school period.

Antecedents in children's own prior behaviour

Ratings of children's senses of humour were generally more strongly predicted by dimensions of their own early behaviour than by early maternal behaviour. While signs of these precursors were evident for the pre-school sample, a much clearer and more consistent pattern of precursors was obtained for the older sample.

   Pre-school sample. Table 8.3 presents the correlations obtained between pre-schoolers' sense of humour measures and the mean of all antecedent child behaviour ratings during the period between the age of three and the child's present age. (Child behaviour ratings from the zero to three-year period were not available.) The general measure of sense of humour was predicted only by the amount of effort exerted in attempts to master intellectual tasks and activities. The exertion of high amounts of effort after the age of three in intellectual games (anagrams, twenty questions, geography names, etc.), puzzles, memorizing poems, learning songs, and perfecting reading, writing, and numerical skills was associated with a 'poorer' sense of humour during the late pre-school years. The importance of such achievement-related activities may lie in the fact that persistence and effort at achievement tasks are generally accompanied by a more serious frame of mind. This frame of mind should be incompatible with humour, or at least reduce the level of appreciation or initiation of humour that occurs (McGhee, 1972, 1977, 1979).

   A similar pattern of prediction was obtained for the amount of effort exerted in attempts to master fine motor skills, although only the predictions of verbal humour and hostility of humour reached significance. Again, children with earlier histories of high effort at fine motor tasks (craft work, puzzles, tinker toys, etc.), made fewer verbal attempts at humour and showed less hostility in their humour. Given these precursors, the prediction of behavioural attempts at humour by the amount of effort directed toward mastery of gross motor skills (large muscle activities, such as running, climbing, jumping, jumping rope,

Table 8.3 Correlations for the nursery-school sample between humour measures and children's own antecedent behaviour after the age of three, sexes combined[a]

Prior child behaviour	Sense of humour	Hostility of humour	Amount of laughter	Behavioural humour	Verbal humour
Unprovoked physical aggression	0.43	0.44	0.23	0.60*	0.31
Unprovoked verbal aggression	0.35	0.55*	0.20	0.55*	0.39
Retaliation to physical and verbal aggression	0.36	0.48*	0.14	0.50*	0.31
Dominance	0.10	0.37	0.26	0.29	0.26
Restless activity	0.25	− 0.60**	0.37	− 0.07	− 0.22
Quantity of speech	0.18	0.19	0.36	0.14	0.13
Quality of language	0.46	0.33	0.17	0.47	0.48*
Instrumental help-seeking (adults)	0.17	− 0.15	− 0.21	0.39	− 0.03
Affection- and emotional support-seeking (adults)	0.15	− 0.23	− 0.24	0.12	0.02
Recognition-seeking for achievement (adults)	− 0.34	− 0.25	− 0.36	− 0.05	− 0.23
Conformity to adult demands	− 0.46	0.06	− 0.22	− 0.36	− 0.35
Imitation	0.06	0.42	0.19	0.11	0.10
Parallel play	0.18	0.28	0.28	0.30	0.18
Associative play	− 0.43	− 0.05	− 0.19	− 0.39	− 0.41
Effort on mastery of fine motor skills	− 0.29	− 0.59**	− 0.08	− 0.44	− 0.52*
Effort on mastery of gross motor skills	0.24	0.25	0.09	0.72**	0.10
Effort on mastery of intellectual activities	− 0.54*	− 0.04	− 0.23	− 0.38	− 0.28
Body co-ordination	0.44	− 0.25	0.26	0.37	0.14
Masculinity-femininity (masculine = high)	− 0.04	0.25	0.33	− 0.23	0.08

[a]$n = 16$
*$p < 0.05$ **$p < 0.01$

baseball, etc.), is especially noteworthy. Children showing greater effort at mastering gross motor skills showed more frequent clowning, silliness, and other behavioural forms of humour. The different predictions obtained from these three achievement areas may lie in the nature of the social interaction patterns associated with each. Gross motor skills typically occur in the context of physically vigorous activity during social play, and are not usually accompanied by a serious frame of mind. Intellectual and fine motor tasks, on the other hand, are less likely to occur in the context of ongoing social play, and tend to be associated with more serious states of mind.

Physical and verbal aggressiveness after three years of age were associated both with more frequent behavioural attempts at humour and with greater hostility in humour among pre-schoolers. These relationships constitute the beginning of a key pattern of antecedents of humour development. It can be seen in the following section that prior aggressive and dominating behaviour are highly predictive of humour measures in elementary-school-aged children. These findings support the Freudian (1916) position that humour is used as a means of expressing hostile feelings or impulses in a socially acceptable way. The negative prediction of hostility of humour from prior levels of restless activity suggests that humour is especially likely to take on aggressive qualities among those children who do not 'work off' some of their aggressive tendencies through vigorous physical activity. It is the inactive three- to five-year-old who is most likely to show hostility in laughter, clowning and joking.

Finally, highly verbal children who showed precocious and expressive language skills were most likely to engage in joking and clowning. This relationship was also obtained for the day-camp sample, suggesting that language facility may play a key role in the development of humour skills generally.

Elementary-school sample. Table 8.4 lists the correlations between day-camp boys' humour ratings and antecedents in their own prior behaviour. A quick glance at this table is sufficient to indicate that a greater number of antecedent behaviours are predictive of humour during the elementary-school years than the pre-school years. The amount of aggression and dominance shown during and after the three- to six-year period was positively related to sense of humour among day-camp boys. However, while verbal and retaliatory (physical only if attacked first) forms of aggression continued to be predictive after the age of six, initiated physical aggression remained predictive only for behavioural forms of humour. More importantly, the unusually high correlation with hostility from the six$^+$ age period suggests that these behavioural attempts at humour were usually of a highly aggressive nature. Verbal and retaliatory aggression after the age of six, on the other hand, were only predictive of laughter and humour lacking these hostile qualities. Thus, a generally heightened early level of aggression appears to play a central role in humour development, perhaps because aggressive boys learn early that hostile feelings are more successfully expressed in the context of joking or clowning.

The findings for the pre-school sample (see Table 8.3) suggest that these hostile behaviour patterns are directed into behavioural forms of humour very early. There appears to be little in the way of attempts to disguise this hostility initially, although some children show signs of beginning to disguise it after the age of six. Only those boys who remained physically aggressive after the age of six showed high levels of hostility in their humour in the elementary-school years. It should be noted that this relationship is almost exclusively due to their behavioural

Table 8.4 Correlations for the elementary-school sample between humour measures and boys' own antecedent behaviour between three to six years of age and after the age of six (6+)

Prior child behaviour	Sense of humour		Hostility of humour		Amount of laughter		Behavioural humour		Verbal humour	
	3 to 6[a]	6+[b]	3 to 6	6+	3 to 6	6+	3 to 6	6+	3 to 6	6+
Unprovoked physical aggression	0.55**	−0.03	0.58**	0.90**	0.44*	−0.03	0.50**	0.86**	0.48**	0.19
Unprovoked verbal aggression	0.64**	0.55**	0.59**	0.34	0.52**	0.52**	0.48**	0.51*	0.54**	0.64**
Retaliation to physical and verbal aggression	0.59**	0.61**	0.53**	0.27	0.52**	0.59**	0.44*	0.48*	0.52**	0.73**
Dominance	0.57**	0.77**	0.45*	−0.16	0.47**	0.75**	0.45*	0.22	0.62**	0.86***
Restless activity	0.05	0.84**	0.03	−0.49*	0.11	0.83**	0.02	−0.12	0.03	0.80**
Quantity of speech	0.39	0.85**	0.28	−0.13	0.20	0.84**	0.31	0.26	0.50**	0.90**
Quality of language	0.46*	0.60**	0.21	−0.03	0.31	0.60**	0.40*	0.18	0.41*	0.67**
Instrumental help-seeking (adults)	0.56**	0.50*	0.56**	−0.41	0.38	0.47*	0.53**	−0.19	0.64**	0.49*
Affection- and emotional support-seeking (adults)	0.28	0.27	0.19	−0.28	0.31	0.29	0.17	−0.01	0.43*	0.28
Recognition-seeking for achievement (adults)	0.52**	0.65**	0.43*	−0.52*	0.44*	0.63**	0.54**	−0.17	0.67**	0.62**
Conformity to adult demands	0.31	0.50*	0.31	−0.16	0.33	0.40	0.14	−0.12	0.29	0.51*
Imitation	0.59**	0.69**	0.48**	0.04	0.50**	0.66**	0.46*	0.29	0.61**	0.79**
Parallel play	0.29	0.62**	0.36	−0.31	0.26	0.57**	0.34	−0.05	0.32	0.63**
Associative play	0.24	0.30	0.42*	−0.39	0.27	0.21	0.26	−0.37	0.20	0.18
Effort on mastery of fine motor skills	−0.39	0.09	−0.39	−0.88**	−0.31	0.08	−0.38	−0.80**	−0.22	−0.12
Effort on mastery of gross motor skills	0.31	0.61**	0.28	0.00	0.24	0.60**	0.26	0.22	0.34	0.58**
Effort on mastery of intellectual activities	−0.06	0.52*	0.10	−0.50*	0.02	0.48*	−0.03	−0.33	−0.05	0.38
Body co-ordination	−0.09	0.35	−0.12	−0.59**	−0.25	0.40	0.00	−0.33	−0.06	0.25
Masculinity-femininity (masculine = high)	0.19	0.51*	0.18	−0.13	0.28	0.44	0.02	−0.14	0.12	0.50*

[a] $n = 23$ [b] $n = 17$
*$p < 0.05$ **$p < 0.01$

attempts at humour, as was the case for the nursery-school sample. Boys whose aggression was of a verbal or retaliatory nature, on the other hand, gave evidence of developing more benign humour patterns; that is, hostility of humour was not significantly related to these forms of aggression after the age of six. Since these forms of aggression were predictive of hostile humour in the pre-school sample, and in the day-camp sample from the three- to six-year period, it may be that humour is more effective at rechannelling verbal and reactive forms of aggression than overt physical aggression.

The fact that day-camp children with a more developed sense of humour also had a history of dominating their peers suggests that humour may have been adopted as a means of maintaining dominant forms of social interaction in a manner that is socially acceptable. In this respect, humour can be conceptualized as a means of capturing and maintaining social power. The skilled and persistent clown or joker is usually successful at holding the attention of those present, and can easily control the strings of social interaction. As was the case with measures of verbal and retaliatory aggression, the amount of dominating behaviour was no longer predictive of hostility of humour after six years of age. The positive prediction of sense of humour by amount of masculinity (traditionally defined) in the child's behaviour undoubtedly is due to the early pattern of dominance and aggression.

The positive relationship between the amount and quality of language shown by the child from three years onwards and boys' subsequent sense of humour supports the view advanced earlier that language facility may play a central role in humour development. Again, there is no evidence of high levels of hostility associated with the humour of those boys with greater verbal skills.

An additional cluster of antecedent behaviours suggests that boys with more developed senses of humour had a prior history of heightened sensitivity to adult attention and reactions. Sense of humour was positively related both before and after six years to the amount of prior instrumental help-seeking (asking adults for help when trying anything new or difficult, when having conflicts with other children, etc.), recognition-seeking for achievement (in crafts, puzzles, painting, reading, counting, climbing, etc.), and conformity to adult demands. The amount of verbal humour was also positively related to the frequency of attempts to gain affection and emotional support from adults during the three- to six-year period. These findings suggest that boys with early concerns about obtaining positive adult reactions may have begun to use humour as a means of getting adult attention and approval. Given their inclination toward more aggressive forms of behaviour, adults may have responded especially favourably to their attempts at humour precisely because of the absence of overt hostility in such behaviour. The fact that instrumental help-seeking for achievement predicted hostility of humour positively from the three- to six-year period, but negatively after six years, suggests that boys learned that hostile forms of humour were not very effective in producing positive reactions from adults.

Further evidence of the reversal of behavioural antecedents of hostile humour after the age of six may be seen in the pattern of predictions from early play behaviour. While the amount of parallel and associative play before the age of six were positively related to subsequent hostility in boys' humour, they were negatively related after the age of six (separate analyses revealed that the correlations from the two age periods were significantly different from one another for each type of play behaviour). The general measure of sense of humour was not significantly related to the amount of associative play at either prior age level (although it was positively predicted by the amount of parallel play after the age of six). This is surprising, since highly developed social skills are generally assumed to be a component of a strong sense of humour. The consistent association of sense of humour with high levels of prior imitation of other children suggests that boys subsequently rated high on humour measures did not initially possess good interactive social skills. Of course, this imitation may have also been designed to obtain favourable reactions from peers. This would mean that boys with strongly developed senses of humour were highly sensitive to both peer and adult attention and reactions.

Boys with a well-developed sense of humour also tended to have had high energy levels after six years of age. They were restless and had difficulty sitting still or sticking with one activity for long periods of time. In spite of this restlessness, however, these boys showed less hostility in their humour than their more sedentary peers. The association of lack of body co-ordination during this period with the subsequent development of hostile forms of humour suggests that this sedentariness may have partially resulted from the children's awareness that their physical skills were inadequate compared to those of their peers. Thus, high levels of physical activity may have provided an outlet for the aggressive tendencies of restless boys, while sedentary boys had no such outlet.

Consistent with the findings for the nursery-school sample, the exertion of high amounts of achievement-related effort (at fine motor and intellectual tasks) after six years was associated with reduced levels of hostility in elementary-school boys' humour. In the case of intellectual achievement activities, however, the non-hostile aspects of boys' sense of humour were positively related to efforts at mastery. This is a surprising finding, in the light of the expectation that achievement effort should produce a more serious frame of mind, which should, in turn, lead to reduced initiation and appreciation of humour. But this inhibitory effect on humour only occurred with respect to effort at fine motor skills (see Tables 8.4 and 8.5). The strongest positive relationship between prior achievement effort and subsequent measures of non-hostile forms of humour occurred with respect to gross motor skills (this was also the case for the pre-school sample and day-camp girls). This consistent positive association with effort at gross motor skills may be due to the greater opportunities for laughter and joking during gross motor activities, without producing any accompanying disruption of the task at hand.

The antecedents of day-camp girls' humour in their own behaviour are listed in Table 8.5. The general pattern of prediction from both prior age periods was similar to that obtained for males, although the reversal of direction of prediction of hostile humour noted for several variables in males before and after the age of six was not obtained for females. Girls with more developed senses of humour showed a consistent history of physical and verbal aggression, along with dominance over peers of the same sex. Among boys, only elevated levels of physical aggression after the age of six continued to be associated with hostile humour. In the case of girls, however, all four measures of aggression and dominance were strongly predictive of the amount of hostility shown in humour. These relationships were positive at the three- to six-year period, but were stronger after the age of six. If humour does provide a means of vicariously expressing hostility, then, girls seem to be less successful than boys at disguising the aggressive nature of their laughter and humour.

The amount of speech shown by girls in free play during the three- to six-year period was positively related to all aspects of their later humour. This is consistent with the dominating tendencies already discussed, but the same relationships approach zero after the age of six. This is the reverse of the pattern obtained for boys, whose sense of humour was more strongly predicted by talkativeness after than before six years. Only the qualitative aspects of girls' speech predicted sense of humour after six years. Verbally precocious and expressive girls who had larger vocabularies and expressed themselves clearly showed both increased laughter and joking. Again, it should be noted that both the amount of speech at three- to six-years-old and the quality of speech after the age of six were equally strongly associated with hostile and non-hostile forms of humour. In males, these dimensions of early language behaviour were only associated with subsequent non-hostile forms of humour.

Females also differed from males in the earliness at which attention- and recognition-seeking behaviours became positively predictive of subsequent humour measures. While instrumental help-seeking and recognition-seeking for achievement from adults predicted sense of humour before and after six years among boys, they did not become predictive among girls until after six years. Humour development among girls was also associated with attempts to gain affection and emotional support from adults after the age of six. These findings are especially interesting in the light of the poor relationship humour-oriented girls had with their mothers before the age of six. Girls who showed high levels of laughter, clowning and joking tended to have mothers who did not come to their aid in conflict situations, and did not try to protect them from exposure to hazards and difficult situations. Their homes also tended to be full of conflict and strife in the first three years. It may be, then, that these girls lacked confidence in their mothers' love for them, and that they developed humour as a means of increasing their chance of securing affection and attention from both parents and other adults. The fact that antecedent attention- and

Table 8.5 Correlations for the elementary-school sample between humour measures and girls' own antecedent behaviour between three to six years of age and after the age of six (6+)

Prior child behaviour	Sense of humour		Hostility of humour		Amount of laughter		Behavioural humour		Verbal humour	
	3 to 6[a]	6+[b]	3 to 6	6+	3 to 6	6+	3 to 6	6+	3 to 6	6+
Unprovoked physical aggression	0.58**	0.74**	0.56**	0.76**	0.57**	0.62**	0.62**	0.78**	0.64**	0.82**
Unprovoked verbal aggression	0.46*	0.81**	0.34	0.85**	0.43*	0.69**	0.45*	0.90**	0.56**	0.83**
Retaliation to physical and verbal aggression	0.45*	0.86**	0.46*	0.87**	0.41	0.76**	0.41	0.88**	0.57**	0.81**
Dominance	0.56**	0.82**	0.41	0.92**	0.45*	0.72**	0.56**	0.82**	0.65**	0.72**
Restless activity	0.02	−0.02	−0.09	0.06	0.12	−0.03	0.00	−0.18	0.06	0.00
Quantity of speech	0.58**	0.20	0.46*	0.22	0.60**	0.20	0.52**	−0.02	0.67**	0.10
Quality of language	0.23	0.58**	0.07	0.55**	0.22	0.60**	0.23	0.45	0.26	0.50*
Instrumental help-seeking (adults)	0.16	0.60**	−0.08	0.82**	0.16	0.51*	0.12	0.55**	0.18	0.67**
Affection- and emotional support-seeking (adults)	0.17	0.46	−0.09	0.60**	0.15	0.45	0.14	0.33	0.21	0.47*
Recognition-seeking for achievement (adults)	0.21	0.60**	0.01	0.86**	0.14	0.54**	0.31	0.60**	0.13	0.57**
Conformity to adult demands	0.16	0.15	0.31	0.26	0.05	0.25	0.13	0.14	0.29	0.04
Imitation	0.55**	0.85**	0.42	0.86**	0.49*	0.79**	0.50**	0.84**	0.64**	0.76**
Parallel play	0.23	0.04	−0.07	0.13	0.25	−0.03	0.20	−0.08	0.20	0.02
Associative play	0.03	−0.29	−0.05	−0.18	−0.01	−0.20	−0.02	−0.21	0.10	−0.45
Effort on mastery of fine motor skills	−0.11	−0.76**	−0.31	−0.68**	−0.14	−0.66**	−0.09	−0.86**	−0.22	−0.78**
Effort on mastery of gross motor skills	0.04	0.48*	0.07	0.51*	0.08	0.44	0.09	0.30	0.02	0.48*
Effort on mastery of intellectual activities	−0.15	−0.14	−0.27	0.06	−0.13	−0.13	−0.17	0.03	−0.20	−0.23
Body co-ordination	0.21	0.05	0.23	0.05	0.24	0.06	0.13	−0.04	0.30	0.13
Masculinity-femininity (masculine = high)	0.14	0.33	0.19	0.46	0.03	0.35	0.15	0.18	0.23	0.23

[a] n = 20   [b] n = 17
*p < 0.05   **p < 0.01

affection-seeking behaviours were more strongly predictive of hostile than of benign forms of humour suggests that girls may not have been completely successful in obtaining the desired favourable adult reactions with their humour.

Like boys, girls with more developed senses humour showed a consistent pattern of imitation of other children during play activities. This is surprising in the light of their otherwise dominating and aggressive patterns of behaviour, and suggests that both sexes may have had some concern about gaining positive reactions from peers, as well as adults. Since dominating and aggressive behaviour is more likely to create enemies than friends, these girls may have developed imitative patterns of behaviour because they offered a means of playing without evoking negative reactions from other children. There was limited support for the view that these girls had poorer skills at social play, in that the amount of verbal humour was negatively related (narrowly missing significance) to the amount of associative play shown after six years of age.

Antecedent achievement-related behaviour showed the same general pattern of prediction of non-hostile forms of humour as was obtained for boys. The exertion of high amounts of effort at tasks requiring fine motor skills was negatively associated with humour development, while the same effort at gross motor skills was positively predictive. However, achievement effort at fine motor skills was incompatible with all aspects of humour development among girls (including hostile forms of humour), while it only interfered with behavioural attempts at humour among boys.

Finally, amounts of prior restless activity and body co-ordination among girls were not related to humour development. These findings contrast sharply with those obtained for boys, where restless activity was positively associated with subsequent benign forms of humour and body co-ordination was negatively predictive of hostility of the child's humour.

Relationship to concurrent measures of intelligence and physical growth

Nursery-school sample. Table 8.6 presents the correlations obtained between pre-schoolers' humour ratings and both their most recent IQ test scores and their current growth measures. There is no evidence that higher levels of measured intelligence either facilitate or interfere with pre-schoolers' humour development. Children's physical status, however, does appear to have an impact on the child's development of initiated forms of humour. Taller and heavier children showed more pronounced humour development, mainly in connection with initiated (as opposed to reactive) forms of humour. The negative prediction by the child's height/weight ratio indicates that it is children who are especially heavy for their height who show the greatest humour development. While this finding provides some support for the view that stocky or fat individuals have a better sense of humour, it should be noted that this prediction was not significant

Table 8.6 Correlations for the nursery-school sample between humour measures and concurrent measures of intelligence and physical growth (sexes combined)

IQ and growth measures	Sense of humour	Hostility of humour	Amount of laughter	Behavioural humour	Verbal humour
Merrill–Palmer IQ score[a]	− 0.20	− 0.12	− 0.09	− 0.17	− 0.08
Stanford–Binet IQ score[b]	− 0.39	0.02	− 0.10	− 0.39	− 0.13
Height[c]	0.48**	0.27	0.31	0.32	0.54**
Weight[c]	0.54**	0.25	0.30	0.53**	0.47*
Height/weight ratio[c]	− 0.51**	− 0.19	− 0.24	− 0.62**	− 0.33

[a]$n = 21$ [b]$n = 18$ [c]$n = 22$
*$p < 0.05$ **$p < 0.01$

for the amount of laughter exhibited by children. The most important conclusion to be drawn from the finding of increased humour initiation among children with greater body mass may be that this helps to account for the consistent finding that early measures of dominance and aggression are predictive of subsequent humour development. Because of their increased physical stature, stocky children should have experienced more success in getting away with aggression than their more frail peers.

Elementary-school sample. Among the six- to eleven-year-old sample, IQ scores at the age of six (Stanford Binet) were not significantly related to any of the five humour measures (correlations ranged from − 0.10 to 0.21). Four measures of physical growth were available for this sample, including (i) weight at the ages of three and six, (ii) height at the ages of three and six, (iii) chest diameter at the ages of three and six, and (iv) height/weight ratio at the ages of three and six. In contrast to the findings for younger children, these physical growth measures were not significantly related to any of the humour measures for either sex (correlations ranged from − 0.16 to 0.36). Thus, greater body mass does not appear to contribute to humour development beyond the pre-school years.

SUMMARY AND DEVELOPMENTAL PROFILE

Precursors of children's sense of humour were generally more abundant in their own early behaviour than in prior maternal behaviour. Several clusters of early child behaviour were associated with subsequent humour development. The single most striking quality of the prior behaviour of children who showed increased laughter, joking, and clowning in the elementary-school years was their dominance and aggressiveness toward their peers. These behaviours were consistently predictive of sense of humour for both sexes, both before and after six years of age. Even among the pre-school sample, children with a prior history of verbal and physical aggressiveness made more frequent attempts at behavioural forms of humour. Level of aggression did not become predictive of the other two components of sense of humour until the elementary-school years.

Parallelling the strong prediction by dominance and physical and verbal aggressiveness, sense of humour was anteceded in both sexes by a heightened quantity and quality of speech. Thus, children who showed greater humour development were not only more talkative than their peers, but also had larger vocabularies, were more expressive, and were generally precocious in their language development. The lack of prediction by early IQ scores suggests that this early facility with language cannot be attributed to superior intelligence in children who became especially humour-oriented. Rather, it appears to have developed because of the key role played by language in dominating forms of behaviour. In the case of boys, there was also evidence of antecedent restlessness after the age of six. While this high activity or energy level undoubtedly contributed to the development of assertive behaviour patterns, it cannot account for their origin since socially assertive behaviour became predictive of sense of humour earlier than did restlessness. The greater height and weight of pre-schoolers who were more initiating of humour may have played a role in establishing physical and verbal aggressiveness, but these physical measures did not turn out to be predictive for the older sample of children. It is difficult, then, to draw any firm conclusions from children's own early behaviour regarding the origins of aggressive and dominating behaviour. We can only conclude that children who do develop these characteristics by the early pre-school years are more likely than their less physically and verbally assertive peers to show elevated humour development later on. Whether these behaviours also predict level of humour development among adults must remain an open question, since we have no assurance that the reactive and initiating aspects of humour exhibit a high level of continuity between the elementary and high-school or college years.

The patterns of early maternal behaviour predictive of subsequent humour development may help to account for children's early dominating and aggressive behaviour. In the case of the pre-school sample, a combination of high babying and protectiveness by mothers who were generally approving, but not affectionate, was associated with heightened humour development. While it is difficult to speculate on how maternal babying, protectiveness, and approval directly lead to laughter and humour initiation in children, it is not difficult to see how a lack of maternal affection in connection with these behaviours might lead to increased aggressiveness. The important issue here, though, is probably not the original source of the aggression, but how aggressiveness and assertiveness might lead to humour once they are established.

Freud's (1916) early insights on humour provide an adequate explanation for how humour might develop out of a pattern of early physical and verbal aggressiveness. Even in the early pre-school years, children who have developed physically and verbally assertive patterns of behaviour toward their peers must encounter frequent negative reactions both from adults and from other children.

In order to maintain smooth and friendly interchanges with other children, the aggressive child must learn to channel hostility into a form of behaviour which will not alienate other children or produce reprimands from adults. Humour provides an ideal vehicle for achieving this end, since it is usually easy to disguise aggressive intent in jokes. Even if the aggressive nature of a joke or act becomes apparent, the child can always claim to have been only joking or playing around. Freud was probably correct in his belief that humour provides a means of vicariously expressing repressed or suppressed hostility, but the findings of this study suggest that children developed an increased focus on humour before they began to suppress their aggression. Assuming that most children begin to feel social pressure to curb or control their aggression by the age of three or so, it appears that more aggressive children began to become more initiating of humour just at the point these pressures were beginning. Clowning activity and silly word changes or distortions not only (presumably) failed to meet with negative reactions from peers and adults; they were probably greeted with great enthusiasm. Once this pattern of reinforcement was established, the path to the development of a young humorist was begun.

The fact that the sense of humour is most fully developed (at least in a quantitative sense) in children who were aggressive, dominating, and talkative suggests that humour might be effectively conceptualized in terms of a means of maintaining social assertiveness or power over others. By consistently clowning or joking, the individual can remain in charge of the flow of conversation or other interaction. By initiating a joke, anecdote, or comic behaviour, the humorist puts others in a situation where they are obliged to react in some way. If the efforts at humour are successful, this will not really seem like an obligation, since others present will find themselves laughing spontaneously and genuinely. Even if the humour is perceived to be inane or annoying, though, most people feel obliged to give some token reaction. Thus, the initiator of humour holds a unique form of power over others. When the comedian is 'on', others present become delegated to the role of responders. The early childhood pattern of dominance in social interactions, then, is continued within the playful framework of humour.

A second cluster of antecedent childhood behaviours suggests that children who showed greater amounts of humour-related behaviour were also especially sensitive to adult attention and reactions. In both boys and girls, sense of humour was predicted by high levels of prior affection and emotional support-seeking, instrumental help-seeking, and recognition-seeking for achievement. Among boys, a high level of conformity to adult demands was also associated with elevated humour development. All of these behaviours point to a concern about pleasing adults and getting favourable reactions from them. The prediction of sense of humour by imitation of peers (for both sexes) might be interpreted to mean that there was an accompanying concern about securing positive reactions from peers. However, as we noted earlier, aggressive and dominating children may have had difficulty at times in getting other children to continue playing with them. Imitation might have evolved as a means of continuing play with children who were otherwise 'put off' by dominating and aggressive behaviour. The fact that boys' sense of humour was positively related to the amount of parallel play after the age of six, but not the amount of associative play, strengthens the view that the aggressive and dominating children who subsequently developed a strong sense of humour did not possess good skills at interactive play with other children. This may have contributed to these children's greater preoccupation with gaining attention and positive reactions from adults. In the case of girls, poor early home adjustment may have contributed to a concern about adult approval. Humour should provide an ideal means of gaining favourable adult reactions, and these reactions should further strengthen the habit of producing humour.

The amount of effort exerted in achievement-related activities provided a third cluster of antecedent behaviours predictive of sense of humour. The only consistently positive association along these lines was obtained with respect to activities requiring gross motor skills. Effort at such tasks was positively related to sense of humour development in both sexes in the elementary-school sample, and was positively related to behavioural forms of humour in the pre-school sample. The reverse order of prediction was obtained for fine motor tasks, both in the pre-school sample (verbal humour) and among girls in the elementary-school sample. It seems likely that persistent effort at fine motor tasks serves to isolate the child from the kinds of social contact and interaction conducive to humour development, while effort at gross motor tasks increases social contact. Also, tasks requiring fine motor skill may be more conducive to putting the child in a serious frame of mind, which would lead to reduced frequency of humorous interchanges even when the opportunity arose.

It should also be noted that a larger number of behaviours were predictive of the general measure of sense of humour in the elementary-school sample than in the pre-school sample. In the latter case, only one antecedent behaviour predicted sense of humour, although seven additional behaviours predicted either behavioural or verbal forms of initiated humour. Within the elementary-school sample, fewer behaviours from the pre-school period (eight for boys and six for girls) predicted sense of humour than from the period beginning after six-years-old (fourteen for boys and ten for girls). This suggests that the most important influences on humour development may occur after the pre-school years. This also helps to account for the relative lack of antecedents in maternal behaviour during the first six years. On the other hand, the key pattern of dominance and aggressiveness is established as a predictor of sense of humour during the three- to six-year period for both sexes, as is the tendency toward talkativeness and imitation. The pattern of attention-, recognition-, and affection-seeking from adults also begins during this period for boys (but not until after the age of six for girls). Thus, these behaviours appear to predispose children to a greater likelihood of humour development as early as three years of age.

The antecedents of increased hostility in humour generally closely paralleled those of sense of humour (ratings of laughter and verbal and behavioural initiation of humour did not consider the hostility dimension). This is a surprising finding, unless one adopts the view that most humour has an underlying base in aggression. The consistent prediction by antecedent high levels of physical and verbal aggression supports this interpretation, especially in the case of girls. In the elementary-school sample, the precursors of sense of humour and hostility of humour were identical after the age of six and nearly identical between the ages of three to six. Only boys in the elementary-school sample showed reverse directions of prediction (after the age of six) of sense of humour and hostility of humour. While restless boys showed increased humour development in general, it was sedentary boys whose humour became hostile. Boys with poorer body co-ordination also developed more hostility in their humour. While sense of humour was positively predicted by recognition-seeking for achievement efforts, hostile forms of humour were associated with a lack of recognition-seeking for such efforts. While high amounts of effort at intellectual tasks anteceded sense of humour, low effort at such tasks anteceded hostility in humour. Finally, while all measures of dominance and aggression predicted sense of humour, only high amounts of physical aggression were associated with hostile humour in boys. Thus, a distinctive developmental history may be identified for hostile humour in boys, but not in girls.

REFERENCES

Baldwin, A. L., Kalhorn, J., and Breese, F. H. (1949). The appraisal of parent behavior. *Psychological Monographs*, **63**, No. 4.

Bergler, E. (1937). A clinical contribution to the psychogenesis of humor. *Psychoanalytic Review*, **24**, 34–53.

Freud, S. (1916). *Wit and its Relation to the Unconscious*. New York: Moffat Ward.

Fry, W. F., and Allen, M. (1975). *Make 'Em Laugh*. Palo Alto, California: Science and Behavior Books.

Janus, S. S. (1975). The great comedians: personality and other factors. *American Journal of Psychoanalysis*, **35**, 169–174.

McGhee, P. E. (1972). On the cognitive origins of incongruity humor: fantasy assimilation versus reality assimilation. In J. H. Goldstein and P. E. McGhee (Eds.), *The Psychology of Humor: Theoretical Perspectives and Empirical Issues*. New York: Academic Press.

McGhee, P. E. (1977). A model of the origins and early development of incongruity-based humour. In A. J. Chapman and H. C. Foot (Eds.), *It's a Funny Thing, Humour*. Oxford: Pergamon Press.

McGhee, P. E. (1979). *Humor: It's Origin and Development*. San Francisco: Freeman.

Middleton, R., and Moland, J. (1959). Humor in negro and white subcultures: a study of jokes among university students. *American Sociological Review*, **24**, 61–69.

Pollio, H. R., and Edgerly, J. (1976). Comedians and comic style. In A. J. Chapman and H. C. Foot (Eds.), *Humour and Laughter: Theory, Research and Applications*. Chichester: Wiley.

Robbins, L. C. (1963). The accuracy of parental recall of aspects of child development and of child-rearing practices. *Journal of Abnormal and Social Psychology*, **66**, 261–270.

Shultz, T. R. (1976). A cognitive-developmental analysis of humour. In A. J. Chapman and H. C. Foot (Eds.), *Humour and Laughter: Theory, Research, and Applications*. Chichester: Wiley.

Smith, E. E., and Goodchilds, J. D. (1959). Characteristics of the witty group member: the wit as leader. *American Psychologist*, **14**, 375–376.

Wenar, C., and Coulter, J. (1962). A reliability study of developmental histories. *Child Development*, **33**, 453–462.

Wilde, L. (1968). *The Great Comedians*. Secaucus, New Jersey: Citadel Press.

Wolfenstein, M. (1954). *Children's Humor*. Glencoe, Illinois: Free Press.

Children's Humour
Edited by P. McGhee and A. Chapmar
© 1980, John Wiley & Sons, Ltd.

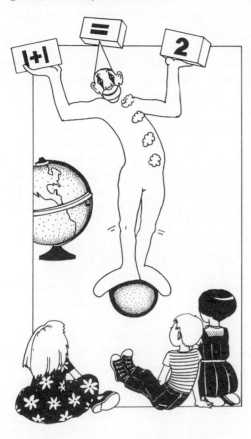

CHAPTER 9

Humour and its Effect on Learning in Children

ANN P. DAVIES
and
MICHAEL J. APTER

The idea that humour should be taken seriously in teaching children is one which appears today to be widely accepted amongst teachers and educationalists. For this reason, trainee student teachers are often encouraged to attempt to introduce humour in appropriate ways into their classroom lessons. Of course the view that teaching should be 'fun' for children goes back a long way in the history of educational thought. But the view that it should sometimes be 'funny' would appear to be a rather newer one. A good example of the influence which this view is coming to have is the use of humour in recent educational television programmes like *Sesame Street, The Electric Company,* and *Potty Time.*

Clearly humour of one kind or another can make lessons, or teaching programmes, or indeed any kind of learning situation, more enjoyable. But does it actually help children to learn? It is to this question that our chapter is primarily directed. Unfortunately, although there is a great deal of anecdotal evidence, comparatively little in the way of systematic research has been carried out on the question. Thus even the research on *Sesame Street* carried out by Ball and Bogatz (1970) does not look specifically at the effect of humour, although Lesser (1972, 1974) has emphasized the importance of humour in this programme.

In the next part of this chapter we look briefly at those few studies which have been carried out on this question, or questions related to it. In the succeeding section we describe more fully an experiment which one of us (Davies, 1978) has carried out in Cardiff and which, we believe, examines the question in more depth than any other study up to the present. In the final section of the chapter we discuss some factors which it was not possible to look at in the Cardiff research but which might well influence the nature of the relationship between humour and learning. These factors will therefore need to be investigated in the future if a full answer is to be given to the question of whether, and how, humour influences learning in children. (A number of these factors have also been discussed by McGhee, 1980, specifically in relation to learning from television programmes by adults as well as children.)

Before this, however, we should set the rest of the chapter in context by looking briefly at the ways in which, in principle, humour might be expected to influence learning, either negatively or positively. This can be done from four standpoints: the social effects of humour, the cognitive effects of humour, the effects of humour on arousal, and humour as a reinforcer. Clearly these four are closely interlinked.

First of all, at the social level a classroom which is characterized by humour is likely to be a happy one, unless the humour is used vindictively by the teacher against the pupils. If humour makes the classroom situation a less threatening one, especially to the less able pupils, then this, in turn, may help to create positive attitudes both to particular subjects and to learning in general. On the negative side, humour may produce an atmosphere which is too 'easy going' and the children may never make the discovery that some intellectual rewards come from hard work and application. The use of humour with children in the classroom usually provokes a great deal of laughter and noise and this may also have advantages and disadvantages. On the one hand the laughter may play a crucial role in the development of a happy classroom atmosphere. Further, it has been demonstrated (e.g. Chapman, 1976; Foot and Chapman, 1976) that social situations facilitate laughter; but it is also possible that laughter itself amplifies further the effects of social facilitation on other ongoing behaviours including learning (cf. Foot, Sweeney and Chapman, 1978). On the other hand, the laughter, and the noise which goes with it, may be distracting and make it more difficult for children to concentrate, particularly on difficult problems. It may also make it physically impossible to hear what the teacher is saying.

In terms of cognition, humour may play several roles. It may in the first place help to attract attention to the teacher and to what he is saying. It may then help to maintain that attention over a period of time. In other words, it may help what is called 'selective attention', which is the ability to attend to one thing rather than another. This may occur in two ways. Firstly, if the humour is closely integrated with the material being taught it may help to maintain interest in it and prevent distraction. Secondly, if the humour is not relevant it may nevertheless help if used at appropriate times by providing a socially condoned interlude; the children may then be able to attend again without distraction afterwards. In a rather different way, humour may help learning through perceptual distinctiveness, emphasizing certain information and helping it to stand out from the rest in a way which makes it easy to remember. (The effect of perceptual distinctiveness on learning has been demonstrated, for example, by Postman and Phillips, 1954.) On the negative side the humour may, especially if it is not closely integrated with the subject matter of the lesson, actually distract from it by setting up incompatible trains of thought. And perceptual distinctiveness may relate to the joke itself, which is remembered, but not to the material with which it was supposed to be associated (cf. Chapman and Crompton, 1978).

Concentration is not only a cognitive phenomenon but also an affective one; it depends not only on 'selective attention' but also on arousal. That is, concentration requires effort (Apter and Murgatroyd, 1975), and effort may be supposed to depend on physiological arousal. Anything which helps to produce and maintain this arousal may therefore help the child to concentrate (other things being equal) and this may in turn help him or her to learn. If humour helps to produce arousal, through surprise and incongruity, for example, then advantage may be taken of this in the classroom. The relationship of humour to arousal is of course one which is still not well understood despite a great deal of theorizing and research. (Our own particular view of this is provided by reversal theory: Apter and Smith, 1977.) If humour does help to bring about arousal, this may also have negative features. For one thing, voluminous research over the last fifty years has generally vindicated the Yerkes–Dodson law. This says, effectively, that as arousal increases so performance improves up to a certain point, but after that it deteriorates; this optimal point depends on the complexity of the task, the point coming lower on the arousal dimension as the task becomes more complex. Humour, therefore, may help to raise arousal beyond its optimum level, especially in cases where the learning task is a difficult one.

Finally, humour is something which people find pleasant. In stricter terminology, it is reinforcing. Its reinforcing properties may therefore be used in teaching for example through operant conditioning. For various reasons operant conditioning is difficult to use in the classroom situation, especially because it is unlikely that all children have made the correct response together at the correct moment. But in certain circumstances it is possible that humour may be a convenient and practicable reinforcer for the teacher. On the negative side, unless it is used judiciously, the wrong behaviour may be reinforced. For example, if the teacher uses humour in an attempt to regain attention in an unruly class, he may simply be reinforcing the unruly behaviour and lack of attention.

Now that we have looked in a general way at some of the varied effects which humour may be expected to have, directly or indirectly, on learning in children, let us look at research which has actually been carried out on the question of whether it does, in fact, influence learning.

PREVIOUS RESEARCH ON HUMOUR AND LEARNING

Of the research which has been done the single study which most directly bears on the theme of this chapter is that of Hauck and Thomas (1972) in the United States. They studied, to quote the title of their paper, 'The relationship of humor to intelligence, creativity, and intentional and incidental learning'. They took as their subjects eighty elementary schoolchildren in the fourth, fifth, and sixth grades (i.e. approximately nine, ten, and eleven years of age). The task they used was this: subjects were presented with ten items, each with three drawings of common objects (e.g. shoe, hat, and glove), labelled with their names. They responded to each item by choosing two out of the three objects and writing a few sentences to associate the two for some use. There were three groups of subjects. One was instructed to say how the objects could be used humorously, another to say how they could be used in an unusual but not humorous manner, and the third group, which was treated as a control, to indicate usual or common uses. Twenty-four hours later a test was given of recall of object labels. This was carried out in such a way that incidental learning and intentional learning could be measured separately: each test was made up of a randomly selected set of ten of the twenty items chosen and used by each subject in the earlier part of the experiment (i.e. each test was made up specially in this way for each subject). The subject was then asked if he could remember the other two objects in the same item; one of these, in each case, was of course the item he used in his associations, the other was not. Memory of the former was interpreted as intentional and of the latter as incidental.

The results were analysed in various ways, taking into account the intelligence and creativity scores of the subjects (especially since the experimenters were also interested in the relationship between creativity, intelligence, and a sense of humour in their subjects). One of their main results was that subjects who made unusual associations recalled significantly more information in both incidental and intentional learning than those making usual or humorous associations. However, it was also found that humour facilitated retention resulting from incidental learning but not intentional learning. The results of the experiment in relation to humour are therefore somewhat equivocal. And the reason for the effect of humour on incidental learning may simply have been an artifact of the difficulty involved in coming up with humorous associations. In other words, it is likely that the children in the humorous condition had to play around with (and therefore attend roughly equally to) all three objects in each item in combinations of two until they eventually hit on a humorous connection in one of the pairs. They therefore spent longer considering the object which in fact was not used in the response pair in the humorous condition than was done in the control condition. In any case, one might ask whether what Hauck and Thomas call intentional learning really is intentional: after all, the subjects, in all these conditions, merely because they chose one object rather than the other, did not presumably intend thereby to learn it; from this point of view the whole experiment is really about incidental learning alone. It is also difficult to draw conclusions from such a study for classroom methods: for example, usually in the classroom the humour comes from the teacher rather than the children. Nevertheless, this remains the most germane study of those which have been carried out up until the study which we shall describe in the next section.

Another relevant study, but with older children, is that of Curran (1973). As part of a larger study of responses to cartoon humour, he attempted to show that humorous visual aids (i.e. cartoons) facilitated retention of verbal material to a greater degree than non-humorous visual aids or no visual aids at all. His subjects in this part of his study consisted of three groups of twenty-four subjects (twelve males and twelve females) from the sixth grade (i.e. aged about eleven) and an equal number from the ninth grade (i.e. aged about fourteen). Each group was exposed to one of three visual aid conditions (humorous visual aid, non-humorous visual aid, and no visual aid); pre- and post-retention testing were used. Results did not substantiate the contention that humorous visual aids facilitate learning to a greater extent than non-humorous ones. A measure of the subjects' expressed motivation indicated a trend toward greater interest for either visual aid condition than for the no visual aid condition.

One other study which should be mentioned because it involves the use of humorous material with children in the classroom is that of Hinson (1970) who was concerned with children's appreciation of humorous verse. His subjects were two hundred and twenty-four pupils up to the age of fourteen years from a junior school and a comprehensive school. This study was concerned more with children's preferences in relation to different types of humorous verse than with learning, and he found that situation humour was the most consistently popular with all age groups, while poems using satire or using word play had much less appeal. Hinson argues that his study is relevant to teaching since his experience is that carefully chosen humorous verse often provides a palatable introduction to more serious poetry for pupils who normally regarded poetry as boring or 'cissy'.

A number of studies, such as those of Gibb (1964), Taylor (1964), Weinberg (1973) and Kaplan and Pascoe (1977), have studied the effectiveness of humour in learning, but with subjects of older age levels, especially university students. Since such little work has been done on humour and learning in younger children we are forced to look briefly at such studies since they may have some relevance. Just how far one can generalize results from these studies to young children remains, however, arguable. It is quite possible, for example, that humour is more important at the primary-school level than with older children. In this respect it is interesting to note that Cattell (1931) found that a greater number of infant and elementary schoolteachers and heads rated a sense of humour as important amongst the qualities of a good teacher, than did secondary schoolteachers and heads. The reason for this is not clear although it could be that at a younger age the need for novelty and stimulation as an aid to concentration is far greater than at a later stage. Humour providing this novelty may help younger children's concentration.

Gibb (1964) found that university students learned more from a lecture on biology when it contained humour than when it did not. Gruner (1976) has criticized this experiment, pointing out in particular that time of day was not controlled for and that the results may have reflected this rather than the presence or absence of humour.

Slightly younger subjects were used in an experiment with high-school summer students by Taylor (1964). He used two speeches about the influence on contemporary thinking of an eighteenth-century minister, one of the speeches containing humour and the other not. No advantage was found for humour. It should be noted, though, that each speech lasted only seven minutes; this may have been too short a time for differences to emerge.

Weinberg (1973), working with one hundred and forty college students, aimed to determine the effect on subsequent test scores of interjecting humorous examples into a factual presentation of psychological subject matter. He hypothesized that humour would lower a subject's anxiety during learning so that he would be more receptive to the material, making him feel more competent and less anxious in the testing situation. His results showed that humour did interact significantly with anxiety and intelligence in different ways, although not always in the direction predicted. Neither high-anxious students of superior intelligence nor low-anxious students of inferior intelligence were affected one way or another by humour. Low-anxious students of high intelligence benefited significantly by humour but high-anxious students of lower intelligence were significantly penalized by it. These results show that humour is not necessarily an aid to learning, although it can be under the right conditions.

As we saw earlier, one factor which might seem to be relevant to whether humour does aid learning or not is that of whether the humorous material is intimately related to the material which is being learned or whether it is unrelated. Kaplan and Pascoe (1977) took up this question with university students.

The sample consisted of five hundred and eight students. Classes attended either a serious lecture or one of three versions of a humorous lecture, all making use of humorous examples. In one case these examples were related to the concepts in the lecture, in the second case the examples were unrelated to the concepts, and in the third case there was a combination of both related and unrelated examples. In the test given immediately afterwards it was found that comprehension was not aided by the use of humorous examples. But on retesting six weeks later, it was found that although total test scores were not significantly different, groups viewing lectures with concept-related humour did significantly better on items testing recall of the humorous examples than did the serious lecture group.

A number of studies have been carried out in which the primary interest was in humour as an aid to attitude change in persuasive speeches. Some of these, for example, Gruner (1967, 1970), Kilpela (1961), Youngman (1966), Kennedy (1972), and Markiewicz (1972) also checked for audience recall of the speech material. For a good recent review of this area, see Gruner (1976).

Taken together, the various studies carried out in the area of humour and learning, both with children and students, have therefore produced somewhat equivocal results. This is presumably, among other things, because of the different ways in which humour has been used in these different studies.

THE CARDIFF STUDY

The study described and discussed here basically sought to test whether children who view a humorous slide-tape teaching programme actually learn more than children who view an equivalent but otherwise non-humorous programme. In all, two hundred and eighty-five junior schoolchildren (i.e. aged between eight- and eleven-years-old) from four schools in the Cardiff area of Wales took part in the study.

Initially all children were given a series of pre-tests to complete. These were:

1. Pre-tests for knowledge in each of the subject areas being taught;
2. Torrance Test of Creativity;
3. Porter and Cattell Children's Personality Questionnaire;
4. The Junior Eysenck Personality Inventory.

Having completed these they were then randomly divided into two groups. One group viewed humorous versions of audio-visual slide-tape teaching programmes and the other group viewed non-humorous but otherwise identical versions of the teaching programmes. There were about eighty slides in each programme, and each programme lasted approximately twenty minutes.

In the humorous version of the programmes, approximately one quarter of the slides, spread through the programme, consisted of cartoons. These cartoons made much use of caricature, visual incongruity and slapstick—all varieties of humour which a preliminary study showed to be rated high in humour by children of the age in question. These humorous additions were only minimally relevant to the topic being taught. For example, in the humorous version of a slide showing a dentist, a caricatured dentist is shown standing on the patient to get leverage to extract a tooth. In the humorous version of people skating, a caricatured young man is shown falling through the ice, while the sun has a face with an expression of surprise on it. In the non-humorous version of the programmes, all the slides consisted of non-humorous diagrams and illustrations. In both types of programme the commentary on the tape was identical, and the slides changed at the same points on the tape in each case.

Four deliberately varied subject areas were taught to the children. These were:

1. General knowledge;
2. Science;
3. Language;
4. Geography/History.

Under the heading 'General knowledge' the topic chosen was 'Signs and Symbols in Everyday Life'; the programme on 'Science' dealt in a simple way with topics like 'day and night' and 'solids, liquids, and gases'; the 'Language' programme taught sixteen everyday words in Latvian; and, finally, the 'Geography/History' programme took Afghanistan as its topic. The particular topics, although perhaps a little 'unusual' for these children, were chosen for this very reason. In other words, they were chosen to ensure that there was little prior knowledge and that the situation was therefore a genuine learning situation. In fact, with these particular topics, scores from the pre-tests of knowledge of the topics were never more than one correct out of a possible twenty-five.

The four programmes (in either their humorous or non-humorous versions) were presented throughout one school day (i.e. between 9.30 a.m. and 4.0 p.m. with normal school morning, lunch and afternoon breaks). Post-tests in each topic were given immediately after viewing each programme, as was a test of attitude to each programme.

The experiments were therefore carried out in class during the normal school day and the children who took part were made to feel that the programmes were simply an extension of the school curriculum. In general, the present study achieved as far as possible a close approximation to a 'real world' rather than a laboratory setting. Retention tests were given at intervals of one and nine months after exposure to the programmes.

Analysis of the post-test data by means of Analysis of Variance techniques produced results which support the view that learning is greater in subjects exposed to a humorous learning programme than their counterparts' programme ($p < 0.001$). (The full details of this analysis and other analyses referred to in this chapter are to be found in Davies' unpublished doctoral dissertation, University of Wales, 1978. Further data and analyses not presented in the present chapter can also be found in that dissertation.) This, the main finding of the study, therefore strongly supports the position that humour can be used in such a way as to aid learning.

As far as attitude is concerned, analysis of scores on the 'attitude to the programme' tests supported the view that humour would produce a more favourable attitude to the programme ($p < 0.001$). This variable of attitude is one which appears not to have been investigated in previous studies but is one which, as noted at the outset to this chapter, is likely to be important in the classroom setting. It may indeed have contributed directly to the significant difference in learning scores found in this study and referred to above. Even if it does not contribute directly to immediate learning it may, in any case, have more long-term and indirect effects—for example through motivating children to work harder and longer on the topics concerned.

In terms of retention it was found that humour was still beneficial in aiding retention after an interval of one month had elapsed since the programmes were viewed. However, whereas there was a difference in immediate post-test scores significant at the 0.1 per cent level between the experimental conditions (i.e. $p < 0.001$), the main effect of humour on retention scores after one month was found to be significant only at the two-and-a-half per cent level (i.e. $p < 0.025$). After nine months there was no significant main effect for humour on retention scores. This might be taken to suggest that humour is most beneficial as an aid to memory over relatively short periods of time. But it is notoriously difficult to draw conclusions from long-term retention tests since so many 'contaminating' factors may come into effect during the intervening period.

Clearly the relationship of humour to learning is not a straightforward one and may involve a large number of different factors. Part of the reason for the equivocal finding of the previous studies referred to above may well have been due to differences in the experimental designs in relation to these factors. In the present study, therefore, a number of factors which may be hypothesized to be germane to the main question were also investigated, the aim being to paint a fuller picture of the relationship of humour to learning. We shall now discuss these factors and the results obtained in relation to them.

Topic differences

Humour would clearly appear to be easier to introduce into some school topics rather than others (e.g. see discussion by Highet, 1951), but the question arises as to whether, having been introduced, it facilitates learning more in some areas than others. This was looked at in a preliminary way in the present study by using four different subject areas in the research.

The results of the study suggest that topic may indeed be an important variable. The Latvian and Afghanistan programmes, while benefiting from the addition of humour, did not benefit to as great an extent as the 'Signs and Symbols' programme and the Science programme. However, it would be unwise to draw any general conclusions from this. For one thing it was not possible to balance the programmes for difficulty or interest; for another, it is debatable just how representative the material used in these programmes was for the subject-matters involved.

There are of course other questions that relate to topic which it was not possible to deal with in the present study, including the following:

1. Is the interest of the topic to the learner an important factor in the effectiveness of humour as an aid to learning? If an interest in the subject area being taught is apparent before exposure to a teaching programme, then perhaps humour may not be as great an aid to learning. But, as noted earlier, humour may act to sustain an interest which might otherwise have been lost.
2. Is humour effective with a completely new subject area by acting as a means of gaining initial interest in the topic?
3. Does humour facilitate learning of, or promote a more favourable attitude to, related fields? For example, after teaching geography humorously would areas of geography other than those already taught be responded to more readily?

Elapsed time

Previous experimental studies have usually presented only one relatively short programme or set of learning materials to their subjects. It may well be that the effects of humour on learning change over time and that the effects over short periods of time are not representative of the full effects of humour as time elapses. In the present study, as we said earlier, four different programmes were shown during the course of one school day, and it was therefore possible to examine this topic experimentally.

The design was such that each class saw either the humorous versions of the programme throughout the experiment or the non-humorous versions. In each of the four schools the order of the topic was changed so that each of the programmes (both humorous and non-humorous) was presented first in one of the schools, second at another school, and so on. In other words, a Latin Square design was used so that the effects of serial position could be looked at in a manner which was independent of topic.

The results are shown in Table 9.1. Inspection of the table shows that both forms of the programme became less effective over the period of the day. Statistical analysis in fact shows that for both the humorous and the non-humorous conditions, differences in scores between the first and fourth presentations are significant at the 0.1 per cent level (i.e. $p < 0.001$). This was of course to be expected, especially since the novelty of the situation may have worn off over time. Of more interest was the fact that the humorous versions of the programmes held up much better over time than the non-humorous versions, the differences between the two experimental conditions reaching the 0.1 per cent level of significance for the second, third, and fourth presentations. The difference between the two experimental conditions for the first presentation, by

Table 9.1 Mean post-test scores, and differences between them, for the four programmes presented to children in the course of a school day, in terms of the order of their presentation.

	First presentation	Second presentation	Third presentation	Fourth presentation
Mean post-test scores, humorous condition	14.51	14.70	13.92	12.02
Mean post-test scores, non-humorous condition	11.84	8.90	9.08	7.44
Differences between means	2.67	5.80	4.84	4.58

contrast, only reached the one per cent level of significance (i.e. $p < 0.01$). Presumably at this initial stage children under both experimental conditions were working well and showing high attention and interest, partly because they were fresh and partly because of the excitement of the novelty of the situation; under these conditions the effect of the humour may have been masked or even reduced, only to become more apparent as factors like fatigue and boredom took increasing effect. This was one of the most interesting results of the whole experimental study, and goes to show the importance of looking at the effects of humour over a reasonably large time span.

Duration of each programme

The question of time-span also arises in relation to the length of each individual programme. The presentation time for learning materials in most previous studies has been rather short, and this might explain why in many cases differences have not emerged between subjects exposed to humorous and non-humorous versions of the materials concerned. This would be particularly true if humour was most effective after a period of exposure to the learning material which is nearly as great as the subject's normal maximum concentration span. Most teachers appear to agree that at the very maximum the concentration span for primary schoolchildren at any one time is approximately between fifteen and twenty minutes. In the present study, the duration of the programme was not itself varied. But since the presentation time was twenty minutes it was reasonable to suppose that, on the hypothesis above, humour may have been more effective towards the end of the programme in each case than it was earlier.

In order to test this, the data were re-analysed by breaking the post-test down into blocks of questions which related to different parts of the programme. Specifically, the post-test consisted for each programme of twenty-five items, made up of five blocks of five items each, each block relating to each of the five four-minute periods of the programme. The scores on each of these blocks were then compared across programmes. The hypothesis was that the differences between the scores obtained as a result of viewing either the humorous or non-humorous version of a programme would vary, depending on the period of the programme to which the question items and the scores on them related. Analysis along these lines, however, did not support the hypothesis.

Age differences

In the present study, three age levels as measured by educational level (i.e. UK junior school, years 2, 3, and 4) were compared. No significant difference was found in the differences between the effectiveness of the humorous and the non-humorous versions of the programme in relation to this age variable. This does not, of course, mean that age differences would not be found between children more dissimilar in age (and in Piagetian stages of cognitive development) or between children and adults.

Sex differences

The sex of subjects in previous research on humour and persuasion and on humour and learning is another variable which has been largely ignored, but which was looked at in the present study. No significant differences were found, however, in relation to the effectiveness of humour in promoting learning.

Personality differences

In order to establish whether there were any personality differences in the effectiveness of humour in a learning situation, the children who acted as subjects were asked to complete three personality tests (counting the creativity tests as a personality test). These personality tests, as listed earlier, covered a fairly broad spectrum of personality and comprised nineteen different measures between them. No significant relationships were found in terms of any of these dimensions, even in respect of the Neuroticism and Extraversion/Introversion dimensions of the Junior Eysenck Personality Inventory.

RECOMMENDATIONS FOR FUTURE RESEARCH

Although the study just described looked at a number of factors which might have been supposed to be related to the effects of humour on learning, many other factors could not be looked at in this design. In the final section of this chapter we list some of these further factors. We do this both in order to suggest lines along which further research on this topic may be pursued, and also to bring out even more strongly some of the complexities of the situation which were indicated at the beginning of this chapter.

Type of humour

Is the type of humour used important in the effect that humour has on learning? For example, is 'harmless' humour, such as that employed as far as possible in the present study, more effective as a facilitator of learning than 'tendentious' humour, such as satire and sarcasm tends to be? It is notable that the majority of studies concerned with the effectiveness of the addition of humour to either a learning situation or a persuasive communication have, as Markiewicz (1972) has noted, employed satire as their form of humour.

It might also be asked if long time-span humour (Giles and Oxford, 1970) is less effective than short time-span humour as an aid to learning. Since long time-span humour is more cognitively demanding, this could act to distract subjects from the actual lesson or learning material. In these terms it might be argued that it would be preferable to use short, quick, obvious witticisms rather than long involved stories which may attract attention to themselves and away from the material to be learned. (In the Cardiff study, short time-span humour was used.)

Relevance of the humour

The humour used in a learning situation may be highly relevant to the topic being taught or be totally irrelevant and brought in in arbitrary ways, or it may have some degree of relevance somewhere between these two extremes. An important question which arises, therefore, is that of whether the degree of relevance is related to the effectiveness of the humour for learning purposes, or whether it might not in certain circumstances even have a negative effect. A similar and related question is that of how closely integrated the humour should be to the material being taught. Must it appear to arise out of it naturally, or can it stand apart and contrast with the rest of the material? (This, in turn, relates to the next factor to be considered—that of the temporal insertion of the humour in the material.) This question was not looked at in the Cardiff study in which the humour was in general only rather arbitrarily related to the topic being taught.

As we have seen earlier, Kaplan and Pascoe (1977) have already carried out a first study of relevance with university students, but no one, as far as we are aware, has yet studied it using children as subjects. The Children's Television Workshop, however, in making such programmes as *Sesame Street* have assumed that humour must be meaningfully related to the material to be learned (Gibbon, Palmer, and Fowles, 1975; Lesser, 1972, 1974). One difficulty in studying the problem of the relevance of humour is that of measuring with any kind of precision the degree to which a joke or other form of humour in a particular instance is relevant to the information being taught. This problem is further complicated by individual differences among the subjects, since some subjects may see relevance where others see no relevance at all. In particular, we would expect more creative subjects to see connections which escape less creative subjects.

Temporal position of insertion of the humour

Are the positions of insertion of humour in the learning situation of importance? In particular, should humour come immediately before or after the information to be learned? Or should the information to be learned in some way be contained within it? This raises broad theoretical issues of the kind discussed at the beginning of this chapter, about the nature of the effect of humour. If the effect of humour is supposed to be essentially one of attracting attention, or raising arousal, then its optimum position will be at some stage before the material to be learned. If, on the other hand, its function is supposed to be mainly that of a reinforcer, then its optimum position is likely to be after the learning material. This does not preclude humour having other functions, too, and a number of these were listed in the introduction to the chapter. For example, humour might aid learning through adding elements of perceptual distinctiveness at appropriate points, or through changing negative attitudes to the subject-matter. But the question of timing would still be important in these cases too.

Amount of humour

Is the amount of humour used during any given period of teaching important? By 'amount of humour' here we mean both the number of humorous incidents and their funniness. This question may be important from two standpoints:

1. The amount of humour introduced to a single learning programme. It is quite possible that there is an optimal level of humour that is effective in any given learning situation. In our investigations approximately a quarter of the slides in the humorous versions of the programmes were humorous. Future research using greater or lesser amounts of humour, in both of the senses indicated above, is advocated to test this hypothesis further.
2. The number of humorous lessons that are taught during any given learning period, for example, the school day. Ball and Bogatz (1970) note that teachers argue that it is variety that is important in a learning situation.

Medium of presentation

Is the medium of presentation of the teaching a salient factor when introducing humour? For example, is humour more effective in the context of audio-visual presentation of the learning material than it is when the learning material is presented by a teacher in a typical classroom setting or when children read the material themselves?

It has been shown (Perl, 1933) that the medium of presentation of humorous material affects the amount of humour that subjects find in the content of the material presented. Little research relevant to the present studies has been done on the effects of medium of presentation of humorous material on learning and attitude change. An exception is the work of Curran (1973) who, as mentioned earlier, did find that subjects exposed to a learning programme with visual aids showed greater interest (but not greater learning) than subjects exposed to a learning programme with no visual aids.

Group versus individual conditions

Is humour more effective in aiding learning when teaching is presented to a group (e.g. in a class lesson or television programme shown in group conditions) than when it is presented to subjects individually (e.g. by means of a book or teaching machine programme)? It is possible that humour helps to bring about social facilitation. Therefore humour may encourage learning in a group situation, for this reason if for no other. In any case, as implied at the beginning of this chapter, the social context may need to be taken into account for a full understanding of the effects of humour on learning.

Overt laughter

Is learning greater the more the laughter that a humorous lesson generates? As noted early in the chapter, laughter may produce a pleasant atmosphere which encourages learning. On the other hand, as was also noted, it is possible that too much laughter might distract subjects from the lesson or even make it physically inaudible.

Ecological factors

More extensive research into ecological factors which may affect the facilitative effect of humour in a learning situation are necessary. Research in varying types of schools, with careful consideration of the salient features of these schools, may also yield much relevant information.

CONCLUDING REMARKS

All psychological questions, however simple they may be to ask, turn out to be highly complex to answer. The question posed in this chapter—*Does humour help children to learn?*—is no exception. Indeed, from the beginning of the chapter we have implied that there can be no simple answers and that the question should specify what kind of humour, under what kind of conditions, with what kinds of subjects and in relation to what kind of learning. Some of this complexity has been brought out by means of the list of possible influencing factors which has been presented in the final section of the chapter and the list of factors investigated in the study described in the previous section. Nor should it be supposed that the factors mentioned in this chapter, taken together, constitute an exhaustive set or that they act independently. However, despite this complexity we feel that some progress is being made, and that this will be facilitated by the greater interest being taken currently by psychologists in the field of humour research as a whole.

REFERENCES

Apter, M. J., and Murgatroyd, S. (1975). Concentration, personality and self-pacing in programmed learning. *Programmed Learning and Educational Technology*, **12**, 208–215.

Apter, M. J., and Smith, K. C. P. (1977). Humour and the theory of psychological reversals. In A. J. Chapman and H. C. Foot (Eds.), *It's a Funny Thing, Humour*. Oxford: Pergamon.

Ball, S. A., and Bogatz, G. A. (1970). *The First Year of Sesame Street: An Evaluation*. Princeton, New Jersey: Educational Testing Service.

Cattell, R. B. (1931). The assessment of teaching ability. *British Journal of Educational Psychology*, **1**, 48–71.

Chapman, A. J. (1976). Social aspects of humorous laughter. In A. J. Chapman and H. C. Foot (Eds.), *Humour and Laughter: Theory, Research and Applications*. Chichester: Wiley.

Chapman, A. J., and Crompton, P. (1978). Humorous presentations of material and presentations of humorous material: a review of the humour and memory literature and two experimental studies. In M. M. Gruneberg, P. E. Morris and R. N. Sykes (Eds.), *Practical Aspects of Memory*. London: Academic Press.

Curran, F. W. (1973). A developmental study of cartoon humor appreciation and its use in facilitating learning. Unpublished Doctoral Dissertation, Catholic University of America.

Davies, A. P. (1978). The importance of humour in childhood learning. Unpublished Doctoral Dissertation, University of Wales.

Foot, H. C., and Chapman, A. J. (1976). Social responsiveness to humour in young children. In A. J. Chapman and H. C. Foot (Eds.), *Humour and Laughter: Theory, Research and Applications*. Chichester: Wiley.

Foot, H. C., Sweeney, C. A., and Chapman, A. J. (1978). Effects of humour upon children's memory. In M. M. Gruneberg, P. E. Morris and R. N. Sykes (Eds.), *Practical Aspects of Memory*. London: Academic Press.

Gibb, J. D. (1964). An experimental comparison of the humorous lecture and non-humorous lecture in informative speaking. Unpublished Master's Thesis, University of Utah.

Gibbon, S. Y., Palmer, E. L., and Fowles, B. R. (1975). 'Sesame Street, 'The Electric Company', and reading. In J. B. Carroll and J. S. Chall (Eds.), *Toward a Literate Society: A Report from the National Academy of Education*. New York: McGraw-Hill.

Giles, H., and Oxford, G. S. (1970). Towards a multidimensional theory of laughter causation and its social implications. *Bulletin of the British Psychological Society*, **23**, 97–105.

Gruner, C. R. (1967). Effect of humor on speaker ethos and audience information gain. *Journal of Communication*, **17**, 228–233.

Gruner, C. R. (1970). The effect of humor in dull and interesting informative speeches. *Central States Speech Journal*, **21**, 160–166.

Gruner, C. R. (1976). Wit and humour in mass communication. In A. J. Chapman and H. C. Foot (Eds.), *Humour and Laughter: Theory, Research and Applications*. Chichester: Wiley.

Hauck, W. E., and Thomas, J. W. (1972). The relationship of humor to intelligence, creativity, and intentional and incidental learning. *Journal of Experimental Education*, **40**, 52–55.

Highet, G. (1951). *The Art of Teaching*. London: Methuen.

Hinson, M. (1970). The assessment of children's appreciation of humorous verses. *Educational Review*, **22**, 198–204.

Kaplan, R. M., and Pascoe, G. C. (1977). Humorous lectures and humorous examples: some effects upon comprehension and retention. *Journal of Educational Psychology*, **69**, 61–65.

Kennedy, A. J. (1972). An experimental study of the effect of humorous message content upon ethos and persuasiveness. Unpublished Doctoral Dissertation, University of Michigan.

Kilpela, D. E. (1961). An experimental study of the effects of humor on persuasion. Unpublished Master's Thesis, Wayne State University.

Lesser, G. (1972). Assumptions behind the production and writing methods in 'Sesame Street'. In W. Schramm (Ed.), *Quality Instructional Television*. Honolulu: University of Hawaii Press.

Lesser, G. (1974). *Children and Television: Lessons from Sesame Street*. New York: Random House.

Markiewicz, D. (1972). The effects of humor on persuasion. Unpublished Doctoral Dissertation, Ohio State University.

McGhee, P. E. (1980). Toward the integration of entertainment and educational functions of television: the role of humor. In P. H. Tannenbaum (Ed.), *The Entertainment Functions of Television*. New York: Lawrence Erlbaum Associates.

Perl, R. E. (1933). The influence of a social factor upon the appreciation of humor. *American Journal of Psychology*, **45**, 308–312.

Postman, L., and Phillips, L. W. (1954). Studies in incidental learning. I. The effects of crowding and isolation. *Journal of Experimental Psychology*, **48**, 48–56.

Taylor, P. M. (1964). The effectiveness of humor in informative speeches. *Central States Speech Journal*, **5**, 295–296.

Weinberg, M. D. (1973). The interactional effect of humor and anxiety on academic performance. Unpublished Doctoral Disseration, Yeshiva University.

Youngman, R. C. (1966). An experimental investigation of the effect of germane humor versus non-germane humor in an informative communication. Unpublished Master's Thesis, Ohio University.

CHAPTER 10

The Clinical Use of Humour in Work with Children

JACOB LEVINE

Clinicians have not waited for the fruits of scientific investigations or theories about humour to make use of it in their diagnostic or therapeutic work. They have applied to clinical situations what might be characterized as commonsense understanding of the manifold ways in which humour is used in everyday life. The recent upsurge of interest in humour has as yet had little impact upon its clinical applications, perhaps because most of the research and theorizing has been concerned with the essence of humour rather than its uses. It is the thesis of this chapter that some of the findings of recent experimental and clinical studies on humour and its development can have considerable usefulness in clinical work with children. We discuss the contributions that humour can make to two primary clinical areas, developmental assessment and psychotherapy.

The use of humour in the assessment of cognitive functions and personality has a relatively long history. Intelligence tests like the Stanford–Binet have included items of humorous incongruity. A number of tests of sense of humour have been devised: they examine humour as a desirable personality trait and relate it to other personality variables. These studies, going back about fifty years, have been carried out as isolated empirical investigations without apparent relevance to theories of humour. In recent years, interest in humour has risen, with primary emphasis on the cognitive aspects. From the cognitive viewpoint, humour has been found to be an integral part of the developmental process reflecting the various stages of cognitive development. It would appear that humour must play an important role in the psychological growth of the child, but as yet we know little about what contribution, if any, humour makes.

On the other hand, the importance of cognitive development in children's responses to humour appears to be well-established. Little systematic research has been done, however, on other components of humour such as the affective or motivational. Some clinical studies have been carried out, principally from the psychoanalytic viewpoint, but they are for the most part unsystematic and based largely on single instances. It is difficult to draw general conclusions from most of these studies, although they do suggest that emotional and motivational factors which relate to a child's developmental level play a significant role in his/her selective responsiveness to humour in its various forms. In many of these cases, the children were presented as cases which were treated therapeutically for their disturbances and the humour they displayed was either symptomatic of their psychopathology or incidental to it. The difficulties in relating the motivational or the emotional components of children's humour responses are formidable particularly since we really have no systematic formulations, other than the psychoanalytic, about these aspects of child development.

DEVELOPMENTAL ASSESSMENT

Responses to humorous stimuli like cartoon absurdities and incongruities have long been used in measuring intelligence, especially with children. The Stanford–Binet Intelligence Test, which is the most widely used children's test, contains a sub-test composed of humorous pictorial absurdities, for children who are aged seven or more. Five pictures are shown to a child and s/he is asked to tell 'what is funny (foolish) about the picture?'. For children aged nine to twelve, verbal instead of picture absurdities are used in the sub-test. An example of such absurd statements is 'Bill Jones' feet are so big that he has to pull his trousers on over his head'. The items used in this sub-test were chosen on the basis of careful sampling and test reliability and validity. McNemar's (1942) factor analysis of the items of each sub-test was comprehensive and showed the high loadings of the intellectual functions they were selected to measure. The conclusion was reached that 'his findings support the view that a single common factor would explain performance on the Stanford–Binet'. It is evident from the studies reported in the 1972 Norms Edition that the absurdities sub-test shares with the other sub-tests the ability to measure general intelligence.

The comprehension of humorous stimuli can thus be used to measure intellectual development. However, the relation between the comprehension of humorous stimuli and intelligence is not without conflicting findings. Some investigators have found high correlations whereas others have not. Omwake

(1939) found that the comprehension of jokes was significantly related to a test of intelligence, to the ability to think abstractly, and to the ability to discover embedded figures. Levine and Redlich (1960) found that the comprehension of cartoons correlated highly with the Wechsler Adult Intelligence Scale (WAIS) for both psychiatric patients and normal subjects. Zigler, Levine, and Gould (1966a, b) found a significant relation between the comprehension of cartoons and cognitive level. They administered a children's form of the Mirth Response Test (Redlich, Levine and Sohler, 1951) to sixty-four children of average intelligence in the second, fourth, and fifth grades. They also obtained similar results in comparisons between normal, institutionalized, and non-institutionalized children who were matched for mental age (MA). Other investigators also have found a positive, significant relation between amount of laughter and mental development (Brackett, 1934), ability to recognize absurdities (Brumbaugh, 1939), and the ability to recognize incongruities (Behan and Bevan, 1956). However, still other investigators have failed to find a significant relation between intelligence and humour comprehension (Cattell and Luborsky, 1947; Cunningham, 1962; Hester, 1924; Kambouropoulou, 1926; Omwake, 1939). Some have concluded that intellectual development is not a deciding factor in the appreciation of humour (Brackett, 1934; Ding and Jersild, 1932; Gregg, 1928; Landis and Ross, 1933; Omwake, 1939). One explanation for the apparent discrepancies was pointed out by Flugel (1954) who noted that investigators like Wynn-Jones (1927), Piret (1940) and Mones (1939), though emphasizing the importance of cognitive development in humour, recognized that its operation is masked by temperament, attitude, and other emotional factors.

Despite the conflicting data correlating intelligence and the understanding of humour, there is no one who will contest the fact that cognitive competence to meet the cognitive requirements to understand a joke is a precondition for its appreciation. Although the controversy is over the magnitude of the correlation between intelligence test scores and the comprehension of humorous stimuli, no one appears to dispute the importance of cognitive processes in the appreciation of humour. For some theorists, the essential structure of humour is based upon the cognitive process of resolving an incongruity (Kant, 1790; Koestler, 1964; Maier, 1932; Rothbart, 1976; Schopenhauer, 1905; Shultz, 1976). Freud (1960) has pointed out that cognition also contributes to the experienced pleasure by the activation of the cognitive process and from the experiencing of cognitive mastery comparable to the solving of a puzzle or a problem.

The statement that getting the point of a joke is in itself a source of pleasure is not a startling insight. However, it does reflect the awareness that there are multiple sources of pleasure in the enjoyment of humour. The fact that there is pleasure in successfully responding to the challenge of getting the point of a joke serves to account for, among other things, the importance of the perishability of a joke. The first hearing of a joke is funny. From then on the pleasure gain is from sharing it with others. Once the incongruity is resolved, the surprise is gone, the puzzle is solved, and the gratification comes from the recall of its resolution.

Perhaps the only systematic attempt to apply theoretical formulations of cognitive development to humour has been made by those investigators who have used Piaget's ideas of stages. McGhee (1972, 1979), Shultz (1976) and Rothbart (1976) have applied Piaget's stages of cognitive development to the development of cognitive processes in the development of humour. In Shultz's (1976) view the recognition and the resolution of incongruity is a sufficient condition for the appreciation of humour. Using the usual definition of incongruity as a cognitive conflict between what is expected and what actually occurs in a joke, Shultz (1976) maintains that the concept of incongruity is the basic structural characteristic of a joke and accounts for the surprisingness of the punchline. From his view-point, humour is more than just the discovery of an incongruity, it requires a second phase of resolving the incongruity. It is this second phase of incongruity that distinguishes humour from nonsense which is pure unresolvable incongruity. According to his analysis the creation of humour involves cognitive processing in reverse of that involved in the response to humour. The findings of Jones (1970) support this view of the importance of incongruity in the humour response. He compared the ratings of one group of subjects for the incongruity of a number of cartoons with the rating for funniness by a second group of subjects and found a positive linear function between the two ratings.

The importance of incongruity in humour has long been recognized, but it is only recently that it has become the primary focus of research by behavioural scientists. Efforts to explain all humour in terms of incongruity have posed some difficulties, particularly with respect to those incongruous situations which are clearly not humorous and lead not to laughter but to puzzlement or exploratory behaviour. Clearly, either only certain forms of incongruity are experienced as humorous or factors in addition to incongruity are necessary.

The continued use of such items as cartoon absurdities in intelligence tests has been based primarily on pragmatic grounds, and on their high correlations with other types of intelligence test measures as well as with overall IQ scores. The humour items have been selected on intuitive grounds and graded on the basis of complexity and difficulty in the resolution of the incongruity. Recently, an increasing number of investigators have begun to focus on the structural characteristics of incongruity in humour in order to provide an empirical base for a cognitive approach to humour. These investigators have no interest in refining the use of humorous stimuli in intelligence testing. However, it is readily apparent that the demonstration of an orderly developmental progression of the various forms of humorous stimuli closely associated with progressive stages of cognitive development will prove of great value in developmental assessment.

Investigators have applied Piaget's conceptualizations of the stages of cognitive development to the development of humour. Piaget (1950) has identified four stages of cognitive development: The first stage is the sensory-motor-from birth to two years of age. In this stage the infant moves from a primarily reflexive response in an undifferentiated way to his/her environment to 'a relatively coherent organization of sensory-motor actions *vis-à-vis* his immediate environment' (Flavell, 1963). The second stage Piaget identifies as pre-operational thought—from two to seven years—in which the child begins to deal with symbols and representational thought. The child's conceptual framework is made up of his/her own subjective perceptions and experiences, and his/her judgments are not reflective or logical. The third stage is that of concrete operations—from seven to twelve years—in which the child begins to use logic in his/her reasoning and s/he now has an orderly conceptual framework which s/he applies in a systematic fashion to the world around him/her. The fourth and final stage is that of formal operations—from twelve to fifteen years—in which the child is now able to conceptualize and to abstract relations.

What humour contributes to the psychological growth of the child is unknown and unexplored. A good 'sense of humour' is prized as one of the most desirable personality attributes, even in children. The comprehension of humour stimuli is useful as one cognitive ability in measuring intelligence. There is suggestive evidence that the ability to create humour is a talent like other creative processes (see Chapter 5). We also have considerable clinical evidence showing that responses to humour can serve as critical indices of psychopathology (Levine, 1978). For example, the inability to enjoy humour is an important sign of a depressive state. Pathological laughter has long been recognized by neurologists as pathognomic of brain damage. But we still know little about how essential the development of humour is, particularly as it is reflected in its emotional, expressive and motivational components, to the normal psychosocial growth of the child.

Having a good sense of humour is a valuable personal asset in interpersonal relations. It suggests that the person is able to relate to another in a positive playful way, expressing in laughter or smiling, the sharing of a pleasurable experience. Whether or not a good sense of humour can be developed through experience is a mystery. How children can be helped to develop or learn to use their sense of humour is not known. From clinical observations, early experiences of social deprivation and lack of opportunity for positive emotional expression (including laughter and smiling), result in psychopathology in later development (Provence and Ritvo, 1961; Putnam, Rank and Kaplan, 1951; Spitz and Wolf, 1946).

Further suggestive evidence of the importance for development to express emotions freely, especially playfulness, was found in the study by McClelland, Constantian, Regalado, and Slone (1978). They found that one of the two dimensions of major importance in children becoming socially and morally mature was the freedom of emotional expression and the lack of strictness with which parents controlled their children's behaviour. 'A child was less apt to become socially and morally mature when his parents tolerated no noise, mess, or rough-housing in the home, when they reacted unkindly to the child's aggressiveness toward them, sex play or expressions of dependency needs. In other words, when parents were concerned with using their power to maintain an adult centered home, the child was not likely to become a mature adult' (McClelland *et al.*, 1978, p. 52).

These conclusions were based on the findings obtained by McClelland *et al.* from interviews and psychological tests given to individuals, thirty-one years of age, whose mothers had been interviewed about child-rearing practices twenty-five years before. McClelland's other general finding was that what these individuals did and thought and how they behaved as adults was not determined by specific techniques of child-rearing in their first five years. It was the emotional climate of the home that was critical.

The clinical literature contains many descriptive references to the humour behaviour of children of different ages which could be useful in developmental assessment. However, most of these descriptions, which are sometimes verbatim, are incidental to the purposes of the clinical case studies, and therefore provide little in the way of diagnostic evaluation. Nevertheless, one can often make clinical inferences from these reports about a child's emotional problems, anxieties, interests, and cognitive abilities. These inferences are based upon the kinds and specific themes of the humour the child laughs at or expresses. Most of these clinical case studies are to be found in the psychoanalytic literature and are therefore presented in that context. The absence of any attempts to systematize these observations prevents them from being used generally in developmental assessments. Examples of these descriptions will be presented in the section on the use of humour in psychotherapy.

The psychoanalytic viewpoint about humour is that its pleasure is partly derived from already-mastered anxiety. As Kris (1940) put it, 'What was feared yesterday and mastered is laughed at today' (p. 213). Thus, the child enjoys humour about actions and functions only after s/he has mastered them. Kris further stated, 'A feeling of anxiety over one's own powers of mastery or more accurately, the memory of an averted superfluous anxiety seems to accompany the comic' (p. 209). As an adaptive process, humour provides the child with an opportunity to re-experience the gratifications of motoric, linguistic, cognitive, and interpersonal mastery at his/her age-appropriate level of development. The child learns that humour is a source of pleasure at each stage of development by momentarily re-experiencing the mastery of functions and activities of earlier stages. For example, it is when children are just beginning to master language that their joking involves playing with words. Piaget (1951) commented that the first experience of cognitive success by the infant was expressed by a smile.

Probably the most extensive observational study of children's humour was done by Wolfenstein (1954) who observed and interviewed children between six and twelve years of age to find out the kinds of jokes they liked to tell. She hypothesized that a basic motive of a child's joking is a wish to transform a painful experience into a pleasurable one. Using a psychoanalytic framework, she connected what children at different ages required for satisfactory joking with the kinds of problems and interests appropriate for their age. At the age of four, children find the shifting of names from boy to girl a good joke which she traced to the fact that three-year-olds often called a boy a girl and a girl a boy. A good naughty joke for a child of four or five is to tease another child with 'you're a doody' or 'you make pee pee on the floor'. She found a sharp change in the style of joking from five to six in which there is less improvization and more use of ready-made jokes. She related this shift to the onset of latency requiring more inhibition and hiding. Children become more preoccupied with intellectual abilities and their jokes involve issues of smartness and dumbness. Moron jokes and riddles become favourite modes of joking. She observed that there is an increasing indirectness of expression in children's jokes as they go through various stages of mental, moral, and emotional development.

Wolfenstein (1954) has described in some detail what she considers to be the developmental phases of joking and the use of the joke facade. According to her, the child must find ways to gratify his/her impulses while disclaiming responsibility for them. S/he does this by an increasing indirectness of expression. S/he will attribute the performance of naughty deeds to other children rather than to him/herself and ultimately to an entirely fictitious character. Frequently, even authority figures are made responsible for the deeds. As an illustration, she describes a sequence of dirty jokes of children aged between four and eleven to demonstrate the increasing complexity of the joke façade. She uses excretory activities as the theme since this is what children are largely preoccupied with in their dirty jokes. 'For a four-year-old, it is a good dirty joke to shout at someone: "Hello, Doody!" or with slightly more subtle mockery: "Hello, Mr. Doody!".'. That the child finds this funny shows that he already has some misgiving about saying it. But in moments of weakened inhibition or strengthened impulse, which easily occur in his unstable inner economy, he can enjoy such a breakthrough of the forbidden without requiring any elaborate façade. However, there is already some indirectness in this seemingly blunt attack. Instead of putting his excreta on the victim, the child has substituted a verbal expression. He has embarked on the first stage of the development which will eventuate in the more complicated froms of wit' (p. 21). Thus, up to four years of age, it is the actual act which is a joke.

It is clear from naturalistic observations that children learn to laugh and joke about all areas of functioning over which they have just achieved mastery. These include body functions, language and verbal fluency, motor skills and, finally, interpersonal interactions. Children's jokes about excreta, plays on words, riddles, puns, clowning and pratfalls, all reflect these steps in development.

Adolescents between twelve and eighteen years of age are perhaps the most interesting group of children to study from the point of view of humour behaviour. They are in the process of reaching the full flowering of their cognitive abilities and they are more socialized. They have learned to appreciate and use the diverse forms of humour in social situations. Their maturing sexuality, independence, and conflicts with parental authority, and developing ego identity with its problems all find overt expression. Humour is one of the few socially acceptable outlets for their aggressive and sexual feelings as well as for their continuing need to free themselves from the constraints of reality and maturity. Their humour behaviour therefore becomes a rich source of data about the individual adolescent's ability to cope with all his conflicting needs and feelings.

It is unfortunate that few clinical or observational studies have been published about the humour behaviour of adolescents, particularly since it could prove useful in illuminating their developmental problems. One study by Ransohoff (1975) illustrates the potential usefulness to developmental assessment of the careful observation of the spontaneous joking, laughter, and giggling of adolescents. She studied two small groups of adolescent girls between twelve and fourteen years of age who met once a week over a seven-month period. The purpose of these meetings was simply to talk about matters of the girls' common interest, with Ransohoff serving as an observer. In general, the humour erupted spontaneously, accompanied by much laughter and giggling, and resonated with current developmental issues. The most prominent of these issues were bodily changes such as beginning of menarche and enlarging breasts, early relationships with boys, disguised masturbatory wishes, and ambivalent feelings toward mothers. She found that these girls' sexual preoccupation was striking, finding expression in curiosity about adult sex, boys getting 'fresh', pregnancy, and body display—like having big breasts. There was a burgeoning of sexual curiosity at about twelve which was expressed by favourite jokes dealing with peeking at adults and making fun of them. A number of jokes failed to evoke laughter, but did evoke anxiety which was handled through motoric discharge (gestures) as by caricaturing the way a man handles his genitals. With these indirect references, the girls did lots of giggling with mounting excitement and anxiety. Their talk and fantasy about sexual behaviour was expressed as a dangerous attack, or through magical word avoidances (e.g. 'his you know what', 'his thing').

The peer group giggling was infectious and served as reassurance when topics that were anxiety-arousing came up. Issues that were too remote from their current development and which aroused much anxiety dealt with adult bodies and male penetration. Most laughter came out as expressions of pride in developing female sexuality.

An interesting psychodiagnostic tool sometimes used by clinicians is to ask a child his/her favourite joke (Wolfenstein, 1954; Yorukoglu, 1977; Zwerling, 1955). It is based upon the assumption that a person's favourite joke is related to a central probelm or emotional conflict, which can then be used diagnostically or in therapy. The limited usefulness of this technique arises from the fact that many children either do not have a favourite joke or report the first one that comes to mind. The validity of this technique is therefore open to question and probably can be used only as supportive of more reliable clinical evidence.

Investigators have explored other facets of children's personality in relation to their humour behaviour. McGhee has been particularly interested in such characteristics as sex-role identification and moral development (McGhee, 1974a; McGhee and Grodzitsky, 1973). In one study, his findings supported clinical observations that in pre-school children 'higher levels of sex-role mastery play an important role in determining appreciation of humor based on sex inappropriate behavior' (McGhee and Grodzitsky, 1973, p. 192). In another series of studies, McGhee applied Piaget's formulations of levels of moral development to children's appreciation of humorous stories: the children were from grades two, four, and eight. He found that children at the earlier levels of moral development (heteronomous) found funniest those stories having highly damaging outcomes. In contrast, children with higher levels of moral development (autonomous) enjoyed the more damaging stories only when the damage was unintentional. He concluded that 'while increased naughtiness or moral unacceptability of an outcome or event adds to its funniness for heteronomous children, it detracts from humor appreciation in adults and morally more mature autonomous children'. These findings are consistent with psychodynamic views of the increase in inter-nationalization of moral values and socialization with ego development. McGhee (1974b) also investigated the development of children's ability to create the joking relationship. He found that children progressing from grades one, two, four, and eight increased their ability to create joking answers to riddles based on word play and absurdity.

PSYCHOTHERAPY

Probably the most valuable clinical use of humour in working with children is in the conduct of psychotherapy. The major obstacle to doing therapy with children, particularly young children, is getting their co-operation. The difficulties of establishing a therapeutic relationship with children are numerous and often insurmountable. The child sees no need for such a communicative relationship since s/he has no reason to trust the adult therapist and has no real understanding of the purposes of therapy or of any therapeutic benefits. The therapist is therefore hard pressed to overcome the reluctance of the disturbed child to talk to him/her and may even have difficulty getting the child to agree to making the visit. The child has usually had to submit to parental pressure to agree to the visit.

Because of this resistance by the child, the therapist has to use whatever tools s/he can in order to establish a therapeutic relationship. Unquestionably the most valuable tool that therapists have developed in their work with children is *play*, and this is now the universal medium of therapeutic communication. In the context of play in therapy, the child reveals his/her problems, anxieties, and conflicts. The child is helped within the context of creative play to communicate these fears and conflicts and work them through. As Ekstein (1966) put it, paraphrasing Freud's referral to dreams, 'the royal road to the unconscious of the child patient is his play, [which is] his best means of the communication of the unconscious conflict' (p. 169).

No one questions the clinical usefulness of play in child therapy despite the fact that play and being playful are primarily identified as distractive to serious work; and, if it is anything, psychotherapy is serious work. But some therapists will take strong exception to using humour in any therapeutic relationship, adult or child (cf. Kubie, 1971). Kubie has presented at least sixteen cogent reasons for eschewing humour in psychotherapy because of its destructive potential. From this viewpoint one must be especially concerned about any techniques that might be destructive in working with children because of their vulnerability. But it is partly as a consequence of their vulnerability to adult actions that the interventions of humour in therapy may be particularly helpful to the therapeutic process.

Just like play, humour is not necessarily an extraneous or distracting intervention in psychotherapy with children. Since humour is a form of play and has many of the salient characteristics of play, it is helpful to consider the use of play as well as humour in child therapy. With regard to the definitions of play and humour, what St. Augustine said in his *Confessions* about time is appropriate to play and humour: he stated that he knew what time was only as long as nobody asked him. We know that play is the primary activity of childhood and is essential to normal development. Children who cannot play or whose play is developmentally arrested have been found to be emotionally and intellecutally handicapped. We may well find that children who have difficulty in enjoying humour may also be impaired in their development (cf. Levine, 1972).

We know that in adults the inability to laugh and enjoy joking is ordinarily pathognomonic of emotional difficulties, sometimes of a serious nature. In any case, it is because children have such an enormous need to play, and in their play express their pleasure by laughter and humorousness that they will relate readily to others, even strangers, who will play with them.

The value of play in child therapy is clinically well-established because it is the best means of establishing and continuing a communicative relationship. To begin with, in most instances, children see no need for therapy. Their difficulties at home or school are viewed by them as arising out of circumstances external to themselves. For them, it is a question of blame or being treated unfairly. His/her misbehaviour, interpersonal or learning difficulties, are the consequences of others' actions. Thus for the child, therapy is not an activity s/he feels, s/he wants or needs, particularly since s/he has no real understanding of its benefits.

Other difficulties in the way of conducting child therapy are also readily apparent. Children who are troubled are unwilling to share their troubles with adults, especially strangers to whom they are brought by their parents to 'treat them'. From a psychoanalytic viewpoint, the child ordinarily has no need to establish a transference relationship with the therapist since s/he already has his/her parents immediately available to interact with. The establishment of a transference neurosis becomes a difficult, even unlikely, event. Above all, it is not within the capacity of the usual troubled child to discuss his/her difficulties or feelings directly or to be reflective in conversational terms about his/her problems. It is for these and probably many other reasons that child therapy must be carried out in an atmosphere of friendliness, playfulness, and good humour. As Weeks and Machs put it (1978) 'Unlike adults who use conversation, younger children may communicate their emotional conflicts and feelings only indirectly through play' (p. 505).

Both play and humour are activities whose primary purpose intrinsically is to obtain pleasure, whatever other purposes may be involved. To obtain the pleasure in these activities they must be carried out by a detachment from reality. In the context of playfulness and being 'in humour' all things are accepted as possible, even the impossible. As in play, in humour a psychological condition or state is thus created in which the real world is ignored. The creation of a therapy situation in which play and humour are media of communication offers both therapist and child a communicative intimacy in which they share a common freedom from the constraints of a painful reality. Winnicott (1971) in describing his play technique of *Squiggle* in child therapy noted the sense of humour displayed by a child, and characterized it in this manner, 'This sense of humor is evidence of a freedom, the opposite of a rigidity of the defenses that characterizes willingness. A sense of humor is the ally of the therapist, who gets from it a feeling of confidence and a sense of having elbow-room for maneuvering. It is evidence of the child's creative imagination and of happiness' (p. 32). It is this ability to assume a humour attitude as it is identified by Freud that represents a shift in state of mind from one of conflict and anxiety to a sense of mastery and compensatory wish fulfillment.

What Freud (1960) calls the humour attitude is essentially the same as Bateson's (1952) psychological frame although Bateson is more concerned with the cognitive paradoxical aspects than with the psychodynamic as was Freud. For Freud, the humour attitude is essentially a psychological shift from reality to the world of the imagination where anything goes. This shift in world view is not altogether voluntary as are most normal playful retreats into the world of imagination. One cannot voluntarily assume a humorous attitude and joyfully laugh at situations as though they are funny if they are not experienced as humorous. As Freud (1960) and Kris (1952) recognized, humour cannot overcome strong emotional states like depression, rage, and terror. To be able to be in a humorous frame of mind one must feel master of the situation and not overcome with fear. It is in this sense that Freud and others considered humour to be liberating.

Bateson (1952) considered humour and play from a cognitive-perceptual viewpoint in which a psychological frame is established which is comparable to an Epiminedes paradox. These paradoxes, formally analysed by Bertrand

Russell, arise when a message about the message is contained in the message. Thus, 'The man who says "I am lying", is also implicitly saying, "The statement which I now make is untrue". Those two statements, the message and the message about the message criss-cross each other to complete an oscillating system of notions, if he is lying, then he is telling the truth; but if he is telling the truth, then he is not lying; and so on' (p. 163). Thus, according to Bateson 'this is play' or 'this is humor' conveys the messages or signals in play or humour which are in a certain sense untrue or non-existent. It is a message which contains a negative statement which itself contains an implicit negative meta-statement. It is extraordinary that such paradoxes have required the genius of a Russell, to be properly understood and analysed, but as Bateson has pointed out, young mammals in their play intuitively grasp the message 'This is play'. For Bateson, these paradoxes are also the prototypic paradigm of humour.

Interestingly, Bateson saw psychotherapy as a similar communicative use of these paradoxes which characterize play and humour. He considers the 'fantastic exchanges that go on within it (Therapy) as paradoxical' (p. 165) and the setting of the therapy as having a regular relationship with reality. 'The therapy situation is a place where the freedom to admit paradox has been cultivated as a technique but on the whole this flexibility exists between two people whenever, God willing, they succeed in giving each other a freedom of discussion. That freedom to entertain illogical alternatives, the freedom to ignore the theory of types, is probably essential to comfortable human relations' (p. 165).

It is important to note that for Bateson the implicit content of message constitutes the content of the unconscious in the psychoanalytic sense. But this premise is based on his view of the so-called Schadenfreude theories of humour—the pleasure which we feel in somebody else's pain. That is, for Bateson, the repression and release of repression which characterizes Schadenfreude is due to the fact that we do not want to acknowledge our implicit enjoyment of another's pain.

The implications of these views of humour for the use of humour in therapy with children are clear. They also suggest that the abuse of humour in therapy may originate from the pleasure obtained from the enjoyment of the child's pain. Making fun of the child and his or her childish acting-out is a mild form of this Schadenfreude in which a therapist may be indulging himself without being aware of it. A good example of the anti-therapeutic effects of humour is the misuse of banter in which, in the guise of affectionate teasing by gross exaggeration, the therapist fails to realize that the patient is in no state of mind to appreciate any teasing as humorous.

It is helpful to consider the use of humour in child therapy from the viewpoint of the meta-conversation, 'I am joking'. This message about the message is an invitation to the child also to join the therapist in assuming the humour attitude or frame of mind. The message then, if it is understood, is not as a true message but as an untrue one requiring a shift in state of mind, a humour illusion. The cues for the meta-message are implicit or the meta-message may require an explicit statement, 'I am telling you a joke'. The troubled child or depressed adult in therapy may not be able or willing to shift to a humour frame of mind and therefore not be able to appreciate the joke. The message is then for the child a true statement and is taken seriously. The willingness of the child to join the therapist in the humour frame of mind depends upon his or her feelings about the therapist and the child's notion about the therapist's intent.

Humour and laughter may erupt spontaneously and naturally in the course of play therapy. When it happens, the sharing of a joke accompanied by laughter ordinarily reflects a climate of friendliness and perhaps of growing intimacy, even if it occurs in the context of a competitive game. Such spontaneous humour events tend to reduce barriers to communication by promoting mutuality and even intimacy. Humour in psychotherapy, whether it is spontaneous or intentional, reduces the psychic distance between patient and therapist thereby affecting the professional relationship.

It is a fact that as a professional relationship psychotherapy places many constraints upon both patient and therapist, but much more upon the latter. Unlike social or friendship relationships, the primary task for the therapist is to help the patient without any *quid pro quo*. For some therapists the proper standard of conduct in maintaining a constructive working relationship is to be reserved and objective, without being unfriendly. Even in play therapy with children such therapists may remain businesslike and firmly professional. For them, humour is rightly inappropriate, since it violates their view of the proper standard of conduct which the therapist must maintain. It may be that few child therapists take such an extreme stance with respect to humour, particularly intentional humour, but it does highlight the issues in considering the clinical use of humour in child therapy.

One must acknowledge that not every therapist is comfortable with the use of humour in therapy as a tool to relieve the stress of the situation. It is also true that not everyone is capable of using humour as a tool to obtain constructive intimacy so that it cannot be a universal technique. Not everyone has the gift of being humorous. But most clinicians consider that the obstacles to the establishment of a therapeutic alliance can best be overcome in a climate of playfulness and humour. It is not so much the pleasure in the levity of humour that fosters this alliance as it is in the sharing of a state of mind affectively communicated. This shared state of mind shifts the emphasis from a painful reality to the liberating state of the imagination. It is the essence of the artistic or aesthetic illusion.

THE CHILD'S USE OF HUMOUR IN THERAPY

The intentions of the child in using humour in therapy are different from those of the therapist. The child says something funny either as a defence or as a disguised expression of hostility. The therapist tells a joke and makes a witty remark when he thinks it will promote the therapeutic process. The child, unlike the therapist, is unaware of and unconcerned about the purposes of humour when it occurs. It is a moment of playful amusement. Ordinarily, neither adult nor child is interested in analysing or reflecting on the motives for telling a joke. Freud (1960) recognized that a person does not necessarily have to know the precise intention of a joke in order to enjoy it. We know that analysing a joke kills the humour and we therefore avoid it. For the child then, joking in therapy is simply to be playful, whatever his/her covert intention may be. For the therapist, the pleasure is secondary. S/he is concerned primarily with using humour to promote the therapeutic process. Even if it is the child who introduces humour in the therapy, the therapist may laugh, but his/her interest is in understanding the covert motive of the humour. It is the disregard of this consideration by the therapist that may result in the humour being destructive or at least distractive to the therapy.

The clinical literature contains a number of examples which can illustrate these points. The cases selected show how normal as well as troubled children use humour for defensive or aggressive purposes. But it is obvious that not all children have that talent or ability. Perhaps the most informative examples are given by those children who show real talent as comedians or as caricaturists and their humour in therapy is a symptom of their psychopathology. The covert motives of their clowning and humorous imitations are understood as resistances and are dealt with as issues in therapy.

Given the artificiability and constraints of the therapeutic situation humour cannot have the range of purposes found in everyday life. Nevertheless, both child and therapist are generally able to use humour for many purposes, subject always to their ability to create or to remember a joke or a funny remark in the context of the situation.

A partial list of some of these purposes for which children have used humour may be helpful in demonstrating range and depth. Thus the child may express through humour: (i) a desire to create a friendly relationship with the therapist; (ii) a need to disarm the therapist whom s/he fears by making an amusing self-disparaging remark or telling a joke on him/herself; (iii) a wish to make the therapist laugh as signifying approval and even affection; (iv) indirect hostility towards the therapist; (v) a defence against anxiety; (vi) an attempt to transform fear into pleasure; (vii) an attempt to provoke the therapist by teasing; (viii) an attempt to provoke the therapist by assuming the role of teasee, that is, to make the therapist tease him/her; (ix) a relief of the tension arising from the session; (x) self-disparagement and/or self-contempt, symptomatic of depression; (xi) mastery of anxiety or ability to take distance from personal concerns or disturbing feelings; (xii) establishment of communicative intimacy with the therapist by sharing a joke; and (xiii) an avoidance of painful or anxiety-laden discourse.

This list of purposes is clearly only representative of the many others one could conjure up. In the absence of any systematic study designed to classify and establish frequencies of the potentially large number of motives for using humour by children in therapy, this sample illustrates the complexity of the problem of trying to discuss how humour is used in therapy.

Orfandis (1972) reported a study of children's use of humour in psychotherapy. Taped interviews of children aged between seven and ten who were seen in a child guidance clinic were analysed in regard to target, form, function, and relationship to the child's personality and development. Based upon these analyses but without statistical treatment because of the small sample, Orfandis concluded that the results indicated that for the children, humour was used as a way of sharing feelings of fear and aggression, of breaking down social barriers, and mastering one's anxieties. She also found that the children who had a serious developmental impairment showed a greatly reduced ability to enjoy and use humour creatively. These results supported the findings of others that certain cognitive and psychosocial levels of development are required for a child to be able to use humour actively and creatively.

Domash (1975) described the therapy of a borderline psychotic boy of nine who was encouraged to use humour in his treatment. The therapist felt that this boy's use of wit and the comic had ego-strengthening effects by permitting him both to express his hostile feelings and to defend himself against the accompanying anxieties. She responded to the boy's witty remarks not by analysing them, but by letting him know that she genuinely enjoyed them. As an encouraging audience, she reinforced his ability to delight and entertain a significant adult. He thereby became aware of his ability to establish a positive intimate contact with another person. He was therefore able to develop his sense of humour. The therapist felt that the boy, Danny, was able to master adaptively the eruption of primitive impulses and feelings. As he was able to transform these impulses into witty remarks he improved considerably.

Danny was nine-and-a-half years of age when he was referred to the outpatient pediatric clinic by his school because he did little academic work, withdrew into his own fantasy world, became easily panicked and got into fights. At first testing he functioned at a borderline level and showed serious thought disorder. He appeared confused, anxious and seemed to have little control of his thoughts and impulses. He was seen weekly for one year and then twice a week for one-and-a-half years.

From the beginning, the patient's communications were characterized by wit and often psychotic condensations. As the relationship developed, the therapist become more of a 'straight man' for the boy's jokes and comic play which were frequently hostile. His humour became less obscure and the hostility more clear. Domash considered that Danny's ability to use humour was not only an important factor in his therapeutic progress, but it was also an index of that progress.

Just as the types and themes of humour vary as the child grows, the techniques and devices of joking change. Since one of the functions of these joke techniques is to mask or distort the true intent or the butt of the joke, the amount of the disguise required for an acceptable joke increases with the development of cognitive abilities. For example, the aggressive or the sexual content of jokes become more indirect and allusive. The incongruities are more subtle and less easily resolved. With maturation comes the progressive internalization of moral and social restraints, and the child becomes more inhibited in his or her actions and speech. Furthermore, the humorous puzzle qualities of the incongruities of jokes require more of a cognitive challenge to be enjoyed as the child develops. In short, joking and humour become more complicated as the child grows up. Wolfenstein's major assumption in her extensive clinical study of ninety middle-class children was that a basic motive for joking by children is the wish to transform a painful experience into a pleasurable one. This assumption is shared by many psychoanalytic writers (e.g. Brenman, 1952; Dooley, 1941; Grotjahn, 1969; Jacobson, 1946; Kris, 1952; Reich, 1949; Sperling, 1953), and was originally formulated by Freud. It is the primary thesis of these psychoanalytic theorists that humour is a defensive, but adaptive pleasure. According to this formulation, humour is a mode of coping with suffering which, unlike other defences, does not deny the awareness of the pain and the suffering but rather minimizes it. The humour attitude views the threat and the anxiety as inconsequential, even absurd, thereby permitting us to 'laugh it off'. The momentary pleasure obtained by this laughter is reassurance that we have mastered the fears. Humour is then a fantasy defence which, unlike other psychological defences attempting to cope with anxiety, is not an expression of ego weakness, but on the contrary is a reflection of ego strength. It is on this basis that Freud regarded humour as liberating and an expression of the invulnerability of the ego, as exemplified by gallows humour. As such, the ability to use humour is a narcissistic triumph. Clinical examples taken from therapeutic situations can readily be found in the psychoanalytic literature which illustrate these for-mulations. In most of these case reports the child used humour to defend himself or herself against the anxiety associated with forbidden impulses or feelings. In some instances the humour took the form of clowning and making self-disparaging jokes as ways of provoking approval and sympathy. In other cases, the joking and laughter of the child, often severely troubled or psychotic, served multiple functions as defences and as controlled releases of overwhelming negative affect transformed into positive feelings.

In a clinical case report, Wolfenstein (1955) described the explosive laughter of a psychotic six-year-old boy whom she treated in psychotherapy. His incessant laughter, which he could produce at will, was not only an attempt to deny and ward off unbearable anxiety but also served as a 'means of attack, a provocation, and an expression of impulses which could not find other outlets. It was associated with a reduction of verbal articulateness, with the shouting of isolated incomprehensible words and phrases, and also with incoordinated motor activity as he threw himself on the floor and rolled about' (p. 381). The substitution of laughing for crying is a universal phenomenon, often occurring in adults as well as children. Though the affects are reversed, the proximity of laughing and crying has frequently been noted. Intense laughter often develops into crying.

The use of humour by children as a defence against anxiety is not pathognomonic of psychosis or of severe emotional disturbance. It is observable in normal children faced with momentary anxiety. In her book on children's humour, Wolfenstein (1954) provided many examples of the joking of normal children defending themselves against situational anxiety. In these instances, the joking was seen by Wolfenstein as reflecting age-appropriate anxieties and joking themes. One example (p. 23) was that of a five-year-old boy left in the kindergarten sitting anxiously waiting for his mother. All the other children had left with their mothers or siblings. The teacher asked the boy, 'Who is calling for you today, Eugene? Your mother or Betty?'. The boy smiled and replied, 'My mother is coming, and Betty is coming, and Kay is coming, the whole family is coming, except me, because I'm here already'. He laughed at his joke. The boy thus transformed feeling of anxiety about being abandoned into a joke, which seemed to reassure him and reduce his anxiety. At this time the little boy was particularly vulnerable because his father had died in the past year.

A six-year-old boy, bright and intellectually ambitious, as a response to the strong stimulation of his parents, saw them carrying his baby sister (Wolfenstein, 1954, p. 31). He became very jealous and asked to be carried too. He was told he was too big. He then made up a riddle, 'Why did the moron write on a piece of paper?' 'Because he could't walk yet'. He laughed at his joke as a paradox. 'What an absurd idea to be able to write and not be able to walk yet.' The riddle seems to represent the little boy's dilemma—his intellectual developments rob him of the opportunity to be treated like the baby. The riddle represents the fulfillment of both wishes.

A ten-year-old boy who was afraid about his father dying (Wolfenstein, 1954, p. 26) read stories with tragic endings and thought they were all funny. When asked *why*, he replied 'because he died'. He then proceeded to write a story in which two crooks robbed a candy store and shot the proprietor whose body was laid in a bier. The boy then made up a funny remark, 'a bier marked Rheingold'. This play on words changed his anxiety into humour. In another case, a twelve-year-old drew a picture of a man with a fruit stand. He gave the picture the title, 'Custer's last stand'. He transformed a picture of piles of corpses into an appetizing heap of fruit.

Brenman (1952) reported the case of a fifteen-year-old depressed girl whom she treated and whom she characterized as a 'comic teasee'. In her constant clowning and need to make others laugh by provoking them to tease her, she was able to satisfy her hostile and masochistic needs as well as her simultaneous need to win approval.

The urge to make others laugh sometimes reaches the proportions of an irresistible need. Professional comedians, like Bert Lahr, have been known to be constantly under pressure to make an audience laugh. As Zolotov (1952), Lahr's biographer, described him 'it is this unsatisfied yearning for love in the form of an audience approval, that drives Lahr to work so hard for a big laugh'. For many of these comedians audience applause and laughter is their all-consuming drive, often equated with love. In the absence of this applause they become deeply depressed. The clinical literature contains a number of case reports of adults and children who have had similar needs to make others laugh. In the case of children, clowning and joking have also served to provoke laughter in others primarily as a means of coping with their anxieties and interpersonal problems.

The clinical cases discussed below were published as instances in which a troubled child, often psychotic, behaved humorously in order to make the therapist laugh. The compulsive nature of this intent to make others laugh characterized the child's behaviour generally and reflected the multiple purposes of his humour as ways of coping with his problems. The therapist, in recognizing the symptomatic use of humour and its potential to subvert the therapy, dealt with it as a resistance and effectively helped the patient to give up these uses of humour in therapy. The therapy became the theatre for the children's comic acts and the therapist was put in the role of appreciative audience or as the object of the humour. If the therapist accepted either role passively without comment, the child's humour behaviour usually subverted the therapy, since the child was repeating his symptomatic acting-out of his problems in the therapy without resolution or learning. However, the therapist could, and in most cases did, properly intervene, not necessarily by helping him or her to recognize the underlying intent. The child became aware that his/her use of humour may not have been the most adaptive way of coping with his/her problems. The humour served to mask or distort the underlying feelings or the motives. In most instances, the child was unaware of the problems s/he was trying to resolve by the use of humour but only felt the urge to make others laugh. From such cases it is evident that not all humour behaviour in therapy that is initiated by the patient, or by the therapist, is constructive.

Brenman (1952) reported in detail the treatment of the fifteen-year-old severely disturbed girl whom she characterized as a 'comic teasee'. She continually provoked others to tease her and to laugh at her clowning witty acts. Sometimes her clowning appeared as simple clumsiness. She provoked others to tease her by her caricature of extreme deference to them, with please-don't-hit-me expressions in her behaviour. Her previous therapist and other staff members responded to this feigned terror by teasing her. 'On one occasion this first therapist was sufficiently provoked by this manner to say, "Did you notice all the heads stuck on spikes as you came up the stairs? Those are my previous victims" ' (p. 267). While this was all in 'good fun' and appreciated as such by the patient, the translation of this just seemed to be: 'You behave as if I am such a bloodthirsty monster by your caricature of terror that I might be expected to have decapitated my previous patients. If you make so hostile an accusation, I will punish you by replying: "Yes, I am just such a monster and your head will be next" ' (p. 267). The therapist actually found her to be a 'lovable youngster' and met her exaggerated cowering with active reassurances but he became aware of her overwhelming demands. He at first tried to meet these demands but they were never fully satisfied. Her caricature of terror provoked him to make teasing jokes such as that describing his previous 'victims'.

She did her charming witty acts to please her mother, who disliked and rejected her. Thus her actions though funny often served to distress her parents. For example, since her family was very proper upper-class, they took great pains to teach her proper 'lady-like' behaviour. She was carefully taught to curtsey, but at her debut she bowed so low she fell flat on her face, distressing her parents but evoking great laughter among the guests. This type of incident characterized her repeated clowning which seemed to be unintentional since she appeared to try hard to do the job correctly. In her therapy, she was helped to become aware that though she had intended to perform a perfect curtsey she had actually made a mockery of it—by producing a 'live caricature of the behaviour they were demanding and directing attention to herself as an awkward but lovable buffoon'. She thereby exposed her parents as shallow and pretentious. 'She became an object of ridicule by her mother who would taunt her as ugly, fat and awkward'. According to Brenman, she made herself into a comic figure which permitted her to mock her parents by caricaturing them, but it was disguised as humour. The hostile aggression she felt towards her parents could be denied and projected on to them—they were the ones who were hostile to her. The teasing she provoked in others, including her therapists, served a similar purpose, to prove that her therapist also hated and rejected her.

Her early talents as a comic figure were used by her to obtain applause and laughter from people which she equated with affection, but at the same time expressing in her humour her rage at her parents by caricaturing them. Her need to give extravagantly of herself only to provoke rejection repeatedly confirmed her characteristic projection of her needy hostile impulses. Her extreme servile manner was itself a caricature and a reaction formation of her great hostility. Brenman reported that in her therapy Alison became less of a teasee, though she continued to be humorous. She demanded less of others and became more mature in her interpersonal relations.

From these detailed examples, the uses of humour by a child in the therapeutic situation may present the therapist with a problem of resistance, which must be worked through if the therapy is to progress. Those instances are unquestionably rare in which the child displays special comic talents which permit him/her to use humour to express salient aspects of his/her psychopathology. But always in the masked form of humour Alison felt she had the licence to be outrageous in her hostility, which ostensibly she was performing to entertain and evoke laughter.

In his play therapy with troubled children, Winnicott (1971) considered the expression of a sense of humour by the child as a very positive sign and an ally of the therapist. He described one such instance of a five-year-old boy who completed the therapist's squiggle by drawing a funny pig. Winnicott stated, 'this sense of humour is evidence of a freedom, the opposite of a rigidity of the defenses that characterizes illness. A sense of humour is the ally of the therapist, who gets from it a feeling of confidence and a sense of having elbow-room for maneuvering. It is evidence of the child's creative imagination and of happiness'. It is not possible to express more clearly and succinctly the value of humour in child therapy. In several other cases he discussed, Winnicott recognized the child's ability to display a sense of humour as indicative of health and freedom. In some cases where a sense of humour was lacking, Winnicott felt that he probably would not be able to play with the child since s/he lacked the necessary flexibility. In one case he reported, the lack of play and of sense of humour persisted despite continued efforts by Winnicott to engage the thirteen-year-old boy. He finally gave up. Winnicott noted that this boy did not play for pleasure.

THE THERAPIST'S USE OF HUMOUR IN THERAPY

On the assumption that the child therapist is intent upon using humour in therapy, the question arises as to the proper purposes and conditions. Not all possible ways of using humour are appropriate as Kubie (1971) has so effectively demonstrated. The only general rule of thumb is that the therapist will intentionally use humour when s/he considers that it will facilitate the therapeutic relationship and process.

The purposes of the child therapist are generally different from those of the child when s/he uses humour. Unlike the child, s/he must be aware of his/her intent. Overall, the therapist's primary purpose is in furthering the therapeutic process and in dealing with the child's resistances. Thus, s/he may joke or make a witty remark when s/he has the following purposes:

(i) to reduce the child's tension or anxiety; (ii) to create a more intimate communicative relationship; (iii) to dramatize a point that is too difficult to communicate directly; (iv) to create a less solemn, more playful climate; (v) to communicate his/her empathic understanding of the child's concerns; (vi) to deal with difficult or forbidden feelings or issues; (vii) to facilitate emotional expressiveness; and (viii) to present an insight to the child affectively.

The question of whether or not to use humour in child therapy is reminiscent of the remarks made by the character in Molière's play *Le Bourgeois Gentlehomme* who discovered with surprise that he had been speaking prose for over forty years without knowing it. If they thought about it, therapists would probably also discover that they have been using humour without being fully aware of it. Humour is expressed in so many forms and is so ephemeral that a mild jest or ironic remark is quickly passed over as inconsequential and forgotten. Yet its impact may be lasting.

In child therapy, playful teasing is a form of humour that is difficult to block, if it is ever desirable to do so. For the child a gentle teasing remark may be his/her way of expressing a growing sense of intimacy or trust. An appropriately timed teasing remark may be reassuring to an anxious child. An example may be found in a published clinical case report by Lopez (1974) of a therapeutic encounter with a blind boy of about five with limited intelligence. From the beginning he had passed air repeatedly during sessions without comment. In the course of the therapy, the boy, who was very anxious and easily frightened, showed signs of growing emotional attachment to the therapist. 'In one session he voluntarily passed a loud flatus. He then stopped short as if in anxious anticipation of my reaction. When I responded by jokingly saying, "Ronny made a . . . (imitation of flatus)", his face lit up in a broad smile. Then, also in a spirit of good humour, he repeated what I had said, at the same time jumping happily up and down.'

One of the few forms of humour which has been presented as an effective intervention in therapy is banter. Coleman (1962) has suggested the use of banter by insecure therapists in dealing with patients who tend to make them uneasy by their indirect or masochistic complaining, self-depreciation and implied questioning of the therapist's competence. The therapist is encouraged to exaggerate the self-belittling remarks of the patient to the point of sounding ridiculous. As Coleman (1962) put it, 'When a patient complains, in one way or another, about not being liked, or being ugly, the therapist may say, "Who can like you anyway?" Or, "Why did I have to get stuck with you?" Or, "You're the worst patient I ever had". This is said in a friendly tone and tends to agree with the patient's self-devaluative fears that he is unloved, and thus appears to be rejecting in its quality. It is obviously not felt as a rejection by the patient when he responds by laughing and becoming visibly more relaxed. Actually, the therapist is not addressing himself to the patient's feelings of worthlessness and unattractiveness but to his aggression. The patient says in effect, "You have to like me, or pretend to even if you think I'm unattractive, because it's your job and you have no choice". With his response, the therapist pricks the patient's pride of ugliness and unattractiveness and gives the patient the opportunity to relax the pressure of his angry demands' (pp. 3–4).

'Who can like you?' is a bantering comment. It carries implications of both good humour and ridicule. The therapist echoes the patient's complaint with amiable exaggeration. He plays the role of the patient's super ego with that touch of friendly chaffing which turns the crown of thorns into a corn of clowns.

These uses of banter have been particularly helpful to inexperienced therapists in mastering their anxieties in therapeutic situations, especially when they feel a patient's challenge of their competence. A bantering comment often makes the therapist feel that s/he is in command of the situation. This intervention by bantering also may help the therapist learn to be aware of his/her disturbed reactions to a patient's provocative behaviour and thereby not to react to the content of the patient's remarks. The transformation of the assault into a humorous interchange can be useful.

However, as with all intentional humour used by the therapist, banter can be destructive to the therapeutic process, especially if the therapist is not sensitive to the state of mind of the patient. For instance, if the patient is too depressed or anxious to be able to recognize the banter as humour, s/he may take the hyperbole seriously. The inability to adopt a humorous attitude results in increased distress. A few clinical examples taken from supervisory sessions with inexperienced therapists will illustrate these destructive effects.

A female patient was preoccupied for many therapeutic hours with innumerable physical complaints for which no organic basis could be found. She described in great detail her aches and pains which prevented her from functioning and for which she sought sympathy and help. She could not accept any psychological basis for her physical symptoms. In one particular hour she spent much of the time describing her headaches and chest pains, etc. At this point, her therapist suggested in a joking manner that perhaps a neighbour was angry with her and had fabricated a doll into which he was putting pins in various places in voodoo fashion. The patient took it seriously and remarked, 'Do you really think this is so?'. She became agitated and anxious, obviously unable to see any humour in the suggestion. The therapist had to explain that he was only joking and did not entertain such a notion as voodoo.

In another case, a female patient, depressed and beset by her feelings of inadequacy and of not being lovable, spent her therapy hours describing what a worthless person she was. She felt no one liked her. In one particular hour she suggested that no doubt the therapist also did not like her, was not really interested in her. She went on to suggest further that perhaps she ought to get another therapist, someone who might like her more. To this the inexperienced therapist replied in a bantering manner, 'who would be interested in treating you? We are stuck with one another, for no self-respecting therapist would want to treat you'. The intent of these bantering remarks was to demonstrate how unrealistic her attitude was. She took these remarks very seriously and became upset for she felt that what the therapist had said was true—nobody could be interested in her.

A patient spent many hours berating himself and describing himself as an idiot who could not do anything right. Finally, the therapist remarked that the patient's statements reminded him of the lawyer who in his final summation before the jury stated, 'My client talks like an idiot and acts like an idiot. Do not be deceived, gentlemen, he really is an idiot'. This supposed joke was understood by the patient to mean that the therapist thought little of him and considered him really stupid.

A female patient suffering from a prolonged depression with suicidal tendencies explained her tardiness to the therapy hour by jokingly describing to her therapist the difficulties she was having with her car. 'What a car! Everything is wrong with it. The brakes don't work; the starter is broken; the steering wheel is loose and the tires are worn.' She laughed as she elaborated on the terrible and dangerous state of her car. The therapist commented that she was probably hoping to have a bad accident so that she could blame him for it. The patient was startled by this remark and distressed that the therapist thought that she blamed him for her suicidal impulses.

OTHER CLINICAL USES OF HUMOUR

In the absence of any systematic studies of the many ways people use humour in everyday life for purposes other than playfulness, there is not much that can be said about the clinical uses of humour other than psychodiagnosis and psychotherapy. Based upon ordinary observation one can say that the myriad uses of humour in everyday human affairs can be and are also found in every clinical setting. Unlike the restraints imposed by the special purposes of the therapeutic relationship most other clinical situations permit staff and clients to employ humour in its many forms as a means of communication and influence. Generally, in clinical settings involving children the staff often use such forms of humour as teasing, banter, and 'kidding' to control acting out or to reduce group tension.

An example of such 'kidding' was discussed by Redl and Wineman (1952) in a book which addressed techniques for the treatment of aggressive children. In their account of working with delinquent and disturbed children at a residential centre, they described various methods of controlling pathological temper tantrums and reducing tension and found that humour was often very effective. They admit that they do not understand why the technique of 'humorous decontamination' works but speculate that it is the result of a combination of factors: (i) the adult's use of humour demonstrates his/her invulnerability and attitude of self-assurance in his/her ability to cope with the situation; (ii) the humour response reassures the child so that s/he is saved the guilt and fear by which s/he was about to be overcome in the attack and problem behaviour s/he was about to act out; (iii) the possibility of face-saving as when the child had to act tough and belligerent; and (iv) the humour diverts the child by the funniness of the moment from the strong emotions which threaten to overcome him/her. Redl and Wineman considered that the humorous reaction to problem behaviour, through its tension-decontamination effect, is often more efficient than any other technique.

Thus, clinicians use humour for a number of purposes other than for developmental assessment and in psychotherapy. In settings and institutions where the clinician is interested in influencing the child and their relationships, humour has proved to be helpful. The kinds and conditions of clinical situations in which humour may be helpful are basically no different from those we find in everyday life. Max Eastman, a well-known humorist, in a moment of seriousness postulated two basic laws which all comic experiences obey: (i) it is necessary to be or become playful in order to perceive anything whatever as funny; and (ii) in everything that we do perceive as funny, there is an element which, if we were serious and sufficiently sensitive and sufficiently concerned, would be unpleasant.

(Eastman, 1936). As one explores humour and thinks about it as a clinical tool, the conviction grows that humour is a vital component of living and of human affairs. Its powers as a liberating and constructive force are often acknowledged, but never fully exploited. It restores perspective on any human activity, institution or person whose image has become overblown or distorted. Strangely, though humour liberates us from the rational, it helps us to be more rational. It helps us to cope more effectively with life and its trials. As the patient who lacked a sense of humour declared in a consultation with a psychiatrist, 'Doctor, I have neither illusions nor delusions. My problem is that I exist day after day in a world of grim reality'.

REFERENCES

Bateson, G. (1952). The position of humor in human communication. In H. von Foerster (Ed.), *Cybernetics*. New York: Josiah Macy Jr. Foundation.

Behan, I., and Bevan, W. (1956). The perception of incongruity by young children. *Acta Psychologica*, **12**, 342–348.

Brackett, C. W. (1934). Laughter and crying in preschool children. *Child Development Monographs*, No. 14, 119–126.

Brenman, M. (1952). On teasing and being teased: and the problem of 'moral masochism'. *Psychoanalytic Study of the Child*, **7**, 262–285.

Brumbaugh, F. (1939). Stimuli which cause laughter in children. Unpublished Doctoral Dissertation, New York University (cited by Flugel, 1954).

Brumbaugh, F., and Wilson, F. T. (1949). Children's laughter. *Journal of Genetic Psychology*, **57**, 3–29.

Cattell, R. B., and Luborsky, L. B. (1947). Personality factors in response to humor. *Journal of Abnormal and Social Psychology*, **42**, 402–421.

Coleman, J. V. (1962). Banter as a psychotherapeutic intervention. *American Journal of Psychoanalysis*, **22**, 69–74.

Cunningham, A. (1962). Relation of sense of humor to intelligence. *Journal of Social Psychology*, **57**, 143–147.

Ding, G. F., and Jersild, A. T. (1932). A study of laughing and crying in preschool children. *Journal of Genetic Psychology*, **40**, 452–472.

Domash, L. (1975). The use of wit and the comic by a borderline psychotic child in psychotherapy. *American Journal of Psychotherapy*, **29**, 261–270.

Dooley, L. (1941). The relation of humor to masochism. *Psychoanalytic Review*, **28**, 37–47.

Eastman, M. (1936). *Enjoyment of Laughter*. New York: Simon and Schuster.

Ekstein, R. (1966). *Children of Time, of Space, of Action and Impulse*. New York: Appleton-Century-Crofts.

Flavell, J. H. (1963). *The Developmental Psychology of Jean Piaget*. Princeton, New Jersey: Van Nostrand.

Flugel, J. C. (1954). Humor and laughter. In G. Lindzey (Ed.), *Handbook of Social Psychology*. Vol. 2. Reading, Masschusetts: Addison-Wesley.

Freud, S. (1960). *Jokes and Their Relation to The Unconscious*. Complete Works (Standard Edition), Vol. 8. London: Hogarth.

Gregg, A. (1928). An observational study of humor in three-year-olds. Unpublished Masters Thesis, Columbia University (cited by Perl, 1933).

Grotjahn, M. (1969). Laughter in psychotherapy. *Voices*, **5**, 4–7.

Hester, M. (1924). Variations in the sense of humor according to age and mental condition. Unpublished Masters Thesis, Columbia University (cited by Perl, 1933).

Jacobson, E. (1946). The child's laughter: theoretical and clinical notes on the function of the comic. *Psychoanalytic Study of the Child*, **2**, 39–60.

Jones, J. M. (1970). Cognitive factors in the appreciation of humor: a theoretical and experimental analysis. Unpublished Doctoral Dissertation, Yale University.

Kambouropoulou, P. (1926). Individual differences in the sense of humor. *American Journal of Psychology*, **37**, 268–278.

Kant, I. (1790). *Critique of Judgment*. New York: Hafner.

Koestler, A. (1964). *The Act of Creation*. New York: Macmillan.

Kris, E. (1940). Laughter as an expressive process. *International Journal of Psychoanalysis*, **21**, 314–341.

Kris, E. (1952). *Psychoanalytic Explorations in Art*. New York: International Universties Press.

Kubie, L. (1971). The destructive potential of humor in psychotherapy. *American Journal of Psychiatry*, **127**, 861–866.

Landis, C., and Ross, J. (1933). Humor and its relation to other personality traits. *Journal of Social Psychology*, **4**, 158–175.

Levine, J. (1972). The role of humor in development. Paper presented at meeting of the American Psychological Association, Honolulu.

Levine, J. (1978). Humor and psychopathology. In C. E. Izard (Ed.), *Emotions, Conflict and Defense*. New York: Plenum.

Levine, J., and Redlich, F. C. (1960). Intellectual and emotional factors in the appreciation of humor. *Journal of General Psychology*, **62**, 25–35.

Lopez, T. (1974). Psychotherapeutic assistance to a blind boy with limited intelligence. *Psychoanalytic Study of the Child*, **29**, 277–300.

Maier, N. R. F. (1932). A Gestalt theory of humour. *British Journal of Psychology*, **23**, 69–74.

McClelland, D., Constantian, C. A., Regaldo, D., and Slone, C. (1978). Making it to maturity. *Psychology Today*, **12**, 42–53.

McGhee, P. E. (1972). On the cognitive origins of incongruity humor. In J. H. Goldstein and P. E. McGhee (Eds.), *The Psychology of Humor: Theoretical Perspectives and Empirical Issues*. New York: Academic Press.

McGhee, P. E. (1974a). Moral development and children's appreciation of humor. *Developmental Psychology*, **10**, 514–525.

McGhee, P. E. (1974b). Development of children's ability to create the joking relationship. *Child Development*, **45**, 552–556.

McGhee, P. E. (1979). *Humor: Its Origin and Development*. San Francisco: Freeman.

McGhee, P. E., and Grodzitsky, P. (1973). Sex-role identification and humor among preschool children. *Journal of Psychology*, **84**, 189–193.

McNemar, Q. (1942). *The Revision of the Stanford–Binet Scale*. Boston: Houghton-Mifflin.

Mones, L. (1939). Intelligence and a sense of humor. *Journal of Exceptional Child Psychology*, **5**, 150–153.

Omwake, L. (1939). Factors influencing the sense of humor. *Journal of Social Psychology*, **10**, 94–104.

Orfandis, M. M. (1972). Children's use of humor in psychotherapy. *Social Casework*, **53**, 147–155.

Perl, R. E. (1933). A review of experiments on humor. *Psychological Bulletin*, **30**, 752–763.

Piaget, J. (1951). *Play, Dreams and Imitation in Childhood*. New York: Norton.

Piaget, J. (1952). *The Origins of Intelligence in Children*. New York: International Universities Press.

Piret, A. (1940). Recherches genetiques sur le comique. *Acta Psychologica*, **2**, 103–142 (cited by Flugel, 1954).

Provence, S., and Ritvo, S. (1961). Effects of deprivation on institutionalized infants: disturbance of development of relationship to inanimate objects. *Psychoanalytic Study of the Child*, **16**, 189–205.

Putnam, M. C., Rank, B., Kaplan, S. (1951). Notes on John I: A case of primal depression in an infant. *Psychoanalytic Study of the Child*, **6**, 38–58.

Ransohoff, R. (1975). Some observations on humor and laughter in young adolescent girls. *Journal of Youth and Adolescence*, **4**, 155–170.

Redl, F., and Wineman, D. (1952). *Controls from Within: Techniques for Treatment of the Aggressive Child*. New York: Free Press.

Redlich, F. C., Levine, J., and Sohler, T. P. (1951). A mirth response test: preliminary report on a psychodiagnostic technique utilizing dynamics of humor. *American Journal of Orthopsychiatry*, **21**, 717–734.

Reich, A. (1949). The structure of the grotesque-comic sublimation. *Bulletin of the Menninger Clinic*, **13**, 160–171.

Rothbart, M. K. (1976). Incongruity, problem solving and laughter. In A. J. Chapman and H. C. Foot (Eds.), *Humour and Laughter: Theory, Research and Applications*. Chichester: Wiley.

Schopenhauer, A. (1905). *The World as Will and Idea*. London: Kegan, Paul, Trench, Trubnen and Company.

Shultz, T. R. (1976). A cognitive-developmental analysis of humour. In A. J. Chapman and H. C. Foot (Eds.), *Humour and Laughter: Theory, Research and Applications*. Chichester: Wiley.

Sperling, S. J. (1953). On the psychodynamics of teasing. *Journal of the American Psychoanalytic Association*, **1**, 458–483.

Spitz, R., and Wolf, K. M. (1946). Anaclitic depression: an inquiry into the genesis of psychiatric conditions in early childhood. *Psychoanalytic Study of the Child*, **2**, 313–342.

Weeks, E., and Machs, J. E. (1978). The child. In A. M. Nichols (Ed.), *The Harvard Guide to Modern Psychiatry*. Cambridge, Massachusetts: Harvard University Press.

Winnicott, D. W. (1971). *Therapeutic Consultations in Child Psychiatry*. New York: Basic Books.

Wolfenstein, M. (1954). *Children's Humor*. Glencoe, Illinois: Free Press.

Wolfenstein, M. (1955). Mad laughter in a six-year-old boy. *Psychoanalytic Study of the Child*, **10**, 381–394.

Wynn-Jones, L. (1927). The appreciation of wit. *Report of the British Association for the Advancement of Science*, p. 323.

Yorukoglu, A. (1977). Favourite jokes of children and their dynamic relation to intra-familial conflicts. In: A. J. Chapman and H. C. Foot (Eds.), *It's a Funny Thing, Humour*. Oxford: Pergamon Press.

Zigler, E., Levine, J., and Gould, L. (1966a). Cognitive processes in the development of children's appreciation of humor. *Child Development*, **37**, 507–518.

Zigler, E., Levine, J., and Gould, L. (1966b). The humor response of normal, institutionalized retarded and noninstitutionalized retarded children. *American Journal of Mental Deficiency*, **71**, 472–480.

Zolotov, M. (1952). Broadway's saddest clown. *Saturday Evening Post*, New York, 31 May.

Zwerling, I. (1955). The favorite joke in diagnostic and therapeutic interviewing. *Psychoanalytic Quarterly*, **24**, 104–114.

CHAPTER 11

Children's Humour: Overview and Conclusions

PAUL E. McGHEE
and
ANTONY J. CHAPMAN

The contributions to this volume are highly varied with respect to the areas of behaviour to which humour is related; and they are also varied in terms of the extent to which data, theoretical views and an integration of findings are presented. As a means of summarizing these varied contributions, this chapter recapitulates some of the key points of each preceding chapter; at the same time, it draws attention to continuing areas of controversy, and makes suggestions for future research directions. This overview is not intended to summarize fully or systematically the contents of each chapter.

CHAPTER 1: DIANA PIEN AND MARY ROTHBART

INCONGRUITY HUMOUR, PLAY, AND SELF-REGULATION OF AROUSAL IN YOUNG CHILDREN

Pien and Rothbart raise the important issue of the point at which infants first become capable of experiencing humour. They have specifically argued against the view of McGhee (1979) and Shultz (1976) that incongruity humour depends upon the acquisition of symbolic capacities during the second year. The only prerequisites for humour, in their view, are the capacity for play and the ability to detect incongruities. Since each of these has been observed as early as four months of age, they conclude that four-month-old infants must experience humour.

Perhaps the most important point to be made in connection with any attempt to establish a position on the original appearance of humour concerns the matter of definitions. There is little agreement about just how humour should be conceptualized and defined. Goldstein and McGhee (1972) noted at the beginning of the recent resurgence of interest in humour research that most investigators or writers simply define humour in terms of their own specific theoretical framework. Pien and Rothbart rightfully point out that there seems to be widespread agreement regarding the importance of both play (or playfulness) and the perception of incongruity in most views of humour. Thus, while these appear to be necessary prerequisites for humour, the question is whether they are sufficient to assure the capacity for humour. If we adopt the assumption that they are sufficient, then it does follow that four-month-olds should be capable of humour.

Within this view, critical supporting evidence should demonstrate playful assimilation of incongruous events as early as four months of age. However, the evidence discussed by Pien and Rothbart (see Sroufe and Waters, 1976; Sroufe and Wunsch, 1972) does not point to a playful interpretation of incongruity until eight or twelve months of age. While vigorous auditory and tactile stimulation is most strongly associated with laughter in four-month-olds, it is not until eight months that some infants begin to laugh at events that might be construed as incongruous (e.g. mother crawling on the floor or pulling a cloth from her mouth). An even stronger case can be made for twelve-month-olds, who laugh at events like mother sucking a bottle or walking like a penguin. Moreover, all of the cases of laughter described by Piaget in his book *Play, Dreams and Imitation in Childhood* occur in connection with familiar or congruous events before eight months of age. Thus, within the criteria for humour established by Pien and Rothbart, future investigations of infant smiling and laughter should direct special attention to reactions to incongruity between four and eight months of age.

Pien and Rothbart do not equate humour with the affect shown during sensory motor play activities, as described by Piaget (1951). This seems appropriate since, without invoking the concept of humour, Piaget provides a satisfactory explanation for the laughter and smiling that typically accompany play. Very young infants repetitively exercise their schemas in play because of the 'function pleasure' experienced in the process. By around four months of age, 'the pleasure of being the cause' is added to this source of pleasure. Piaget discusses these playful repetitions of actions in terms of the sense of joy and power that results. This then, and not humour, is what is behind early play. This further supports their view that it may be the age at which the playful interpretation of incongruities begins which marks the onset of humour.

It is difficult to specify how the issue of the importance of symbolic capacities for humour might be resolved. There is full agreement that a new form of behaviour (namely, pretend or make-believe) occurs with the onset of primitive image-based symbolic capacities. Children between twelve and eighteen months of age begin to treat objects *as if* they were some other object, and yet they show signs of being very aware and confident of the inappropriateness of their actions. McGhee (1977, 1979) has argued that this awareness and confidence is central in leading the child to see the incongruous behaviour as humorous. While this type of behaviour is clearly different from the laughter of twelve-month-olds described by Sroufe and his associates, it is just as clear that a laughter-accompanied playful reaction to incongruity is occurring in each case.

The explanation of smiling and laughter patterns in infancy offered by Sroufe and Waters (1976) further complicates any attempt to determine the origins of humour. They argue that developmental trends in both smiling and laughter can be explained in terms of underlying changes in tension (or arousal). In both cases, this tension is initially produced by the physical properties of stimuli, but is later associated with cognitive interpretation of events. They agree with Tomkins' (1963) view that laughter differs from smiling only in terms of its greater and more rapid build-up of tension. They are in further agreement with Rothbart (1973, 1976) that it is the infant's evaluation of the overall context in which this arousal occurs which determines whether the tension is released in the form of laughter or crying (see Sroufe, Waters, and Matas, 1974). Thus, laughter or smiling can be expected if the situation is perceived as safe or non-threatening, while crying or wariness should result if it is perceived as dangerous or threatening. Sroufe and Waters argue that laughter serves the important function of lowering arousal back into a normal range once it has been elevated, thereby restoring the infant's capacity to attend actively to, or interact with, the arousing stimulus. The importance of this explanation of smiling and laughter lies in the fact that it holds similarly throughout infancy. Thus, the infant undoubtedly experiences elevated arousal upon seeing its mother suck on a bottle, shake her hair, or crawl on the floor. These are new stimulus events, bearing a high amount of discrepancy from the infant's stored schemas involving the mother. The fact that the mother is involved with these discrepant events may make them especially involving. Is this arousing event in a familiar or safe context qualitatively different from other arousing-but-unthreatening events in younger infants? Is laughter in this situation a satisfactory index of humour?

Further theoretical and empirical attention is required to resolve these issues. Play, incongruity and arousal fluctuations undoubtedly have a central role in the earliest forms of humour, just as they are central to humour generally (Berlyne, 1972). The main issue for future consideration seems to be whether these must be combined with the make-believe activities which accompany symbolic thinking to produce humour, or whether they are sufficient to produce humour perceptions before the onset of symbolic capacities.

The most important contribution of the second half of Chapter 1 may be the finding that smiling in infants could be associated with either approach or avoidance behaviour. The arousal-regulating function of avoidance behaviours proposed by Pien and Rothbart deserves attention in future studies, but it would appear that we are a long way from fully understanding the relationship between the infant's cognitive evaluation of stimuli, accompanying affect, and subsequent physical or cognitive orientation toward the stimulus. While we agree with Pien and Rothbart that their findings support 'pleasure in mastery' theories, it is less clear that their findings support arousal theories of humour. They noted that 'there were not enough data for a meaningful analysis of the relation between arousal and laughter'. While smiling did occur in connection with 'pop-ups' of the Jack-in-the-box, this does not provide convincing evidence of humour perception. Does an experimenter's prior definition of an event occurring in a playful context as an arousing and incongruous event provide sufficient foundation for categorizing the reaction as one of humour if laughter does not occur?

Finally, this chapter draws attention to a long-neglected issue among researchers studying infancy. Berlyne (1960), Shultz (1976) and others have questioned the meaning of terms like 'novelty', 'incongruity', and 'discrepancy'. Are these equivalent from the infant's point of view? There is clear evidence in support of Pien and Rothbart's claim that infants can detect and react affectively to changes in the content of stimuli as early as the fourth month. However, do young infants merely perceive altered stimuli as discrepant? Or do they perceive the event as incongruous, relative to what is remembered from past similar events? In speculating about the origins of humour, we might benefit by distinguishing between *mis*expected and *un*expected events, between active and passive expectations regarding an event, and between the child's level of awareness of the unusualness of the event. Does the cognitive-affective quality of the child's reaction depend on a growing awareness that some discrepant or incongruous events are more surprising and puzzling than others?

CHAPTER 2: RONI BETH TOWER AND JEROME SINGER

IMAGINATION, INTEREST, AND JOY IN EARLY CHILDHOOD: SOME THEORETICAL CONSIDERATIONS AND EMPIRICAL FINDINGS

This chapter marks an important early step towards an understanding of the role of fantasy or imagination in children's humour. Tower and Singer conceptualize humour as evolving out of make-believe or imaginative activity. Once humour is seen as merely one form of imaginative play, it follows that the various cognitive, social and affective outcomes of imaginative play described must hold for humour as well. Since humour research has not focused on many of the 'benefits' listed by Tower and Singer, it would be of value to determine whether frequent engagement in humour is more or less beneficial to children than frequent engagement in non-humorous forms of imaginative play. Given the positive relationship between amount of general fantasy play and frequency of humour initiation and laughter (see Chapter 5), considerable overlap in such benefits should occur. The most valuable contribution of research along these lines might result from a determination of which benefits are of a generalized nature, and which are distinctive to humorous and to non-humorous forms of imaginative play.

Of the seven affective functions of imaginative play described by Tower and Singer, the one most widely attributed specifically to humour consists of the provision of increased avenues of expression for fear and anger. According to Freud (1960) and other psychoanalytic writers, humour provides a means of releasing aggressive impulses in a socially acceptable fashion. Wolfenstein (1954) and others have emphasized humour's role in helping children cope with anxiety and other forms of distress. By dealing with the source of anxiety in the safe and playful context of joking, the child is able to master the anxiety.

Tower and Singer argue convincingly that more imaginative children tend to be happier than less imaginative children. The tendency of imaginative children also to show more laughter and initiation of humour further suggests that children showing an early orientation towards humour must also display more positive affect generally. This early association of humour with signs of happiness is incompatible with the psychoanalytic view that humour has some form of disturbance at its motivational base, and suggests that humour results from a positive frame of mind rather than a negative one (see Keith-Spiegel, 1972, for a review of positions on the healthy versus unhealthy attributes of humour). On the other hand, evidence presented in Chapter 8 suggests that girls who developed more pronounced senses of humour came from homes which were poorly adjusted in the early pre-school years. The debate on this issue has been going on since the turn of the present century. The failure to resolve this question may indicate that an increased preoccupation with humour in childhood can actually result from either a very happy or unhappy childhood.

Tower and Singer offer several lines of argument and evidence in support of the view that imaginative play facilitates language development. It is worth noting that this is consistent with the finding reported in Chapter 8 that increased laughter and frequency of initiating humour were associated with precocious language development. Tower and Singer suggest that accelerated language development might be related to a broader tendency for imaginative play to lead to a general desire for increased stimulation. Within this view, it would be the already developed tendency to engage in imaginative play which leads the child to seek out novel and incongruous forms of stimulation. Since humour provides both an intrinsically and socially rewarding means of producing such stimulation, this would account for the positive relationship obtained between frequency of imaginative play and humour initiation among pre-schoolers reported in Chapter 5. McGhee (1979), however, has recently suggested that the reverse developmental sequence might actually occur. That is, some children show greater interest than others in highly novel or discrepant stimulus events as early as the first year of life. Whatever the origins of increased novelty-seeking in these infants, it is this heightened tendency to enjoy the variety of stimulation provided by moderately novel or incongruous events which leads the child a year or so later to become especially involved with imaginative play. Thus, it is an already developed desire for increased stimulation which leads the child to engage in both humorous and non-humorous forms of imaginative play.

Tower and Singer use Tomkins' (1962, 1963) theoretical model to explain the characteristic association of positive affect with imaginative play. According to this view, a sharp decrease in the density of neural firing should evoke the emotion of joy, along with accompanying laughter or smiling. It is the occurrence of moderate increases and sharp decreases in the density of neural firing during imaginative play which lead to the basic affects of interest and joy. Tower and Singer do not, however, satisfactorily explain just how humour fits into this explanatory system.

Within Tomkins' model, it seems clear that humour cannot be considered a primary affect or emotion, although it does seem closely linked to the primary affect of joy. Joy is generally associated with smiling or laughter, the primary overt manifestations of the experience we call humour. Thus, humour produces joy, but joy can also result from other experiences having nothing to do with humour. This position is consistent with other views which emphasize the cognitive nature of humour. Regardless of how one conceptualizes the nature of cognitive processes involved in humour, it follows from Tomkins' model that humour is a cognitive experience—a particular kind of awareness—which produces the basic affect of joy. Tomkins' model suffers from the same problems which plague Berlyne's (1960, 1972) explanation of humour in terms of underlying arousal fluctuations. Just as moderate increases in arousal and arousal jags (an increase followed by a sharp decrease) occur in similar fashion in both humorous and non-humorous experiences, so the sharp decrease in density of neural firing associated with joy may occur in connection with humorous and non-humorous events. Thus, while joy and a sharp decrease in density of firing may indeed characterize humour, this view only accounts for how humour is similar to other sources of joy. It is equally important to determine how humour differs.

CHAPTER 3: THOMAS SHULTZ AND JUDITH ROBILLARD

THE DEVELOPMENT OF LINGUISTIC HUMOUR IN CHILDREN: INCONGRUITY THROUGH RULE VIOLATION

Shultz and Robillard's chapter constitutes the first systematic attempt to examine the relationship between language and linguistic development and children's comprehension and production of humour. By carefully outlining developmental changes in children's usage and awareness of rules governing language usage, and pointing out possible linkages to humour, this chapter provides many avenues for future research on the linguistic aspects of humour. It is especially interesting to note in this respect that the semantic aspects of language seem to be more closely linked to humour than the syntactic aspects. This is consistent with earlier views of children's humour which emphasize the importance of how incongruous or other events are processed or cognitively evaluated. It may be especially rewarding for future investigators to study the relationship between underlying cognitive developmental changes and changes in the semantic properties of linguistic humour.

Linguistic forms of humour might also be used to test theories of humour which emphasize the general importance of mastery for humour (see McGhee, 1979, for a review of these). Shultz and Robillard note that children become aware of incorrect phoneme productions before they can use phonemes correctly themselves. Do such errors with phonemes become occasions for humour as soon as the child becomes aware of incorrect usage, but before s/he can consistently use them correctly? Or does the humour become apparent only after the errors have been corrected in the child's own speech? Evidence in favour of the latter would suggest that cognitive mastery over this aspect of correct language usage is not the most important factor in leading to humour. Rather, it would be the achievement of a physical mastery over the mechanics of producing the correct sound. Prior to the achievement of both forms of mastery over the troublesome phoneme, children may be unable to respond to errors in the playful manner commonly assumed to be necessary for humour.

Shultz and Robillard note that mistakes in the usage of phonemes may involve varying numbers of distinctive features, although minimal distinctive feature differences are most common. Does this pattern also hold for humour? Is humour maximized when distinctive feature differences are high or low? It may also be that there is an optimal moderate number of errors in distinctive features which maximizes humour, since an optimal moderate amount of challenge seems to facilitate humour generally. Finally, the number of feature differences optimally associated with humour might depend on the specific phonemes involved, and may change with increasing age and mastery of the language.

There appears to be little basis for arguing that language plays a central role in the earliest forms of humour, but it does appear that language is used in the service of play and humour as soon as it begins to be mastered. Shultz and Robillard emphasize that the acquisition of language is crucially important because it permits 'ideas to be communicated in a convenient, economical fashion which largely transcends time, space and object'. This is essential, of course, to the social sharing of humour experiences. It may have an even more fundamental role with respect to humour, however, in that the mastery of a language system is essential to achieving quick and easy manipulation of ideas. Without the possession of language, children would be restricted to the image-based forms of humour of the one- to two-year-old child. Language mastery is essential to the development of more abstract and sophisticated forms of humour.

CHAPTER 4: HOWARD GARDNER *ET AL.*

CHILDREN'S LITERARY DEVELOPMENT:
THE REALMS OF METAPHORS AND STORIES

Gardner and his associates have provided a broader scope to the investigation of the role of language in humour development than that provided by Shultz. In combination, these two chapters suggest numerous directions for new research. While Gardner's research does not directly deal with humour development, it nonetheless has an important contribution to make in this volume. Humour based on incongruity shares many properties with metaphors, and fairy tales and stories may be channelled into either humorous or non-humorous directions. Thus, humour researchers can benefit from the varied methodologies and findings relating to the study of children's literary development.

The comprehension and production of both incongruity humour and metaphors require the 'bisociative' form of thinking described by Koestler (1964), since each involves the perceiving of a meaningful relationship between two ideas, concepts, or areas of experience which are not normally considered to be related. Accordingly, there should be some parallel in the developmental patterns associated with production and comprehension of each. There is general support for this view, in that both early humour and early metaphors tend to be based on the perceptual properties of objects and events. It would be surprising if this parallel did not occur, of course, in the light of the strong general influence of perceptual appearances on the child's thinking before the age of six or seven (Piaget, 1952). The first signs of comprehension of more abstract psychological properties of metaphors at the age of seven or eight years corresponds to the timing of children's initial understanding of double meanings in jokes and riddles. While humour researchers have suggested that the acquisition of concrete operational thinking might be responsible for this transition, investigators of the figurative uses of language have not suggested such a connection.

The uncertainty regarding the timing of transition points in the comprehension of metaphors appears to have resulted from the fact that different methodologies point to different transition points. Thus, when children are asked to explain the meaning of a given metaphor, comprehension seems to begin just prior to adolescence. A matching or other non-verbal approach, however, points to comprehension as early as the age of seven. It is essential for researchers in both traditions to realize, therefore, that children usually understand more than they can verbalize. Especially when studying pre-school children, comprehension of a humour event must be determined by some approach which does not require the child to analyse and explain what s/he is laughing at.

The curvilinear relationship noted by Gardner between age and metaphor production is puzzling, since there is no analogous change with respect to humour production. Most surprising is the occurrence of a 'literal stage' during early school years. During this period, children show less appreciation of metaphors and also they produce them less often. This is precisely the time, though, that children become preoccupied with riddles and other forms of jokes based on double meanings. Gardner suggests that children between the age of seven and nine or so are struggling to consolidate the meanings of words, and to determine their range of application. Presumably, they do not begin to enjoy metaphors again until they acquire a greater sense of mastery over these language dimensions. But does not the appreciation of humour based on multiple meanings also require such mastery?

This inconsistency between the developmental patterns for metaphors and humour is even more puzzling in view of Gardner's conclusion that 'precise lexical knowledge of the meanings of words is not a necessary prerequisite to metaphoric understanding'. He argues further that cues provided in the immediate pictorial or linguistic context may be sufficient to lead to metaphoric understanding. If anything, this would lead to the expectation that metaphoric comprehension should precede humour comprehension when the same words are involved, since jokes or cartoons lose their point without precise background understanding of the words or events involved. One need only step into a different sub-culture within a society in order to find oneself standing around wondering what others are laughing at.

One basic structural difference between incongruity humour and metaphors may partially account for different developmental trends in comprehension and production of each. In metaphors, a word or phrase is applied to an event to which it is not literally applicable (as in 'Juliet is my sun'). Humorous incongruities, on the other hand, typically involve the application of one or more peripheral meanings which suggest nonsense or illogicality at the same time as providing a sensible resolution of the incongruity. While the 'tension' Gardner speaks of is probably shared by humour and metaphor comprehension or production, there is no overriding simultaneous awareness of meaningfulness and nonsense when a child fully understands a metaphor. When an incongruity joke based on multiple meanings is understood, however, there is the accompanying realization that the resolution makes sense only within the limited context provided by the joke.

Gardner notes that context and set factors may play crucial roles in distinguishing between humour and metaphor. Humour theorists have especially emphasized the importance of a playful set in this regard. It would be of value for future research along these lines to attempt to produce humorous and non-humorous reactions to the same metaphor by manipulating only set or context factors. Will metaphors automatically become funny under these conditions? Certainly, in the absence of a playful cognitive set, neither joking nor metaphoric communications are likely to be viewed as funny. It may be, however, that in the presence of such a set, jokes will be perceived as humorous (assuming that they are understood) while metaphors will still not be funny. This would at least help to establish or eliminate set and contextual factors as the key factors determining the nature of the child's cognitive and affective reaction to the event.

At this point, virtually no research on humour has been completed which is analogous to that described by Gardner with respect to children's enjoyment and production of fairy tales and stories. Again, each of these seems capable of producing humour reactions in some cases, but not in others. The complexity of these genres, and the accompanying obstacles to controlling important dimensions of the stimulus event, may have prevented humour researchers from tackling these forms of humour in the past. There can be no doubt, however, that stories and anecdotes are common sources of humour in everyday social interaction—especially among older children. The research methodologies and findings described here by Gardner should provide the impetus for humour researchers to begin study of this neglected and important aspect of children's humour.

CHAPTER 5: PAUL McGHEE

DEVELOPMENT OF THE CREATIVE ASPECTS OF HUMOUR

Studies on humour and creativity are sparse, and there are at least two sets of reasons for that. The first has to do with difficulties in researchers knowing how, when, and where to observe and analyse those occasions when fresh humour is spontaneously emitted. Some of the problems confronting the investigator, McGhee notes, are identical to those faced by any investigator of creativity. Contrived research environments have limited potential for circumventing these problems: for humour, they are generally too artificial or sterile for the elicitation of new jokes, punch-lines, cartoon captions or amusing comments, and this is especially so when the subjects are children. Original humour may usually be generated with a minimum of premeditation, and normally the presence of others in social gatherings is a vital catalyst for the formulation of new humour. On the other hand, the assembling of a new joke (but not a 'practical joke') is typically a more private affair. In the world of mass entertainment much humour is conceived by solitary scriptwriters working routine hours behind a desk.

A second set of reasons for the paucity of studies has to do with the assessment and measurement of newly created humour. There can even be a problem about recognizing with certainty that one has borne witness to the creation of humour. A humorous remark which is entirely novel to any one research team may actually be well-rehearsed by the child or adult subject; or an incident may be classified as 'humour' by one group but not by another. Research on humour *responsiveness* is beset by related problems of definition, measurement, and observational environment, but somewhat less acutely so. Consequently, research into humour reactions, cognitive and behavioural, has flourished relative to research into humour and creativity, and this imbalance needs to be redressed. Indeed, it may be timely to remind ourselves that in very young children most forms of humour are self-generated. Also, in lay terms, having a good sense of humour in childhood or adulthood generally reflects at least as much, usually more, on one's ability to initiate humour as it does on one's ability to respond enthusiastically to humour. Most of us experience a special warmth for those of our friends and acquaintances who have a capacity for making witty remarks or recounting everyday happenings in a way that causes us to laugh. Some individuals, even as children, have a talent for detecting and teasing out humorous possibilities in commonplace events and then capitalizing on them for the enjoyment of others.

In Chapter 5, McGhee examines the development of creative aspects of humour and he speculates about the special features of the individual child which are congruent with the ability to create and initiate humour. McGhee intimates that, contrary to what one might confidently expect, humour creation has not been treated as though it were central to an understanding of humour development in children. The empirical studies which have been published are reviewed fully in the chapter and thus, for example, age-related changes in humour are discussed.

A new longitudinal study is reported which is complementary to the broad-based study of individual differences detailed in Chapter 8. (Some general methodological comments about the study are recorded in the section on Chapter 8, below.) This investigation gives reason to think that not until after the age of six are early indications of creativity predictive of frequency of humour initiation. For children at nursery school, somewhat surprisingly, fantasy activity was not related to humour initiation, although it was related to humour responsiveness. Most of the empirical literature is based on older subjects and studies overall tend to confirm that the ability to be humorous matches other creative skills. Links between humour, creativity, and playfulness recur throughout published studies.

Aside from providing a thorough overview of empirical contributions the chapter is of great value in that various theoretical possibilities are explored, linking humour and creativity; and humour production is analysed as an example of a creative act. Singer's work on fantasy and make-believe (see Chapter 2) is brought to bear on more traditional thinking about creativity, and Koestler's (1964) work on bisociation is reviewed briefly. McGhee's own work on cognitive mastery and related psychoanalytic work is also mentioned.

CHAPTER 6: ANTONY CHAPMAN, JEAN SMITH, AND HUGH FOOT

HUMOUR, LAUGHTER, AND SOCIAL INTERACTION

The programme of research undertaken by Chapman, Smith, and Foot has helped to fill a major void in our understanding of children's humour. With the exception of a small number of observational studies of pre-school children in the 1920s and 1930s, social aspects of humour development had been largely neglected. This is surprising, as they note, since virtually everyone who has speculated about humour in a broad sense has acknowledged the importance of social variables for humour. In addition to increasing our understanding of social influences on children's humour, their research has underscored the necessity for all humour researchers to consider the social circumstances in which data are obtained. For example, most investigators studying children's humour have given little or no attention to experimenter effects and to demand characteristics of the experimental situation. Children's humour reactions are sensitive not only to the presence or absence of an adult, but to their general demeanour and appearance as well. If Chapman and his colleagues are correct in their suggestion that the social circumstances surrounding humour have the strongest impact on laughter (stronger than stimulus dimensions or other characteristics manipulated by the experimenter), humour researchers clearly must begin to take social factors into account in designing future experiments.

In the case of the experimenter, is there an optimal behaviour pattern if the study is not primarily directed toward social aspects of humour? Most investigators in the past appear to have made an effort to present a pleasant demeanour, without actually laughing or smiling at the stimuli presented. The data presented in this chapter, however, suggest that this may serve generally to inhibit children's responsiveness to the cartoons or jokes presented. This poses a dilemma for researchers, since the experimenter cannot choose to smile or laugh at some stimuli, but not others. The only options appear to involve showing some form of reaction to all of the stimuli, or reacting to none of them. If the experimenter does show varying degrees of laughter or smiling to all of the stimuli presented, this should generally facilitate subjects' laughter. But, if this influence is as strong as Chapman has suggested, it may mask differences in responsiveness as a function of the independent variables in the study. An alternative approach would be to have a warm-up session in which the experimenter laughs freely at cartoons or jokes, and creates an atmosphere in which children are free to laugh without restraint. If the experimenter is present as additional stimuli are presented, a consistent pattern of smiling may be sufficient to support spontaneous laughter without unduly increasing it through modelling influences. If such facilitation effects are kept at moderate levels, and are homogeneous across experimental conditions, such masking effects should be avoidable. It may be, of course, that comparability of findings across experimenters will be best accomplished by eliminating the presence of adults from the experimental situation when humour materials are presented.

Chapman, Smith, and Foot have also drawn attention to the importance of distinguishing between humorous and non-humorous forms of laughter. While the latter is as interesting and worthy of study as the former, most investigators are interested only in humorous laughter in response to the materials presented.

Most studies probably contain some (undetermined) level of both forms of laughter, but up to this point attempts to determine the relative amounts of each have been rare. Experimenter behaviour constitutes only one source of increased non-humorous laughter. An accurate picture of genuine humour appreciation will be possible only when this and additional sources of non-humorous laughter are controlled. It may prove especially fruitful to study repetition effects in this regard. We continue to know virtually nothing about the effects of repetition on humour appreciation, and how this relationship changes with progressive development. Non-humorous laughter may be encouraged in response to previously heard jokes because of children's awareness that laughter is the socially appropriate response. The data presented in this chapter suggest that group size may have an important influence on the amount of non-humorous laughter occurring in connection with repeated humour.

The consistently high positive correlation obtained by Chapman and his associates between funniness ratings and overt expressions of affect should be noted, since most investigators tend to obtain different findings for these two measures of appreciation. It seems unlikely that Cardiff children are simply more consistent in their intellectual and affective reactions to humour than American children. It is more likely that careful attention to social factors in their studies account for the consistency obtained. Progress in research on humour should be speeded up by specifically investigating those factors which influence degree of reliability between these appreciation measures. Future investigators might then adopt experimental procedures which maximize the probability of obtaining a high correlation between them. This would make interpretation of findings easier, since we would not need to specify the particular measure of appreciation used.

Chapman et al. have taken an intriguing position with regard to sex differences in children's humour. In their view, sex differences may be entirely social in origin. They argue that social facilitation effects for both sexes are mainly due to a sharing of the social situation, not a sharing of the humour stimuli presented. Girls, however, seem to have a greater concern about sharing the social situation than boys do. Girls are more likely than boys to direct their responsiveness to their companions, while boys are more likely than girls to laugh mainly in response to the actual humour event. They have further proposed that girls prefer relatively high levels of social intimacy, while boys prefer lower levels. They concluded that 'girls used laughter and smiling to gain and maintain the attention of companions', presumably producing a socially more intimate situation in the process. Boys are more likely to use laughter to reduce the intimacy of a situation. For both sexes, uncomfortably high levels of arousal are considered to result when the prevailing intimacy level gets too high (boys) or too low (girls). If girls' humour reactions are less exclusively a result of the humour materials presented than those of boys, researchers will need to consider this too in interpreting their data.

While the research of Chapman, Smith, and Foot has made a major contribution to our understanding of the social aspects of children's humour, it should be noted that they are primarily concerned with the achievement of an understanding of children's social behaviour. Humour has been adopted as an ideal area in which to study social behaviour because laughter and smiling are such highly social events. Given this point of origin of their research, it has not focused on developmental issues in connection with the social aspects of children's humour. An understanding of the social psychology of children's humour can, however, provide the impetus for developmental research along these lines. It should be similarly fruitful to initiate developmental investigations of the models of adult humour set forth by La Fave (1972), Martineau (1972) and Zillmann and Cantor (1976).

CHAPTER 7: DAVID BRODZINSKY AND JONATHAN RIGHTMYER

INDIVIDUAL DIFFERENCES IN CHILDREN'S HUMOUR DEVELOPMENT

Brodzinsky and Rightmyer have pointed to the need for research on individual differences in children's humour and its development. As they have emphasized, most investigations of children's humour have adopted the nomothetic approach and have simply treated important areas of individual differences as sources of error variance. It is not surprising that researchers would study global developmental trends in their initial attempts at understanding a phenomenon as complex as humour, since typically these are easier to identify and measure. There can be little doubt about the importance of studying sources of individual differences in humour responsiveness and development, however, since one's sense of humour is totally unique. While there may be commonalities with the patterns of humour responsiveness of others, the differences are usually more striking. The longitudinal study reported by McGhee in Chapter 8 is the only study of its kind; it specifically examines the question of the origins of individual differences in humour responsiveness in prior child and maternal behaviour. In addition to such antecedent developmental influences, we must begin to examine the relationship between concurrent physical, personality, gender, cognitive and other sources of individual differences in humour. To this point, we have focused most of our empirical attention on determining how children's humour development is similar, as a function of important cognitive and other developmental variables. As the authors of this chapter point out, this approach only gives us half the total picture. We will not fully understand children's humour and its development until we determine how and why children differ in their senses of humour.

In spite of the obvious importance of gender as a potential source of individual differences in humour development, Brodzinsky and Rightmyer note that no systematic attempt has been made to study sex differences in children's humour. While analyses of sex differences are often reported, they have rarely been the main focus of studies. The efforts of Chapman and his associates in connection with the social aspects of humour (Chapter 6), and of McGhee in connection with antecedent developmental influences (see Chapter 8, and McGhee, 1979) constitute important steps toward correcting this condition.

Brodzinsky and Rightmyer note that the level of cognitive challenge offered by a cartoon or joke contributes to individual differences in humour appreciation, since children with varying cognitive abilities should all tend to prefer humour which is moderately challenging. Prior research has shown that children with similar cognitive capacities show similar levels of appreciation of jokes which require those capacities for comprehension (McGhee, 1976a). Most jokes and cartoons, however, do not require specifiable single cognitive capacities. This makes the cognitive challenge notion an interesting one theoretically, but it is difficult to demonstrate its operation in the typical jokes told and appreciated by children. Until some means of determining the amount of cognitive challenge offered by different types of humour stimuli to children of different cognitive levels is achieved, investigations of this source of individual differences in humour appreciation will be impossible. The early efforts of Zigler, Levine, and Gould (1967) mark a valuable first step toward equating levels of cognitive challenge for children at different age levels, but their approach is weakened by relying on comprehension scores as a means of determining level of challenge.

The main sources of individual differences in humour appreciation are considered to stem from children's tendencies to prefer humour at some optimal moderate level of difficulty. It is quite possible, however, that different children might come to prefer varying difficulty levels in humour as they get older. Among adults, some individuals appear to prefer highly abstract and challenging jokes, while others prefer simpler, easy to process jokes. While it might be argued that the easy jokes are actually moderately challenging to the latter group, it is more likely that some people simply prefer to keep their humour simple and less 'intellectual'. Individuals may also differ in the extent to which tendentious themes in humour modify the preferred level of challenge. While some individuals may prefer more challenging jokes regardless of the presence of sex, aggression, or other emotionally salient themes, others may increase their enjoyment of less taxing humour in the presence of such themes. Development of a means of assessing the match between complexity of a joke and the cognitive processing abilties of the recipient (i.e. of assessing level of cognitive challenge) will also enable researchers to determine the reliability of preferred level of challenge between childhood and adulthood.

The most promising direction of current research on individual differences in children's humour is that based on cognitive styles. Reflective children have shown greater comprehension than impulsive children of the cartoons and jokes that have been presented to them, but impulsives have consistently shown more laughter. Since prompting (asking children to think again about what is funny about a joke) eliminated the differences in comprehension without eliminating differences in laughter, and since impulsives also laugh more than reflectives at non-humorous control stimuli, there is no doubt about differences in appreciation being due solely to differences in children's threshold for laughter as a general social reaction. This personality dimension does not pose a problem for researchers in the nomothetic tradition, since the random assignment of children to experimental conditions should balance these opposing influences. It does, however, raise the beast that humour researchers have generally preferred not to come to grips with, namely, what is the nature of humour appreciation, and how should it be measured?

If appreciation is defined in terms of amount of overt affect, do impulsive children consistently experience greater appreciation of humour than reflectives? This seems unlikely, since we know that impulsives' laughter is in great part simply a general style of responding to events. In our view, humour is most essentially a cognitive experience. Children with comparable intellectual experiences of humour may show widely varying laughter and other social reactions. We have seen in this volume that both personality and social factors may influence the public response of laughter. But an intellectual rating may fail to capture the spontaneous enjoyment that is central to the experience of humour. The actual process of asking children to rate jokes or cartoons for funniness may interfere with the very event we are interested in measuring. For the time being, it seems safest to conclude that each dependent measure taps a different aspect of humour appreciation. The fact that most investigators typically find different predictions for the two measures makes it essential that we continue to obtain both measures in all studies. The fact that Chapman, Smith, and Foot (see Chapter 6) seem to be the only investigators able to consistently obtain a high positive relationship between amount of smiling/laughter and funniness ratings suggests that researchers might profitably scrutinize their experimental procedures. As noted earlier, their careful attention to social aspects of the experimental situation may be responsible for the consistency of findings between the two measures.

In the final analysis, the comprehension and appreciation of humour must be a totally individual affair. Possessing the cognitive prerequisites to understand a joke is no guarantee of comprehension, and comprehension is no guarantee of appreciation. Assuming full comprehension of a cartoon or joke (although it is not always clear just what this means), an individual's prior developmental history, current physical, biological, and social needs, and general frame of mind combine to determine funniness at that particular moment. To humour researchers, the study of individual differences in appreciation is certainly no joke.

CHAPTER 8: PAUL McGHEE

DEVELOPMENT OF THE SENSE OF HUMOUR IN CHILDHOOD: A LONGITUDINAL STUDY

The study of individual differences reported by McGhee is unique in the humour literature and, as indicated above, this is readily apparent by comparing it with any reviewed by Brodzinsky and Rightmyer in Chapter 7. McGhee's is a longitudinal, correlational study conducted at the Fels Research Institute, and it draws upon a wealth of background data already available from permanent Fels' files. Because the children and their mothers were observed over a period of years prior to the conception and instigation of the humour study, McGhee has been able to formulate and address a series of questions about the origins of humour which are fundamental to a full understanding of humour development. They concern how early behaviours and early mothering relate to later humour responsiveness and humour initiation.

His total sample comprised boys and girls in two age groups, and in both groups a variety of socioeconomic backgrounds was represented. The first group was attending Fels Nursery School and members were aged between three and five-and-a-half years: the information already on file concerned, first, antecedent maternal behaviours from birth onwards and, second, the children's behaviours from the age of three onwards. The second group was attending Fels Day Camp and members were aged between six and eleven years. The same sorts of data were also on file for these older children: there were details about antecedent maternal behaviours from birth until the age of six and details about the children's behaviours from three onwards. Most of the humour data, but not all, were collected specially for the study while the boys and girls were at the nursery school or day camp. Under both circumstances the children engaged in play which was non-structured and non-adult-directed.

The findings and their interpretation are of course discussed in full, and in summary, in the chapter itself. In referring to the results here we do no more than outline the principal findings in the broadest terms. More than any other, Chapter 8 details a single study and hence we shall review selected features of the research methodology in order to highlight the major innovations and limitations of that study.

A broad-based approach is especially valuable in any longitudinal research which is unlikely to be repeated, yet it is unavoidable that some major methodological constraints are introduced in order that such studies should remain manageable. McGhee has kept these constraints to a minimum but, for example, the oldest subjects in his study were aged eleven and there is no claim that the conclusions would have any generality beyond that age. Then again, childrearing and humour data were not available for fathers but, as McGhee notes, humour initiation is more characteristic of men than women; and, therefore, fathers may be the more potent humour models, especially for boys.

Also, in such a comprehensive observational study it is to be expected that the sample size was not large ($n = 43$); and the adoption of humour indices which are of undetermined reliability and validity is not uncharacteristic of the humour literature generally.

To date this is the only longitudinal study of individual differences in humour, and one of its main strengths is that it organizes immense amounts of data. As far as it was possible the social conditions were matched for the two groups although, perhaps inevitably, there must be some question about equivalence of test conditions across ages. For instance, one arrangement (the day camp, say) may typically be more conducive than the other arrangement to particular classes of behaviour—such as aspects of humour. Also, it is feasible, for example, that a day camp promotes activities which are more characteristic for six- to eleven-year-olds than are nursery-school activities for younger children. In such an event, some children may be unusually carefree and sociable; and, more importantly, some children may be more inclined to manifest their humour, while others may not. In other words, not only may there be group differences in quantity and quality of humour under the two observation conditions (because of psychological and environmental factors governing those conditions), but individuals are unlikely to be predisposed to react uniformly to changes in social conditions. On a related point, there is some likelihood that the children at the two age groups, and within those age groups, were differentially influenced by the presence of the observers. Over and above these factors, the observers' degrees of participation in the children's activities probably varied according to the age of the children and according to the interactants *per se*. But most of these points are to some degree inherent in all naturalistic, longitudinal research, especially when it is combined with a cross-sectional design, as in this study. Given that two groups of children were observed, the eleven-year-olds could obviously not be reintroduced to the younger children's nursery school; but there are environments in which both age groups feel comfortable.

It has already been said in this concluding chapter that there is little agreeement about how humour should be conceptualized and defined. Psychologists, no less than laymen, tend to define humour in multitudinous ways and, following work such as that of Pien and Rothbart in Chapter 1, some researchers might want to argue that definitions of children's humour should take account of subjects' ages. This is not a view to which we would subscribe, yet the McGhee study might be interpreted as offering support for the view that a child's 'sense of humour' should to an extent be defined according to age. Intercorrelations between measures of humour were large and significant for the older group but small and non-significant for the younger group. Four observers were employed to record humour measures, two for each age group, and inter-observer reliabilities were high. The strategy of weighting the measures equally in a composite 'sense of humour' index is therefore deserving of research in its own right; it may be more legitimate for one age group than for the other. Also, when dealing with vast numbers of statistical relationships—more than 800 correlation coefficients are reported—there is a question about what level of probability is acceptable for results to be considered 'significant': if one adopts a 5 per cent criterion level then one would expect *by chance* to find that about 40 of the correlations were 'significant' beyond $p < 0.05$. McGhee's study has yielded many more than 40 significant correlations at the 1-tailed 0.05 level (over 65 in all), and more than 150 are significant at the 0.01 level.

It is crucial for humour research that we achieve an understanding of the development of individual differences, and each of the methodological comments proffered here is important to bear in mind in a follow-up, or partial follow-up, of McGhee's study. As already intimated, that study in itself constitutes a major step forward. One body of data points to links between aggression and humour: there are indications that children who display humour most are also the children who are verbally and physically aggressive in the first years of life. A second body of correlational data suggests links between children's humour behaviours and their early sensitivity to maternal reactions. These and other findings are analysed within a framework of humour theory and developmental theory generally. The tables of correlation coefficients provide a rich source of information for further speculation and research. In those tables, and in McGhee's discussion, are many promising clues about the origins of humour. These clues should now be investigated by taking parts of the McGhee study and extending them. The study provides a much-needed basis for experimental work on humour development through which causative links can be determined.

CHAPTER 9: ANN DAVIES AND MICHAEL APTER

HUMOUR AND ITS EFFECT ON LEARNING IN CHILDREN

The research programme of Davies and Apter marks the beginning of an important new direction of humour research. Most of this volume is devoted to gaining an understanding of basic processes associated with children's humour and its development. However, this chapter and the chapter on clinical applications of humour suggest that humour may have important practical applications with children as well. While psychologists and others have been studying influences upon children's learning for decades, surprisingly, virtually no attempt has been made to determine whether humour might somehow aid learning and memory. This is especially puzzling in view of the obvious fact that children's attention is readily piqued by humour. The timeliness of research into the relationship between humour and learning is evident from a recent study of humour researchers' views about areas in need of additional research (McGhee, 1976b). More investigators listed the relationship between humour and learning/memory as a neglected but worthy area of research than any other single research topic.

Davies and Apter note that humour might be especially beneficial in classroom settings. For many children, schools have in recent years become sources of anxiety and dread, rather than opportunities for experiencing the joy of learning. It is painfully obvious that many schools are in need of change and revitalization, but there is not always agreement as to what changes are needed. Because of the universal senses of joy experienced in connection with humour, it may prove beneficial to search for innovative ways to introduce humour into the curriculum. Since many teachers are aware of the importance of humour in the classroom, why has there not been a greater reliance on it as a teaching technique? The findings reviewed in this chapter suggest that teachers may be aware of the fact that humour can backfire when not used expertly. That is, instead of arousing interest and a desire to learn about a subject, it may create a general mood of playfulness—a state which is generally incompatible with learning. It may be this outcome which makes teachers hesitant to develop some form of humour into their teaching style.

Both prior theory and research yield conflicting views regarding the facilitatory versus inhibitory effects of humour upon learning. This inconsistency appears to have resulted from the fact that most of the dimensions stressed by Davies and Apter have not been given consideration. Conflicting findings are likely to continue until a systematic research programme is undertaken to study these dimensions. Investigators planning such research might benefit from an informal examination of the uses of humour in the fields of children's television programmes and television advertising (see McGhee, 1980). Davies and Apter note that successful children's educational programmes like *Sesame Street* and *The Electric Company* commonly use humour to aid in the teaching of basic concepts. While the assumption that humour helps maintain attention to the programme appears to be a sound one, no attempt has been made to determine whether humour in these programmes does, in fact, facilitate learning. Arguments outlined in their chapter make inhibitory effects equally plausible. The techniques used by the Children's Television Workshop in developing these programmes (see Lesser, 1974), however, provide a good starting point for investigators interested in determing those characteristics of the humour situation optimal for learning in young children.

In the world of television advertising, creators of advertisements are primarily concerned about having viewers remember key items of information about the product advertised. There have been notorious flops as well as successes in using humour to sell products, leaving most writers of advertisements with the conviction that using humour in this connection is an art, rather than a science. An experienced individual can presumably predict how successful a given advertisement will be, but there are no clear guidelines for predicting what will work and what will not. This view has undoubtedly resulted from the fact that, as Davies and Apter have shown, numerous qualities of the humorous communication can influence the impact of the message. Investigators developing research programmes aimed at examining the relationship between humour and learning might profitably begin by attempting to isolate the peculiar qualities of successful humorous advertisements.

In short, there is every reason to believe that humour can be an effective teaching/learning technique, if it is used in the correct fashion. Davies and Apter have provided a framework for starting to determine how conditions associated with facilitatory influences differ from conditions associated with inhibitory influences.

CHAPTER 10: JACOB LEVINE

THE CLINICAL USE OF HUMOUR IN WORK WITH CHILDREN

Levine has effectively drawn attention to the fact that while little empirical attention has been devoted to clinical uses of humour, many therapists are convinced by their own clinical experience that humour has much to offer in connection with therapy and with both diagnostic and developmental assessment measures. Levine shares this view and draws upon both developmental and clinical studies for supporting evidence. In the case of using humour for the purpose of developmental assessment, he notes that items of a humorous nature have a long history of usage on the Stanford–Binet intelligence test. This test includes a pictorial absurdities sub-test for younger children and a verbal absurdities sub-test for older children. The items on these sub-tests are, in fact, similar to the stimuli used in many humour studies. The high correlation between performance on this sub-test and total test score suggests that more intelligent children should show better comprehension of most cartoons and jokes. Generally speaking, the data are consistent with this conclusion. The fact that there are exceptions to this trend, however, is not surprising, since most investigators do not control for complexity or amount of challenge offered by the stimuli used. The strength of the positive relationship obtained should decrease as progressively simpler cartoons and jokes are used. Even if complexity and other important stimulus dimensions were adequately controlled in measures of intelligence based on humour, test performance and relationships to performance on other humour measures would appear to have little to contribute to our understanding of humour development beyond the finding that more intelligent children are more likely to understand (or achieve a higher level of understanding of) whatever cartoons or jokes are presented to them.

Humour appreciation measures also appear to hold little promise as a means of assessing intellectual development, since we have only begun to identify factors which influence humour appreciation in children. Even if we fully understood the role played by complexity and cognitive challenge in determining humour appreciation, control would have to be exercised over additional influencing factors, such as degree of emotional salience of the content to the child (e.g. the amount of sex or aggression depicted), familiarity of the joke, and degree of identification with aggressors and victims involved in the humour. Because of the probable interaction of these and additional factors in determining appreciation, it is unlikely that future studies will yield either a satisfactory test of intelligence based on humour appreciation or consistently significant relationships between standardized tests of intelligence and appreciation. At best, efforts along these lines might demonstrate that higher levels of intellectual development are associated with greater appreciation of particular types of humour (e.g. more complex). It would be most surprising, however, if this relationship were strong enough to use level of appreciation as an index of the child's intellectual level.

The greatest potential for using humour measures as a means of assessing intellectual level may lie in more qualitative conceptualizations of intelligence, such as that developed by Piaget. As Levine notes, performance on particular Piagetian tasks has been found to relate to comprehension of humour related to the concepts assessed by those tasks. Since the experience of humour based on the violation of a given concept requires the confident possession of that concept, jokes or cartoons based on such violations might provide an effective means of determining whether the concept has been acquired. Attempts along these lines must rely on comprehension only, however, since children occasionally show laughter and give high funniness ratings to cartoons and jokes which they do not understand.

No attempt has been made to develop humour-based measures of social, emotional, or personality development. Similarly, there have been no efforts to develop diagnostic tests based on humour for use in clinical work with children. Studies of the diagnostic potential of humour with adults have produced mixed results. For example, some investigators have failed to find significant differences in humour appreciation among traditional diagnostic groups, such as neurotics, schizophrenics, and normals (Derks, Leichtman, and Carroll, 1975; Verinis, 1970). Other evidence suggests, however, that schizophrenic and neurotic patients are more likely than normals to be disturbed by cartoons and jokes (Levine and Abelson, 1959). The most typical finding in studies using adult clinical populations is that humour stimuli closely related to the area of conflict are rated very low in funniness (Ecker, Levine, and Zigler, 1973; Redlich, Levine and Sohler, 1951). This pattern does not appear to be restricted to clinical populations, since both psychiatric and highly intelligent normal individuals have been found to show a puzzling inability to understand normally easily-understood cartoons when they touch off strong emotional conflicts (Levine and Redlich, 1955). The central issue with such studies (using children as well as adults) lies in whether humour measures can be developed which will prove to be of genuine diagnostic value. While it is interesting to note differences in humour responsiveness among individuals already assigned to psychiatric categories, it remains to be demonstrated that certain dimensions of humour comprehension or appreciation can be used reliably to assign patients to initial categories.

Levine has noted that the most promising clinical use of humour with children up to this point has been the 'favourite joke' technique. The fact that many children's favourite joke is often related to underlying sources of conflict or distress points to the importance of the coping functions of humour. Levine shares the common psychoanalytic view that humour helps children overcome conflict and anxiety. By playfully confronting distressful situations in the context of humour, many children appear to be able to master the anxiety associated with those situations. Similarly, recently mastered conflict situations tend to be the source of joking because (in Levine's view) of the pleasure derived from re-experiencing mastery over a previously anxiety-arousing situation. Thus, humour is considered both to assist in the coping process and to reflect the mastery achieved over recently mastered conflicts.

Perhaps the most important conclusion to be drawn from the clinical views and studies reviewed by Levine is that humour can be used effectively by therapists to assist children in dealing with their conflicts, although care must be taken in doing so. The use of humour to promote the goals of therapy appears to be a skill which a therapist must develop. By creating a more playful and relaxed frame of mind, the adroit introduction of humour by the therapist may increase the child's willingness to confront the source of his or her anxiety. The establishment of this frame of mind is more likely to produce a feeling of comfort and trust regarding the therapist—an essential step if therapy is to be successful.

Finally, the findings discussed by Levine raise the inevitable question of the relationship between humour responsiveness and mental health. It is generally assumed that the possession of a 'good sense of humour' is a prerequisite for healthy adjustment. While there is no agreement on what it means to have a good sense of humour, a case can be made for the position that either the extreme presence or absence of humour and laughter is likely to be associated with poor adjustment in some respect. Unfortunately, no attempt has been made to relate children's mental health to humour responsiveness between these two extremes. The limited data available for adults support the view that a positive relationship between humour and measures of mental health generally holds (O'Connell, 1960; O'Connell and Cowgill, 1970; O'Connell and Peterson, 1964). While supporting data for children are lacking, it follows that if humour does help children to release aggressive and sexual impulses in a socially acceptable way, and facilitates attempts to master sources of anxiety and distress, it must foster the achievement of good mental health. Similarly, it must facilitate the adjustment to demands for rational, moral, and generally conventional behaviour by providing periodic freedom from the stifling restrictiveness of those demands. It does not necessarily follow, however, that children who laugh, joke or clown frequently are better adjusted than their less humour-oriented peers. Those peers may encounter less anxiety and conflict, and so be less motivated to adopt humour as a coping mechanism. It can only be concluded that laughter and humour appear to produce a better state of mental health than might have otherwise existed in those children who suffer from high levels of mental stress. Even this conclusion, however, awaits a systematic test.

REFERENCES

Berlyne, D. E. (1960). *Conflict, Arousal and Curiosity.* New York: McGraw-Hill.

Berlyne, D. E. (1972). Humor and its kin. In J. H. Goldstein and P. E. McGhee (Eds.), *The Psychology of Humor: Theoretical Perspectives and Empirical Issues.* New York: Academic Press.

Derks, P. L., Leichtman, H. M., and Carroll, P. J. (1975). Production and judgment of 'humor' by schizophrenics and college students. *Bulletin of the Psychonomic Society,* **6**, 300–302.

Ecker, J., Levine, J., and Zigler, E. (1973). Impaired sex-role identification in schizophrenia expressed in the comprehension of humor stimuli. *Journal of Psychology,* **83**, 67–77.

Freud, S. (1960). *Jokes and Their relation to The Unconscious.* New York: Norton.

Goldstein, J. H., and McGhee, P. E. (Eds.) (1972). *The Psychology of Humor: Theoretical Perspectives and Empirical Issues.* New York: Academic Press.

Keith-Spiegel, P. (1972). Early conceptions of humor: varieties and issues. In J. H. Goldstein and P. E. McGhee (Eds.), *The Psychology of Humor: Theoretical Perspectives and Empirical Issues.* New York: Academic Press.

Koestler, A. (1964). *The Act of Creation.* New York: Dell.

La Fave, L. (1972). Humor judgments as a function of reference group and identification classes. In J. H. Goldstein and P. E. McGhee (Eds.), *The Psychology of Humor: Theoretical Perspectives and Empirical Issues.* New York: Academic Press.

Lesser, G. (1974). *Children and Television: Lessons from Sesame Street.* New York: Random House.

Levine, J., and Abelson, R. (1959). Humor as a disturbing stimulus. *Journal of General Psychology,* **60**, 191–200.

Levine, J., and Redlich, J. (1955). Failure to understand humor. *Psychoanalytic Quarterly,* **24**, 560–572.

Martineau, W. H. (1972). A model of the social functions of humor. In J. H. Goldstein and P. E. McGhee (Eds.), *The Psychology of Humor: Theoretical Perspectives and Empirical Issues.* New York: Academic Press.

McGhee, P. E. (1976a). Children's appreciation of humor: a test of the cognitive congruency principle. *Child Development,* **47**, 420–426.

McGhee, P. E. (1976b). The humour questionnaire: an analysis of humour researchers' views of appropriate directions for future research. Paper presented at the British Psychological Society, Welsh Branch, International Conference on Humour and Laughter, Cardiff, July.

McGhee, P. E. (1977). A model of the origins and early development of incongruity-based humour. In A. J. Chapman and H. C. Foot (Eds.), *It's a Funny Thing, Humour.* Oxford: Pergamon Press.

McGhee, P. E. (1979). *Humor: Its Origin and Development.* San Francisco: Freeman.

McGhee, P. E. (1980). Toward the integration of entertainment and educational functions of television: the role of humor. In P. H. Tannenbaum (Ed.), *Entertainment Functions of Television.* Hillsdale, New Jersey: Erlbaum.

O'Connell, W. E. (1960). The adaptive functions of wit and humor. *Journal of Abnormal and Social Psychology,* **61**, 263–270.

O'Connell, W. E. and Cowgill, S. (1970). Wit, humor and defensiveness. *Newsletter for Research in Psychology*, **12**, 32–33.
O'Connell, W. E., and Peterson, P. (1964). Humor and repression. *Journal of Existential Psychology*, **4**, 309–316.
Piaget, J. (1951). *Play, Dreams and Imitation in Childhood*. New York: Norton.
Piaget, J. (1952). *The Origins of Intelligence in Children*. New York: International Press.
Redlich, F. C., Levine, J., and Sohler, T. P. (1951). A mirth response test: preliminary report on a psychodiagnostic technique utilizing dynamics of humor. *American Journal of Orthopsychiatry*, **21**, 717–731.
Rothbart, M. K. (1973). Laughter in young children. *Psychological Bulletin*, **80**, 247–256.
Rothbart, M. K. (1976). Incongruity, problem-solving and laughter. In A. J. Chapman and H. C. Foot (Eds.), *Humour and Laughter: Theory, Research and Applications*. Chichester: Wiley.
Shultz, T. R. (1976). A cognitive-developmental analysis of humour. In A. J. Chapman and H. C. Foot (Eds.), *Humour and Laughter: Theory, Research and Applications*. Chichester: Wiley.
Sroufe, L. A., and Waters, E. (1976). The ontogenesis of smiling and laughter: a perspective on the organization of development in infancy. *Psychological Review*, **83**, 173–189.
Sroufe, L. A., Waters, E., and Matas, L. (1974). Contextual determinants of infant affective response. In M. Lewis and L. A. Rosenblum (Eds.), *The Origins of Fear*. New York: Wiley.
Sroufe, L. A., and Wunsch, J. P. (1972). The development of laughter in the first year of life. *Child Development*, **43**, 1326–1344.
Tomkins, S. (1962). *Affect, Imagery and Consciousness*. Vol. 1. New York: Springer.
Tomkins, S. (1963). *Affect, Imagery and Consciousness*. Vol. 2. New York: Springer.
Verinis, J. S. (1970). Inhibition of humor enjoyment: differential effects with traditional diagnostic categories. *Journal of General Psychology*, **82**, 157–163.
Wolfenstein, M. (1954). *Children's Humor*. Glencoe, Illinois: Free Press.
Zigler, E., Levine, J., and Gould, L. (1967). Cognitive challenge as a factor in children's humor appreciation. *Journal of personality and Social Psychology*, **6**, 332–336.
Zillmann, D., and Cantor, J. R. (1976). A disposition theory of humour and mirth. In A. J. Chapman and H. C. Foot (Eds.), *Humour and Laughter: Theory, Research and Applications*. Chichester: Wiley.

Bibliography of Studies on Children's Humour, Laughter, and Smiling

PAUL E. McGHEE

and

ANTONY J. CHAPMAN

CHILDREN'S HUMOUR

Ames, L. B. (1949). Development of interpersonal smiling responses in the preschool years. *Journal of Genetic Psychology*, **74**, 273–291.

Athey, C. (1977). Humour in children related to Piaget's theory of intellectual development. In A. J. Chapman and H. C. Foot (Eds.), *It's a Funny Thing, Humour*. Oxford: Pergamon Press.

Bariaud, F. (1977). Comprehension and emotional adhesion in the genetics of humour. In A. J. Chapman and H. C. Foot (Eds.), *It's a Funny Thing, Humour*. Oxford: Pergamon Press.

Bender, L. (1944). The psychology of children's reading and the comics. *Journal of Educational Sociology*, **24**, 34–53.

Bever, T. (1968). Associations to stimulus-response theories of language. In T. R. Dixon and D. L. Horton (Eds.), *Verbal Behavior and General Behavior Theory*. Englewood Cliffs, New Jersey: Prentice Hall.

Bird, G. E. (1925). An objective humor test for children. *Psychological Bulletin*, **22**, 137–138.

Blatz, W. E., Allin, K., and Millichamp, D. (1936). A study of laughter in the nursery school child. *University of Toronto Studies: Child Development Series*, No. 7.

Bliss, S. (1915). The origin of laughter. *American Journal of Psychology*, **26**, 236–246.

Brackett, C. W. (1933). Laughing and crying of preschool children. *Journal of Experimental Education*, **2**, 119–126.

Brackett, C. W. (1934). Laughing and crying in preschool children. *Child Development Monographs*, No. 14, 119–126.

Brodzinsky, D. M. (1975). The role of conceptual tempo and stimulus characteristics in children's humor development. *Developmental Psychology*, **11**, 843–850.

Brodzinsky, D. M. (1977). Conceptual tempo as an individual difference variable in children's humour development. In A. J. Chapman and H. C. Foot (Eds.), *It's a Funny Thing, Humour*. Oxford: Pergamon Press.

Brodzinsky, D. M., Feuer, V., and Owens, J. (1977). Detection of linguistic ambiguity by reflective, impulsive, fast-accurate, and slow-inaccurate children. *Journal of Educational Psychology*, **69**, 237–243.

Brodzinsky, D. M., and Rightmyer, J. (1976). Pleasure associated with cognitive mastery as related to children's conceptual tempo. *Child Development*, **47**, 881–884.

Brumbaugh, F. (1940). The place of humor in the curriculum. *Journal of Experimental Education*, **8**, 403–409.

Brumbaugh, F., and Wilson, F. T. (1940). Children's laughter. *Journal of Genetic Psychology*, **57**, 3–29.

Bryant, J., and Meyer, T. P. (1977). A developmental analysis of children's favourite jokes. In A. J. Chapman and H. C. Foot (Eds.), *It's a Funny Thing, Humour*. Oxford: Pergamon Press.

Carr, P. (1958). Can comic books be used in education? *Education*, **79**, 57–61.

Chandler, K. A. (1902). The sense of humor in children. *Century*, **42**, 959–967.

Chapman, A. J. (1973). Social facilitation of laughter in children. *Journal of Experimental Social Psychology*, **9**, 528–541.

Chapman, A. J. (1974). An experimental study of socially facilitated 'humorous laughter'. *Psychological Reports*, **35**, 727–734.

Chapman, A. J. (1975a). Eye contact, physical proximity and laughter: a re-examination of the equilibrium model of social intimacy. *Social Behavior and Personality*, **3**, 143–155.

Chapman, A. J. (1975b). Humorous laughter in children. *Journal of Personality and Social Psychology*, **31**, 42–49.

Chapman, A. J. (1976). Social aspects of humorous laughter. In A. J. Chapman and H. C. Foot (Eds.), *Humour and Laughter: Theory, Research and Applications*. Chichester: Wiley.

Chapman, A. J., and Chapman, W. A. (1974). Responsiveness to humor: Its dependency upon a companion's humorous smiling and laughter. *Journal of Psychology*, **88**, 245–252.

Chapman, A. J., and Crompton, P. (1978). Humorous presentations of material and presentations of humorous material: a review of the humour and memory literature and two experimental studies. In M. M. Gruneberg, P. E. Morris, and R. N. Sykes (Eds.), *Practical Aspects of Memory*. Oxford: Pergamon Press.

Chapman, A. J., Smith, J., and Foot, H. C. (1977). Language, humour and intergroup relations. In H. Giles (Ed.), *Language, Ethnicity and Intergroup Relations*. London: Academic Press.

Chapman, A. J., and Speck, L. J. M. (1977a). Birth order and social responsiveness in young children. In A. J. Chapman and H. C. Foot (Eds.), *It's a Funny Thing, Humour*. Oxford: Pergamon Press.

Chapman, A. J., and Speck, L. (1977b). Humorous laughter and relief of anxiety in first-born children. *Journal of Individual Psychology*, **33**, 37–41.

Chapman, A. J., and Wright, D. S. (1976). Social enhancement of laughter: An experimental analysis of some companion variables. *Journal of Experimental Child Psychology*, **21**, 201–218.

Chukovsky, K. (1963). *From Two to Five*. Berkeley: University of California Press.

Cunningham, A. (1962). Relation of sense of humor to intelligence. *Journal of Social Psychology*, **57**, 143–147.

Davies, A. P. (1977). Humour as a facilitator of learning in primary school children. In A. J. Chapman and H. C. Foot (Eds.), *It's a Funny Thing, Humour*. Oxford: Pergamon Press.

Dearborn, G. V. N. (1900). The nature of the smile and laugh. *Science*, **2**, 851–856.

Ding, G. F., and Jersild, A. T. (1932). A study of the laughing and smiling of preschool children. *Journal of Genetic Psychology*, **40**, 452–472.

Domash, L. (1975). The use of wit and the comic by a borderline psychotic child in psychotherapy. *American Journal of Psychotherapy*, **29**, 261–270.

Ellis, G. T., and Sekyra, F. (1972). The effect of aggressive cartoons on the behavior of first grade children. *Journal of Psychology*, **81**, 37–43.

Enders, A. C. (1927). A study of the laughter of the pre-school child in the Merrill-Palmer Nursery School. *Papers of the Michigan Academy of Science, Arts and Letters*, **8**, 341–356.

Felker, D. W., and Hunter, D. M. (1970). Sex and age differences in response to cartoons depicting subjects of different ages and sex. *Journal of Psychology*, **76**, 19–21.

Fine, G. A. (1977). Humour in situ: the role of humour in small group culture. In A. J. Chapman and H. C. Foot (Eds.), *It's a Funny Thing, Humour*. Oxford: Pergamon Press.

Foot, H. C., and Chapman, A. J. (1975). Laugh and the world laughs with you. *Psychology Today* (UK), **1**, 42–45.

Foot, H. C., and Chapman, A. J. (1976). The social responsiveness of young children in humorous situations. In A. J. Chapman and H. C. Foot (Eds.), *Humour and Laughter: Theory, Research and Applications*. Chichester: Wiley.

Foot, H. C., Chapman, A. J., and Smith, J. R. (1977). Friendship and social responsiveness in boys and girls. *Journal of Personality and Social Psychology*, **35**, 401–411.

Foot, H. C., Chapman, A. J., and Smith, J. R. (1980). Patterns of interaction in children's friendships. In H. C. Foot, A. J. Chapman and J. R. Smith (Eds.), *Children's Friendships and Social Relations*. Chichester: Wiley.

Foot, H. C., Smith, J. R., and Chapman, A. J. (1975). Boys and girls come out to play: Sex differences in the social interaction of young children. *New Behaviour*, **1**, 418–420.

Foot, H. C., Smith, J. R., and Chapman, A. J. (1977). Sex differences in children's responses to humour. In A. J. Chapman and H. C. Foot (Eds.), *It's a Funny Thing, Humour*. Oxford: Pergamon Press.

Foot, H. C., Sweeney, C. A., and Chapman, A. J. (1978). Effects of humour upon children's memory in solitary and group situations. In M. M. Gruneberg, P. E. Morris, and R. N. Sykes (Eds.), *Practical Aspects of Memory*. Oxford: Pergamon Press.

Fowles, B., and Glanz, M. E. (1977). Competence and talent in verbal riddle comprehension. *Journal of Child Language*, **4**, 433–452.

Fry, W. F. Jr. (1974). Psychodynamics of sexual humor: sexual views of children. *Medical Aspects of Human Sexuality*. September, 77–80.

Garvey, C. (1977). *Play*. Cambridge, Massachusetts: Harvard University Press.

Gentile, L. M., and McMillian, M. M. (1978). Humor and reading programs. *Journal of Reading*, **21**, 343–351.

Gesell, A., and Ilg, F. (1946). *The Child From Five to Ten*. New York: Harper and Brothers.

Gibbon, S. Y. Jr., Palmer, E. L., and Fowles, B. R. (1975). 'Sesame Street,' 'The Electric Company,' and reading. In J. B. Carroll and J. S. Chall (Eds.), *Toward a Literate Society: A Report from The National Academy of Education*. New York: McGraw-Hill.

Graham, L. R. (1958). The maturational factor in humor. *Journal of Clinical Psychology*, **14**, 326–328.

Gregg, A., Miller, M., and Linton, E. (1929). Laughter situations as an indication of social responsiveness in young children. In D. S. Thomas (Ed.), *Some New Techniques for Studying Social Behavior*. New York: Teachers' College.

Groch, A. S. (1974). Joking and appreciation of humor in nursery school children. *Child Development*, **45**, 1098–1102.

Grotjahn, M. (1957). *Beyond Laughter*. New York: McGraw-Hill.

Harms, E. (1943). The development of humor. *Journal of Abnormal and Social Psychology*, **38**, 351–369.

Hauck, W. E., and Thomas, J. W. (1972). The relationship of humor to intelligence, creativity, and intentional and incidental learning. *Journal of Experimental Education*, **40**, 52–55.

Hayworth, D. (1928). The social origin and function of laughter. *Psychological Review*, **35**, 367–384.

Heckel, R. V., and Kvetensky, E. D. (1972). The development of humor in children. *Psychology*, **9**, No. 2.

Hetherington, E. M. (1964). Humor preferences in normal and physically handicapped children. *Journal of Abnormal and Social Psychology*, **69**, 694–696.

Hooff, J. A. R. A. M. van (1972). A comparative approach to the phylogeny of laughter and smiling. In R. Hinde (Ed.), *Nonverbal Communication*. Cambridge: Cambridge University Press.

Hoult, T. (1949). Comic books and juvenile delinquency. *Sociology and Social Research*, **33**, 279–284.

Hunter, W. (1977). Humour and the deprived child. In A. J. Chapman and H. C. Foot (Eds.), *It's a Funny Thing, Humour*. Oxford: Pergamon Press.

Jacobson, E. (1946). The child's laughter: Theoretical and clinical notes on the function of the comic. *Psychoanalytic Study of the Child*, **2**, 39–60.

Jones, M. C. (1926). The development of early behavior patterns in young children. *Pedagogical Seminary*, **33**, 537–585.

Justin, F. (1932). A genetic study of laughter provoking stimuli. *Child Development*, **3**, 114–136.

Kappas, K. H. (1967). A developmental analysis of children's responses to humor. *Library Quarterly*, **37**, 67–77.

Kenderdine, M. (1931). Laughter in the pre-school child. *Child Development*, **2**, 228–230.

Kimmins, C. W. (1921). An investigation of the sense of humor in school children. *Reports of the British Association for the Advancement of Science*, No. 449.

Kimmins, C. W. (1922a). The sense of humor in children. *Strand Magazine*, **63**, 52–57.

Kimmins, C. W. (1922b). Visual humor: Sights that children laugh at. *Strand Magazine*, **63**, 294–299.

King, P. V., and King, J. E. (1973). A children's humor test. *Psychological Reports*, **33**, 632.

Kreitler, H. and Kreitler, S. (1970). Dependence of laughter on cognitive strategies. *Merrill-Palmer Quarterly*, **16**, 163–177.

Kris, E. (1938). Ego development and the comic. *International Journal of Psychoanalysis*, **19**, 77–90.

Laing, A. (1939). The sense of humor in childhood and adolescence. *British Journal of Educational Psychology*, **9**, 201.

Lesser, G. (1974). *Children and Television: Lessons from Sesame Street*. New York: Random House.

Leuba, C. (1941). Tickling and laughter: two genetic studies. *Journal of Genetic Psychology*, **58**, 201–209.

Leventhal, H., and Mace, W. (1970). The effect of laughter on evaluation of a slapstick movie. *Journal of Personality*, **38**, 16–30.

Levin, G. (1960). Children's smiles and laughter. *Ofakim*, **14**, 128–131.

Levine, J. (1967). Humor in play and sports. In R. Slovenko and J. A. Knight (Eds.), *Motivation in Play, Games and Sports*. Springfield, Illinois: Charles C. Thomas.

Levine, J. (1977). Humour as a form of therapy: Introduction to Symposium. In A. J. Chapman and H. C. Foot (Eds.), *It's a Funny Thing, Humour*. Oxford: Pergamon Press.

Lieberman, J. N. (1965). Playfulness and divergent thinking: An investigation of their relationship at the kindergarten level. *Journal of Genetic Psychology*, **107**, 219–224.

Lieberman, J. N. (1976). Playfulness in play and the player: A behavioral syndrome viewed in relation to classroom learning. *Contemporary Educational Psychology*, **1**, 197–205.

Lieberman, J. N. (1977). *Playfulness: Its Relationship to Imagination and Creativity.* New York: Academic Press.

Lockard, J. S., Fahrenbruch, C. E., Smith, J. L., and Morgan, C. J. (1977). Smiling and laughter: different phyletic origins? *Bulletin of the Psychonomic Society,* 10, 183–186.

Loewald, E. (1976). The development and uses of humor in a four-year-old's treatment. *International Review of Psycho-Analysis,* 3, 209–221.

Maw, W. H., and Maw, E. W. (1972). Differences between high- and low-curiosity fifth-grade children in their recognition of verbal absurdities. *Journal of Educational Psychology,* 63, 558–562.

McComas, H. C. (1923). The origin of laughter. *Psychological Review,* 30, 45–55.

McGhee, P. E. (1971a). Cognitive development and children's comprehension of humor. *Child Development,* 42, 123–138.

McGhee, P. E. (1971b). The role of operational thinking in children's comprehension and appreciation of humor. *Child Development,* 42, 733–744.

McGhee, P. E. (1971c). Development of the humor response: A review of the literature. *Psychological Bulletin,* 76, 328–348.

McGhee, P. E. (1972a). Methodological and theoretical considerations for a cross-cultural investigation of children's humor. *International Journal of Psychology,* 7, 13–21.

McGhee, P. E. (1972b). On the cognitive origins of incongruity humor: Fantasy assimilation versus reality assimilation. In J. H. Goldstein and P. E. McGhee (Eds.), *The Psychology of Humor: Theoretical Perspectives and Empirical Issues.* New York: Academic Press.

McGhee, P. E. (1974a). Moral development and children's appreciation of humor. *Developmental Psychology,* 10, 514–525.

McGhee, P. E. (1974b). Development of children's ability to create the joking relationship. *Child Development,* 45, 552–556.

McGhee, P. E. (1974c). Cognitive mastery and children's humor. *Psychological Bulletin,* 81, 721–730,

McGhee, P. E. (1976a). Sex differences in children's humor. *Journal of Communication,* 26, 176–189.

McGhee, P. E. (1976b). Children's appreciation of humor: A test of the cognitive congruency principle. *Child Development,* 47, 420–426.

McGhee, P. E. (1977a). A model of the origins and early development of incongruity-based humour. In A. J. Chapman and H. C. Foot (Eds.), *It's a Funny Thing, Humour.* Oxford: Pergamon Press.

McGhee, P. E. (1977b). Children's humour: A review of current research trends. In A. J. Chapman and H. C. Foot (Eds,), *It's a Funny Thing, Humour.* Oxford: Pergamon Press.

McGhee, P. E. (1977c). Humor development in children. In B. Wolman (Ed.), Vol. 5, *International Encyclopedia of Neurology, Psychiatry, Psychoanalysis and Psychology.* New York: Van Nostrand Reinhold.

McGhee, P. E. (1979a). The role of laughter and humor in growing up female. In C. Kopp and M. Kirkpatrick (Eds.), *Growing up Female.* New York: Plenum.

McGhee, P. E. (1979b). *Humor: Its Origin and Development.* San Francisco: Freeman.

McGhee, P. E. (1980). Toward the integration of entertainment and educational functions of television: role of humor. In P. H. Tannenbaum (Ed.), *Entertainment Functions of Television.* New York: Erlbaum.

McGhee, P. E., and Grodzitsky, P. (1973). Sex-role identification and humor among preschool children. *Journal of Psychology,* 84, 189–193.

McGhee, P. E., and Johnson, S. F. (1975). The role of fantasy and reality cues in children's appreciation of incongruity humor. *Merrill-Palmer Quarterly,* 21, 19–30.

Mones, L. (1939). Intelligence and a sense of humor. *Journal of Exceptional Child Psychology*, **5**, 150–153.

Moursund, J. P. (1976). *Learning and the Learner*. Monterey, California: Brooks/Cole. (Chapter 13: 'Humor'.)

Norris, D. (1971). Crying and laughing in imbeciles. *Developmental Medical Child Neurology*, **13**, 756–761.

Omwake, L. (1937). A study of sense of humor: Its relation to sex, age and personal characteristics. *Journal of Applied Psychology*, **21**, 688–704.

Orfandis, M. M. (1972). Children's use of humor in psychotherapy. *Social Casework*, **53**, 147–155.

Pien, D., and Rothbart, M. K. (1976). Incongruity and resolution in children's humor: A re-examination. *Child Development*, **47**, 966–971.

Pien, D., and Rothbart, M. K. (1977). Measuring effects of incongruity and resolution in children's humour. In A. J. Chapman and H. C. Foot (Eds.), *It's a Funny Thing, Humour*. Oxford: Pergamon Press.

Posen, I. S. (1974). Pranks and practical jokes at children's summer camps. *Southern Folklore Quarterly*, **38**, 299–309.

Prentice, N. M., and Fathman, R. E. (1975). Joking riddles: A developmental index of children's humor. *Developmental Psychology*, **11**, 210–216.

Prerost, F. J. (1977). Environmental conditions affecting the humour response: Developmental trends. In A. J. Chapman and H. C. Foot (Eds.), *It's a Funny Thing, Humour*. Oxford: Pergamon Press.

Pustel, G., Sternlicht, M., and Siegel, L. (1972). The psychodynamics of humor, as seen in institutionalized retardates. *Journal of Psychology*, **80**, 69–73.

Raley, Sister A. L., and Ballman, C. (1957). Theoretical implications for a psychology of the ludicrous. *Journal of Social Psychology*, **45**, 19–23.

Ransohoff, R. (1975). Some observations on humor and laughter in young adolescent girls. *Journal of Youth and Adolescence*, **4**, 155–170.

Rothbart, M. K. (1973). Laughter in young children. *Psychological Bulletin*, **80**, 247–256.

Rothbart, M. K. (1976). Incongruity, problem-solving and laughter. In A. J. Chapman and H. C. Foot (Eds.), *Humour and Laughter: Theory, Research and Applications*. Chichester: Wiley.

Rothbart, M. K., and Pien, D. (1977). Elephants and marshmallows: A theoretical synthesis of incongruity-resolution and arousal theories of humour. In A. J. Chapman and H. C. Foot (Eds.), *It's a Funny Thing, Humour*. Oxford: Pergamon Press.

Sachs, L. J. (1973). On crying, weeping and laughing as defences against sexual drives, with special consideration of adolescent giggling. *International Journal of Psychoanalysis*, **54**, 477–484.

Schaffer, L. F. (1930). Children's interpretations of cartoons. *Contributions to Education*, No. 429. New York: Teachers College, Columbia University.

Schaier, A. H., and Cicirelli, V. C. (1976). Age changes in humor comprehension and appreciation. *Journal of Gerontology*, **31**, 577–582.

Shaw, C. R. (1961). The use of humor in child psychiatry. *American Journal of Psychotherapy*, **15**, 368–381.

Sheppard, A. (1977). Developmental levels in explanations of humour from childhood to late adolescence. In A. J. Chapman and H. C. Foot (Eds.), *It's a Funny Thing, Humour*. Oxford: Pergamon Press.

Sherman, L. W. (1975). An ecological study of glee in small groups of preschool children. *Child Development*, **46**, 53–61.

Sherman, L. (1977). Ecological determinants of gleeful behaviours in two nursery school environments. In A. J. Chapman and H. C. Foot (Eds.), *It's a Funny Thing, Humour*. Oxford: Pergamon Press.

Shultz, T. R. (1972). Role of incongruity and resolution in children's appreciation of cartoon humor. *Journal of Experimental Child Psychology*, **13**, 456–477.

Shultz, T. R. (1974). Development of the appreciation of riddles. *Child Development*, **45**, 100–105.

Shultz, T. R. (1976). A cognitive-developmental analysis of humour. In A. J. Chapman and H. C. Foot (Eds.), *Humour and Laughter: Theory, Research and Applications*. Chichester: Wiley.

Shultz, T. R., and Horibe, F. (1974). Development of the appreciation of verbal jokes. *Developmental Psychology*, **10**, 13–20.

Singer, D. L., and Rummo, J. (1973). Ideational creativity and behavioral style in kindergarten-age children. *Developmental Psychology*, **8**, 154–161.

Sinnott, J. D., and Ross, B. M. (1976). Comparison of aggression and incongruity as factors in children's judgments of humor. *Journal of Genetic Psychology*, **128**, 241–250.

Smith, J. R., Chapman, A. J., and Foot, H. C. (1975). Seeing the gag. *New Behaviour*, **1**, 62.

Smith, J. R., Foot, H. C., and Chapman, A. J. (1975). What makes us laugh? *Psychology Today* (UK), **3**, 18–23.

Smith, J. R., Foot, H. C., and Chapman, A. J. (1977). Nonverbal communication among friends and strangers sharing humour. In A. J. Chapman and H. C. Foot (Eds.), *It's a Funny Thing, Humour*. Oxford: Pergamon Press.

Sutton-Smith, B. (1975). A developmental structural account of riddles. In B. Kirschenblatt-Gimblet (Ed.), *Speech Play and Display*. Hague, Netherlands: Mouton.

Terry, R. L., and Woods, M. E. (1975). Effects of humor on the test performance of elementary school children. *Psychology in the Schools*, **12**, 182–185.

Tibbetts, S. (1973). What's so funny? Humor in children's literature. *California Journal of Educational Research*, **24**, 42–46.

Tolor, A. (1966). Observations of joke-telling by children in therapy. *Mental Hygiene*, **50**, 295–296.

Walker, M. A., and Washburn, M. F. (1919). The Healy–Fernald picture completion test as a test of the perception of the comic. *American Journal of Psychology*, **30**, 304–307.

Wells, R. E. (1934). A study of tastes in humorous literature among pupils of junior and senior high schools. *Journal of Educational Research*, **28**, 81–91.

Whitt, J. K., and Prentice, N. M. (1977). Cognitive processes in the development of children's enjoyment and comprehension of joking riddles. *Developmental Psychology*, **13**, 129–136.

Williams, J. M. (1946). An experimental and theoretical study of humour in children. *British Journal of Educational Psychology*, **16**, 43–44.

Wilson, D. G., Rust, J., and Kasriel, J. (1977). Genetic and family origins of humor preferences. *Psychological Reports*, **41**, 659–660.

Witty, P. (1941a). Children's interest in reading the comics. *Journal of Experimental Education*, **10**, 100–104.

Witty, P. (1941b). Reading the comics—a comparative study. *Journal of Experimental Education*, **10**, 105–110.

Witty, P. (1942). Some observations from studies of the comics. *Bulletin of the Association of Arts in Childhood*.

Wolfenstein, M. (1951). A phase in the development of children's sense of humor. *Psychoanalytic Study of the Child*, **7**, 336–350.

Wolfenstein, M. (1953). Children's understanding of jokes. *Psychoanalytic Study of the Child*, **9**, 162–173.

Wolfenstein, M. (1954). *Children's Humor*. Glencoe, Illinois: Free Press.

Wolfenstein, M. (1955). Mad laughter in a six-year-old boy. *Psychoanalytic Study of the Child*, **10**, 381–394.

Wright, D. S. (1977). Children's humour: discussion. In A. J. Chapman and H. C. Foot (Eds.), *It's a Funny Thing, Humour*. Oxford: Pergamon Press.

Yalisove, D. (1978). The effect of riddle structure on children's comprehension of riddles. *Developmental Psychology*, **14**, 173–180.

Yorukoglu, A. (1974). Children's favorite jokes and their relation to emotional conflicts. *Journal of Child Psychiatry*, **13**, 677–690.

Yorukoglu, A. (1977). Favourite jokes of children and their dynamic relation to intrafamilial conflicts. In A. J. Chapman and H. C. Foot (Eds.), *It's a Funny Thing, Humour*. Oxford: Pergamon Press.

Zigler, E., Levine, J., and Gould, L. (1966a). The humor response of normal, institutionalized retarded, and noninstitutionalized retarded children. *American Journal of Mental Deficiency*, **71**, 472–480.

Zigler, E., Levine, J., and Gould, L. (1966b). Cognitive processes in the development of children's appreciation of humor. *Child Development*, **37**, 507–518.

Zigler, E., Levine, J., and Gould, L. (1967). Cognitive challenge as a factor in children's humor appreciation. *Journal of Personality and Social Psychology*, **6**, 332–336.

Zillmann, D., and Bryant, J. (1975). Viewers' moral sanction of retribution in the appreciation of dramatic presentations. *Journal of Experimental Social Psychology*, **11**, 572–582.

Zippin, D. (1966). Sex differences and the sense of humor. *Psychoanalytic Review*, **53**, 209–219.

Ziv, A. (1976). Facilitating effects of humor on creativity. *Journal of Educational Psychology*, **68**, 318–322.

SMILING AND LAUGHTER IN INFANCY

Ainsworth, M. D. S. (1964). Patterns of attachment behavior shown by the infant in interactions with his mother. *Merrill-Palmer Quarterly*, **10**, 51–58.

Ainsworth, M. D. S. (1967). *Infancy in Uganda*. Baltimore: Johns Hopkins Press.

Ambrose, J. A. (1960). The smiling and related responses in early human infancy: an experiment and theoretical study of their significance. Unpublished Doctoral Dissertation, University of London.

Ambrose, J. A. (1961). The development of the smiling response in early infancy. In B. M. Foss (Ed.), *Determinants of Infant Behaviour*. Vol. 1. London: Methuen.

Ambrose, J. A. (1963). The age of onset of ambivalence in early infancy: indications from the study of laughing. *Journal of Child Psychology and Psychiatry*, **4**, 167–181.

Brackbill, Y. (1958). Extinction of the smiling response in infants as a function of reinforcement schedule. *Child Development*, **29**, 115–124.

Brossard, L. M., and Decarie, T. G. (1968). Comparative reinforcing effect of eight stimulations on the smiling response of infants. *Journal of Child Psychology and Psychiatry*, **9**, 51–59.

Church, J. (Ed.) (1966). *These Babies: Biographies of Cognitive Development*. New York: Random House.

Cicchetti, D., and Sroufe, L. A. (1976). The relationship between affective and cognitive development in Down's Syndrome infants. *Child Development*, **47**, 960–979.

Clark, L. L. (1976). The expression of emotion by the blind. *The New Outlook*, May–June.

Dargasies, S. (1962). The first smile. *Developmental Medicine and Child Neurology*, **4**, 531–533.

Dearborn, G. V. N. (1900). The nature of the smile and laugh. *Science*, **11**, 851–855.

Dennis, W. (1934). A description and classification of the responses of the newborn infant. *Psychological Bulletin*, **31**, 5–22.

Dennis, W. (1935). An experimental test of two theories of social smiling in infants. *Journal of Social Psychology*, 6, 214–223.

Ekerman, C. O., and Whatley, J. L. (1975). Infants' reactions to unfamiliar adults varying in novelty. *Developmental Psychology*, 11, 562–566.

Emde, R. N., Gaensbau, T. S., and Harmon, R. J. (1976). Social smiling and a new level of organization. *Psychological Issues*, 10, 86–93.

Emde, R. N., and Harmon, R. J. (1972). Endogenous and Exogenous smiling systems in early infancy. *Journal of the American Academy of Child Psychiatry*, 11, 177–200.

Emde, R. N., and Koenig, K. L. (1969a). Neonatal smiling and rapid eye movement states. *Journal of the American Academy of Child Psychiatry*, 8, 57–67.

Emde, R. N., and Koenig, K. L. (1969b). Neonatal smiling, frowning, and rapid eye movement states, II: sleep cycle study. *Journal of the American Academy of Child Psychiatry*, 8, 637–656.

Emde, R. N., McCartney, R. D., and Harmon, R. J. (1971). Neonatal smiling in rapid eye movement states, IV: premature study. *Child Development*, 42, 1657–1661.

Foley, H. (1977). When do pre-term and light-for-date babies smile? *Developmental Medicine*, 19, 757–760.

Fraigberg, S. (1970). Smiling and stranger reaction in blind infants. In J. Hellmuth (Ed.), *Exceptional Infant: Studies in Abnormalities*. New York: Brunner/Mazel.

Freedman, D. G. (1964). Smiling in infants and the issue of innate vs. acquired. *Journal of Child Psychology and Psychiatry*, 5, 171–184.

Freedman, D. G., and Keller, B. (1963). Inheritance of behavior in infants. *Science*, 140, 196.

Gewirtz, J. L. (1965). The course of infant smiling in four child-rearing environments in Israel. In B. M. Foss (Ed.), *Determinants of Infant Behaviour*. Vol. 3. London: Methuen.

Gesell, A. (1937). Early evidences of individuality in the human infant. *Scientific Monthly*, 45, 217–225.

Goldstein, K. (1957). The smiling of the infant and the problem of understanding the other. *Journal of Psychology*, 44, 175–191.

Greenfield, P. M. (1972). Playing peekaboo with a four-month-old: A study of the role of speech and nonspeech sounds in the formation of a visual schema. *Journal of Psychology*, 82, 287–298.

Haith, M. M. (1972). Forgotten message of the infant smile. *Merrill-Palmer Quarterly*, 18, 321–332.

Hayashi, K. (1972). The development of the smile in infancy. *Japanese Journal of Child Psychiatry*, 13, 317–322. (English summary.)

Hopkins, J. R., Zelazo, P. R., Jacobson, S. W., and Kagan, J. (1976). Infant reactivity to stimulus-schema discrepancy. *Genetic Psychology Monographs*, 93, 27–62.

Jones, M. C. (1933). Emotional development. In C. Murchison (Ed.), *A Handbook of Child Psychology*. Second edition. Worcester, Massachusetts: Clark University Press.

Kagan, J. (1971). *Change and Continuity in Infancy*. New York: Wiley.

Kagan, J. (1974). Discrepancy, temperament and infant distress. In M. Lewis and L. A. Rosenblum (Eds.), *The Origins of Fear*. New York: Wiley.

Kagan, J., Henker, B., Hen-tov, A., Levine, J., and Lewis, M. (1966). Infants' differential reaction to familiar and distorted faces. *Child Development*, 37, 519–532.

Killbride, J. E., and Killbride, P. L. (1975). Sitting and smiling behavior of Baganda infants—influence of culturally constituted behavior. *Journal of Cross-Cultural Studies*, 6, 88–107.

Korner, A. F. (1969). Neonatal startles, smiles, erections and reflex sucks as related to state, sex, and individuality. *Child Development*, 40, 1039–1053.

Landau, R. Spontaneous and elicited smiles and vocalizations of infants in four Israeli environments. *Developmental Psychology*, **13**, 389–400.

Leuba, C. (1941). Tickling and laughter: two genetic studies. *Journal of Genetic Psychology*, **28**, 201–209.

Lewis, M. (1969). Infants' responses to facial stimuli in the first year of life. *Developmental Psychology*, **1**, 75–86.

Lewis, M. and Goldberg, S. (1969). The acquisition and violation of expectancy: an experimental paradigm. *Journal of Experimental Child Psychology*, **7**, 70–79.

Ling, A. H. (1974). Communication development in the first three years of life. *Journal of Speech and Hearing*, **17**, 146.

MacDonald, N. E., and Silverman, I. W. (1978). Smiling and laughter in infants as a function of level of arousal and cognitive evaluation. *Developmental Psychology*, **14**, 235–241.

McCall, R. B. (1972). Smiling and vocalizations in infants as indices of perceptual-cognitive processes. *Merrill-Palmer Quarterly*, **18**, 341–348.

McCall, R. B., and McGhee, P. E. (1977). The discrepancy hypothesis of attention and affect in infants. In I. C. Uzgiris and F. Weizmann (Eds.), *The Structuring of Experience*. New York: Plenum.

Melson, W. H., and McCall, R. B. (1970). Attentional responses of five-month-old girls to discrepant auditory stimuli. *Child Development*, **41**, 1159–1171.

Modarres, T., Emde, R. N., Grensbauer, T. J., and Harmon, R. J. (1978). Emotional expression in infancy: a biobehavioral study. *Journal of Nervous and Mental Disease*, **166**, 226–230.

Polak, P. R., Emde, R. N., and Spitz, R. A. (1964a). The smiling response to the human face, I: methodology, quantification, and natural history. *Journal of Nervous and Mental Disease*, **139**, 103–109.

Polak, P. R., Emde, R. N., and Spitz, R. A. (1964b). The smiling response, II: visual discrimination and the onset of depth perception. *Journal of Nervous and Mental Disease*, **139**.

Pontius, A. A. (1975). Developmental phases in visual recognition of human face pattern, exemplified by smiling response. *Experentia*, **31**, 126–129.

Salzen, E. A. (1963). Visual stimuli eliciting the smiling response in the human infant. *Journal of Genetic Psychology*, **102**, 51–54.

Shirley, M. M. (1931–1933). *The First Two Years: A Study of Twenty-Five Babies*. Minneapolis: University of Minnesota Press.

Shor, R. E. (1978). Production and judgment of smile magnitude. *Journal of Genetic Psychology*, **98**, 79–96.

Shultz, T. R., and Zigler, E. (1970). Emotional concomitants of visual mastery in infants: the effects of stimulus movement on smiling and vocalizing. *Journal of Experimental Child Psychology*, **10**, 390–402.

Soderling, B. (1959). The first smile: a developmental study. *Acta Paediatrica*, **48**, supplement 117, 78–82.

Spitz, R. A., and Wolf, K. M. (1946). The smiling response: a contribution to the ontogenesis of social relations. *Genetic Psychology Monographs*, **34**, 57–125.

Spritzer-Griffith, S. E. (1976). Mutual vision regard of Down's syndrome and normally developing infants in interaction with a familiar and an unfamiliar adult. *Dissertation Abstracts International*, **36**, 18-B, 4181.

Sroufe, L. A., and Waters, E. (1976). The ontogenesis of smiling and laughter: a perspective on the organization of development in infancy. *Psychological Review*, **83**, 173–189.

Sroufe, L. A., and Wunsch, J. P. (1972). The development of laughter in the first year of life. *Child Development*, **43**, 1326–1344.

Super, C. M., Kagan, J., Morrison, F. J., Haith, M. H., and Weiffenbach, J. (1972). Discrepancy and attention in the five-month infant. *Genetic Psychology Monographs*, **85**, 305–331.

Tautermannova, M. (1973). Smiling in infants. *Child Development*, **44**, 701.

Teele, A. S. (1973). Maternal influences on the development of social smiling in early infancy. *Dissertation Abstracts International*, **34**, 4-B, 1763.

Thompson, J. (1941). Development of facial expression of emotion in blind and seeing children. *Archives of Psychology*, **37:264**, 1–47.

Washburn, R. W. (1929). A study of smiling and laughter in infants in the first year of life. *Genetic Psychology Monographs*, **6**, 396–537.

Watson, J. S. (1966). Perceptions of object orientation in infants. *Merrill-Palmer Quarterly*, **12**, 323–340.

Watson, J. S., and Ramey, C. (1972). Reactions to response-contingent stimulation in early infancy. *Merrill-Palmer Quarterly*, **18**, 219–227.

Wilson, J. P. (1960). Nursing experience and the social smile. Unpublished Doctoral Dissertation, University of Chicago.

Wolff, P. H. (1959). Observations on newborn infants. *Psychosomatic Medicine*, **21**, 110–118.

Wolff, P. H. (1963). Observations on the early development of smiling. In B. M. Foss (Ed.), *Determinants of Infant Behaviour*. Vol. 2. London: Methuen.

Zelazo, P. R. (1967). Social reinforcement of vocalizations and smiling of three month old infants. Unpublished Doctoral Dissertation, University of Waterloo.

Zelazo, P. R. (1971). Smiling to social stimuli: eliciting and conditioning effects. *Developmental Psychology*, **4**, 32–42.

Zelazo, P. R. (1972). Smiling and vocalizing: a cognitive emphasis. *Merrill-Palmer Quarterly*, **18**, 349–365.

Zelazo, P. R. (1976). From reflexive to instrumental behavior. In C. P. Lipsitt (Ed.), *Developmental Psychobiology: The Significance of Infancy*. Hillsdale, New Jersey: Erlbaum.

Zelazo, P. R., and Komer, M. J. (1971). Infant smiling to nonsocial stimuli and the recognition hypothesis. *Child Development*, **42**, 1327–1339.

Subject Index

Affiliation 21
Aggression 184, 198, 204, 224, 228
Animal humour 134–135
Antecedents of humour
  adjustment of home 204, 219, 222, 228, 285
  affection seeking 198, 226, 228
  aggression 198, 204, 224, 228, 299
  attention seeking 226, 228
  body co-ordination 198, 227, 230
  developmental profile 231–235
  dominance 198, 204, 226
  effort, fine motor skills 198, 222, 227, 230
  effort, gross motor skills 222–223, 227, 230
  effort, intellectual skills 222, 227
  energy level 198, 204, 227, 230
  imitation 198, 227, 230
  language development 224, 228, 285
  masculinity 226
  maternal approval 217
  maternal babying 204, 217, 219
  maternal joking 219
  maternal protectiveness 217, 219
  maternal rejection 217
  sex differences 204
  social play 198, 204, 227, 230
  talkativeness 228
Anxiety 260–262, 269–270, 274, 303
Approach-avoidance 10–21
Arousal
  boost 2–3, 12–13
  early humour and 283
  effect on learning 239
  jag 2–3
  self-regulation of 18–20
Arousal-safety model 2–7, 10–11, 14, 17, 21, 145
Atypical development 198–201, 207
Authoritarianism 196

Bisociation 120–122, 288, 291

Clinical uses of humour
  anxiety 260, 262, 270, 274, 303
  bantering 275–276
  conflict 262

coping 222, 262, 272, 303
  developmental assessment 256–263, 301
  diagnostic uses 302–303
  disguised intent 269–270
  mastery of anxiety 260–261, 303
  need for love 271–272
  play in therapy 263–266, 303
  psychoanalytic view 260
  psychopathology 259, 264, 269
  psychotherapy 263–277, 303
  purposes of joking 268
Cognitive challenge 188–192, 295
Cognitive congruency principle 188–192, 295
Cognitive development 132–133. 185, 187–193, 205, 207, 258–259, 302
Cognitive styles 185, 187, 193–196, 205–207, 295–296
Collative variables 2, 9–10
Comedians 135
Conceptual tempo 193–196
Concrete operational thought 188–192, 259
Conflict 183, 198, 203–204, 262
Conservation 189–191, 207
Conservatism 196
Creativity
  bisociation and 120–122, 288, 291
  cognitive development and 132–133
  cognitive nature of 120–121
  creating humour and 124–127, 206–207, 259, 289–290
  humour development and 119–136, 290–291
  make-believe and 121, 291
  playfulness and 123–124, 291
  research methodology 129–130, 290
  tests of 120

Definitions of humour 2, 281–282, 298
Demand characteristics 158–159, 170
Developmental assessment 256–263
Differential approach 183–185, 206
Divergent thinking 120–121
Dogmatism 196
Down's syndrome 200–201

Emotionally disturbed children   199–200
Empathy   197–198
Ethnic humour   144
Experimenter effects   158–160
Exploration   9–10, 42

Fantasy assimilation   2–6
Fantasy play
    aggression and   129
    antecedents   127–129
    assertiveness and   129
    humour and   123, 127
Function pleasure   282

Idiographic approach   183–185, 206
Imagery and
    acculturation   36
    anxiety reduction   38
    attention span   30
    cognitive benefits   30–34
    communication   37
    emotional expression   37–38
    empathy   35
    integration of experiences   33
    language   33
    making plans   32–33
    mastery   39
    organization of information   31
    perceptual elaboration   32
    poise   35
    positive affect   39
    reflection-impulsivity   31
    self-control   22
    self-entertainment   36
    sensitivity to others   34–35
    social benefits   34–37
    social interaction   35
    spontaneity   38
    transformation of information   32
Imaginary friends   45, 49
Imaginative play
    activity level and   47
    cognitive-affective theory and   40–45
    cognitive benefits of   30–34, 284
    controlled novelty and   44–45
    creativity and   51
    emotional benefits of   37–40, 285
    humour and   42, 51, 284
    joy and   43–44, 285–286
    language development and   285
    modelling influences   49
    origins of   29, 282
    self-generated   30
    social benefits of   34–37, 284

social class and   50
television influences on   45–47, 50–51
training of   50
Incongruity
    humour   1–21
    linguistic   60–61, 69, 72–73, 83, 85–86
    morphological   74–75
    phonological   69–73
    resolution of   2, 3, 7, 60, 82
    semantic   79–81
    syntactic   82
Individual differences (in humour)
        181–207, 294–299
    atypical development   198–201
    cognitive challenge   188–192, 295
    cognitive development   185, 187–193,
        205–207
    cognitive style   193–196, 205–207,
        295–296
    intelligence   186–187, 189
    origins of   213–235, 294, 297, 299
    personality   196–198, 205–207,
        295–296
    rationale for study   182–183
    research strategies   183–185
    sex differences   154–155, 165–169,
        171–172, 201–204, 293, 295
Infant
    approach/avoidance   9–23
    crying   10, 16–18, 22
    distress   9, 16–19, 22
    fear   9–12, 16, 20, 23
    games   3, 8
    gaze aversion   14, 18–20, 23
    laughter   2–3, 6–7, 14, 200–201
    object concept   4
    smiling   6–8, 13–17, 28
    symbolic play   2–6, 20
    wariness   10, 17, 20–21
Intelligence   186–187, 189, 230–231,
        256–258, 301–302
Introversion-extroversion   184, 196

Joke façade   183, 207, 261
Joy   28, 36–40
Joyful play   28, 36–39

Laughter   2–3, 6–7, 14, 148, 152–153,
        157, 165–166, 181, 186, 189–190,
        195–196, 198–202, 204, 261–262,
        264, 270–272, 282–283, 292, 296,
        303
Learning, effects of humour on
    advertising   300

amount of humour 250
anxiety reduction 242
arousal effects 239
atmosphere in classroom 238, 300
attention 238–239
cognitive effects 238–239
concentration 239–242
distinctiveness of information 239
distraction 239
duration of programme 247–248
elapsed time 246–247
incidental learning 240–241
interest in topic 246
medium of presentation 250–251
persuasion 243
playfulness 300
reinforcement 239
relevance 242–243, 249
short-term retention 245
social effects 238, 251
television uses 300
timing 250
topic differences 245–246
types of humour 249
visual aids 241
Linguistic humour 59–86
early mastery 260, 287
incongruity and 60–61, 69, 72–73, 83, 85–86, 289
linguistic ambiguity 195
linguistic rules 60–67, 73–74, 76–77, 81, 83
literary development 91–115
metalinguistics 60, 69
metaphor 85, 94–102, 113, 288
morphology 73–75
paradigmatic relations 92
phonology 61–73, 287
pragmatics 83–86
semantics 76–81, 286–287
syntagmatic relations 92, 112
syntax 81–82, 287
Literary development 91–115
Locus of control 196
Longitudinal study 213–235, 297–299
Ludic assimilation 7–8, 21

Mastery
of anxiety 260–261, 269, 303
cognitive 122–123, 133
linguistic humour and 287
make-believe 282
pleasure in 2, 7–9, 14–16, 20, 283

Maternal behaviour 193, 207
Memory 193, 207
Mental health 303
Mental retardation 200–201, 203
Metaphor development 85, 94–102, 113–114, 132, 288–290
comprehension 94–95, 98–102, 288
core meaning 100–101
definition 94
developmental paradox 96
dual function adjectives 100
end state 94–95
humour 85, 91–94, 112–115, 288–290
language mastery 289
literal stage 97–98, 288–289
origins 98
perceptual similarities 99
production 96–98, 288–289
psychological metaphors 99–104
traditional view 96
Moderate novelty 41
Moral development 192, 263
Morphology 73–75
grammatical morphemes 73–74
humour 74–75
inflections 73–74
obligatory contexts 73
over-extension 74
over-regularization 74
Pig Latin 75
play languages 74–75
rule awareness 74
rule use 73–74
segmentation 75

Nomothetic approach 183–185, 206, 294
Novelty 2–3, 8–9, 284–285

Optimal stimulation 125
Origins of humour 1, 3–6, 16–21, 133–135, 281–283

Personality factors 183, 193, 196–198, 205–207, 263, 295–296
Phonology 61–73
alliteration 69, 73
allophones 61
combination rules 67–69
distorted articulation 69
humour 69–73
immature articulation 69–70
metre 72–73
phonemes 61–73
phonemic assymetry 63

phonemic frequency   63
poetic language   69
rhyme   69, 73
rule use   61–67
substitution rules   65–67, 70–71
tongue twisters   69, 71–72
verse   72–73
Physical growth   230–231
Play (playful attitude)   2–9, 28–40, 45,
   124, 259, 263–266, 282
Pleasure in mastery   7–8
Positive affects   28, 36–51
Pragmatics   83–86
   conversational postulates   83–86
   humour   85–86
   metaphor   85
   overliterality   85
   request forms   83–85
   rule awareness   84
   rule use   83–84
Production of humour   6, 186, 198,
   203–207, 263
Psychotherapy   263–277

Reality assimilation   2–5, 9
Reflection-impulsivity   31, 48, 187,
   193–196, 207, 295–296
Resolution of incongruity   2–3, 60, 82,
   257

Schizophrenia   197
Self-concept   197
Semantics   76–81
   humour   79–81
   Jabberwocky   79
   name-switching   80–81
   rule awareness   77–79
   rule use   76–77
   selection restrictions   76–80
   semantic anomolies   78, 80
   semantic features   76–80
   semantic relations   77
   tangletalk   79
   under-extension   77
   word-referent relations   77–79, 81
Sense of humour
   antecedents   215–230
   developmental profile   231–235
   importance   242, 259
   mental health   303–304
   operationally defined   298
Sex differences   154–155, 165–169,
   171–172, 204, 248, 293, 295
Sex role   197, 263

Sexual arousal   196
Simile development   132
Smiling   6–8, 13–17, 196, 201–202,
   282–283
Social aspects of humour
   adult humour   142–149, 150, 171
   age effects   160–163
   aggression   147
   children's humour   149–170, 291–294
   communication   143
   companion effects   158–160
   competition   168–169, 171–172
   demand characteristics   158–159, 170,
      292
   ethnic humour   144
   experimenter effects   158–160, 292
   friendship   165–169
   group processes   143–145
   group size   160–163
   laughter functions   148, 152–153, 157,
      165–166, 292
   learning and retention   238, 251
   sex differences   154–155, 165–169,
      171–172, 293
   smiling   167
   social facilitation   153, 157–163, 196,
      202–203, 292
   social functions   143–145; 150–154,
      171
   social interaction   145, 149, 172
   social intimacy   153, 158, 163–169
Social power   226
Stories   102–112
   competence levels   103–106
   defining criteria   103–104
   developmental stages   105
   early storytelling   109–112
   fairy-tale genre   107–109, 290
   grammar approach   105–107
Symbolic play   2–6, 20, 133–135
Syntax   81–82
   humour   82
   rule awareness   82
   rule use   81
   syntactic incongruity   82
   word order   81–82

Theories   1–7, 16–21, 183, 184, 187–188,
   196, 204–205
Therapy   183, 199, 263–278
Tickling   151

Warm-up effects   161, 163, 172